Praise for Joel C. Rosenberg

"Everyone who cares about the future of Israel and the Middle East should read this book. Rosenberg is a shrewd observer of the tectonic changes underway in the region. And his rare and unique access puts you inside the room with some of the most powerful Arab, Israeli, and American leaders shaping the future of war, peace, and religious freedom in our time."

MIKE PENCE, former vice president

"If there's one book you read about the Middle East this year, this should be it. Few people understand the scope and scale of change in the region better than Joel C. Rosenberg. This guy gets it!"

MIKE HUCKABEE, former governor of Arkansas

"*Enemies and Allies* should be required reading in the White House, Congress, and the Knesset. Rosenberg lays out in fascinating and vivid detail why more and more Arab leaders want to make peace with Israel, even as the terror masters in Tehran want to bring about a second Holocaust. And Rosenberg is right—what's needed now is a new and far more robust strategic alliance between the U.S., Israel, and the Sunni Arab world to defend Western civilization against the perils of the Persian Bomb."

DANNY AYALON, former Israeli ambassador to the United States and deputy foreign minister

"It is unusual for an ordinary Israeli citizen with no position of power— no political or diplomatic or intelligence credentials—to be invited to meet with some of the most consequential leaders in the Arab world. Yet it happened. Not once but over and over again. This is a huge story. Joel C. Rosenberg has spent hour upon hour with Arab kings and crown princes, presidents and prime ministers, even His Royal Highness Mohammed bin Salman, heir to the Saudi throne, and his inner circle. A recent immigrant to Israel and an evangelical, Rosenberg has built trust with these leaders. Befriended them. Listened to them. And was even granted permission to share these unprecedented conversations with the rest of us. He has worked tirelessly urging them to expand religious freedom for Jews and Christians, visit the Holy City of Jerusalem, and make peace. This is an amazing tale—so amazing that I suspect *Enemies and Allies* is going to be widely read not just in America and in Israel, but throughout the Arab world—probably in Tehran, Moscow, and Ankara, too—as well it should. Rosenberg has written a significant and insightful book about the future of the Middle East."

MAJOR GENERAL Aharon Ze'evi Farkash, IDF, retired, former head of Israeli military intelligence

"Two decades after 9/11, the Middle East is in the midst of some of the most profound changes in modern history. While new and grave threats are rising, so are new opportunities for security, peace, and prosperity for the region. My friend Joel—an evangelical from a Jewish background— develops a spellbinding narrative in *Enemies and Allies* by recounting his many providential encounters with the most prominent leaders in Israel and the Arab Muslim world. The impact of these engagements will continue to shape U.S. policies in the region for years to come. I can think of few intelligence operatives, much less *New York Times* bestselling authors, who have a keener sense of what is happening, what it means, or why it matters than Joel C. Rosenberg. *Enemies and Allies* is proof of that."

DAVID SHEDD, former acting director of the U.S. Defense Intelligence Agency

"I've known Joel Rosenberg for more than twenty years. I've traveled with him on the historic delegations he has led to meet with the top leaders in the Arab world. And I can tell you this is a man who truly gets what's happening in the Middle East and cares deeply about advancing the cause of peace and human rights for Jews and Christians and for Muslims. His new work, *Enemies and Allies*, is the most important book about Israel, Iran, and the Arab world in years, and I can't recommend it highly enough."

J. KENNETH BLACKWELL, former U.S. ambassador to the U.N. Human Rights Commission, former Ohio secretary of state, and member of the Council on Foreign Relations and the board of advisors of the Jewish Institute for National Security Affairs (JINSA)

"Rosenberg nails it! *Enemies and Allies* is timely and terrifying. The definitive, must-read book for every patriot who cares about the future of freedom. Based on his exclusive and extensive conversations with senior U.S., Israeli, and Arab leaders and intelligence officials, Rosenberg reveals what the mainstream media won't tell you: why the single greatest threat in the Middle East to the national security of the American people, Israel, and our Arab allies is the apocalyptic, genocidal regime in Iran. But Rosenberg goes further, explaining how exponentially more dangerous Tehran becomes as it builds alliances with the dictators of Russia, Turkey, North Korea, and China. And why the clock is ticking for the free world to act to strengthen our allies and neutralize our enemies before it's too late."

> **RICK SANTORUM,** former senator and member of the Senate Armed Services Committee

"*Enemies and Allies* is a highly engaging journey through the pitfalls and possibilities of the modern Middle East in which Israel is emerging as a true asset for security and stability, not seen as the source of all trouble. Joel offers readers his front-row seat to history through personal conversations with all the key personalities shaping the future of the region, from Netanyahu to Trump to MBS. A must-read for anyone who wants to understand the genesis of the Abraham Accords and their aftermath."

> **VICTORIA COATES,** former U.S. deputy national security advisor for Middle Eastern and North African affairs at the National Security Council

"This informed account of Mideast travail by a qualified front-row witness will cheer the peacemakers and frustrate the appeasers and apologists. There is no denying that Joel Rosenberg's chronicle of his journey through these pivotal historic events puts critical pieces of the puzzle credibly on the table. That he finishes with an optimistic outlook is encouraging and testimony to his deep faith."

> **PORTER GOSS,** former director of the Central Intelligence Agency

"In *Enemies and Allies*, my friend Joel C. Rosenberg takes you where few people get to go—inside meetings with powerful Arab and Israeli leaders who are literally reshaping the future of the Middle East. I've been at his side as he has asked these leaders hard questions, pressed for peace, championed religious freedom, and done so with deep conviction and genuine respect. This is a fascinating book that will take you behind the scenes during a whirlwind of unlikely yet momentous events that are raising critical questions that must be answered soon: Who exactly are our enemies? Who are our allies? And where does all this fast-moving change go from here?"

JOHNNIE MOORE, commissioner on the U.S. Commission on International Religious Freedom (USCIRF) and author of *Defying ISIS: Preserving Christianity in the Place of its Birth and in Your Own Backyard*

ENEMIES *and* ALLIES

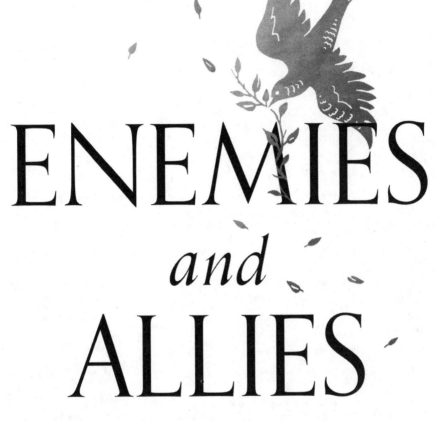

ENEMIES
and
ALLIES

An Unforgettable Journey inside the Fast-Moving
& Immensely Turbulent Modern Middle East

JOEL C. ROSENBERG

Tyndale House Publishers
Carol Stream, Illinois

Visit Tyndale online at tyndale.com.

Visit Joel C. Rosenberg's website at joelrosenberg.com.

Tyndale and Tyndale's quill logo are registered trademarks of Tyndale House Ministries.

Enemies and Allies: An Unforgettable Journey inside the Fast-Moving & Immensely Turbulent Modern Middle East

Designed by Libby Dykstra

Views and opinions expressed in *Enemies and Allies* are the author's and not necessarily those of the publisher.

Unless otherwise indicated, all Scripture quotations are taken from the (NASB®) New American Standard Bible®, Copyright © 1960, 1971, 1977, 1995, 2020 by The Lockman Foundation. All rights reserved. www.lockman.org.

Scripture quotations marked NIV are taken from the Holy Bible, *New International Version,*® NIV.® Copyright © 1973, 1978, 1984, 2011 by Biblica, Inc.® Used by permission. All rights reserved worldwide.

Scripture quotations marked NLT are taken from the *Holy Bible*, New Living Translation, copyright © 1996, 2004, 2015 by Tyndale House Foundation. Used by permission of Tyndale House Publishers, Carol Stream, Illinois 60188. All rights reserved.

For information about special discounts for bulk purchases, please contact Tyndale House Publishers at csresponse@tyndale.com or call 1-855-277-9400.

Library of Congress Cataloging-in-Publication Data

A catalog record for this book is available from the Library of Congress.

ISBN 978-1-4964-5381-5

Printed in the United States of America

27	26	25	24	23	22	21
7	6	5	4	3	2	1

To my amazing team at All Israel News and All Arab News—Israelis, Palestinians, Lebanese, and Americans—what an honor it is to cover the unfolding story of enemies and allies in this part of the world with you each and every day. May God bless you for your dedication to seeking and reporting the truth, come what may.

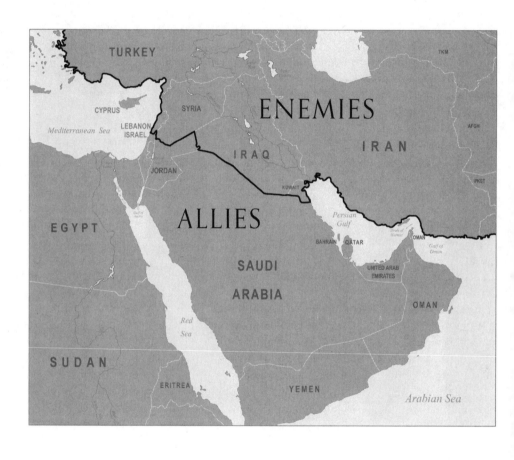

Contents

Preface

It has long been said, "What happens in Vegas stays in Vegas."

Nobody says that about the Middle East.

What happens there—for better or worse—affects the entire world. Ever-fluctuating oil prices affect how much it costs to fill up the family car with gas. Ever-shifting stock market valuations affect the future of our retirement savings. Ever-evolving airport security procedures affect the time and hassle it takes just to board an airplane. Ever-increasing defense and homeland security budgets affect the taxes we are required to pay just to keep ourselves safe. Never-ending wars and rumors of war affect so many of us who have to send our sons and daughters to the military to confront our enemies and defend our allies.

We could wish it were not so. Yet such matters are not in our hands. Time and again, the eyes of the world are drawn back to the Middle East and North Africa, the epicenter of the momentous events that are shaking our world and shaping our future.

Two decades after the horrific terrorist attacks against the United States on September 11, 2001, which shifted our focus to the Middle East yet again, the region is undergoing sweeping, historic, tectonic transformations. We ignore them at our peril.

Some of the changes have been unspeakably brutal:

- In Afghanistan, the seemingly endless war has killed more than 150,000 people since 2001.[1]
- In Iraq, the war that began in 2003—followed by the insurgency and the rise and fall of the Islamic State—has left upwards of 330,000 civilians and combatants dead, cost the American people more than $2 trillion, and still has not brought peace.[2]
- In Syria and Yemen, ongoing civil wars have left close to a half million dead and millions more homeless and running for their lives.[3]
- The so-called Arab Spring led to the collapse of regimes in Egypt, Tunisia, Libya, and Yemen—and thousands of dead and injured.
- In Gaza, a well-meaning but premature experiment with local elections in 2006 put the Hamas terrorist organization in power. Together with their jihadist allies, they have proceeded to fire more than 12,000 rockets and mortars at civilian population centers in southern Israel, drawing round after round of retaliatory attacks by the Israel Defense Forces, leading to death and injury and untold trauma on both sides of the border.[4]

Other changes are fostering hope for newfound peace, security, and prosperity:

- The Abraham Accords—historic peace, normalization, trade, and tourism agreements between Israel and the United Arab Emirates, the Kingdom of Bahrain, the Republic of the Sudan, and the Kingdom of Morocco—were successfully brokered by the U.S.
- More Arab and Muslim nations are showing interest in making peace with Israel and building strategic alliances together. Even the Kingdom of Saudi Arabia.
- Arab states are no longer leveraging the price of oil against the U.S. and Israel. Instead, they are doing so against the tyrants in Tehran.
- Deeper strategic alliances are being forged between the U.S. and Israel and between the U.S. and the Arab world.
- At the same time, numerous Arab nations have embarked upon unprecedented domestic reform programs designed to create more

economic freedom and opportunity for their people—most notably the Vision 2030 initiative in Saudi Arabia.

Today, political, financial, business, and faith leaders—indeed, people of all kinds, from tourists to day traders, from military officials to our intelligence communities, from human rights activists to leaders of global ministries—are watching events in the Middle East with a mixture of apprehension and awe. They are also asking critical questions:

- Where is the Middle East heading—toward catastrophic new wars or a captivating new era of peace and prosperity?
- Who exactly are our enemies today, and who are our allies?
- What are the most serious threats in the region, and what are the most exciting opportunities?
- Is there a new "gold rush" coming as CEOs, entrepreneurs, and investors surge into a new Middle East—one focused not on war and terror but on technology, trade, and tourism?
- What does the future hold for the security of Israel—amid all this change, will the Jewish State be safer or more in danger?
- How will the rapidly changing dynamics in the Arab and Muslim world affect the future of religious minorities, including the millions of Christians who live in the region?
- And who are the major agents of change in the region—for good or for evil? Who should we be watching, what are their aims, and how far will they go to achieve their ambitions?

Over the past two decades, I have crisscrossed the Middle East and North Africa as an author, a columnist, a documentary filmmaker, and a follower of Jesus Christ from a Jewish background. I traveled from Morocco in the west to Afghanistan in the east. Lived in Egypt. Explored Jordan. Taught the Bible in Turkey. Helped build a Christian radio station in Iraq. Sold our home in the Washington, D.C., area and moved to Israel with my family in the middle of a rocket war. Became a dual U.S.-Israeli citizen. Bought an apartment in Jerusalem. Sent two of my sons to the Israeli army. Along the way, I have had the rare fortune to meet with kings and crown princes, presidents and prime ministers, spy chiefs and diplomats—spending hours in conversation behind closed doors. At their request, I have brought delegations of evangelical Christian leaders to meet with them—often the first Christian delegations in history to meet with the leaders of these Arab Muslim countries. We have not gone seeking headlines or photo ops but to pursue long-term friendships and to listen, learn, and pray. We have also used these opportunities to encourage our hosts to take even bigger steps to advance peace, religious freedom, and human rights—in their nations and throughout the region.

At the same time, I have also been honored to meet with pastors and priests, imams and rabbis, generals and ex-jihadists, wise men and warlords, business owners and factory workers, billionaires and the poorest of the poor. Together, we've enjoyed countless cups of coffee and tea. We've talked for hours—for days—sometimes deep into the night. I have asked them pointed, direct questions, and they have given me candid, heartfelt answers.

What do you want?

Whom do you fear?

Who are your enemies?

Who are your allies?

What are your dreams for your children and grandchildren?

What are the obstacles in your way?

What do you think of Jews?

What do you think of Jesus and those who follow him?

Can there ever be peace between Israel and the Arab Muslim world?

How can I pray for you?

May I take a moment and pray for you right now?

Over the course of several decades, I have seen the answers begin to change. Attitudes are shifting. Not just on the street but also in the palaces—in the corridors of power that few outsiders ever see.

Fascinated by the speed and scale and scope of change, and wanting more people to hear these compelling stories, I launched two new websites—All Israel News (allisrael.com) and All Arab News (allarab .news) on September 1, 2020. With a team of Israeli, Palestinian, and Lebanese reporters, editors, videographers, and web designers, we are tracking and explaining what is happening and why it matters. From our first days in operation, we were able to break exclusive stories and publish original interviews with some of the most influential newsmakers in the region. Our stories have been cited by Israeli, Arab, American, and other reporters around the world. They have also been retweeted by government officials, journalists, religious leaders, and everyday citizens who are exasperated by the extreme bias in too much of the media today and are hungry for credible, fair, balanced, and unique reporting and analysis about Israel and the Arab Muslim world.

Yet even two websites cannot adequately explain the scope of the changes we are witnessing. Daily news coverage of specific events is pointillism. What is needed is context.

That is why I wrote this book. It is the product of my journeys. In these pages, I will take you inside royal courts and capitals and introduce you to the most powerful figures in the region. Love them or hate them, these are the players driving the change. These are the leaders to keep your eye on. I've spoken with many of them at length, and I will share my observations and assessments. Most important, however, I will let you hear them in their own words through never-before-published transcripts of our conversations.

Here are some of the leaders you will meet:

- **Saudi Crown Prince Mohammed bin Salman:** Universally known by his initials, MBS, he is the richest, most mysterious, and most controversial Muslim leader on the face of the planet. Only in his thirties, he is positioned to assume the throne and lead his nation for the next half century. Is he the bold reformer that he and his admirers claim? Is he truly advancing the most audacious economic, social, and geopolitical changes in the history of the kingdom in order to make it a magnet for trade, investment, and tourism? Or is he, as his critics contend, a "reckless and dangerous" rogue, an "impetuous and dangerous young royal," a "wrecking ball," a "toxic" figure who must be removed from the line of succession?[5]

  In November 2017, a thirty-year veteran of the Central Intelligence Agency and expert on the Saudi kingdom wrote a 272-page book without meeting or interviewing MBS.[6] In the spring of 2020, a *New York Times* reporter published a 384-page biography of MBS without meeting or interviewing him.[7] In September 2020, two *Wall Street Journal* reporters published a 368-page biography of MBS, also without meeting or talking to him.[8]

I had the opportunity to meet with MBS twice. I have spoken with him at length and on the record. The first time was in his palace in Riyadh, the capital of the kingdom, where our meeting lasted for two hours. The second time was in Jeddah, the kingdom's summer capital, where we met for another two hours. I also spent many more hours with his most senior advisors. In the first book of its kind, then, I will take you inside those conversations. You will hear the crown prince answer direct and difficult questions in his own words.

- **Egyptian president Abdel Fattah el-Sisi:** His admirers hail him as a hero who is saving the world's largest Arab country from radical Islamists hell-bent on transforming Egypt into a Sunni version of the Shia terrorist regime in Iran. Supporters praise him for advancing a moderate and tolerant vision of Islam, working hard to revitalize the once-moribund Egyptian economy, working closely with Israel to fight terrorism and promote regional peace, and working consistently to protect the largest Christian population in the Middle East from being butchered by the radicals. He also commissioned the construction of the largest church in the history of the region and presented it as a gift to his nation's Christians on their Christmas Eve. His critics, however, denounce him as a modern-day "Pharaoh" and a cruel dictator who has made Egypt more dangerous than at any time in recent history. Who is right? And what does the future hold? Events in Egypt are moving so quickly that few books have yet tackled the topic. One was published in 2018 by a *New York Times* reporter who did not meet or interview President Sisi.[9] I have had the opportunity to meet President Sisi on five separate occasions, and I'll take you inside the palace and let you hear him make his case in his own words.

- **United Arab Emirates Crown Prince Mohammed bin Zayed:** Widely known by his initials, MBZ is one of the most private yet influential leaders in the Arab world. He almost never gives interviews or speeches, preferring to work quietly behind the scenes. Few know that he was born in an evangelical medical missionary hospital. Few know how he and his family—notably his father—built the UAE into one of the most advanced and tolerant nations in the Arab world. Fewer still know how he and his colleagues came to stun the world by signing the first peace treaty with Israel in more than a quarter of a century. Yet, having met with MBZ for hours and having built friendships with members of his inner circle, I will introduce you to MBZ and explain his importance in the new Middle East.

- **Jordanian King Abdullah II:** He is a monarch. A Muslim. And a moderate. He is a direct descendant of the prophet Muhammad. With an English mother. And he governs half of the Holy Land. He has been in power longer than any other leader in the Arab world. He is a faithful friend and ally of the United States. A trusted peace partner with Israel. Even so, few really know who he is, what he believes, or how he sees the future of the region. After five meetings with this remarkable man, I will take you inside his palace and his kingdom and let you meet him for yourself.

- **Former president Donald J. Trump:** How was it possible that a presidential candidate with no prior political or foreign policy experience—a man who called for a complete ban on all Muslims entering the United States (a position I publicly denounced during the 2016 campaign)—went on to become the most pro-Israel, pro-Arab president in American history, crushing the Islamic State, withdrawing from the dangerous Iran nuclear deal, forging deep alliances with the Sunni Arab world, and brokering not one but four astonishing Arab-Israeli peace deals, more than any American president in history? His strategy to advance peace and security in the Middle East was routinely mocked and dismissed every step of the way. Why, then, is it working? And how did it come about that a once "Never Trumper" like me was invited to meet with the president, vice president, secretary of state, and members of the White House's Mideast policy team and even attend the historic

Abraham Accords signing ceremony on the South Lawn of the White House? I'll take you behind the scenes and tell you the inside story.

- **President Joe Biden:** After the most expensive, contentious, and controversial presidential election in American history, everything in Washington changed yet again. Though he had served in Washington for half a century as senator and vice president, most Americans—and certainly most Israelis, Arabs, and others in the Middle East—were asking: Who is Joe Biden? What is his track record in the Middle East? How will he deal with our enemies and our allies? Is he determined to follow unwaveringly the policies of President Barack Obama? Or have Biden and his team learned critical lessons from the flaws and failures of the Iran nuclear deal? Are they absorbing and properly analyzing how rapidly the Middle East is changing and the implications of those changes? With such high stakes, I interviewed American and foreign officials who have worked closely with Biden for years and have known him well, and I will take you inside his world and let you hear his views in his own words.

Buckle up.

In my experience, a journey into the epicenter can be a bumpy ride. Certainly today, the change underway in the region is coming fast and furious—and it is far from over. But I trust you will find, as I have, that it is worth the trip. Nearly 600 million people live in the Middle East and North Africa. My hope is that when you have finished this book, you will have a better appreciation for the immense challenges they face and how your future and your fortunes are uniquely and inextricably connected to theirs. I also hope you will join me in heeding the words of Psalm 122:6—praying faithfully and fervently for "the peace of Jerusalem" and for all who live in the nations around her. Never have such prayers been more needed, for our enemies as well as our allies.

Joel C. Rosenberg
Jerusalem, Israel
March 1, 2021

Part One

THE THREATS

1

WHAT ARE THE MOST SERIOUS THREATS WE FACE TODAY IN THE MIDDLE EAST?

*My conversations with Mike Pompeo,
former CIA director and secretary of state*

I first met Mike Pompeo in June 2016, when he was serving his third term as a congressman from Kansas. One of his staff members had contacted me and asked if I would like to meet her boss the next time I was in Washington, D.C. She said Pompeo had been reading my books and was interested in my views on the dramatic changes underway in the Middle East.

As it happened, I had just arrived in the U.S. from my home in Israel to speak at a series of conferences and events. I readily accepted the invitation and we set the meeting for Friday, June 10.

Pompeo struck me as a down-to-earth, no-nonsense straight shooter who had seen his share of difficult times, and he intrigued me for several reasons. He was a U.S. Army vet who served on the House Intelligence Committee. He was also a devout Christian who had once taught fifth-grade Sunday school and whose faith shaped his worldview.

Pompeo was also one of the more outspoken members of Congress in opposition to the nuclear deal that President Barack Obama had negotiated with Iran, calling it "a historic mistake" and "a surrender."[1] Particularly impressive to me was that Pompeo and Senator Tom Cotton of Arkansas had discovered and exposed the stunning fact that the Obama team had allowed Iran to negotiate secret side deals with the International Atomic Energy Agency (IAEA) without revealing the existence or the substance of these deals to Congress or the American people.[2]

When we met for coffee in his Capitol Hill office, we did not spend much time discussing our personal lives. Mostly we focused on Iran and the campaign of genocide being waged by the Islamic State of Iraq and Syria (ISIS).[3]

I brought Pompeo two of my most recent novels as gifts—*The Third Target*, published in January 2015, and *The First Hostage*, published in December 2015. They were the first two installments of a trilogy I was writing about ISIS, portraying the group not simply as a terrorist threat but as a genocidal threat fueled by the group's apocalyptic eschatology, a subject too few in Washington were focused on at the time.

In *The Third Target*, ISIS jihadists capture a cache of chemical weapons in Syria and begin a series of attacks throughout the region. Feverishly seeking to expand the territorial reach of their Islamic kingdom known as a caliphate, they also try to assassinate the king of Jordan, blow up his palace, take over his kingdom, and fly their black flags over Amman.

During our conversation, I explained to Congressman Pompeo that while I was researching and writing the book in 2013 and early 2014, President Obama was publicly dismissing ISIS as a "jayvee team" that posed no serious threat to the U.S. or our allies.[4]

However, as early as the summer of 2014—still months before my novel was released—it was becoming apparent that genocidal conditions were emerging, and the jihadists were willing to annihilate all who stood in their way as they tried to establish their Islamic State. As I was then saying publicly, this was as dark a time as any I had ever seen in the modern Middle East. ISIS had captured half of Iraq and was forcing Christians there to convert or die. More than 170,000 people had been murdered in Syria, and millions of Syrians had fled their homes to escape the violence.[5]

By the time *The Third Target* was released, the ghastly atrocities committed by ISIS were worsening exponentially. I used my book tour— including an address to the National Religious Broadcasters convention—to explain and speak out against the apocalyptic theology driving the leaders of ISIS, calling on the Obama administration to formally declare the actions of ISIS as genocide and urging the White House to take far more decisive military action to end the slaughter of Christians, Yazidis, and Muslims.[6]

Obama didn't get it.

But Mike Pompeo did. I had heard the congressman sound the warning bells against ISIS, and I was grateful to now have the opportunity to discuss it with him.

In September 2015, for example, Pompeo had cosponsored a congressional resolution, "expressing the sense of Congress that those who commit or support atrocities against Christians and other ethnic and religious minorities, including Yezidis, Turkmen, Sabea-Mandeans, Kaka'e, and Kurds, and who target them specifically for ethnic or religious reasons, are committing, and are hereby declared to be committing, 'war crimes,' 'crimes against humanity,' and 'genocide.'"[7]

When President Obama failed to take decisive action, Pompeo wrote to Secretary of State John Kerry, urging the administration to do more to protect Christians and other religious minorities.

"Since launching its caliphate, ISIS has executed, enslaved, abducted, displaced, and forcibly converted thousands of Christians," Pompeo wrote. "In areas that ISIS controls, Christians face three stark choices: pay the ruinous *jizya* tax, convert to Islam, or be murdered. Worse still, even Christians who pay this tax are eventually stripped of their property and killed."[8]

Still, Obama and his team vacillated.[9]

Representative Jeff Fortenberry of Nebraska (the resolution's lead author), Pompeo, and their colleagues in the House decided it was time to turn up the heat. On March 14, 2016, they brought their resolution to the House floor, where it passed unanimously, 393 to 0. Democrats abandoned the president en masse and joined their Republican colleagues in demanding action from the administration.

Finally, on March 17, Secretary Kerry held a news conference in which he acknowledged that ISIS "is genocidal by self-proclamation, by ideology, and by actions in what it says, what it believes, and what it does."[10] Now, of course, the question was, How serious would the administration be about crushing ISIS and stopping the genocide once and for all?[11]

Tragically, Obama still refused to order decisive military action.

As Pompeo and I discussed the situation, I said, "Congressman, one of the central themes in my novels is this: *To misunderstand the nature and threat of evil is to risk being blindsided by it.*

"Americans were blindsided by the Imperial Japanese on December 7, 1941. Neither we nor our leaders truly understood the evil intentions or capabilities of the Japanese military until they hit us at Pearl Harbor.

"Americans were blindsided again on September 11, 2001. *The 9/11 Commission Report* makes it clear that the success of the attacks by al Qaeda weren't so much the failure of intelligence—looking back, all the signs were there—but a failure of imagination. Our leaders simply couldn't imagine that anyone would hijack jet planes and turn them into ballistic missiles by flying them into buildings. Now we have leaders who have been blindsided again. Everything in ISIS doctrine and theology tells us this is a group determined to use genocide to bring about the End of Days, establish their caliphate, and welcome the coming of the so-called savior, the Mahdi. But Obama, Biden, Kerry, and their team can't or won't see it."

Pompeo replied that the only hope to confront and crush such evil was to elect a serious, experienced Republican commander in chief who was prepared to handle himself on the world stage from day one in office. I agreed, but at that moment it seemed impossible. Donald Trump, with no previous political experience, had already been declared the presumptive winner of the Republican nomination, awaiting only confirmation at the national convention in July.

Neither Pompeo nor I had backed Trump during the primaries. Indeed, we had both been sharply critical of him and had supported other Republican contenders. At that time, I considered myself a Never Trumper.

"I'm curious," Pompeo said as our conversation drew to a close, "how did you get the idea of writing novels about ISIS when they weren't even a household word?"

I explained that the idea had come from talking to two former directors of the Central Intelligence Agency—James Woolsey, a Democrat who had served under President Bill Clinton, and Porter Goss, a Republican who had served under President George W. Bush. Both had become friends of mine, and when I'd asked them what kept them up at night—who the new "bad guys" were in the Middle East that I ought to be writing about—each had, in separate conversations, told me that al Qaeda in Iraq was morphing into something particularly dangerous.

That had intrigued me, so I did some research and ended up writing the books, based on their advice.

Little could I have imagined as I gave those two novels to Mike Pompeo—sitting in his office in the Cannon House Office Building on that Friday in June 2016—that I was talking to the next director of the CIA, a future secretary of state, and a man who would play a critical role in helping President Trump withdraw from the Iran nuclear deal, create a strategy of "maximum pressure" against the regime in Tehran, destroy the Islamic State, crush the caliphate, liberate its enslaved victims, revitalize our tattered alliances with Israel and the Sunni Arab states, and broker the most significant Arab-Israeli peace treaties in more than a quarter of a century.

Life truly is stranger than fiction.

THE WAR AGAINST AL QAEDA

After Mike Pompeo became secretary of state, he and I connected every few months to talk about trend lines in the Middle East. Usually we talked by phone or corresponded through a back channel. Occasionally we met in person, whether in his seventh-floor office at the State Department, at the White House, at the opening session of the U.N. General Assembly in Manhattan, at a conference in Des Moines, or in Cairo at the opening of the largest cathedral ever built in the Middle East.

Over time, my respect for Pompeo deepened. When I began working on this book, I asked if he would give me his take on the status of the Middle East. He graciously agreed. It was the first on-the-record interview we'd ever had.

"I would love to understand where you were on 9/11," I began. "How did the horrific events of that day impact you and lead you as CIA director—and, of course, as secretary of state?"

"I was in Wichita, Kansas, in the central offices of Thayer Aerospace [a company he founded]. I got a call from my wife, Susan, who said, 'Flip on the TV.' I did and I remember being, like most Americans, horrified, angered—and recognizing that there had been this enormous assault on the American people by Islamic jihadists, Islamic terrorists, and knowing that it would have an enormous impact on the lives of every American for years to come. That anger, that raw emotion we felt that day is something I still feel when I think about what happened in New York. And it drove the work I did when I was director of the CIA, to ensure that we were continuing to prosecute all those jihadists who intended to put harm on the United States of America."[12]

I asked Pompeo how he assessed the war against al Qaeda.

"They still exist and are still intent on conducting jihad," he replied. "But we have not only taken senior leader after senior leader off the battlefield, we have created conditions where the network is not as capable and not as powerful today as it was a number of years ago."

True enough.

On September 14, 2019, it was confirmed that Hamza bin Laden, the thirty-year-old son of Osama bin Laden, had been killed in a U.S. operation.[13]

On February 6, 2020, news broke that Qassim al-Rimi, the founder of al Qaeda in the Arabian Peninsula, had been killed in a U.S. operation in Yemen.[14]

On June 3, 2020, Abdelmalek Droukdal, emir of al Qaeda's North African affiliate, was killed by French forces in Mali.[15]

On June 14, 2020, Khalid al Aruri, leader of al Qaeda in Syria, was killed by a U.S. drone strike.[16]

On August 7, 2020, Abu Mohammed al-Masri, the second-highest ranking operative in al Qaeda, was killed in Tehran.[17]

Some 27,614 members of al Qaeda in Syria have been killed on the battlefield.[18]

U.S. intelligence now believes that as a result of the relentless work of American and NATO forces, there are now fewer than a couple hundred al Qaeda terrorists left in Afghanistan, a country that was once the organization's home base of operations.[19]

"They have fewer resources available," Pompeo continued, "and we have built out a global system [of counterterrorism]. Some of this preceded the Trump administration, but we certainly continued the pace to build out an information network and intelligence network [to] find al Qaeda [members] in the Arabian Peninsula or al Qaeda members in Iran or al Qaeda members that remain in Afghanistan or in Southeast Asia. The network is good. We have absolutely decreased risks to the homeland here in the United States and to threats from al Qaeda in other parts of the world."

Intelligence experts such as David Shedd, former acting director of the Defense Intelligence Agency (DIA) during the Obama administration, backed up Pompeo's assessment. In an interview for this book, Shedd told me he had been working at the White House on the National Security Council staff on 9/11, "that fateful day," and it became instantly "clear to me that America was at a turning point," that we were facing "a different type of adversary than what we had known throughout the Cold War.[20]

"The U.S. was not unfamiliar [with] or immune from international terrorism over the two decades before 2001," Shedd told me, but he conceded that this new enemy—Islamist extremism—"was poorly understood" in Washington and throughout the U.S. And for some reason, he said, the suicide bombing attack by Hezbollah—a Shia Islamist group—against the U.S. Embassy in Beirut in April 1983 (which killed sixty-three people, including seventeen Americans) and Hezbollah's bombing of the U.S. Marines barracks in October 1983 (which killed 241 U.S. military personnel) had not proved to be a sufficient wake-up call. Nor had the attacks by al Qaeda—a Sunni Islamist group—against American embassies in Kenya and Tanzania in August 1998 (which killed 224 people and injured more than 4,500 others). Nor, apparently, had al Qaeda's attack against the USS *Cole* warship in October 2000 (which killed seventeen U.S. sailors and injured thirty-nine more).

"It took the large-scale attacks of September 2001," he said, to create a "great awakening" and "shift dramatically the course of America's security posture."

Today, Shedd told me, "the U.S. not only understands extremist Islamic-led terrorism much better, but it has also built up the intelligence and security capabilities and capacity to counter the terrorism threats at scale."

Still, "the U.S. and its allies cannot rest on the laurels of the past two decades, claiming that Islamic extremism under any banner has been defeated," Shedd said. But there is no question that "al Qaeda was weakened significantly with the 2011 killing of Osama bin Laden at his compound in Abbottabad, Pakistan." He added that "America's intelligence and security apparatus has been effective in disrupting the communication lines among the remaining senior echelon members of al Qaeda" and that "perhaps no better example exists than the fact that al Qaeda's leader, Ayman al-Zawahiri, has not been able to plan, plot, and communicate effectively while in hiding or on the run."

Even critics of the Trump administration concurred with Pompeo and Shedd's assessment. For example, thirty-year CIA veteran Bruce Riedel, a member of the Brookings Institution, agreed that "the al Qaeda organization that carried out [the 9/11 attacks] is a shell of its previous self. The global campaign against Osama bin Laden's creation has achieved notable success. The ideas that inspired bin Laden and his followers have lost some, but not all, of their attractiveness. There is no place for complacency, but the threat is different."[21]

Ben Rhodes, who served as deputy national security advisor to President Obama and was a fierce critic of Trump, also agreed. "Yes, we have a continued need to fight terrorist groups," he wrote in 2020, "but the greatest threats we face going forward will come not from groups like al Qaeda or ISIS."[22]

THE WAR AGAINST THE ISLAMIC STATE

What about ISIS, the even more brutal successor to al Qaeda? I asked Pompeo.

"We should think about them jointly because they are not as disconnected as is sometimes thought," he replied. "They [al Qaeda and ISIS] will compete against each other, but when the common enemy raises its head—the 'Great Satan' of the United States of America—I can assure you that the two of them would find a pathway to work alongside of each other against us.

"With respect to ISIS, we came in [to office in January 2017] when it was going strong," Pompeo noted. "Your audiences will remember Americans being beheaded. Americans in cages being set on fire. An enormous caliphate—a piece of real estate the size of the United Kingdom—controlling, operating, taxing, running a government in eastern Syria and western Iraq."

However, Pompeo explained, from the moment Donald Trump took office, he "gave our intelligence community and military all the tools we needed to destroy the caliphate, and we did that. We took it down in its entirety."

Pompeo conceded that "ISIS cells remain in multiple parts of the world," and he emphasized the need for the U.S. and its allies not to lower their guard. "But every place we find them," he said, "the president has given us the tools and the power and the authority to go after them so we can protect America."

Again, the public record confirmed Pompeo's assessment. The Trump strategy of all-out, gloves-off war against the Islamic State worked, whereas the Obama strategy of pinpricks and half measures had not.

During the Obama years, ISIS was completely on offense and intoxicated with victory, eventually gaining control of 40 percent of Iraq and one-third of Syria. By the end of Trump's first year in office, ISIS was on the ropes. It had lost 95 percent of its territory, including its capital in the Syrian city of Raqqa, as well as Mosul, the second largest city in Iraq.[23]

By March 2019, the caliphate had been completely destroyed. Sixty high-value targets and one hundred other ISIS officials had been killed. In Syria alone, 39,736 ISIS fighters had been killed.[24]

On October 26, 2019, U.S. military forces hunted down and killed Abu Bakr al-Baghdadi—the caliph, or leader, of the Islamic State—in a daring special forces operation led by Delta Force commandos in northwest Syria.[25]

This was a huge deal. Baghdadi had been ISIS's most fearsome and strategic leader. Taking over after the death of AQI founder Abu Musab al-Zarqawi in 2006, it was Baghdadi who really unleashed the genocide for which the world came to know ISIS.

William McCants, a former Brookings Institution scholar who authored the 2016 book *The ISIS Apocalypse: The History, Strategy, and Doomsday Vision of the Islamic State*, told me it was Baghdadi's theology—and even more important, his apocalyptic eschatology—that inspired jihadists from all over the world to join ISIS not only to rape, torture, and kill their enemies but to build an Islamic kingdom on earth and wage a campaign of annihilation against Jews, Christians, and even Muslims who didn't share ISIS's cultlike views.

By building a caliphate from scratch and slaughtering everyone in their way, McCants explained, ISIS had hoped to usher in the End of Days and the coming of the Islamic savior known as the Mahdi.[26]

The takedown of the caliphate was an extraordinary victory, one that will be studied by military strategists and intelligence operatives for decades. It came about through an alliance of eighty-three nations, but Pompeo was right: It was an American-led victory and one of the enduring legacies of the Trump presidency.

Again, David Shedd concurred.

"The U.S. strategy to 'find, fix, and finish' the leadership of these extremists—who are intent on using terrorism to promote their ideology—has been highly effective," he told me. "I can say with a high degree of confidence that the removal of the leadership of al Qaeda and ISIS as enemy combatants by killing them has proven highly effective in disrupting their operational capabilities."[27]

Yet, like Mike Pompeo, Shedd was adamant: "The U.S. cannot relent."

2

WHY IS IRAN A THREAT
LIKE NO OTHER?

*My conversation with Israeli prime minister
Benjamin Netanyahu*

On March 3, 2015, I arrived early at the U.S. Capitol Building, cleared security, and took my seat in the gallery in the U.S. House of Representatives.

The speaker that day would be Israeli prime minister Benjamin "Bibi" Netanyahu, and all 435 members of the House and 100 members of the Senate were expected to attend. I was grateful that Congressman Lynn Westmoreland of Georgia—a member of the House Intelligence Committee and a friend—had invited me to attend this joint session of Congress. After all, this was the hottest ticket in town.

The topic was the Iran nuclear threat, and there was electricity in the air. Everyone present knew we were about to witness a geopolitical showdown like few others in modern history.

From the moment that Speaker of the House John Boehner had issued the invitation in late January, a political firestorm had erupted. President Obama's staff said they had not been consulted about a possible Netanyahu speech and felt blindsided by the notion that an Israeli leader was coming to directly challenge a foreign policy position of the president of the United States in his own capital city.

Almost immediately, the White House announced that neither Obama nor Secretary of State John Kerry would meet with Netanyahu when he was in Washington. The official reason given was that, as a matter of policy, the president did not meet with foreign leaders close to their elections, and the Israelis were going to the polls on March 17. But everyone knew the real reason: Obama was furious that Boehner and Netanyahu were doing an end run around him, taking their case regarding the gravity of the Iranian threat directly to Congress and the American people.[1]

Vice President Joe Biden, who as president of the Senate had missed only one joint session of Congress since 2009, quickly announced he would not attend Netanyahu's address and would be "traveling abroad" instead.[2]

"A TRAIN WRECK IS COMING"

Tensions had been escalating since the very start of the Obama administration, but now they were reaching a fever pitch.

On April 14, 2009, less than three months after Obama's first inauguration, I warned in an interview on the Fox News Channel that "a train wreck is coming between the United States and Israel over how to handle Iran."[3]

That very day, Obama had blinked in the face of growing Iranian aggression.

As David Sanger, a national security correspondent for the *New York Times*, wrote at the time:

> The Obama administration and its European allies are preparing proposals that would shift strategy toward Iran by dropping a long-standing American insistence that Tehran rapidly shut down nuclear facilities during the early phases of negotiations over its atomic program, according to officials involved in the discussions.
>
> The proposals . . . would press Tehran to open up its nuclear program gradually to wide-ranging inspection. But the proposals would also allow Iran to continue enriching uranium for some period during the talks. That would be a sharp break from the approach taken by the Bush administration, which had demanded that Iran halt its enrichment activities, at least briefly to initiate negotiations. . . .

In warning against a more flexible American approach, a senior Israeli with access to the intelligence on Iran said during a recent visit to Washington that Mr. Obama had only until the fall or the end of the year to "completely end" the production of uranium in Iran. The official made it clear that after that point, Israel might revive its efforts to take out the Natanz plant by force.[4]

I told the Fox News interviewer that this was the worst moment in U.S.-Israeli relations in sixty-one years.

"Netanyahu understands that there is an apocalyptic, genocidal death cult running Iran right now," I said. "They are determined to get the nuclear weapons and destroy Israel. [But remember], Israel is only the Little Satan. The United States is the Great Satan. . . . The leaders of Iran want to annihilate the United States. And the idea that we will drop this precondition and not force Iran to stop enriching uranium before we sit down and talk is a huge mistake. I would describe it as appeasement."[5]

The supreme leader of Iran, Ayatollah Ali Khamenei, and his inner circle embrace a fanatical and genocidal form of eschatology I describe as apocalyptic Islam, something far more dangerous than mere radical Islam. Whereas radical Islamists use violence to pursue their political and theological objectives (such as driving Western forces out of the Middle East and reclaiming Palestine for Muslims), apocalyptic Islamists want to use violence to try to annihilate the State of Israel, neutralize the United States, decimate Christendom, and hasten the establishment of their global Islamic kingdom and the coming of their savior, the Mahdi.

These objectives are similar to those later adopted and preached by ISIS leader Abu Bakr al-Baghdadi. In Baghdadi's Sunni version of apocalyptic Islam, the coming of the Mahdi to earth could be accelerated by immediately starting to build the caliphate and immediately launching a campaign of genocide to eradicate Christians and Jews. There was no need to wait. Jihadists were commanded to use whatever weapons were at hand—even simple swords and knives.

By contrast, Khamenei's Shia version of apocalyptic Islam holds that the way to hasten the coming of the Mahdi is not to launch an immediate genocidal war against Jews and Christians but, rather, to methodically acquire weapons of mass destruction and *then* launch the war that will bring about the consummation of the End of Days.[6]

"The leaders of Iran believe that the end of the world is here," I explained during the Fox News interview. "They believe that the Islamic messiah, the Twelfth Imam, is coming imminently—that's the word they're using: *imminent*. And they believe their mission in life is to hasten or speed up the coming of the Islamic messiah by destroying Judeo-Christian civilizations as we know it. . . .

"Prime Minister Netanyahu understands this. . . . I've talked to him about it. . . . But [the Obama-Biden] administration does not."[7]

In the months that followed, U.S.-Israeli tensions worsened.

When George W. Bush left office in January 2009, 88 percent of Israelis said Bush was pro-Israel. By August 2009, however, a *Jerusalem Post* poll found that only 4 percent of Israelis believed Barack Obama was pro-Israel.[8]

THE SPEECH HEARD ROUND THE WORLD

Now Netanyahu was making his case on Obama's home turf. Addressing a joint session of Congress and a live global television audience, he said:

> Tomorrow night, on the Jewish holiday of Purim, we'll read the book of Esther. We'll read of a powerful Persian viceroy named Haman, who plotted to destroy the Jewish people some 2,500 years ago. But a courageous Jewish woman, Queen Esther, exposed the plot and gave for the Jewish people the right to defend themselves against their enemies. The plot was foiled. Our people were saved.
>
> Today the Jewish people face another attempt by yet another Persian potentate to destroy us. Iran's supreme leader, Ayatollah Khamenei, spews the oldest hatred, the oldest hatred of anti-Semitism with the newest technology. He tweets that Israel must be annihilated. . . .
>
> But Iran's regime is not merely a Jewish problem, any more than the Nazi regime was merely a Jewish problem. The 6 million Jews murdered by the Nazis were but a fraction of the 60 million people killed in World War II. So, too, Iran's regime poses a grave

threat, not only to Israel, but also the peace of the entire world. To understand just how dangerous Iran would be with nuclear weapons, we must fully understand the nature of the regime. . . .

I'm standing here in Washington, D.C., and the difference is so stark. America's founding document promises life, liberty, and the pursuit of happiness. [Revolutionary] Iran's founding document pledges death, tyranny, and the pursuit of jihad. . . .

Now, this shouldn't be surprising, because the ideology of Iran's revolutionary regime is deeply rooted in militant Islam, and that's why this regime will always be an enemy of America. . . .

Iran and ISIS are competing for the crown of militant Islam. . . . They just disagree among themselves who will be the ruler of that empire. . . .

The difference is that ISIS is armed with butcher knives, captured weapons, and YouTube, whereas Iran could soon be armed with intercontinental ballistic missiles and nuclear bombs. . . .

We can't let that happen.[9]

At one point, when the crowd in the gallery was on its feet applauding—myself included—the gentleman to my right, whom I did not know, leaned over and said to me, "This is an amazing speech. It's like one of Joel Rosenberg's novels. Have you ever read his novels? Some of them are about the Iran nuclear threat, and I'm telling you, Netanyahu sounds like he's reading from one of Rosenberg's novels."

Stunned, I just stared at him blankly.

Several more times during the speech, the man nudged me and whispered things like "That's crazy; that line sounds like it was ripped out of one of Rosenberg's novels."

Though I was reasonably certain Netanyahu could not hear the man, I shuddered at the thought that he might stop in the middle of his address, look up at us, and say, "Should I wait, or are you two done?"

I politely whispered back to the man that I would be happy to chat with him after the speech, but for now perhaps we could just listen. Netanyahu received twenty standing ovations that day. Not just from Republicans but from some Democrats as well.

HOW OBAMA SAW THE IRANIAN REGIME

While there were many strong lines in Netanyahu's speech, the most important one was this:

> To understand just how dangerous Iran would be with nuclear weapons, we must fully understand the nature of the regime.

Obama was infuriated by the speech. By that line. Indeed, almost everything about Netanyahu rankled him. Part of it was personality. The two leaders handled relationships, disagreements, and interpersonal conflict very differently. Early on, they had lit each other's fuse. The explosion was only a matter of time.

At its core, however, this was a fight over policy, not personality. These men held diametrically opposed views of the nature and goals of the Iranian regime. Netanyahu took Ayatollah Khamenei's murderous, genocidal, apocalyptic language literally. Obama did not. To the contrary, Obama regarded the Iranian leaders as rational actors who could be cajoled, incentivized, and ultimately persuaded by good old-fashioned persistent diplomacy to make a mutually beneficial deal with the community of nations.

Joe Biden was also on record as downplaying the Iranian regime's genocidal, apocalyptic language. While campaigning for president in Iowa in 2007, Biden had said, "My concern is not that a nuclear Iran someday would be moved by messianic fervor to use a nuclear weapon as an Armageddon device and commit national suicide in order to hasten the return of the Hidden Imam. My worry is that the fear of a nuclear Iran could spark an arms race in the Middle East, with Saudi Arabia, Egypt, Syria, and others joining in."[10]

In an address at American University a few months after the Netanyahu speech, President Obama said, "Just because Iranian hard-liners chant 'Death to America' does not mean that that's what all Iranians believe."[11]

To Netanyahu, the fact that most of Iran's 85 million people do not want to annihilate the United States has no bearing on what the "hardliners" who rule the country want to achieve. And as long as the ayatollahs are tweeting that Israel must be annihilated, it's difficult to believe that the majority of Iranian citizens have much say in the matter.

WHAT NETANYAHU TOLD ME

In the interests of full disclosure, I should tell you that I once worked for Benjamin Netanyahu.*

In autumn of 2000, I was running my own small consulting company, advising business and political leaders on messaging and communications strategy. Steve Forbes, the editor in chief of *Forbes* magazine and presidential candidate, had been a client. So was Natan Sharansky, the former Israeli interior minister.

In September, Netanyahu—who had served as Israel's prime minister from 1996 to 1999 but lost reelection to rival Ehud Barak—hired me to join a small group of American consultants to assist with his comeback campaign, hoping to return to the premiership in the winter of 2001.

At the time, I was still living in the U.S.—this was long before I became an Israeli citizen—but I was honored to work for Netanyahu as a media aide. My appointment didn't last long, however. In December, Barak found a way to checkmate Netanyahu, using a loophole in the law that prevented him from running, since he wasn't then a sitting member of the Knesset.

Netanyahu and I never worked closely together. Still, in the spring of 2003, when he was foreign minister, he invited me to visit Israel to discuss the threat of Iran and other forces in the region with him and his advisors. I gladly accepted and found the weeklong trip a treasure trove for future novels and nonfiction books.

A few years later, in January 2007, I asked Netanyahu if I could interview him for a documentary film I was producing, to be released for the fortieth anniversary of the reunification of Jerusalem by Israel in the June 1967 war. He graciously agreed. To this day, I'm fascinated by how that conversation provided a rare and important insight into how Netanyahu sees the Iranian regime and why the train wreck with Obama was inevitable.

As the camera began to roll, I said to Netanyahu, "In your 1995 book, *Fighting Terrorism*, you write that it's only a matter of time before the U.S. gets hit by radical Islam. You talk about the World Trade Center

---

* Mr. Netanyahu's staff declined multiple requests for the prime minister to be interviewed for this book. Thus, I drew upon relevant previous interviews and conversations I had with him. I have not had a meeting with Mr. Netanyahu since 2008.

and the threat of kamikaze attacks. What is it you were able to see in the mid-1990s that so many leaders in the West couldn't see?"

"I think the West misunderstood, and still misunderstands, the threat of [Iran's brand of] Islam," Netanyahu told me. "It is a fanatic, messianic ideology that seeks to have an apocalyptic battle for world supremacy with the West. It seeks to correct what it sees—what its disciples see—as an accident of history, where the West has risen and Islam had declined. The correction is supposed to be done by the resurrection of an Islamic empire and the acquisition of nuclear weapons and the use of nuclear weapons, if necessary, to obliterate Islam's enemies and to subjugate the rest.[12]

"This is a pathological ideology, much like Naziism was," Netanyahu continued. "And it poses a threat, in my judgment, in many ways bigger than Naziism—because Hitler embarked on a world conflict and then sought to achieve nuclear weapons. Whereas, as the leading radical Islamic regime, Iran is seeking to *first* acquire nuclear weapons and *then* embark on a world conflict. And that is what is not yet understood in the West; and certainly, if it's understood, it's not acted upon."

"How should the West deal with such a regime?" I asked.

For starters, Netanyahu told me, it is incredibly dangerous "to think that these people are normal" or that Iran's leaders "conform to the conceptions of deterrents and careful calculation of cost and benefit" and would respond positively to normal international diplomacy.

"You've already seen what the Sunni stream [of radical Islamism] does, which is to smash into buildings in Manhattan with collective suicide, to smash into the Pentagon with collective suicide," he said. "There is no reason to believe that the militant Shiites, once they have atomic weapons, will not be suicidal. They say openly that they intend to remove Israel, the 'Little Satan.' But remember that their goal is to get the United States, the 'Big Satan.' . . . And to have such a regime that believes in apocalyptic Armageddon with the West—in which millions will die on both sides, but the Muslim millions go to a Muslim heaven with all the trappings—to have that crazy ideology in charge of a country that is developing atomic weapons, is unbelievably dangerous and it should stop. Everything else is secondary to this."

"Can you negotiate with, or even successfully deter, someone who

believes that it is his God-given mission to eliminate millions of people?"
I pressed.

"No, it's very hard to rely on deterrents," Netanyahu explained. "It is not
the same as Soviet Russia. It is not the same as China or India or any one
of the nuclear powers today [that] think in terms of cost and benefit. In the
case of an extreme religious cult that has no such calculations, you could,
in fact, face a suicidal regime. Therefore, you cannot rely on deterrents.
You should work on prevention—that is, preventing them from acquiring
the weapons of mass death."

"How much time does the West have to make a decision to act decisively to stop Iran?" I asked.

"Not much—we are running out of time," he said, adding that the
regime "wants to concentrate on completing their nuclear program, because
once they have that, then they could threaten the West in ways that are
unimaginable today. They could take over the Persian Gulf on all its sides
and take control of the oil reserves of the world, most of them. They could
topple Saudi Arabia and Jordan in short order. And of course, Iraq. All
your internal debates in America on Iraq would be irrelevant because [a]
nuclear-armed Iran would subordinate Iraq in two seconds. And of course,
they threaten to create a Second Holocaust in Israel and proceed on their
idea of a global empire, producing twenty-five atomic bombs a year, 250
bombs in a decade, with missiles that they are already working on and
they want to develop to reach the Eastern seaboard of the United States.
This is something that just—everything else pales in comparison to this
development. This has to be stopped, for the sake of the world, not only
for the sake of Israel."

These were the views Netanyahu brought back into office when he
was reelected as prime minister in 2009. But not until Donald Trump was
elected did he have an ally who saw Iran as he did.

THE RISE OF A RUSSIAN-IRANIAN AXIS

*My conversations with senior U.S., Israeli,
and Arab intelligence officials*

Two decades ago, I didn't know a single American or foreign intelligence official.

However, over the course of my career writing political thrillers, non-fiction books, and columns about events in the Middle East, I have gotten to know three directors of the CIA, a director of the DIA, a director of national intelligence, and other key officials throughout the American intelligence community. I have also been fortunate to spend time with a broad range of senior intelligence officials in Israel, Egypt, Jordan, Saudi Arabia, the United Arab Emirates, Bahrain, and other countries in the Middle East.

Few spies will talk on the record—understandably—but the ones I've met have all been willing to talk to me at length on deep background, meaning I could use their input without attributing it to anyone directly.

The good news: They all concur that Iran does not have a nuclear weapon.

The bad news: They all quickly add that evidence continues to mount that the Iranian regime remains determined to build, buy, or steal nuclear weapons.

That, however, is not the only concern.

Many also worry that Tehran has been steadily and successfully build-ing a political, economic, and military alliance with two of the world's most troubling leaders—Russian president Vladimir Putin and Turkish president Recep Tayyip Erdoğan*—as well as with leaders of the People's Republic of China and North Korea. This is a recipe for trouble, made worse by the fact that far too few world leaders are paying sufficient attention to the trend or designing effective strategies to counter it.

I will explain in a moment. First, however, we need to take a brief look at how Israel and the U.S. have thus far managed to slow down Iran's nuclear program and take out some of Iran's key terrorist leaders without starting a full-blown kinetic war, and why Tehran is turning to Moscow and Ankara, hoping to achieve objectives in an alliance that it cannot achieve alone.†

THE WAR IN THE SHADOWS

Over the past decade and a half, key nuclear scientists in Iran have dis-appeared one by one.

On January 15, 2007, an expert in uranium enrichment died mysteri-ously while working at an Iranian nuclear facility in Isfahan.[1]

Three years later, one of Iran's leading nuclear scientists was killed in front of his home when a bomb-laden motorcycle parked next to his car exploded.[2]

Later that year, rumors began seeping out of Iran about a mysterious and highly aggressive malware virus that was suddenly plaguing computer sys-tems at nuclear facilities and other industrial plants throughout the Islamic Republic. As I wrote at the time, "The effect appears to be so severe that Iran had to announce at least a two-month delay in the launch of online operations at its Bushehr Reactor that the Russians helped build. Indeed, an estimated 30,000 computers in Iran have been infected. Neither the CIA nor Israel's Mossad has commented, much less claimed credit. Nor are they likely to do so. Perhaps they are not involved. But it may be that the relative

---

* Erdoğan is pronounced *EHR-doe-ahn*.

† I have been given access to sensitive (though not classified) data and intelligence assessments to write this chapter, but I am not at liberty to cite such material. Therefore, I will quote only what is known on the public record.

success of this ongoing and intensifying covert war inside Iran accounts for why Israel has not taken direct military action [against Iran] thus far."[3]

On July 23, 2011, another Iranian nuclear scientist was killed outside his home by gunmen on motorcycles.[4]

A few months later, a massive explosion at one of Iran's key missile bases killed seventeen people, including a key commander in their long-range missile program.[5]

Eight days later, another enormous explosion rocked Iran, this time at a nuclear facility in Isfahan used for uranium enrichment.[6]

On and on it went.

Meanwhile, however, the Obama administration was opposing congressional efforts to impose tougher economic sanctions on Iran, publicly pressuring Israel not to strike Iran, and publicly dismissing Israel's ability to do any serious damage even if they did attack Iran from the air. This was too much for even the reliably pro-Obama editors of the *Washington Post*. They published an editorial scorching the White House for "waffling" on the Iran issue and "sending the wrong signals to Iran," signals of weakness and indecision.[7]

"A major 'hot war' in the Middle East may be coming in 2012," I wrote at the end of 2011. "But evidence continues to mount of an aggressive 'covert war' already being fought inside Iran and the Middle East. The goal: to neutralize Tehran's nuclear weapons and ballistic missile programs before it's too late."[8]

Whoever was responsible, the attacks were working. Tehran's bid for a nuclear arsenal was being slowed down without a full-blown war. But the mullahs were not dissuaded from continuing to try.

THE STEAL OF THE CENTURY

Zoom ahead to January 2018.

That was when Prime Minister Netanyahu gave the Mossad the green light to break into a top secret Iranian archive facility in the heart of Tehran. The legendary Israeli spy agency wasted no time. At enormous risk to their lives, a team of undercover operatives broke into the building and spent almost six and a half hours opening thirty-two safes with blowtorches that burned at 3,600 degrees.[9]

By the time they were done, the Israeli operatives escaped with a half ton of priceless documents—55,000 pages, 183 compact discs of memos, videos, and plans—the very blueprints and strategy for making nuclear weapons and attaching them to ballistic missiles that the Iranian regime had always denied having.[10]

Independent analysts soon verified that the documents were real and significant.

"The Nuclear Archive [seized by Israel in Iran] contains much new information not previously available to the IAEA (International Atomic Energy Agency) or Western governments . . . about Iran's past work on nuclear weapons," said David Albright, a leading American nuclear expert, in sworn testimony before the U.S. House Subcommittee on National Security in June 2018, after reviewing the materials. "It presents a much more complete picture of Iran's nuclear weapons efforts [and in far more detail] than previously available."[11]

What kind of critical information was found in the archive? Here are the principal items Albright presented to Congress:

- the number and kilotons of nuclear weapons sought by Iran
- the specific amount of highly enriched uranium in nuclear explosive designs
- blueprints for the production of all the components of nuclear weapons
- the location of planned nuclear weapons test sites
- details about a second building at the Parchin site involved in high explosive work related to nuclear weapons in an explosive chamber. This building has not been visited by the IAEA.
- other nuclear weapons related sites and activities
- much more detail about Iran's extensive work on uranium metallurgy including ample evidence of Iran having all the equipment for all the work needed in a nuclear weapons uranium metallurgy program. The information also shows that Iran made all the uranium metal weapons components with surrogate materials.
- small-scale uranium processing for a neutron initiator for a nuclear weapon

- direct evidence that the secret Fordow enrichment site was being built to make weapon-grade uranium[12]

MASTERMINDS NO MORE

Now zoom ahead to December 2019.

Angered by ongoing Iranian and Iranian-backed proxy attacks against Americans and her allies, President Trump ordered the chairman of the Joint Chiefs of Staff to locate and eliminate General Qassem Soleimani, head of the Islamic Revolutionary Guard Corps' elite Quds [Jerusalem] Force.

On January 3, 2020, the Pentagon delivered.

Soleimani was a big fish—one of Ayatollah Khamenei's most trusted advisors. When he was killed in a stunning U.S. drone strike at Baghdad International Airport—along with several of his aides, senior Iranian military officials, and terrorist allies—it was an enormous blow to Khamenei's reign of terror.

Soleimani was "actively developing plans to attack American diplomats and service members in Iraq and throughout the region," a Pentagon spokesman said, adding that the general and his Quds Force "were responsible for the deaths of hundreds of American and coalition service members and the wounding of thousands more."[13]

When the news became public just after New Year's, Mark Dubowitz, a Middle East analyst and head of the Foundation for the Defense of Democracies in Washington, observed that "the strike on Soleimani was more consequential than the killing of Osama bin Laden. The general's experience, savvy, and resources had made him Iran's real foreign minister and close to irreplaceable for Tehran."[14]

The *New York Times*, no friend of the Trump administration, noted that "in killing Soleimani, Trump took an action that Presidents George W. Bush and Barack Obama had rejected, fearing it would lead to war between the United States and Iran."[15]

Now zoom ahead yet again, to November 27, 2020.

That was the day that Mohsen Fakhrizadeh, another Iranian mastermind, was assassinated near Tehran in broad daylight. Fakhrizadeh was not only a brigadier general in the Iranian Revolutionary Guard Corps, he was also the man in charge of Iran's entire covert nuclear weapons development program.

"It's a major operational hit—more or less equivalent to the U.S. hit on Qassem Soleimani," said Uzi Rabi, director of Tel Aviv University's Moshe Dayan Center for Middle Eastern and African Studies.[16]

Unfortunately, there is no sign that, as a result of these losses, Tehran has chosen to abandon its ambition to build or acquire a nuclear arsenal. To the contrary, evidence mounts month by month that Iran is still building more secret nuclear facilities, cheating on the Joint Comprehensive Plan of Action (JCPOA)—the Iran nuclear deal—which is still in force with all signatory countries except the U.S., and accelerating its ability to break out and create fully operational nuclear weapons.[17]

What's more, in his final major address, Secretary of State Mike Pompeo revealed previously undisclosed evidence that "al Qaeda has a new home base: it is the Islamic Republic of Iran," and that, combined with Iran's aggressive nuclear program, "this axis poses a grave threat to the security of nations and to the American homeland itself."[18]

TEHRAN TURNS TO PUTIN

This is where the story takes an ominous turn.

Consistently stymied and stalled—if not fully thwarted—in their bid for the Persian Bomb, the ayatollahs and mullahs in Tehran have turned their eyes to Moscow in recent years.

The Russian Federation, after all, is already a nuclear-armed nation. They currently possess 6,372 nuclear warheads—1,572 deployed, 2,740 in reserve, and an additional 2,060 retired but still intact.[19] What's more, the Russians have some 485 "deployed strategic delivery systems," including short-range, medium-range, and intercontinental ballistic missiles, ten strategic submarines, and sixty-six strategic bombers.[20]

To be clear, U.S. and foreign intelligence officials tell me they're not afraid Putin would sell, much less give, Russian nuclear warheads to the mullahs in Tehran. Nor do they believe the mullahs are specifically seeking Russian warheads. Rather, they believe Tehran wants to dramatically expand the threat it can pose to the U.S., Israel, and the Sunni Arab world by aligning itself in every possible way with Moscow. They want to buy

Russian arms and Russian nuclear technology and know-how, create trade deals with Moscow, and leverage Russian political cover at the United Nations.

Why have they found a willing partner in Putin? The Russian leader has multiple motives. One is that he wants to pull together a vast coalition of nations who hate the U.S., will vote against the U.S. at the U.N., frustrate American foreign policy objectives around the world, and create a counterweight to what Putin regards as an unacceptable unipolar world led by Washington.

"A unipolar world does not exist anymore," Putin said in his annual press conference in December 2019. "After the collapse of the Soviet Union, there was an illusion that this [unipolar] world is possible and could exist for a long time. However, it was just an illusion. I have always said that, and recent events serve as a testament to this."

Putin attributed "the appearance of a multipolar world order" to global economic development. But, he said, the world "cannot have a unipolar structure with just one center that controls the entire global community."[21]

In Khamenei, Putin has embraced one of the leading anti-American figures on the planet. Putin is convinced that the Iranian regime is serving his purposes. But what if Putin miscalculates? What if, by helping Khamenei, Putin inadvertently creates a thermonuclear monster?

These are the questions I put to retired Major General Aharon Ze'evi-Farkash, who served as the head of *Aman*, Israeli military intelligence, from 2002 to 2006. It turned out these are exactly Israel's concerns.

"Iran's strategy is to have a nuclear military capacity as a threat to Israel and the region and the world—for them, it's important to continue the [Islamic] revolution," the general told me. But the Kremlin doesn't see it. "I spoke with leaders in Russia. I met President Putin, and he says, 'You don't have to worry about nuclear military capacity in Iran. We are there. We are close to them. We will control them. We will not give them the opportunity to achieve what they started.' And my answer was 'What happened in China? What happened in India? What happened in Pakistan?'" No one thought those countries could build nuclear warheads and long-range missiles. But they did. And no one knew until they tested. But by then it was too late to stop them.[22]

A CZAR IS BORN

In 2000, three Russian journalists published a book about Putin, titled *First Person*. It is one of the most important books ever written about the Russian president, not because the journalists offered their own analysis or insights into Putin but because they simply let him speak for himself. They interviewed Putin on six separate occasions, each time for about four hours. The book is merely a transcript, and when it comes to understanding Putin's ambitions and approach, it is a gold mine of intelligence.[23]

Putin on his mission in life:

- "My historical mission," he insists, is "preventing the collapse of the country."[24]
- To do this, he vowed to "consolidate the armed forces, the Interior Ministry, and the FSB [the successor to the KGB, the secret police of the Soviet Union]."[25]
- "If I can help save Russia from collapse, then I'll have something to be proud of."[26]

Putin on his style:

- "Everyone says I'm harsh, even brutal," Putin acknowledges, without ever disputing such observations. "A dog senses when somebody is afraid of it, and bites," he observes. "The same applies [to dealing with one's enemies]. If you become jittery, they will think that they are stronger. Only one thing works in such circumstances—to go on the offensive. You must hit first, and hit so hard that your opponent will not rise to his feet."[27]

Putin on the czars of Russia:

- "From the very beginning, Russia was created as a super-centralized state. That's practically laid down in its genetic code, its traditions, and the mentality of its people," said Putin, adding, "In certain periods of time . . . in a certain place . . . under certain conditions . . . monarchy has played and continues to this day to play a positive role. . . . The monarch doesn't have to worry about whether or not he will be elected, or about petty political interests, or about how to influence the electorate. He can think about the destiny of the people and not become distracted with trivialities."[28]

Putin's choice of history's most interesting political leader:

- "Napoleon Bonaparte."[29]

On his rise from spy to president:

- "In the Kremlin, I have a different position. Nobody controls me here. I control everybody else."[30]

Putin is not an ideologue. Though he grew up in the epicenter of communism and was a loyal agent with the Soviet KGB, there is no evidence that at his core he is a Marxist-Leninist-Communist.

Nor is Putin driven by religion. He claims to be a Christian, occasionally attends the Russian Orthodox Church, poses for photo ops with Orthodox priests, and refers in speeches to the church and its importance in Russian life more than any Russian leader since the days of the czars.[31] But there is no evidence that he has a personal relationship with Jesus Christ or that the teaching of the Bible actually shapes or guides his actions. Rather, the evidence suggests Putin is playing on the deep cultural and nationalistic affection the Russian people have for the Russian Orthodox Church to advance his popularity and political power.

I believe there are two ways to explain Putin.

The first possibility is that Putin sees himself as a modern-day czar—a strong, authoritarian, even totalitarian monarch divinely chosen to work for the glory of Mother Russia, for her power, for her expansion, for her riches, for her supremacy in the world. Though he mourns its demise, I don't think he wants to rebuild the Soviet empire. Why bother absorbing all the headaches of the former republics? Since he fears the prospect that Russia could ever appear weak, he looks for low-risk, high-reward military adventures that make Russia—that is, himself—look strong.

The second possibility is that Putin sees himself as a Russian version of *The Godfather*—a gangster, a phenomenally wealthy and murderous mafia boss. But Putin is not the aging Vito Corleone. Nor is he the rash and impulsive Sonny Corleone, who in his anger let down his guard and allowed himself to be assassinated at the tollbooth. Putin is more like Michael Corleone—cold, calculating, driven by an insatiable lust for money, power, vengeance, and respect—ungoverned by the laws of men and willing to intimidate or kill anyone who gets in his way.

Every intelligence official I've spoken to has a slightly different view, but generally they all fall into one of these two camps. I see Putin as a combination of the two. In his heart, he sees himself as a "Mikhail Corleone"; but in his public persona, he portrays himself more as Czar Vladimir IV, trying to put a more nationalistic (and thus a more acceptable) face on his own greed and ambition.

Either way, he is a dangerous man building alliances with other dangerous men.

PUTIN EMBRACES TEHRAN

When Putin became president of the Russian Federation on December 31, 1999, he immediately turned his attention toward Iran.

As the *New York Times* reported in October 2000, "Vice President Al Gore signed a secret agreement [in June 1995] with Viktor S. Chernomyrdin, then the Russian prime minister, calling for an end to all Russian sales of conventional weapons to Iran by the end of 1999."[32]

Putin could not have cared less. It was not his agreement, so soon he was selling hundreds of millions to almost two billion dollars of arms to Iran every year.[33]

Putin also dramatically increased Russia's involvement in helping Iran build its first nuclear power plant, taking over from a German company's earlier efforts.[34] Before long, one thousand Russian nuclear scientists, engineers, and technicians were working in Iran.[35] In time, Russia would ink a deal to help Iran build eight more nuclear facilities.[36]

In 2007, Putin traveled to Tehran to meet with Iranian president Mahmoud Ahmadinejad. It was the first time a Russian leader had visited Iran since Joseph Stalin in 1943.[37] Russia also signed a $800 million deal to sell Iran its most-advanced antimissile system, the S-300.[38]

In 2014, Putin signed a $20 billion trade deal with Iran, directly contravening international economic sanctions levied against Iran in response to Tehran's illegal nuclear program.[39]

In November 2015, Putin made his second trip to Tehran, meeting with Ayatollah Khamenei for ninety minutes.[40]

On and on it goes.

Thus, the question remains: Why is Czar Putin building an alliance with the most dangerous and destabilizing regime in an already-volatile region of the world?

Part of his motive is money. After the collapse of the Soviet Union, the Russians found themselves desperate for foreign currency and awash with weapons they weren't likely to use anytime soon. Meanwhile, after eight years of war with Iraq, the Iranians were lusting after advanced weaponry and nuclear technology—and they had plenty of cash from their oil reserves. Boris Yeltsin didn't recognize the opportunity in the 1990s. But his successor soon did. It was a match made in hell.

But Putin craves more than just cash. Like a mob boss, he also craves power. So with a nuclear arsenal and a massive military machine at his disposal, Putin is determined to pursue his vision of imperial greatness by expanding Russian influence around the world. This is why he invaded the republic of Georgia in 2008, capturing 20 percent of Georgian territory; invaded Ukraine in 2014 and annexed Crimea; sent military forces into Syria in 2015, ostensibly to support his ally, President Bashar al-Assad, but also to make Russia a major—and feared—player in the Middle East. Putin also established a permanent Russian naval base in the Syrian port of Tartus.

Is he done?

Or is he just getting started?

4

WHY THE ADDITION OF TURKEY TO THE RUSSIAN-IRANIAN AXIS IS SO DANGEROUS

Further conversations with senior U.S., Israeli, and Arab intelligence officials

The Russian-Iranian alliance is troubling enough.

Now add in Turkey.

With some 375,000 active-duty soldiers under arms, Ankara has the largest military in Europe and is a member of the North Atlantic Treaty Organization (NATO). Under President Recep Tayyip Erdoğan, however, Turkey is now abandoning its longtime Western allies and turning East.

Historically, Moscow and Tehran are not obvious partners for Turkey, so the alliance bears some examination.

"For Turkish security analysts, no country is dreaded more for its military power and expansionist tendencies than Russia," observes a noted expert on Turkey. "Between 1568, when the Ottomans and Russians first clashed, and the end of the Russian Empire in 1917, the Turks and Russians fought over a dozen large-scale wars. In each encounter, Russia was the instigator, and in most cases the overall victor. . . . Many Turks are woefully aware of Russia's role as their country's historical nemesis."[1]

Indeed, early on, Putin and Erdoğan were not at all close. In 2015, Turkey shot down a Russian fighter jet that had entered its territory. Analysts feared an escalation. Instead, Putin and Erdoğan calmed the situation. When Erdoğan crushed a coup attempt on July 15, 2016, Putin was the first world leader to call and congratulate him. The two subsequently met in St. Petersburg and a friendship was born.[2]

By 2017, Erdoğan had signed a $2.5 billion deal with Putin to buy the S-400 antiballistic missile system, the most state-of-the-art defense artillery in the Russian inventory. Vehement U.S. objections did not dissuade Erdoğan, who saw no problem as a NATO member getting into bed with the Kremlin.

"Turkey is continuing its steady, dangerous march to the dark side," I wrote at the time. "Erdoğan entered office posing as somewhat of a moderate but is emerging as a radical Islamist and a serious and growing challenge to the U.S. and the West."[3]

In November 2017, Putin, Erdoğan, and Iranian president Hassan Rouhani met in Sochi, Russia, for their first summit.

Six months later, the three met again in Ankara.

In September 2018, the three met for a summit in Tehran.

In February 2019, they met in Sochi again.

In September 2019, the three were back in Ankara for yet another summit.

In July 2020, Putin, Rouhani, and Erdoğan held a videoconference together, choosing not to meet in person due to the COVID-19 pandemic.

Ostensibly, the three were simply trying to solve the crisis in Syria. In fact, Putin was building a strategic alliance with two of the most dangerous regimes in the Middle East.

THE SULTAN RISES

Turkey is a gorgeous country, rich in beauty, history, and culture.

I have been there many times to speak, attend conferences, and meet with leaders from all over the Muslim world. I have also enjoyed touring the land, from the ruins of Ephesus to the Byzantine bazaars and medieval mosques of Istanbul. Several times, I took my wife and four sons there to visit. We never once felt uncomfortable, much less in danger, as Americans, as Christians, or as Jews.

To understand why Turkey is changing so rapidly, it is critical to understand the rise of President Erdoğan.

First, a bit of context.

For more than six hundred years, a succession of sultans ruled a regional superpower known as the Ottoman Empire, a kingdom (or caliphate) with vast wealth and great military strength. At the empire's zenith, the Ottomans controlled more than one million square miles on three continents, including the countries we know today as Turkey, Greece, Bulgaria, Egypt, Hungary, Macedonia, Romania, Jordan, Israel, Lebanon, Syria, parts of the Arabian Peninsula, and the coastal regions of North Africa.[4]

By the end of World War I, however, the Ottoman Empire had been defeated by the British-American alliance. In 1923, Mustafa Kemal—a Turkish general who had helped remove the last sultan and led a revolution to liberate his country—founded the modern Republic of Turkey. Elected its first president, Kemal built it into a pro-Western, pluralistic democracy respectful of its Muslim heritage yet decidedly secular in its governance and military ranks. As his reforms succeeded in rebuilding the humbled nation, Kemal's popularity grew. People began calling him Atatürk, meaning "Father of the Turks," and the moniker stuck.

Mustafa Kemal Atatürk died in 1938, but his vision had taken hold. Turkey emerged over the course of the twentieth century as a rare model for Muslim reformers. By 1952, Turkey was welcomed into the NATO alliance. It became a destination of choice for European tourists and even for Israelis, who flocked to Turkey's southern beach resorts for inexpensive yet lovely and even luxurious vacations.

Not anymore.

"Whereas Atatürk . . . envisioned Turkey as European, Erdoğan has pivoted the country toward the Middle East and often practiced Islamist solidarity in foreign policy to make Turkey a great regional power," writes Soner Cagaptay, a Turkish political analyst based in Washington, D.C., in his 2017 biography of Erdoğan, *The New Sultan: Erdogan and the Crisis of Modern Turkey*. "Across the Middle East, Erdoğan [threw] his support exclusively behind the Muslim Brotherhood," the region's original and largest Islamist movement, and "amassed powers sufficient to undermine Atatürk's legacy."[5]

Born in Istanbul in 1954 to a lower-middle-class family, the young Erdoğan regarded himself as a pious Muslim. A *New York Times Magazine* profile noted that he "would practice his fiery rhetoric on abandoned ships, facing into the wind as he rehearsed his salutation: 'My sacred brothers, whose hearts beat with the excitement of a big future Islamic conquest. . . .'"[6]

Erdoğan became convinced that the only way to restore Turkey to the right path was to enter politics and change the system from within. But to do so in such a highly secularized society, he would have to hide his true beliefs. He began by transferring from a religious high school to a secular public high school to build a more mainstream résumé, even while quietly joining an Islamist study group committed to weaponizing Muslim religious doctrine to achieve political objectives.[7]

In 1994, Erdoğan finally achieved his first victory, and it was a stunning one: He was elected mayor of Istanbul, Turkey's largest city.[8]

Reflecting the nation's commitment to secularism, Erdoğan, ever the pragmatist, wore suits, not clerical robes. His wife did not wear a headscarf in public. He stayed focused on improving the "buses, rubbish collection, pollution, [and] water," not trying to impose Sharia law.[9]

In 1997, however, he let his mask slip.

At a political rally in a poor, highly religious community in southeastern Turkey, Erdoğan recited an Islamist poem to fire up the crowd.

The mosques are our barracks,
the domes our helmets
the minarets our bayonets,
and the faithful our soldiers.[10]

And he didn't stop there. In his speech, as reported in the *New York Times Magazine,* "Erdoğan went on to proclaim that Islam was his compass and that anyone who tried to stifle prayer in Turkey would face an exploding volcano."

In "playing to the crowd," Erdoğan was "prodding the military. And the military took the bait. Erdoğan was charged with inciting hatred on the basis of religion and convicted."[11]

As *Time* magazine reported, Erdoğan "served four months in prison and was barred for life from public office."[12]

To closet Islamists all across Turkey, Erdoğan was now part martyr, part hero, and his popularity surged.

THE MASK COMES OFF

Upon his release from jail, Erdoğan began plotting his comeback.

First he would run for prime minister and then for president. To get there, however, Erdoğan knew he would have to become more disciplined. In 2001, he established a new "moderate" Islamic movement called the Justice and Development Party (AKP).[13]

"We are not an Islamist party," one member insisted. "We are for democracy, good economics, and social justice."[14]

It worked. Fourteen months later, the AKP won almost two-thirds of the seats in Turkey's Grand National Assembly.

With Erdoğan barred by law from the premiership, deputy chairman Abdullah Gül initially became prime minister. But the party quickly amended the Turkish constitution to allow Erdoğan to take over the reins in March 2003.

Assiduously cultivating his image as a pragmatist, Erdoğan made a dozen trips to Washington and attended NATO summits.[15] In 2005, he even made a two-day visit to Israel, toured the Yad Vashem Holocaust memorial, and invited Prime Minister Ariel Sharon to visit Ankara.[16]

But the ruse didn't last for long.

In 2009, Erdoğan chose an annual forum of world leaders in Davos, Switzerland, to deliver a blistering attack on Israeli president Shimon Peres, accusing the Israelis of being expert murderers of the Palestinians.

"When it comes to killing, you know very well how to kill," Erdoğan said directly to Peres as the two men sat side by side in a panel debate over the war underway at that time in Gaza.[17]

In a twelve-minute monologue, Erdoğan blasted alleged Israeli atrocities. When Peres tried to defend himself and his nation, Erdoğan would have none of it. When the moderator tried to close down the discussion, Erdoğan was determined to have the last word—again taking Peres and Israel to task. Then he got up and walked off the stage.[18]

The stunt made headlines. The video was seen by millions. Again Erdoğan's popularity surged.

GAINING POWER

In August of 2014, Erdoğan was elected president of Turkey with 52 percent of the vote. Soon after, he abandoned his image as a moderate and a pragmatist, revealing himself as an Islamist consumed with gathering power to himself. As he did, however, the mood in Turkey began to sour. Under the radar, elements of the Turkish military were becoming convinced Erdoğan was a threat to the security and well-being of the country.

On July 15, 2016, elite units of the Turkish military launched an operation to forcibly remove Erdoğan from power. Erdoğan, in turn, quickly mobilized army units loyal to him. When the shooting stopped, at least 250 people had been killed and some 2,000 injured.[19]

Erdoğan seized the moment to purge his opponents—and perceived opponents—from government and civil society. In one of the most brutal crackdowns of any professed democracy in the world, he ordered the arrest of at least 160,000 Turks and foreign nationals and fired 170,000 Turkish government employees for allegedly having ties to the coup.[20]

Since then, things in Turkey have gone from bad to worse. We can see the trend in headlines from the past few years:

WITH MORE ISLAMIC SCHOOLING,
ERDOGAN AIMS TO RESHAPE TURKEY
Reuters, January 25, 2018

ERDOGAN'S AMBITIONS GO BEYOND SYRIA.
HE SAYS HE WANTS NUCLEAR WEAPONS
New York Times, *October 20, 2019*

AFTER SIX DECADES, TURKEY IS NOW A U.S. ALLY IN NAME ONLY
The New Yorker, *November 14, 2019*

TURKEY EXPELS PROTESTANT MISSIONARIES
FOR "THREATENING PUBLIC ORDER"
Al-Monitor, July 9, 2020

TORTURE ON THE RISE IN ERDOGAN'S TURKEY
Al-Monitor, July 31, 2020

SULTAN OF CENSORSHIP: TURKEY'S PRESIDENT
CRACKS DOWN ON SOCIAL MEDIA

The Economist, *August 6, 2020*

ISRAELI MILITARY AND INTELLIGENCE ASSESSMENTS
SEE TURKEY AS GROWING THREAT

Jerusalem Post, *August 23, 2020*

TURKISH PRESIDENT RECEP TAYYIP ERDOĞAN: JERUSALEM WAS
BUILT BY THE OTTOMANS; IT IS OUR CITY, A CITY FROM US

Middle East Media Research Institute, October 2, 2020

In April 2017, "a slim majority of Turkish voters agreed . . . to grant sweeping powers to their president, in a watershed moment that the country's opposition fears may cement a system of authoritarian rule within one of the critical power brokers of the Middle East. . . . The constitutional change will allow the winner of the 2019 presidential election to assume full control of the government, ending the current parliamentary political system."[21]

Sure enough, Erdoğan won in 2019 and was quick to savor his victory, telling his supporters, "We are enacting the most important governmental reform of our history." The once-stealth Islamist had brilliantly gamed the Turkish democracy to acquire near-absolute power and pursue his radical agenda.

"Democracy is like a streetcar," he once said. "When you come to your stop, you get off."[22]

REASSESSING ERDOĞAN

Porter Goss served as CIA director from 2004 to 2006. Previous to that, he was chairman of the House Intelligence Committee; as a young man, he had worked as a clandestine officer in the Agency.

I didn't know Goss when he was at the CIA. It was only after he retired that I learned he was a fan of my books. Then, in 2007, he and his wife, Mariel, invited Lynn and me out for dinner with some mutual friends—and we have been meeting ever since. Indeed, for the past decade or so, I have made an annual pilgrimage to the Gosses' home in south Florida. The deal is simple: They critique my latest political thriller and I get to test my ideas for the next one. As you might imagine, over the years we have discussed Russia, Iran, Syria, and Turkey many times.

"I must admit," Goss told me in November 2020, when I interviewed him for this book, "I may not have properly assessed Erdoğan. I always thought he could be brought around. I never thought he would try to put the whole [moderate] change in Turkey back in the bottle and turn Turkey back into an Islamic empire. Trying to get rid of Atatürk? It never occurred to me he would even try that, but actually he is trying to do that."[23]

During Erdoğan's early years in power, Goss noted, Turkey had a very good economy and was doing its part in NATO. "Then all of a sudden, he got this idea that people were turning on him. And, Joel, this I *do* know, because I talked to Erdoğan personally about it."

Goss met with Erdoğan in Turkey during the George W. Bush administration, and he said, "We had a cordial and businesslike discussion. As I was leaving his office, he pulled me aside and gave me a message in very strong language to take back to Washington. Erdoğan does speak some English, and he made it quite clear how deeply hurt he was because his Western allies weren't standing up for him. Europeans were questioning if he was a reliable member of NATO and ridiculing him, in his view. I recall he was especially upset about some Danish cartoons [mocking the prophet Muhammad]. I honestly think that was a benchmark moment for him—he felt kicked in the teeth by the West. And I would guess it added to his suspicions about prominent Turkish dissidents, real opponents of his, some living in the United States."

Erdoğan's mood shifted from that point, Goss told me, and the Turkish leader became far more inclined to go off and do his own thing.

"He has turned to other players who are pleased to exploit his unhappiness for their own agendas," Goss said. "That's why you're seeing relationships emerge with Russia, Iran, and possibly other mischief-makers."

Indeed, even though Turkey, Russia, and Iran have long histories of assorted conflicts with one another, and even though the three leaders—Erdoğan, Putin, and Khamenei—have enormous egos, megalomaniacal ambitions, and conflicting worldviews, what is becoming increasingly clear is that these men share several common objectives. Driven by their own fierce sense of nationalism (among other motives), they are deeply unhappy and increasingly determined to frustrate and neutralize (if possible) American economic, geopolitical, and military power. Not convinced they can effectively challenge American supremacy individually, the three are progressively joining forces and looking for targets of opportunity.

Goss calls it "an unholy alliance."

He believes that Putin and Khamenei, in particular, are working hard to pull other leaders into their orbit—including China, North Korea, Venezuela, and any other anti-American, anti-Western leaders they can round up.

"I see despots working together in illegitimate enterprise," Goss told me. "Their first mission is to stay in power. Their second mission is to enrich themselves. Their third mission is to make sure that nobody is misbehaving at their expense. We're talking about unsteady personalities who are comfortable associating with violence if it brings them something. That's what I mean by an 'unholy alliance.'"[24]

WHAT DOES THE FUTURE HOLD?

Could the nascent Russian-Iranian-Turkish alliance fall apart if one (or more) of its current leaders dies or is otherwise removed from power?

Of course.

But what if they, or their successors, continue building this alliance? They've had a test run learning how to cooperate—fitfully, to be sure—during the takeover of Syria. What might be next? If they truly went all in to join their political, economic, and military assets, how might they threaten American, European, and Israeli interests?

One thing is certain: The growing threat posed by Moscow, Tehran, and Ankara has forced every leader in the region—most specifically the leaders of the Sunni Arab states—to fundamentally rethink: *Who is my friend, and who is my foe?*

As I told the audience at the Values Voter Summit in September 2018, "These [Arab] countries realize that the threat to the region is not the United States; it's not Israel; it's not Christianity. It is Iran and Iran's radical Islamism," along with Iran's growing ties with Russia and Turkey.[25]

And yet there is a silver lining in all this.

Even as Russia, Iran, and Turkey are forming their dangerous alliance, something new and encouraging is developing as a potential counterweight. As far back as 2018, we began to see the rise of an American–Israeli–Sunni Arab alliance—imperfect and not yet fully formed—that offers hope for renewed stability and expanded peace in the Middle East.

Moderate leaders now see that forming close strategic ties with both the United States and Israel is essential to their ability to survive, let alone thrive, and they are taking steps toward that end.

I have had a rare opportunity to observe this process up close and to talk with the very leaders who are working hard to shape a more positive future for the people of the region—leaders such as the king of Jordan, the president of Egypt, and the crown prince of Saudi Arabia, among others. In the next section, I will introduce you to these leaders in the order I met them and give you an opportunity to hear their ideas, dreams, desires—and fears—in their own words.

Part Two

THE
OPPORTUNITIES

5

I HAD NEVER MET A KING BEFORE

My first meeting with Jordan's King Abdullah II

On January 14, 2016, my executive assistant received a cryptic email from someone named Rob Richer:

> A senior foreign official who has read *The First Hostage* has asked me to reach out to Joel to discuss a possible meeting. For sensitivity purposes, I'd prefer to outline by phone.

It was all rather mysterious. The official's name was not mentioned, and I had not heard of the email's author. So of course I googled him.

> Rob Richer retired in November 2005 from the Central Intelligence Agency as the associate deputy director for operations (ADDO). Prior to his assignment as the ADDO in 2004, Richer was the chief of the Near East and South Asia Division, responsible for clandestine service operations throughout the Middle East and South Asia. Mr. Richer currently consults on Middle East and national security issues and is a senior partner with International Advisory Partners.[1]

Intrigued, I made calls to friends in the intelligence and diplomatic community to learn more and heard only good things about Richer. When I learned he was also a former CIA station chief in Jordan and a friend of King Abdullah II, I got right back to him.

We arranged to have lunch the following Monday at the Old Ebbitt Grill in downtown Washington, around the corner from the White House. After sharing a bit of our backgrounds, Richer explained that he had flown to D.C. several weeks earlier to meet with the Jordanian monarch, who was scheduled to meet with President Obama to discuss the war with ISIS, the massive influx of Syrian and Iraqi refugees who were fleeing ISIS and flooding into Jordan, and other critical matters.

While routing through Heathrow Airport, Richer saw a copy of my latest political thriller, *The First Hostage*, in a bookstore window. He had no idea who I was and had not read any of my books. But there was something about the cover and title that caught his interest. He ducked into the shop, bought a copy, boarded the plane, settled in, and began reading the first chapter.

He said he was stunned to find the Hashemite Kingdom overrun by ISIS. Amman in flames. The royal palace destroyed. And the king flying his own Black Hawk helicopter to a military base to coordinate a counterstrike. That's how the novel begins. Upon reaching Washington, Richer said, he headed for the Four Seasons Hotel, went up to the king's suite, cleared security, and handed the novel to the king.

"Your Majesty, you have to read this."

"Why?" asked the king, looking at the cover of the book.

"Because you're in it."

"What do you mean I'm in the book? It's a novel."

"Right, but you're a named character."

When I wrote *The First Hostage,* I decided not to create a fictional character to represent the Jordanian monarch. I was so intrigued by the real King Abdullah's background that I saw no reason to make up a fictional counterpart for my books. As a moderate Muslim, a direct descendant of the prophet Muhammad, a helicopter pilot, a commando, and a onetime commander of Jordan's special forces—who never expected to ascend to the throne but then did—the king was an action hero in real life. So why not make him a character in my series?

Richer then told me the rest of the story.

That weekend, President Obama had canceled his meeting with the king. This was unheard of. The king had not just "popped in" to Washington. He had been invited to meet with the president. Now that the media knew he was there, he couldn't exactly slip out of town quietly and head back to Amman. Moreover, he also had meetings scheduled with cabinet officials and members of the House and Senate.

But now that he didn't have to spend time with his advisors preparing to meet and meeting with Obama, the king had some free time on his hands.

"So he read your book in two days," Richer said.

I was floored, but there was more.

After the king finished *The First Hostage*, he asked Richer, "What do you know about the author?"

Richer had no idea, so the king asked him to find out.

After Richer found my website and read my bio, he turned to my blog. It so happened that I had posted two new articles that day, both of which blasted Obama for snubbing the king.[2]

When Richer brought the stories to the king's attention, the king told him to set up a meeting with me.

THE INVITATION

Over lunch, Richer asked some probing questions.

Why had I chosen to write a series of thrillers involving Jordan? Why had I written about ISIS trying to assassinate the king and overthrow the monarchy? Why had I used the king's real name? These were sensitive topics, to be sure, especially coming from a Jewish-Christian writer with dual U.S.-Israeli citizenship.

"I write about worst-case scenarios," I said. "I have tremendous respect for King Abdullah. He's clearly a man of peace who cares deeply about the people on both sides of the Jordan River. I wanted Americans to get to know him, to understand what an important ally he is and how dangerous it would be not just for Jordan, the Palestinians, and Israel but for the United States and our interests in the region if the king were taken out."

But why a novel? he asked.

"Some people want to be entertained; some want to be educated," I said. "I'm trying to do both."

We agreed to meet for dinner the following night to continue our discussions. When we did, he stunned me again.

"The king would like to meet you."

And not just for coffee. The monarch was inviting my wife and me to visit him in Amman for five days.

FIVE DAYS IN AMMAN

Lynn and I flew from Tel Aviv to Amman on the morning of March 23, 2016.

We were picked up by a royal protocol officer and driven to the Four Seasons Hotel. After unpacking and getting settled in our room, we were informed that a car would soon be picking us up for a lunch meeting. We assumed it would be with another protocol officer or maybe an advisor to the king because our *real* visit wasn't scheduled to start until the following day.

So we freshened up, went down to the lobby at the appointed time, and got into a waiting black Mercedes. As the car moved through the packed streets of Amman, I leaned over to Lynn and whispered, "It's kind of weird, this route we're on."

"Why? What about it?" she asked.

I told her it seemed like the exact route I had described in *The Third Target*, when the main character—J. B. Collins, a *New York Times* foreign correspondent—was picked up by Jordanian intelligence and driven to the royal palace.

"Wouldn't it be wild if—?"

Before I could finish the sentence, we came up over a ridge, around a corner, and through the gates of the very palace that had been destroyed by ISIS in a huge terrorist attack in *The Third Target*. Soon we were entering an enormous courtyard where the king hosts an Israeli-Palestinian peace summit just before the fictional attack. Finally we were dropped off in front of one of the wings of the palace and escorted inside.

Rob Richer was waiting for us. I introduced him to Lynn and he led us into a waiting room. After we chatted for a bit, we were ushered into another room and were greeted by His Majesty King Abdullah II. He was not wearing traditional Arab robes. Rather, he had on a smart blue business suit, light-blue shirt, and salmon-colored tie. Tanned, graying at the temples, and smiling broadly, he gave us each a firm handshake and welcomed us warmly to the Hashemite kingdom.

Lynn handled it like a pro, but I was so flustered at meeting the monarch that I sputtered, "Your Honor, it's great to meet you—I mean Your Majesty."

I felt like a moron. The king, however, could not have been more gracious. Overlooking my faux pas, he led us past the National Crisis Center, a high-tech war room reminiscent of Jack Bauer's fictional Counter Terrorism Unit headquarters on the TV series 24. We entered the Jordanian version of the White House Situation Room and then an adjacent dining room, where a round table was set for four.

We were about to have lunch with a direct descendant of the prophet Muhammad. Just Rob Richer, Lynn, and me. No other advisors. No security.

LUNCH AT THE PALACE

I cannot recall what they served us for lunch.

I do remember the conversation.

As we took our seats, the king said with a slight British accent, "You know, Joel, I was thinking about where it might be fun to meet you for the first time. A number of places came to mind, but given that you did destroy this palace, I thought maybe I should bring you here to see this building that we consider quite special."

I reddened.

"Thank you, Your Majesty—yes, this is a gorgeous palace. And obviously I hope you understand that I don't want anyone to attack or destroy it. I was not predicting it would happen or encouraging it. I was simply trying to show a worst-case scenario. And—"

The king laughed. Yes, he understood, he assured me. Otherwise, I would not be there. He then said that he couldn't help but notice that I had made him a named character in the book.

"But I also see that you have fictional names for all my advisors and staff," he said. "Still, I can see who's who. So I've bought quite a few copies of your book and given them to folks on my staff. I point to where they are in the book—the character that correlates to them—and say, 'Here, that's you. You don't make it through the terrorist attack.'"

Lynn and I laughed, and I began to relax. What followed was a ninety-minute conversation about novel writing, life inside Jordan, the economic and geopolitical challenges facing the kingdom, Jordan's relationship with the U.S. and with Israel, and more. We even talked about the king's hopes of drawing more Hollywood filmmakers to produce their movies in Jordan.

As the lunch began to wind down, the king said, "I'm enjoying our conversation and would love to continue it, but I'm afraid I have some other responsibilities."

We certainly understood. He had a kingdom to run.

But the king wasn't rushing us off. He had something else in mind.

"Actually, I need to be at an army base, near a city called Zarqā," he said. "Our troops are doing a live-fire military exercise out there today. Not many militaries train with live bullets and bombs because they believe it's too dangerous. But I believe our troops need to experience as close to real-combat conditions as possible. We're fighting ISIS, after all. So we take the risks.

"This exercise was supposed to be a demonstration of our ground forces capabilities for Vice President Biden when he visited the kingdom a few weeks ago. But when the Secret Service learned we were going to be using live ammunition and missiles and so forth, they said 'absolutely not.' So we canceled the exercises and rescheduled.

"Now, we didn't reschedule them for *you*; but when I woke up this morning, I was thinking this might interest you both. Would you like to see it?"

I was tempted to quip that we'd rather go shopping or hang out at the hotel pool, but instead I told him we would love that.

Before we left the palace for the helicopter flight to Zarqā, however, I asked the king if we could give him a few gifts we'd brought with us.

We stepped into the Situation Room, where I had left my briefcase with several copies of *The Third Target* inside.

"Your Majesty," I said, "you read *The First Hostage*, but that was actually the second novel in this new series. This one's the first."

He graciously accepted the three copies I handed him and said he looked forward to seeing how the full story began.

Conscious of the time, I said, "May I take just a moment and show you the first sentence of the first page of *The Third Target*? I think you'll find it interesting."

He nodded, acting as if he had all the time in the world. I quickly opened the book and flipped to the first page. As I did, I explained that while the series was mostly about J. B. Collins, the story begins on July 20, 1951, with a first-person account by the journalist's grandfather, who was scheduled to interview—fictionally, of course—the king's real great-grandfather, Abdullah I, in front of the Al-Aqsa Mosque in Jerusalem. Then I pointed to the first sentence.

"I had never met a king before."

The king laughed. And before I realized what he was doing, he pulled a pen from the breast pocket of his suit coat and wrote something on the page.

Well, you have now.

He added his signature and handed the book back to me with a warm smile. Lynn and I were touched by his humor and his generous spirit.

He took one of the remaining copies and asked me to sign it for him, then gave the third copy to his advisor. After thanking him for the lunch and for his time, we were whisked off to a waiting military helicopter.

LIVE-FIRE EXERCISE

Not long after we arrived at the army base and met up with a group of Jordanian high school students who had also been invited, the king arrived, flying his own Black Hawk helicopter, just as he had in *The First Hostage*. The suit was gone, replaced by green camouflage special forces fatigues.

His Majesty briefed us on what was about to happen, and while he was speaking, an air-to-ground missile sliced through the sky, no more than a hundred yards above our heads, and obliterated a small concrete building in a valley beyond us. Soon, all manner of attack helicopters and fighter jets roared overhead. Mechanized ground forces with tanks and armored person-nel carriers roared into the valley with soldiers close behind them, taking up positions and firing on the Potemkin village, representing an ISIS stronghold.

Obviously no one was firing back at the Jordanian forces, but each soldier had to be careful to coordinate his movements with his colleagues to avoid being accidentally shot in the back. The deafening explosions shook the ground. The buzz of machine-gun fire made it even more difficult to hear. But the king motioned for us to come up beside him and began shouting play-by-play coverage of what was happening, along with color commentary of what it meant and why it was important.

Lynn and I had never seen anything quite like it. So often since 9/11, we've heard people ask, "Where are the moderate Muslims willing to take their stand against the radicals?" Now we were standing next to one.

Fifteen months earlier, in December 2014, a Royal Jordanian Air Force F-16 had experienced mechanical troubles over Syria. Forced to eject, the pilot landed near Raqqa, the ISIS capital. Unfortunately, he was soon captured, locked in a steel cage, and later burned alive—all of which ISIS videotaped and posted on the Internet.

The death of twenty-six-year-old First Lieutenant Moaz al-Kasasbeh horrified the kingdom and galvanized the Jordanian people to avenge their pilot's murder and unleash the full fury of the military to destroy the caliphate once and for all.

"The blood of martyr Moaz al-Kasasbeh will not be in vain," King Abdullah said at the time.[3]

The king ordered his air force into battle. Within days, they had launched air strikes against 56 ISIS targets in what it called "Operation Martyr Muath." Within weeks, Jordan completed 946 air strikes and announced it had destroyed 20 percent of ISIS's ground capabilities.[4]

TOURING JORDAN

The next day, two friends of ours—a married couple from northern Virginia—joined us.

The husband had forged a friendship with then-Prince Abdullah in high school, when they attended Deerfield Academy together in Massachusetts. The two had stayed close over the years, typically getting together once a year with several other old classmates. Lynn and I had met this couple in 1991 at McLean Bible Church, where we had attended a Sunday school class for young married couples.

For the next twenty-five years, we had no idea that the husband knew, much less was friends with, King Abdullah, since he had promised the king to be discreet. When the king found out we all knew each other, however, he invited the four of us—and this couple's son—to come visit him together.

The king arranged for his own private helicopter to fly us to military bases all over Jordan for private briefings. When it came to the threat from ISIS and other radicals, he wanted us to understand what the kingdom was up against. And though he never said it in so many words, it became clear that the king wanted to show me he had no intention of allowing the events in my novels to come true.

The king had other objectives, as well. After all, he reigned over the eastern half of the biblical Holy Land. Knowing we were Christians, he sent us all over Jordan to learn its rich Jewish and Christian history. We went to Mount Nebo, where Moses gazed into the Promised Land, even though God denied him entry. One of the very special days for us was visiting the site along the Jordan River where many historians and archaeologists believe John the Baptist lived. Indeed, this was likely the "Bethany beyond the Jordan" where Jesus was baptized by John.[5] We were moved by the sites themselves as well as by the king's kindness and respect for our faith.

We were also blessed to visit King's Academy, an extraordinary and inspiring private school founded in 2007 and modeled after Deerfield Academy, the American boarding school in Massachusetts where Abdullah and our mutual friend spent their formative teenage years. As His Majesty once put it so eloquently, "The knowledge and values that King's instills in its students help shape confident, well-rounded individuals and inspire them throughout their life paths as change-makers of a shared future of peace and opportunity."[6]

Due to previous family obligations that we couldn't change, Lynn was able to stay for only two full days before returning to Israel. However, our friends from Virginia and their son and I were able to stay for the full five days, and we were so glad we did. There were many other features of Jordan that the king wanted us to see.

We toured the ancient Nabataean ruins in Petra, Jordan's most visited tourist site—made famous to most Americans through the third Indiana Jones movie. We also loved touring the ruins at Jerash, one of the best preserved of the ten ancient Roman cities known as the Decapolis, located north of Amman; and Jordan's main archaeological museum in the heart of Amman.

DINNER AT THE PERSONAL PALACE

For our last full evening together in the kingdom, King Abdullah invited us to Beit Al Urdon, his personal palace, for a private dinner with a few of his childhood friends.

When we arrived, we were surprised to find him dressed very causally. He apologized that Queen Rania would not be able to join us.

"There's a lot going on right now," the king explained. "Tomorrow, the U.N. secretary-general is arriving. He's bringing the head of the World Bank. Separately, the prime minister of Turkey is arriving for a visit. We also have the Bulgarian foreign minister coming in. And Bono just landed at the airport. He came for a briefing on the refugee crisis up at the Zaatari camp, and the queen thought it would be good to host a little dinner party for him tonight. Otherwise, she would have loved to have joined us."

For the rest of the evening, what kept going through my mind was "Why in the world is the king spending time with us rather than Bono?"

The king led us into a small and intimate dining room that looked like a Japanese steak house—complete with samurai swords affixed to the wall, a samurai helmet in a case, and lovely Japanese artwork. In the center of the room were tabletop griddles for cooking Japanese food, though the meal we were served was not cooked in front of us.

Over the course of the next two and a half hours, we discussed the current dynamics in the region, the king's philosophy of governing, his relations with the Palestinians and with Israel, and his view of the threat posed by Iran. I talked about my own beliefs and explained the views of evangelical Christians regarding peace in the Middle East. We also conversed about the king's 2011 book, *Our Last Best Chance: The Pursuit of Peace in a Time of Peril*, which I had read and found absolutely intriguing.

We also talked about our families, and particularly our children, and as the evening wound down, I felt comfortable enough to read aloud a personal note from my youngest son, greeting the king and asking for his autograph.

Touched by the request, the king wrote a personal note back to Noah.

Noah—thanks for a lovely letter. Hope to see you soon!

Abdullah II

Later, as the king walked us out to the car that would take us back to the hotel, I realized I had forgotten to bring Noah's note and the king's reply. Slightly panicked, I explained this to the king. Graciously, he sent me back to the dining room with an aide. When we got there, however, the dishes had already been cleared and the tables cleaned. The note was gone. Frustrated with myself for not having been more attentive to something so important to my son, I returned to the car and told the king what had happened.

"Don't worry," he assured me. "We'll find it and I'll get it to you tomorrow."

I shook his hand and got into the Mercedes for the ride back to the Four Seasons.

There's no way I'm getting that note back, I told myself, annoyed that, by my own negligence, I would be returning to Noah empty-handed. The king, after all, was a very busy man, and that would be the furthest thing from his mind.

Our last day in Jordan was exceedingly full. Once again, the king assigned his personal helicopter—the Marine One of Jordan—to fly us to meetings with various military and intelligence officials around the country. When we returned to the Marka air base near Amman, we were greeted by a royal protocol officer. With gloved hands, he was holding a silver tray. On it was a cream-colored envelope bearing the royal seal. Instantly I knew what it was. Sure enough, when I opened the envelope, there was Noah's handwritten note, with the king's handwritten reply.

I found myself becoming emotional, deeply moved that King Abdullah had remembered the lost note amid everything else on his agenda. That small gesture revealed the heart of a father, not just a king.

6

WHO IS KING ABDULLAH II?

*Understanding the vision of the longest-reigning
Arab leader in the region*

King Abdullah II is the longest-reigning Arab leader in the Middle East. Yet because Jordan is a small country—only 10 million people—and doesn't rest on a sea of oil and gas, the king doesn't command the world's attention. But he should. After all, no Arab leader has proved as moderate or as committed to advancing peace and regional security as King Abdullah.

THE ROOTS OF A REFORMER

To understand the son, we must first understand his father—and the royal line.

The Hashemites hail from the Arabian Peninsula. They are direct descendants of the prophet Muhammad, deriving their name from Hashim ibn Abd Manaf, Muhammad's great-grandfather. An elite family of scholars, soldiers, and leaders, the Hashemites ruled Mecca and Medina, the two most sacred cities to Muslims, for eight centuries through one Islamic dynasty after another, including the Ottomans. Then along came

Colonel T. E. Lawrence, the British army officer immortalized by the Academy Award–winning motion picture *Lawrence of Arabia*. Meeting secretly with Hashemite leader Sharif Hussein bin Ali during World War I, Lawrence passed along a message from London that essentially read: *If you help us overthrow the Ottomans, we will give you three kingdoms: Arabia, Mesopotamia, and Transjordan.*

The Hashemites agreed, the British achieved victory, and by 1922, the Ottoman Empire was no more. True to their word, the British granted the Hashemites all three territories, on the belief that London would gain enormous influence, if not effective control, over the oil-rich region.

In short order, however, the British plan unraveled. The military forces of the Saud family—led by Sultan Abdulaziz Ibn Saud—conquered the Hashemites and established the Kingdom of Saudi Arabia, ending more than a thousand years of Hashemite rule in the Islamic holy city of Mecca. King Faisal II of Iraq (Mesopotamia) was assassinated in Baghdad, ending Hashemite rule over the nascent state of Iraq. In London, all eyes were on Transjordan, the last remaining outpost of Hashemite rule.

As one of the sons of Sharif Hussein bin Ali of Mecca, Emir (later King) Abdullah I was the founder of the modern Jordanian nation, securing independence from the British and establishing the Hashemite Kingdom of Jordan on May 25, 1946.[1]

In May 1948, he sent the Jordanian army to join Egyptian, Syrian, and Iraqi forces in attacking the newly reborn State of Israel. To the Jordanian people, he became a hero for fighting the Zionists and capturing the Old City of Jerusalem, including the Haram al-Sharif (known to Jews as the Temple Mount), on which are located the Dome of the Rock and the Al-Aqsa Mosque, making the site the third most sacred to Muslims.

Tragically, however, on July 20, 1951, King Abdullah I was gunned down on that very site—while attending Friday prayers at the Al-Aqsa Mosque—by a Palestinian assassin, amid rumors that the king might be trying to make peace with the Jews.

Abdullah's son Talal assumed the throne but was unable to govern effectively due to a history of mental illness. Talal abdicated the throne thirteen months later, and his eldest son, Hussein, who had witnessed his grandfather's assassination in Jerusalem, received the crown. The weight of the young kingdom was now on the shoulders of the monarch, only seventeen at the time.

Skeptics abounded, inside and outside of Jordan, doubtful that Hussein would survive, much less succeed. Yet over the next five decades, King Hussein proved himself a remarkably shrewd politician and intelligence operative. His spies were loyal to him, always keeping him one step ahead of the many plots against him.

King Hussein's greatest mistake came in joining Egypt and Syria in trying to destroy the Jewish State in 1967. Though privately warned by Israeli officials not to join Cairo and Damascus in their quest to "throw the Jews into the sea," the king nevertheless ordered his generals to attack the Israel Defense Forces, hoping to enjoy the fruit of a lightning-quick pan-Arab victory over the Jews. However, the IDF struck back hard, defeating the Arab forces in six days and seizing the entire West Bank region along with Jerusalem (al-Quds), the Dome of the Rock, and the Al-Aqsa Mosque— the crown jewels of the Arab and Muslim world.

Humiliated, when the king attended the next Arab League Summit, in Khartoum, Sudan, he joined his colleagues in declaring the famous Three Nos: (1) no peace with Israel, (2) no recognition of Israel, and (3) no negotiations with Israel.

For years after the Six-Day War, Arab terrorists—known as the *fedayeen*—used Jordanian territory to launch murderous cross-border raids into Israel. For a time, the king even allowed Yasser Arafat to base his Palestine Liberation Organization (PLO) on Jordanian soil.

To his enormous credit, however, King Hussein eventually turned against the radicals, embarking instead on a courageous, if incremental, series of moderate, peace-making reforms that were unprecedented in the Muslim world.

In 1970, for example, he ordered Yasser Arafat and all PLO terrorist forces out of Jordan. When Arafat refused and launched a coup d'état, King Hussein sent his military forces into battle, successfully driving the PLO out of the kingdom in an operation that became known to Palestinians as Black September.

In the mid- to late-1970s, the king became close friends with Egyptian president Anwar Sadat, who kicked the Soviets out of Egypt, became the first Arab leader to visit Jerusalem (in 1977), and in 1979 became the first Arab leader to forge a historic peace treaty with Israel, known as the Camp David Accords.

On July 31, 1988, the king formally and unilaterally renounced all claims of legal ownership and control of the West Bank, relieving the kingdom of the financial and political burden of trying to govern the highly diverse and sharply divided Palestinian factions.

In 1989, the king began allowing Jordanians to vote for members of Parliament and have a growing say in the day-to-day governance of the country. These moves were hailed by Freedom House as "the Arab world's most promising experiment in political liberalization and reform."[2]

Though he had been an ally of Saddam Hussein during the first Gulf War in 1991, King Hussein later turned against the Iraqi tyrant and became a trusted ally of the U.S. and the West.

On October 26, 1994—after decades of back-channel conversations with the Israelis—the king became the second Arab leader in history to sign a peace treaty with the State of Israel, officially ending all hostilities and establishing formal diplomatic relations between the two countries.

In March 1997, a Jordanian soldier tried to sabotage the treaty by opening fire on a group of Israeli schoolchildren touring the Island of Peace along the Jordan River, murdering seven Jewish girls. The soldier was immediately arrested by Jordanian security forces and sentenced to decades in prison with hard labor. And in a great act of humility, love, and statesmanship unprecedented in the region, King Hussein asked if he could come to Israel, visit the families of the children who had been murdered, and personally express his condolences.

Though tensions between the two nations were running sky high, Prime Minister Netanyahu and the families agreed to the visit. In deeply moving footage that was broadcast throughout Israel, King Hussein, wearing his trademark red- and white-checkered headdress known as a kaffiyeh, knelt before the parents, wept with them, hugged and kissed them, and asked for their forgiveness.[3]

In a press conference with Netanyahu afterward, the king said, "I cannot recall an occasion when Jordanians, members of our armed forces, all of us in Jordan, have felt as angry, ashamed, stained, puzzled, shocked, by what happened to these young children visiting the Island of Peace a few days ago."[4]

He added that he and Netanyahu "had an opportunity to be together probably for a longer period of time than we have ever had, and we have talked frankly and openly, and I can assure you that we will continue to work together for peace in this region and to see it as a reality between us, to see it grow as we have always sought it to be, a peace between people, a warm peace, a real peace, and to encourage others and help them to arrive at the same goal, particularly as regards Palestinians and Israelis."[5]

When His Majesty succumbed to cancer on February 7, 1999, it was a terribly sad day for reformers in the region. Fortunately, just nine days before his death, Hussein appointed his son Abdullah II to succeed him.

THE REGION'S LEADING REFORMER

Abdullah's mother, Princess Muna al-Hussein, née Antoinette Gardiner, is an Englishwoman who worked on the set of *Lawrence of Arabia* while it was being filmed in Jordan. There she met the recently divorced King Hussein, who liked to visit the set because the film was telling the story of his forebears. The two fell in love and married in 1961.

When Abdullah was born on January 30, 1962, he was named crown prince by constitutional decree—as a forty-first-generation direct descendant of the prophet Muhammad and King Hussein's eldest son. But in 1965, with growing unrest in the Middle East, the title was transferred to King Hussein's brother Hassan.

Consequently, young Abdullah did not grow up expecting, much less planning, to become king. Rather, upon finishing his education, he pursued the career he most loved—in the military. Serving as a special forces commando, he learned how to fly helicopters and eventually rose through the ranks to become commander of all Jordanian special forces.

It was, however, King Hussein's desire that Abdullah, not Hassan, assume the throne. At nearly the last minute, King Hussein announced the change.

On the day of his father's death, with no time to mourn, Abdullah ascended the throne, stepping into the giant shoes of a hero and statesman.

Many foreign leaders and intelligence operatives did not believe the thirty-seven-year-old prince was ready. Perhaps many in Jordan felt the same way, as they had never thought of Abdullah becoming the monarch. Nevertheless, King Abdullah II was determined to build on his father's legacy of moderation and progress.

In 2000, he signed a free trade agreement with Washington, the first-ever between the U.S. and an Arab state.

In 2001, he became a vital ally of the U.S. in the battle against al Qaeda.

In 2003, he provided critical intelligence and logistical support to U.S. and allied forces during the liberation of Iraq and the removal of Saddam Hussein, despite polls showing that 88 percent of Jordanians opposed the war.[6]

In 2004, using the weight of his heritage as a direct descendant of the prophet Muhammad, he organized leading Islamic scholars to draft what became known as the Amman Message, a groundbreaking document condemning terrorism and citing verses from the Qur'an to define Islam as a religion of moderation and peace. It was endorsed by 552 Islamic scholars and clerics in eighty-four countries and became a previously unavailable tool in the theological battle against al Qaeda, ISIS, and other radical Islamists.[7]

Two years later, he went further, bringing together Muslim and Christian scholars to draft a document titled "A Common Word Between You and Us." The final version, released at a conference in Jordan in September 2007, was another landmark document, detailing theological principles common to both Islam and Christianity, including the commandments to love God and love your neighbor. This became another important tool in countering the theology of radical Islamists.[8]

Also in 2006, he provided decisive intelligence enabling the U.S. to kill terrorist Abu Musab al-Zarqawi, the Jordanian-born founder of al Qaeda in Iraq, a forerunner of ISIS.

That same year, he became the first Muslim monarch to address the National Prayer Breakfast in Washington, speaking to an audience of more than 3,500 government and religious leaders from around the world about the vital importance of positive and peaceful relations between Muslims and Christians.

"WE ARE ENGAGED IN A THIRD WORLD WAR"

During the rise of ISIS, President Obama refused to say we were fighting against "radical Islamism."[9] He didn't want to offend the world's 1.8 billion Muslims.

King Abdullah, by contrast, was crystal clear about the nature of the enemy. In an interview broadcast on *CBS This Morning* in December 2014, he referred to the battle against violent Islamists as "a third world war by other means."[10]

"This is a Muslim problem," he said. "We need to take ownership of this. We need to stand up and say what is right and what is wrong. This is no reflection on our religion. This is evil."[11] In the king's second address to the National Prayer Breakfast, in February 2017—one that I was honored to attend—he explained why he had not waited for others to act but had made Jordan a leader in the war with radical Islamism.

"For those of us who are Muslim, this fight is very personal," the king told the four thousand assembled guests from all over the world. "These criminals are *khawarej*—outlaws to our faith. People nowadays talk about 'fake news.' The *khawarej* produce 'fake Islam.' They selectively paste together the words of Islamic texts to promote a false and perverted ideology. In reality, everything they are, everything they do, is a blatant violation of the teachings of my faith.

"Together, let's set the record straight," he continued. "Among its many beautiful gifts, Islam, as with other faiths, commands mercy and tolerance, calls on us to honor the dignity of every person, forbids coercion in religion, and demands respect for the houses of God. . . .

"This is the Islam I was taught, and so I teach my children," the king concluded. "And so our faith is taught to Muslim children worldwide. Those outlaws do not inhabit the fringes of Islam—they are altogether outside of it. And I have called on the Muslim world to fight back boldly. We, like other faith communities, have a vast silent majority, and it is time for that majority to get loud and to be clear in their condemnation."[12]

I had flown to Washington from Israel specifically to see how the king would be received by the overwhelmingly evangelical Christian audience, and I was delighted to see him repeatedly receive thunderous applause and two rousing—and much-deserved—standing ovations.[13]

President Trump and Vice President Pence had just been inaugurated, and I was encouraged that King Abdullah was the first Arab leader they invited to meet with them. I was also grateful for the opportunity to meet with the king myself that week. Though I cannot reveal the substance of that conversation, it gave me additional insights into the king's moderate values and hopeful vision for his country and for the region.

THE WARRIOR KING

Upon returning to Israel from that remarkable visit to Jordan in the spring of 2016, I wanted to share some of what I was seeing and hearing.

I wrote a column for the *Jerusalem Post*, headlined "Meeting Jordan's Warrior King." After getting a firsthand look at the king and his national security team, I said, I had come away with three observations.

First, Jordan's king was sitting on a volcano, nearly surrounded by a raging forest fire, bracing for a massive earthquake.
To his north, Syria was imploding. To his east, Iraq had been massively destabilized. Some 1.3 million refugees had poured into Jordan from Syria alone, and more were coming every day, putting enormous pressure on Jordan's struggling economy.

ISIS leaders had publicly vowed to invade Jordan, "slaughter" the king, whom they denounced as an "ally of the Crusaders," and raise their black flags over Amman. Some three thousand Jordanians had joined ISIS, including the son of a member of the Jordanian Parliament.

A poll I commissioned around that time found that 74 percent of Americans feared a major ISIS attack inside the U.S., and 73 percent feared a major ISIS attack in Israel. But nearly two-in-three Americans (65 percent) also feared that ISIS would "try to overthrow the king of Jordan—an important, moderate Arab ally of the United States—and use Jordan as a base camp to launch terrorist attacks against America and Israel."

I pray such scenarios never come to pass. And though the threat posed specifically by ISIS has diminished, there are certainly other radicals gunning for Jordan and its monarch. So I continue to pray every day for the safety and security of the king, his family, and the people of Jordan.

Second, King Abdullah was born for this moment.
As a direct descendant of the prophet Muhammad, the monarch has real credibility when it comes to countering the theological narratives espoused by radical and apocalyptic Islamists.

He strenuously opposes the jihadists' claim that Muslims are required to engage in violent "holy war"—much less genocide—to reestablish the caliphate and bring about the End of Days. What's more, as one of the Islamic world's leading reformers, he is working with clerics and scholars throughout Jordan and the region to define and advance a moderate, tolerant, peaceful vision of Islam.

At the same time, as a career soldier trained at the best British military schools, and a natural leader who rose through the ranks to become the commander of Jordan's special operations forces prior to ascending to the throne, the king is uniquely qualified to protect his people from the terrorist threat. At the time when I wrote the column, Jordanian forces were taking down an ISIS or related cell inside Jordan every week. As a result of excellent intelligence and security work, Jordan has not had a major terrorist attack inside its borders since 2005.

Third, the king is ready, willing, and able to be even more actively engaged in the fight against the radicals, and to continue caring for so many Muslim and Christian refugees, but he needs more international assistance to do this effectively.
Although the international community has committed billions in financial aid to help Jordan shoulder the enormous refugee burden, the needs persist. Jordan still shelters a massive number of Syrian and Iraqi refugees, putting an enormous strain on the kingdom's budget, schools, hospitals, and job markets—all compounded by the COVID-19 pandemic.

Fortunately, the United States and other countries have stepped up their efforts to help. A 2020 report by the Congressional Research Service noted that "annual U.S. aid to Jordan has nearly quadrupled in historical terms over the last fifteen years, [and] total bilateral U.S. aid . . . to Jordan through FY2018 amounted to approximately $22 billion."[14] Jordan also hosts more than three thousand U.S. troops.

In 2011, the United States gave Jordan $665 million in combined economic and military aid.[15] In February 2014, during a visit by King Abdullah II, the Obama administration announced an additional five-year, $1 billion loan guarantee for Jordan.[16] Then, in 2018, the Trump administration signed a five-year Memorandum of Understanding with Jordan, pledging a total of $6.375 billion in foreign assistance through 2022.[17]

Also in 2018, Germany provided Jordan an aid package worth $530 million.[18] Saudi Arabia transferred $334 million to Jordan in 2019, as part of a $2.5 billion aid package put together by the leaders of Saudi Arabia, Kuwait, and the United Arab Emirates.[19]

These were all important moves, but Jordan also needs international assistance to develop more robust industries, expand its export markets, attract more tourists, and grow its private economy.

Will such assistance be forthcoming? At the time of this writing, the U.S. faces enormous budget pressures, due in part to the COVID-19 crisis, and the Gulf States are dealing with historically low oil prices—and thus dramatic revenue shortfalls—also due in large part to the stunning slowdown in demand for oil due to drastically reduced global travel during the pandemic.

What if these and other nations are not as able or willing to stand with Jordan financially as they once were? What if fear and anger among Jordanian citizens grows white-hot as they struggle to make ends meet?

The massive unrest that became known as the Arab Spring has not erupted in Jordan. But one thing the region cannot afford is for the volcano to blow.

THE FIRST DELEGATION

On my last night in Jordan in 2016, I asked the king one final question as we finished our dinner at his private palace.

"Your Majesty," I began, "it isn't every day that a follower of Jesus—much less one from a Jewish background—has an opportunity to meet with and talk for hours with a direct descendent of the founder of Islam. Or that a failed political consultant like me gets to meet a monarch. Or that an Israeli—apart from the prime minister or foreign minister or head of Mossad—gets to begin a friendship with our next-door neighbor, a man of peace, just like his father.

"I hope you could see in my novel that I have such a deep respect for you—even before meeting you—and I must tell you that my respect has only deepened since I've been here. But I feel I would be remiss to keep this experience to myself. I really think there are some very prominent and influential Christian leaders in the U.S. and elsewhere who also have never met an Arab Muslim monarch, but who ought to meet you to understand your heart, your values, and your vision for your country and for peace. Would you ever be open to having a delegation of Christian leaders come for several days to have essentially the experience that Lynn and I have had? I think it could be very important—not only for interfaith relations, but also for the cause of peace and security in the region."

"That's a great idea, Joel," the king replied. "Let's work together to make it happen."

Given our respective schedules, it took some time to schedule. And in the meantime, a new opportunity arose.

7

"LET MY PEOPLE COME"

My first encounter with Egyptian president
Abdel Fattah el-Sisi

I first met Abdel Fattah el-Sisi in Washington, D.C., in April 2017.

It was his first state visit to the United States, though he had come to power four years earlier. President Obama had adamantly refused to invite Sisi to Washington.[1] Indeed, he had effectively banned Sisi from the White House for reasons I will explain over the next two chapters. But let's start with some context.[2]

For decades, Egypt's military leadership had warned that the Muslim Brotherhood, a radical Islamist organization founded in Egypt in 1928, was in fact a terrorist organization that could never be allowed to gain political power or they would destroy the country, impose an extremist version of Sharia law, and try to turn Egypt into a Sunni Islamic version of the Shia terrorist regime in Iran.

Hassan al-Banna, the founder of the Muslim Brotherhood, had written a book called *Jihad,* in which he stated that "fighting the unbelievers involves all possible efforts . . . to dismantle the power of the enemies of Islam including beating them, plundering their wealth, destroying their places of worship, and smashing their idols."[3]

Al-Banna taught that "it is the nature of Islam to dominate, not to be dominated," and "to impose its [Sharia] law on nations and to extend its power to the entire planet."[4] The organization's slogan became "Allah is our objective. The Prophet is our leader. The Qur'an is our law. Jihad is our way. Dying in the way of Allah is our highest hope. Allahu-Akbar [Allah is greater!]."[5] And the group had been responsible for high-profile assassinations of Egyptian leaders, prompting its ban in Egypt in 1948.[6]

When Egypt's President Hosni Mubarak was toppled in the Arab Spring uprisings in 2011, the Muslim Brotherhood ascended to power. At first, most Egyptians were convinced the Brotherhood could bring about positive change, and Mohamed Morsi, the Brotherhood's leader, was elected president in 2012, promising freedom and justice.

RISING FEAR

Barely a year later, however, public opinion in Egypt had shifted dramatically. Having watched Morsi in action, overwhelming majorities of Egyptians were terrified by where the Brotherhood was taking their country. According to a survey by the Arab American Institute in early June 2013:

- 72 percent of Egyptians said Morsi was not "guaranteeing my rights and freedoms"
- 74 percent said Morsi was not "keeping me safe and maintaining order"
- 71 percent said "the Muslim Brotherhood intends to Islamize the state and control its executive powers"
- 71 percent said they no longer had any confidence in Morsi
- By contrast, 94 percent said they had confidence in the Egyptian army.[7]

As fear grew, millions of Egyptians once again turned out on the streets, this time demanding that Morsi and the Brotherhood step down. Morsi refused. By the end of June, some 22 million Egyptians had signed a petition demanding that Morsi step down, yet he still refused.[8] Given that Egypt had no impeachment law and thus no legal way to remove Morsi from power, many feared a civil war was brewing.

What Morsi didn't know, however, was that the man he had appointed in 2012 to serve as his defense minister and commander in chief of the Egyptian military was not a member of the Brotherhood. To be sure, Abdel Fattah el-Sisi was a devout Muslim. He was also a quiet man. As a senior general and head of military intelligence, he had long kept his political views to himself. This apparently confused Morsi, causing him to assume Sisi was part of the tribe.

In fact, Sisi was horrified by what he saw Morsi doing. On July 3, 2013, he and the Egyptian military made their move. They arrested Morsi and thirty-eight senior Brotherhood leaders, seized government ministries from the Islamists, shut down the Brotherhood's satellite TV network, banned the Brotherhood's activities, installed an interim government, and called for new elections. Sisi, however, did not appoint himself as head of the new government. Rather, he took the role of deputy prime minister. Adly Mansour, president of Egypt's Supreme Constitutional Court, was named interim president.

"The generals built their case for intervention in a carefully orchestrated series of maneuvers," the New York Times reported, "calling their actions an effort at a 'national reconciliation' and refusing to call their takeover a coup. At a televised news conference . . . Gen. [Abdel] Fattah el-Sisi said the military had no interest in politics and was ousting Mr. Morsi because he had failed to fulfill 'the hope for a national consensus.'"[9]

At the news conference, Sisi was "flanked by Egypt's top Muslim and Christian clerics as well as a spectrum of political leaders including Mohamed ElBaradei, the Nobel Prize–winning diplomat and liberal icon, and Galal Morra, a prominent Islamist ultraconservative, or Salafi, all of whom endorsed the takeover."[10]

AN EXPLOSION OF ANTI-CHRISTIAN ATTACKS

Almost immediately, violence erupted in Cairo and spread quickly across Egypt as enraged Muslim Brotherhood followers clashed with security forces.

Within a week, an estimated eight hundred people were dead, and the violence only intensified.

By mid-August, the New York Times reported "an explosion of anti-Christian attacks," noting that "supporters of the ousted Islamist president,

Mohamed Morsi, have lashed out across Egypt . . . blocking bridges and highways, storming government buildings, and attacking churches of the country's Christian minority."[11] On August 15, *Christianity Today* reported that some thirty-seven churches and fourteen Christian schools had been attacked across nine provinces.[12]

This was only the beginning.

"This is a real disaster," one Catholic priest told the AFP news agency, warning that Egypt was becoming a "dangerous volcano."[13]

The Obama administration put the blame squarely on Sisi, urging him and his generals to restore Morsi to power. "We are deeply concerned by the decision of the Egyptian Armed Forces to remove President Morsi and suspend the Egyptian constitution," Obama told reporters. "I now call on the Egyptian military to move quickly and responsibly to return full authority back to a democratically elected civilian government as soon as possible through an inclusive and transparent process, and to avoid any arbitrary arrests of President Morsi and his supporters."[14]

Sisi had no intention of putting the Muslim Brotherhood back in charge. Rather, he called for new elections and announced he would run for president. The Brotherhood called for a boycott. Its followers refused to vote. Enormously popular among non-Islamists, Sisi won in a landslide.

OBAMA EMBRACES THE MUSLIM BROTHERHOOD

It was this chain of events that led Obama to ban President Sisi from the White House.

Yet Obama had no problem with the Muslim Brotherhood. Along with Vice President Joe Biden and Secretary of State Hillary Clinton, Obama had backed the Arab Spring protests in 2011 that toppled longtime American ally Hosni Mubarak and had supported bringing the Muslim Brotherhood into Egyptian politics.

"We believe, given the changing political landscape in Egypt, that it is in the interests of the United States to engage with all parties that are peaceful and committed to nonviolence, that intend to compete for the parliament and the presidency," Clinton said in 2011. "We welcome, therefore, dialogue with those Muslim Brotherhood members who wish to talk with us."[15]

They took this step even though the Brotherhood was widely considered an extreme Islamist movement and a growing number of countries in the Muslim world considered it an outright terrorist organization.[16]

When Morsi won the presidency of Egypt in 2012, Obama was not concerned in the slightest. To the contrary, he called Morsi to congratulate him.[17]

This despite the fact that, in 2010, Morsi had declared Israelis and Jews "blood-suckers," "warmongers," and "descendants of apes and pigs" and had called for a boycott of U.S. products.[18]

Morsi had also said, "The Zionists have no right to the land of Palestine. There is no place for them on the land of Palestine."[19]

Further, Morsi had called for "military resistance" against Israel and insisted it was "the only way to liberate the land of Palestine."[20]

Upon taking office in 2012, Morsi said he would "reconsider" the 1979 peace treaty with Israel.[21]

If these comments were not bad enough, Morsi had publicly declared during the campaign, "The Qur'an is our constitution, the prophet Muhammad is our leader, jihad is our path, and death for the sake of Allah is our most lofty aspiration," a sentiment straight out of the radical Islamist playbook.[22]

Morsi came to power in Egypt insisting that "this nation will enjoy blessing and revival only through the Islamic Sharia."[23]

Morsi vowed to "take an oath before Allah and before you all that, regardless of the actual text" of the Egyptian constitution, he would "not accept a text that does not reflect the true meaning of the Islamic Sharia as a text to be implemented."[24]

Morsi told the Iranian Fars news agency that one of his top priorities was to "improve ties with Iran."[25]

To prove it, Morsi became the first Egyptian leader since the Islamic Revolution of 1979 to visit Iran, declaring that "Egypt views Iran as its strategic partner."[26]

Then Morsi literally rolled out the red carpet for Iranian president Mahmoud Ahmadinejad during a stunning and historic visit to Cairo in February 2013—hugging and kissing the Iranian leader in front of the cameras, even though Ahmadinejad had repeatedly called for the annihilation of the U.S. and Israel.[27]

THE TRUMP TURN

During the 2016 campaign, Donald Trump repeatedly warned of the threat of radical Islam and vowed to take an entirely different approach to the Middle East.

To illustrate his point, Trump met with President Sisi in New York when the Egyptian leader came for the opening of the U.N. General Assembly, and he expressed his "strong support for Egypt's war on terrorism." He also promised that, in a Trump administration, the U.S. would be "a loyal friend, not simply an ally, that Egypt can count on in the days and years ahead."[28]

Grateful for the support, Sisi called Trump immediately after the November election to congratulate him on his victory. Trump then invited Sisi to the White House in April 2017 and vowed to work with him to combat terrorism and advance regional peace.

"I just want to let everybody know in case there was any doubt that we are very much behind President el-Sisi," Trump said during a photo op with Sisi in the Oval Office. "He's done a fantastic job in a very difficult situation. We are very much behind Egypt and the people of Egypt."[29]

"You will find Egypt and [me] always beside you in bringing about an effective strategy in the counterterrorism effort," Sisi pledged in return, adding that Egypt—the first Arab country ever to make peace with Israel—was ready to help Trump and his team "find a solution to the problem of the century" between the Israelis and Palestinians, by helping Trump craft "the deal of the century."[30]

As best as I can ascertain, that was the first public mention of the phrase "deal of the century." It wasn't something that Trump or his team coined. It was Sisi. More on the deal later.

MEETING PRESIDENT SISI

As part of his first state visit, President Sisi made an interesting choice.

Rather than meeting only with senior administration officials and congressional leaders, he also chose to meet with a group of about sixty Mideast experts and pro-Israel advocates. The reason was clear enough: He wanted to explain his vision and the progress he was making with his reforms, describe his approach to counterterrorism and the Arab-Israeli peace progress, and push back at the negative press that was dogging him.

The event was held on the morning of April 5 at the Four Seasons Hotel in Georgetown, just down Pennsylvania Avenue from the White House. As an author, columnist, and dual U.S.-Israeli citizen, I was humbled to be included in such a gathering. The room was filled with a wide range of high-profile and influential figures, including former senior U.S. officials from both political parties, mayors of major cities, the heads of various think tanks and Middle East advocacy groups, and about two dozen senior leaders from the American Israel Public Affairs Committee (AIPAC).

I had been invited by Yasser Reda, Egypt's ambassador to the United States. Though Reda and I had not met until that day, we had earlier begun an email correspondence after being connected by a dear mutual friend, Rob Satloff, executive director of the Washington Institute for Near East Policy.

Behind closed doors, before the event began, we were all informed of the ground rules. We could not quote the Egyptian leader directly, nor publicly mention the names of the Americans who were in the room. Beyond that, we could ask President Sisi whatever we wanted. The goal of the session was not to make headlines but to help us get to know Sisi and his views in a setting where we could all speak candidly.

Seeing Abdel Fattah el-Sisi up close and personal for the first time was an interesting and counterintuitive experience. After all, his reputation was larger than life. Both admirers and critics alike saw him as a giant killer, a revolutionary figure who was almost single-handedly changing the destiny of the world's most populous Arab country. Yet he was neither a large nor physically intimidating man. And though he is more than twelve years older than I am, he still had a youthful look about him. His hairline was beginning to recede from a broad forehead, but his dark-brown hair had only a few flecks of gray around the temples. He was trim and fit, with good posture and an air of confidence, but not haughtiness, about him.

In that meeting, and over the next four times I would see him, Sisi struck me as a calm and dignified man, with warm brown eyes and a kind smile (when he allowed himself to smile) and a rare but infectious laugh. He has an authoritative voice but chooses to speak softly, gently, and almost exclusively in precise, classical Egyptian Arabic, unless he is speaking with someone one-on-one, which he can do in flawless, colloquial English, having studied for a time in the United States.

Wearing a dark-blue business suit, crisp white shirt, and violet tie, Sisi made introductory remarks for about fifteen minutes and then took questions for the next hour and a half.

When the event was over, Sisi and his advisors stood up, and I expected the entourage to quickly exit the room. Instead, Sisi began to chat with people at the head table. No one else, however, moved forward to greet him. Given that everyone else in the room was a high-ranking "somebody," they subscribed to the protocol that one should not rush up and "get a selfie with Sisi." Not that selfies were even possible, mind you; the Secret Service had taken our phones when we entered the ballroom. Still, I wanted to meet the president; so I decided that, unless the Secret Service tackled me, I was going to approach the head table and take my chances.

When no one stopped me, I suddenly found myself shaking hands with the president of Egypt and introducing myself.

"Your Excellency, I want to start by thanking you for rescuing 100 million Egyptians from the tyranny of the Muslim Brotherhood," I began.

He brightened and thanked me.

I explained that I had been deeply impressed by the powerful speech he'd delivered two years earlier, on January 1, 2015, when he called for a "religious revolution" in how Islam is taught and practiced—in effect, a Muslim Reformation that would reject radicalism and create a more peaceful, stable, and tolerant Islamic world.

"Is it possible that 1.6 billion people [Muslims] should want to kill the rest of the world's inhabitants—that is 7 billion—so that they themselves may live? Impossible!" Sisi told a group of scholars at Cairo's Al-Azhar University, the Harvard of Sunni Islam. "We are in need of a religious revolution. You, imams, are responsible before Allah. The entire world is waiting for your next move."[31]

To this day, it stands as one of the most courageous and impressive speeches by a Muslim leader against the forces of violent extremism in Islam.

"Your Excellency, though I am from a Jewish background on my father's side and am a dual U.S.-Israeli citizen, by faith I am an evangelical

Christian. And I want to take this opportunity to thank you, sir, for all the actions you have taken to protect Christians in Egypt. I realize there is much more to do, but I can see that you are dispatching security forces to protect churches, especially in Cairo. I see that you are directing the government to rebuild and repair all the churches that were damaged or destroyed by the Brotherhood. You have met with Coptic Orthodox leaders and Roman Catholic leaders, and you even have Pope Francis visiting soon. I honestly can't recall an Egyptian leader ever showing so much respect to the Christian community, and I just want you to know that I'm very grateful."

"You are most welcome, Joel," he replied. "This is the new Egypt. I don't see distinctions between Muslims and Christians. I just see Egyptians and I want to foster unity among all people of all faiths in my country."

"Well, sir, it's very impressive—and I see that you're reaching out to Jewish leaders, those in this room, but you've also welcomed delegations of Jewish leaders to Cairo to meet with you, and this is intriguing and encouraging, as well."

"Again, this is the new Egypt," he replied, "open, inclusive, tolerant of other faiths and other ethnicities. We have a long way to go, but I hope we are going in the right direction."

"I believe you are."

Looking around, I noticed that still no one else had come up to speak with the Egyptian leader, so I kept going.

"That said, sir, I have not seen any reports that you have met with evangelical Christian leaders yet. You may have. Don't get me wrong. It's not a criticism. Perhaps I missed it, or it was not reported."

"No, no, I believe you are right," Sisi replied. "I don't believe I have met with any evangelical leaders."

"Well, Your Excellency, I would encourage you to do so. There are some 60 million evangelical Christians here in the U.S., and some 600 million worldwide. We are a very influential group culturally, spiritually, even politically. You'll notice many evangelicals are in the Trump administration, including Vice President Pence. So it's something to think about."

He nodded.

"A few months ago, King Abdullah invited me to meet with him in

Amman," I continued. "My wife and I had several lovely days together with him and his generals and advisors. We really got to know who he is and what he believes and where he is trying to take his country. And over dinner on the last night in Amman, I asked him if he would be interested in having a delegation of evangelical Christian leaders come and spend time with him, as Lynn and I had done. He loved the idea, and we're working on developing a trip, hopefully for later this year. Perhaps that's something you might consider, as well."

In all honesty, I was simply trying to plant the seed of an idea. I had no expectation that he would respond so warmly or so quickly. But at that moment, Sisi seemed to light up.

"I would love that," he said. "Joel, would you consider bringing such a delegation to Cairo to meet with me? I would be honored to welcome you and your evangelical colleagues."

I was stunned. To my knowledge, Sisi had no idea who I was. Obviously I had been invited to his event. And obviously I had been cleared through whatever vetting his intelligence services and the U.S. Secret Service had done. But with sixty bona fide experts in the room, he could not possibly have known anything about me. Yet here he was, inviting me to bring a delegation of evangelical Christians to Egypt.

"That would be a great honor," I replied.

"Wonderful." He turned to the three men standing next to him and said, "Gentlemen, make it happen."

I shook the president's hand and thanked him again, then stepped aside to meet with Egyptian foreign minister Sameh Shoukry, Ambassador Reda, and Sisi's chief of staff, Abbas Kamel, who would later be promoted to the head of Egyptian intelligence. We chatted warmly for a few minutes, exchanged business cards, and Ambassador Reda was assigned by the others to follow up with me and work out all the details for a visit.

RETURNING TO ISRAEL

I returned to Israel a few days later, just before Passover.

Lynn and our sons and I were invited to celebrate the Jewish holiday at the home of some dear Israeli friends and several other families. During the course of the evening, they were intrigued by the door that had opened for me to meet President Sisi but astonished that Sisi had asked me to bring a Christian delegation to meet with him in Cairo.

"How in the world is that possible?" they asked. The whole thing with King Abdullah had been surreal enough, they said, but how crazy was it that a second Arab leader wanted a delegation as well?

"Insane," I agreed. "But here's the really crazy part: Could you ever imagine a Jewish man standing before the leader of Egypt on the eve of Passover and saying, 'Let my people come'?"

WHO IS ABDEL FATTAH EL-SISI?

*First impressions of Egypt and taking
our first delegation to Cairo*

A few days after I got back to Israel, ISIS attacked two churches in Egypt.

On April 9, Palm Sunday—one of the holiest days on the Christian calendar—suicide bombers hit a Coptic Orthodox church in Alexandria and another in Tanta, a city in the Nile delta. The attacks killed forty-five Christians and wounded more than one hundred.

I immediately wrote to the Egyptian ambassador in Washington and President Sisi's chief of staff, expressing my condolences. Ambassador Reda thanked me for my note and invited me to visit him in Washington the following month to nail down dates for the delegation, draft an itinerary, and discuss whom to invite.

FIRST IMPRESSIONS

At the same time, I was processing my first impressions of President Sisi.

Though I couldn't quote him from the meeting at the Four Seasons, I had spent two hours listening to Sisi make his case and answer questions from many of the leading Middle East experts in the U.S. I had carefully observed his interactions with President Trump, congressional leaders, and American business leaders. I had also talked to several members of the House and

Senate who knew Sisi and had spoken to him at length behind closed doors, and I was reading everything I could get my hands on about him.

Three distinct impressions began to form.[1]

Pro-American and Pro-Growth

The first thing I saw in President Sisi was a man determined to rebrand Egypt as a trustworthy and stable ally of America and the West after years of political chaos and instability.

It is worth remembering that he came to power amid the most catastrophic meltdown of Egypt's social, economic, and political order in living memory. After the Arab Spring uprisings and the fall of Hosni Mubarak, the Muslim Brotherhood and Mohamed Morsi had tried to impose Sharia law and a brutally violent Islamist regime on a nation that had just overthrown an autocrat. Egypt was on fire. People were dying in the streets. Police stations were burning. Churches were being blown up.

Even as the Obama administration had fully backed the extremist Morsi government, private investors had fled, and the Saudis and other Gulf States that were deeply opposed to the Brotherhood had stopped providing support to Egypt. In 2011, Egypt's GDP contracted sharply. During the tumult and uncertainty of the Morsi tenure, economic growth was almost nonexistent.

Yet, from the moment Sisi and the Egyptian military removed the Brotherhood from power and put Morsi and his extremist colleagues in prison, the new government has focused its efforts on restoring order on the streets, reestablishing national stability, and beginning the arduous task of rebuilding investor confidence.

Consider a few numbers:

- Before the Muslim Brotherhood rose to power, Egypt's economy had been growing between 5 percent and 7 percent annually.
- After the overthrow of Mubarak in 2011, the economy nearly went into recession, growing by only 1.7 percent.
- When Sisi came to power and began to implement his reforms, the Egyptian economy rebounded, growing 4.3 percent in 2016. By 2019, Egypt's GDP was growing at a rate of 5.6 percent.[2]

- Unemployment, which was running at more than 13 percent when Sisi took office in 2014, dropped to 8.3 percent over the next five years.[3]

Unfortunately, the coronavirus hit Egypt hard, especially its tourism industry—which accounts for about 12 percent of GDP—and the gas industry, which saw prices plummet. Nevertheless, the economy still grew by 3.3 percent in 2020, while Israel's economy contracted by 6 percent and many countries went into recession.[4]

Far more needs to be done by Sisi and his team to reduce taxes, regulations, government spending and debt, and streamline the bloated bureaucracy. Sisi needs to work harder to create a free-market magnet for foreign direct investment in order to create enough good, well-paying jobs for Egypt's 100 million citizens.

Still, from the moment he came to power, Sisi's message to the international business community was clear: Egypt is once again stable and open for business.

Anti-Islamist

As a devout Muslim who opposes extremism—and as the former commander of the Egyptian military—Sisi came into office well-positioned to make Egypt an effective leader in the fight against terrorism.

To truly defeat radical Islamists—from the Muslim Brotherhood to al Qaeda to the remnants of ISIS and other violent extremist groups—and to build an effective Sunni Arab counterweight to mounting Shia Iranian aggression, Washington needs a strong Egyptian partner. In Sisi, the U.S. has a leader who understands the use and limits of hard power and is not afraid to deploy such power.

The good news is that his counterterrorism efforts have shown signs of progress. In 2019, for example, Egypt finally fell out of the top ten nations in the world ravaged by terrorism, according to the *Global Terrorism Index*. The number of terror attacks fell from 169 to 45, and 592 fewer people were killed by terror attacks in 2019 than in 2018.[5]

Especially encouraging to see was how well Egypt and Israel were collaborating on intelligence and security issues. President Sisi and Prime

Minister Netanyahu immediately began working quietly but closely in the fight against jihadist groups hidden in caves and operating out of small villages throughout the Sinai Peninsula.

Still, Sisi has his work cut out for him.

Jihadists are also operating openly in Libya, Egypt's neighbor to the west. If Sisi and his generals do not maintain the utmost vigilance along the western border, the fear is that chaos and instability could spill over into Egypt. I believe that the U.S. would be wise not to cut military aid to Egypt anytime soon. Cairo needs all the help it can get in the fight against Islamist extremists.

Pro-Peace

As the leader of the first Arab nation ever to sign a peace treaty with Israel, President Sisi believes that Egypt offers a model that can help others in the region make peace with the Jewish State.

Over the course of our meetings together, I have been struck by how much Sisi expresses his admiration for former Egyptian president Anwar Sadat, even though Sadat was assassinated for visiting Jerusalem and agreeing to the Camp David Accords. Most Egyptians opposed the peace deal at the time. Many still do. Nevertheless, Sisi is inspired by Sadat's bold quest for peace. Perhaps this explains why he built such effective lines of communication with Netanyahu and King Abdullah II, has worked so hard to pacify Hamas and other jihadists in the Gaza Strip, and has consistently urged Palestinian leaders in Ramallah to get back to the negotiating table with Israel.

I believe it is important for Washington to honor our allies in Cairo for the significant progress they have made, including their openly expressed desire to be a valued and trusted American security partner, even as the U.S. encourages the Egyptians to push forward with more sweeping reforms, including improving the human rights environment and strengthening religious freedom.

"One thing is for sure: Abdel Fattah Sisi is no politician," I wrote in a column for the *Jerusalem Post* in April 2017. "He doesn't think like one. He doesn't talk like one. He is a general, a man of strategy and action. His strategic objective is to stabilize his country and rebrand Egypt as a friend of America, a friend of the West, a place to do business, and a force for regional peace and reconciliation. He is, therefore, an Arab leader worth watching very closely."[6]

BUILDING A TEAM

Early in May 2017, I flew to Cairo for several days of meetings.

Before heading to Washington, D.C., to meet with Ambassador Reda, I wanted to spend time with several key Egyptian Christian leaders to pray together, let them know about my plans to bring a delegation to Egypt, and seek their counsel as to how this visit might be used to encourage and even strengthen Egypt's estimated 15 million Coptic Orthodox Christians and 2 million Protestants. The meetings went even better than I could have hoped, and I flew to the U.S. with a real sense that the Lord was opening a unique door for my colleagues and me to build a relationship with the president of Egypt and discuss our concerns with him.

Meanwhile, following my February meeting in D.C. with King Abdullah and ongoing discussions with his team, I sensed it might be possible to schedule trips to Egypt *and* Jordan, back-to-back.

As I landed at Dulles airport, a game plan was beginning to take shape, and my goals were becoming more clearly defined. I believed that our delegation needed to pursue seven key objectives:

1. Develop long-term friendships with regional leaders, not seek photo ops.
2. Meet government leaders at the highest possible levels and spend *hours* with them—not just a few minutes. This would give us the best opportunity to truly understand their vision, the challenges and threats they face, and their track record of reform, and also ask them candid and direct questions about matters of human rights and religious freedom (particularly for Christians in their countries), as well as ask about their views toward Israel and the Jewish people.
3. Explain to these government leaders who evangelical Christians are and what we believe, dispel any myths they may have heard, and address any concerns.

4. Pray with and for these government leaders, their families, and their nations, according to 1 Timothy 2:1-3: "First of all, then, I urge that requests, prayers, intercession, and thanksgiving be made in behalf of all people, for kings and all who are in authority, so that we may lead a tranquil and quiet life in all godliness and dignity. This is good and acceptable in the sight of God our Savior."

5. Meet with Muslim clerics and scholars in these countries to better understand their perspectives and build bridges of friendship.

6. Meet Christian pastors and ministry leaders whenever possible for an extended period of time—without government officials present—to better understand their perspectives and the challenges they face, and to have time to pray together.

7. Upon returning home, write and speak about what we see and hear in these countries. Be ready to honor those to whom honor is due, according to Romans 13:7, but also respectfully encourage leaders to press forward with bolder domestic reforms, do more to advance religious freedom, and move courageously toward making (or strengthening) peace with Israel. We also need to help Christians in North America and elsewhere to better understand the historic roots and current needs of the church in the Middle East and to know how best to pray for and support our brothers and sisters in Christ in the region.

The meeting with Ambassador Reda went well, and there were two main takeaways:

- Cairo wanted to limit the size of the group to twelve principal participants (though we could bring a few staffers and spouses).
- Cairo was not looking for a specific message to emerge from this delegation. "I just ask that you tell the truth," Reda told me, adding that he knew his government was not perfect, but he wanted Christians to see they were making progress.

I now needed to come up with criteria for choosing whom to invite on these delegations. Twelve was certainly a biblical number, and it would keep the group intimate enough to engage in meaningful dialogue with the leaders we met. But in a nation of 60 million evangelical Christians, how was I supposed to narrow down a guest list to eleven plus me?

This is what I concluded.

1. They had to be leaders I knew personally and trusted to be sincere followers of Jesus Christ.
2. Some had to have influence with the president, vice president, senior administration officials, or members of Congress.
3. Others had to have influence in various sectors of evangelical Christianity while purposefully staying *out* of politics. This was not, after all, a political or government delegation. Nor was it a lobbying mission. This was about helping Christians outside of the Middle East gain a better understanding of current dynamics in the region.
4. At least some of the leaders had to have national media and social media platforms, allowing us to broadly communicate our findings.
5. We needed a mix of men and women.
6. We needed a mix of pastors and nonprofit leaders.
7. We needed racial and geographic diversity.
8. We needed a mix of people known for their commitment to Israel and some for whom Israel was not a priority.
9. We also needed some leaders with a strong heart of love and compassion for Arabs and Muslims and some with little or no experience in the Arab and Muslim world—yet open to learning.

After much prayer, we set our dates for late October to early November and confirmed the names of the eleven leaders who would join the delegation.

- **Delanyo "Dela" Adadevoh**, vice president of global leadership for Campus Crusade for Christ International (CRU) and a native of Ghana, West Africa.
- **Michele Bachmann**, former congresswoman from Minnesota and a former member of the House Intelligence Committee.

- **William "Jerry" Boykin**, executive vice president of the Family Research Council, retired lieutenant general and former commander of the U.S. Army's Delta Force, and former U.S. deputy undersecretary of defense for intelligence.
- **Mario Bramnick**, pastor of a congregation near Miami, Florida, and founder of the Latino Coalition for Israel.
- **Michael Evans**, founder of the Jerusalem Prayer Team and the Friends of Zion Museum in Jerusalem.
- **Jim Garlow**, pastor of a congregation near San Diego, and his wife, Rosemary.
- **Johnnie Moore**, commissioner with the U.S. Commission on International Religious Freedom (USCIRF), cofounder of the White House Evangelical Advisory Board, former vice president of Liberty University, and author of several books, including *Defying ISIS: Preserving Christianity in the Place of Its Birth and in Your Own Backyard*.
- **Tony Perkins**, president of the Family Research Council, a commissioner with the U.S. Commission on International Religious Freedom, and a pastor of his home church in Louisiana.
- **Larry Ross**, former spokesman for Billy Graham, public relations advisor to numerous U.S. evangelical leaders, and an advisor to the annual National Prayer Breakfast in Washington.
- **Bob Vander Plaats**, president of The Family Leader in Des Moines, Iowa, and his wife, Darla.
- **Michael Youssef**, an Egyptian-American evangelical pastor of a congregation in Atlanta, Georgia, and host of the *Leading the Way* television program, and his wife, Elizabeth.

FIVE DAYS IN EGYPT

Two of my four sons and I flew to Cairo on October 30, 2017.

Jacob and Jonah would serve as our photographers and notetakers. We checked in to the Nile Ritz-Carlton, met with the executives from the tour company we had hired, and began welcoming members of the delegation as they arrived.

Over the next five days, our group (seventeen in all) met with Egyptian business executives, academics, and geopolitical experts. We had dinner with acting U.S. Ambassador Thomas Goldberger and his wife. We visited the pyramids, toured the old Egyptian Museum, and received a fascinating briefing from the famed Egyptian archaeologist Zahi Hawass on the new, sprawling, $1 billion, high-tech Egyptian Museum being built near the pyramids in Giza.

We spent hours with two of the highest-ranking Muslim leaders in the country.

One was Mohamed Mokhtar Gomaa, minister of religious endowments, who oversees Egypt's 120,000 mosques. Once the dean of the faculty of Islamic and Arabic studies at Cairo's famed Al-Azhar University (which has been training clerics for more than a thousand years), and long-known as an advocate of moderate Islam, Gomaa was appointed just weeks after Mohamed Morsi's regime was toppled in 2013.

We were intrigued to learn that Gomaa had moved quickly to ensure that only moderate clerics could preach—and only peaceful, moderate messages were taught—in Egypt's mosques.[7] In 2013 alone, Gomaa fired 55,000 clerics whom he and his staff deemed were preaching extremism.[8] In 2015, Gomaa required all mosques to "remove any books, cassettes, or CDs that incite violence and radicalism" from their libraries.[9] In 2016, he required every cleric in the country to preach only sermons written by the highest and most trusted scholars at Al-Azhar.[10]

We also met with Egypt's grand mufti, Shawki Allam, the nation's highest official overseeing matters of Islamic law and practice in daily life. Also once a faculty member at Al-Azhar, and widely known as a moderate, Allam began combatting radical Islamism theologically from the moment he took the post in 2013. Among other projects, he wrote a book titled *The Ideological Battle: Egypt's Dar al-Iftaa Combats Radicalization*, arguing from the Qur'an that terrorism is forbidden by Islam.[11]

Both men told us they wanted Washington to declare the Muslim Brotherhood a terrorist organization. We were encouraged by their passion to supplement President Sisi's military and law enforcement approach to defeating terrorism by training and deploying clerics to teach moderate Islam. Few Westerners realize the extent to which Egypt's religious scholars are actively implementing Sisi's call for a Muslim reformation, but the effort is both profound and historic.

MEETING WITH EGYPTIAN CHRISTIAN LEADERS

We were especially grateful for the opportunity to meet with Egyptian Christians.

My friend Andrea Zaki, who heads all of Egypt's evangelical Protestant churches, arranged for us to spend half a day with him and about sixty Egyptian pastors and Christian ministry leaders. We got to know their stories; hear their perspectives on Egypt before, during, and after the Arab Spring; and pray with them. We heard firsthand accounts from the pastors and their wives about what a nightmare it had been during and immediately after the Muslim Brotherhood's reign of terror.

- Churches burnt and bombed.
- Christians assaulted and killed.
- Twenty-one Coptic Christians beheaded by ISIS on a beach in Libya.
- Death threats and other forms of intimidation from the Brotherhood.

We also heard testimonies of God's grace and faithfulness to these followers of Jesus, including a new boldness to preach the gospel in Tahrir Square during the Arab Spring and a new passion to live out and communicate their faith, despite the persecution they suffered. Without exception, the pastors and ministry leaders told us how grateful they were that their country had been liberated by Sisi. They also told us that Christians were now being treated with more fairness and respect.

But they refused to paint a rosy picture for us, also sharing the serious challenges they still faced from local government officials, from Islamists, and from the culture more broadly. They asked us to keep praying for them, for all of Egypt, and for their leaders when we returned home. We promised we would, and we did.

TEA WITH MRS. SADAT

One of our other joys was an opportunity to have tea with Jehan Sadat, widow of the late Egyptian president Anwar Sadat.

The visit was not on our original itinerary, but President Sisi insisted that we see Mrs. Sadat, and his staff made all the arrangements.

We visited her in the home where she has lived for forty years, guarded by heavily armed soldiers. This was the same home where her husband planned the surprise attack against Israel on Yom Kippur in October 1973, and the home where he also planned his "peace offensive" toward Israel, beginning with that stunning and historic visit to Jerusalem in November 1977.

Then eighty-four, Mrs. Sadat was a lovely and gracious woman with a dignified, regal bearing. Wearing a silk blouse, gray slacks, and white sandals, she greeted us warmly and led us into her spacious living room, which was decorated with artwork and framed photos of her husband with various world leaders.

A mother and grandmother, a professor, and a compelling storyteller with flawless English, she captivated us with her gracious hospitality. And for me, at least, the hours we spent with her were among the most interesting of our trip. As a new Israeli citizen, I was especially honored to meet her, tour her home, and introduce her to my sons, both of whom served in the Israeli military.

"I want the Israelis to live in peace," she told us. "Anwar really respected Prime Minister [Menachem] Begin for his strength and his courage in the Camp David talks. He told me that the thing that impressed him most during his visit to Israel were the tears he saw in the eyes of Israeli women as they held their children and welcomed him to their country. He could see in their eyes that they were thanking him for bringing an end to the war between our two countries."[12]

She spoke with us quite candidly about her hatred for radical Islamism, her vivid memories of that terrible October day in 1981 when her husband was assassinated, as well as her memories of the 9/11 attacks. She had been in northern Virginia when the news broke, and her children had called to plead with her to come back to Cairo.

She spoke of her revulsion against al Qaeda and its forerunner, the Muslim Brotherhood. As she wrote in her 2009 book, *My Hope for Peace*, she had nothing but contempt for Hassan al-Banna, founder of the Brotherhood, whose followers launched terrorist attacks from its earliest years in the 1920s; and Sayyed Qutb, the Brotherhood's most influential leader and polemicist, who "believed that the only acceptable government was one that cleaved to his strict, fundamentalist vision of Islam and encouraged Muslims to move against any state that deviated from this ideal."[13]

Qutb's book titled *Milestones*, she believed, "provided ideological inspiration for many radical Islamists, including Sheikh Omar Abdel Rahman, Ayman Zawahiri, and Osama bin Laden."[14]

In her book, Mrs. Sadat held out hope that the Brotherhood had changed and had truly become a moderate organization.[15] But by the time we met with her, nearly a decade later, she had painfully concluded that the Brotherhood had been lying all along.

She praised President Sisi for the "courageous decision" to arrest Mohamed Morsi and remove the Brotherhood from power. She told us in no uncertain terms: "It is impossible to reconcile with the Muslim Brotherhood."

9

SITTING WITH SISI

*On the record with the leader of the world's
most populous Arab country*

Our meeting with Egyptian president Abdel Fattah el-Sisi, leader of the world's most populous Arab country, took place on the morning of November 1, 2017.

The session was scheduled to last one hour; it lasted nearly three.

Our principals-only group included the eleven American evangelical leaders I had invited, plus Andrea Zaki, head of the Egyptian Protestants, and me. The president was joined by Khalid Fawzi, then chief of Egyptian intelligence; presidential spokesman Bassam Rady; and the official translator.[1]

After we cleared security, protocol officers led us through the palace to a grand vestibule. When the enormous doors were opened, we entered a great hall with a massive crystal chandelier, gorgeous oriental carpets, and a striking floor-to-ceiling tapestry portraying a map of Egypt, the Nile, and the Red Sea on the far wall. Seventeen gilded armchairs were set up—eight on the left side of the room, seven on the right. The president's chair was centered at the far end, near the Egyptian map. Next to it was an Egyptian flag on a stand, flanked by two gilded end tables. The final chair, the translator's, was positioned behind and slightly to the right of the president's.

Standing in the center of the room was President Sisi, wearing a black suit, white shirt, and burgundy tie. We formed a single file line and Sisi greeted each one of us in turn.

"It is so nice to see you again, Joel," he said in English, with a firm handshake and warm smile. "Thank you for coming. Welcome to Cairo."

"It is my honor, Your Excellency," I replied. "Thank you so much for inviting us."

One of the protocol officers led me to the chair directly to the right of the president's. After each member of the delegation greeted Sisi, he or she was led to an assigned seat. Michele Bachmann was on my immediate right. Directly across from us was the head of Egyptian intelligence. We all remained standing until Sisi took his seat.

Given that Sisi speaks fluent English, had studied at the U.S. Army War College, and had written his thesis in English, I was surprised that he conducted the entire meeting in Arabic—speaking a few sentences or a paragraph at a time and then pausing while we heard the translation.

He had done the same thing at the Four Seasons meeting in Georgetown, and I later learned that he does this so that he can speak as precisely as possible. One benefit was that we had time to take careful notes from each brief snippet of dialogue.

I felt for the translator when occasionally Sisi would stop her in mid-sentence, restate his point in English, and then ask her to continue. She would nod, rephrase, and continue. When the meeting concluded, I thanked her for tackling the challenging task of translating for a world leader who knows exactly what he wants to say in English.

"He keeps me on my toes," she said with a smile.

I was also surprised that Sisi did not make extended opening remarks. Many Arab leaders will give formal speeches to their foreign guests, sometimes lasting upwards of an hour or more. Sisi was different. He thanked us for coming and then asked me to make an opening statement on behalf of the group. He also took a moment to express his condolences for the savage terror attack in Manhattan the day before, when a radical Islamist terrorist from Uzbekistan killed six foreign tourists and two Americans and wounded a dozen others before being shot by a police officer.[2]

GOD LOVES EGYPT

"Thank you, Your Excellency," I began. "We want to thank you for inviting us to meet with you. We want to thank you for your leadership in rescuing Egypt from the Muslim Brotherhood and for your condolences on the attack in New York. We are in the same fight and we need each other.

"Mr. President, we want you to know that we love the nation of Egypt. But as followers of Jesus Christ, our love for Egypt is not based on a specific leader or policy. We love Egypt because God loves Egypt. As you well know, the Lord Jesus Christ and his parents lived in Egypt for a time. Moses, Joshua, and the children of Israel lived in Egypt. Other important biblical leaders and prophets lived in or visited Egypt. In fact, Egypt is mentioned in the Bible more times than any other country except Israel, showing us how important Egypt is to the heart of God. So that's first.

"Second, we want you to know that we are not looking simply for a single meeting with you, Your Excellency, but are hoping to build a bridge of friendship to the leaders and people of Egypt. Evangelicals play an influential role in the U.S. and around the world, and we believe it's important to build a relationship with you. We also want you to know that we are praying for and standing with Dr. Andrea Zaki and the Protestant Christians of Egypt, as well as with the Coptic Orthodox and other Christians of Egypt, and we are glad that Dr. Zaki could join us today."

The president turned to his left and welcomed Zaki—in his black suit, distinctive purple shirt, and white clerical collar—sitting to the left of the intelligence chief.

When Sisi turned back to me, I added, "Sir, I also want you to know that, before coming here, I briefed my friend Vice President Pence on our delegation and what we would be doing here in Egypt and later in Jordan. He sends his greetings and looks forward to his visit with you in December."

Sisi nodded and smiled. "I aspire to a friendship with you all," he said. "I was very keen to hold an open and frank dialogue with you, and I look forward to seeing the vice president, as well. The U.S.-Egyptian strategic relationship, as you know, has involved forty years of stability.

The difficulties of the last few years [under President Obama] represent a cloud that will disperse. Indeed, I am keen to strengthen this relationship.

"I believe in transparency and plurality," he continued, speaking directly to me but occasionally glancing at others around the room. "God created us differently. We hold different values. You will never be us, and we will never be you. Terrorists believe they have the absolute truth. They want absolute power over mankind. But God created us with full freedom. What faith do we embrace? I am a Muslim. You are Christians. Together, we must oppose those who try to impose their views on the world."

He paused and then addressed my point about God's love for Egypt.

"Egypt has a high position in God's eyes. Abraham married an Egyptian.* Moses was born and nurtured in Egypt. Moses' dialogue with God in Sinai—glorified and honorable—was on the territory of Egypt. Jesus fled oppression and came to Egypt with the Virgin Mary and Joseph, spending three years here. This is a sign of the high position of Egypt in God's view.

"The problem is that terrorism and extremism are driven by false ideologies," he continued. "Either people believe the same things believed by the terrorists, or they are killed. This is not appropriate to God's graciousness. God doesn't need people to impose religion on others. People must believe voluntarily. If you see a great man, people will rush to him for photographs. But if you try to force someone to have photos taken with a man, this will be resisted.

"Terrorism is our greatest enemy," he concluded. "We are engaged in efforts to defeat ISIS in Syria and Iraq. We are engaged in fighting terrorists here in Egypt. The mission is still long and has not been accomplished yet."

That said, he expressed confidence that Egypt and the free world would prevail.

When he had completed his remarks, he invited me to ask an opening question.

"I would be happy to, Your Excellency. But first, on behalf of the entire delegation, I want to wish you a very happy birthday."

"Your visit is my gift," he replied.

---

* Sisi's reference was to Hagar, Sarah's servant and the mother of Ishmael. See Genesis 16:1-15.

FIFTY MORE MUSLIM EMBASSIES IN ISRAEL?

Having noted that November 19 was both the president's birthday and the fortieth anniversary of President Sadat's historic visit to Jerusalem in 1977, I began by asking President Sisi to comment on his views of the peace process in light of Egypt's experience as the first Arab nation to make peace with Israel.

"I witnessed the pre-Islamist phase, before 1967," he said, "when Nasser was saying Israel must be thrown into the sea. I also witnessed the post-'77 phase, the current phase, as an Egyptian citizen. It is marvelous, and it could be replicated."

How so?

"We are committed to the safety and integrity of Israel, without any menace to them," Sisi explained. "But there could be fifty or more embassies of Muslim countries in Israel and vice versa—open borders, economic relations."

He was referring to the 2002 Arab Peace Initiative, which stated that once Israel and the Palestinians concluded a formal peace treaty, the entire Organization of Islamic Cooperation (OIC), comprising fifty-seven Muslim-majority countries, was ready to sign peace treaties with Israel as well.

"This was the dream and vision of President Sadat," he said, "and Prime Minister Begin helped get it started."

Sisi went on to describe how closely Egypt and Israel were now working together to fight terrorism, and about his warm relationship with Prime Minister Netanyahu. Indeed, he went on at some length about his appreciation for Netanyahu and for Ron Dermer, then-Israel's ambassador to the U.S. and one of Netanyahu's most trusted and valued advisors.

Sisi noted that the peace accord specified exactly how many and what kind of troops and weapons Egypt could have in Sinai. But he emphasized that "Israel has been willing for us to fight terrorism in Sinai with more troops and additional weapons" than specified in the treaty "because there is trust, because there is a good relationship between our two countries.

"Perhaps Sadat didn't have the opportunity to see it all come to pass, but I hope we can," he said. "I want to build on the peace that President Sadat began. Egypt has no problem with Israel. Egypt had a disagreement with

President Obama and Secretary Kerry. They believed that we should press Israel to make concessions. We don't believe this is the right way to go. I'm not speaking about dreams that cannot happen, but our own experiences. We have experience in making peace with Israel, and we can help others."

Unprompted, Sisi commented on relationships between Muslims, Jews, and Christians in Egypt.

"We have a Jewish synagogue [in Alexandria] that we have restored," he said. "All people are valued and appreciated in the new Egypt, including Jewish people. We are taking practical steps toward peace. Christians are our brothers. We don't make a distinction between an Egyptian Coptic Christian or a Muslim. We are keen to treat all Egyptians alike."

ADVANCING RELIGIOUS FREEDOM FOR ALL

As the conversation continued, Sisi described to us a new law he had signed, which permitted Christians to construct and improve church buildings. This, he said, was something that had not been permitted under Egyptian law for 150 years.

"Everyone has a fundamental right to worship God in his own house in Egypt," he said, noting that "the largest cathedral in Egypt will be built in our new capital city."

The president told us that the new city planners had shown him a design for a large mosque in the capital, but that he had insisted there must be a Christian church, too.

"In the Arab world, it might seem weird to help build and rebuild churches," he said. "Perhaps this will be extended to other Arab Muslim countries."

Immediately, I thought of Saudi Arabia, where not a single church building exists, though that is a story for a different chapter.

Sisi then asked me to moderate the discussion, choosing who would ask the next question. Surprised but willing, I decided to honor our Egyptian Christian friend and asked Dr. Zaki if he would like to go next.

"Thank you, Joel," he replied. "Actually, I do not have a question, but I would like to thank the president for signing the recent law to build, enlarge, and license new churches and to legalize church buildings that were previously unlicensed."

Zaki noted that there were some 1,500 evangelical Protestant churches in Egypt. He also noted that, before President Sisi was elected, about 60 percent of these—a thousand or so—churches were not licensed to operate. Now, however, he said that Egyptian Christians were allowed to apply for church licenses to operate freely and were receiving "full cooperation of the government because of the president's support for this law.

"I believe the president was selected by God and elected by the people," Zaki added. "The Muslim Brotherhood thought they were going to be in power for five hundred years. But General el-Sisi rescued the country. The president truly believes in religious freedom."

I asked former congresswoman Michele Bachmann to speak next.

"You are the George Washington of Egypt," she began, saying that he had led the Egyptian revolution against the tyranny of the Muslim Brotherhood and was doing everything he could to stabilize the country and get it headed in the right direction.

She reminded him that, in 2014, while still in Congress, she had authored a bill for the U.S. to designate the Muslim Brotherhood as a "foreign terrorist organization," and she emphasized the importance of continuing to press forward with such legislation, which has still not passed Congress. Then she shifted gears and thanked Sisi for all he was doing to protect Egypt's Christian community, the largest in the Arab world.

"When I came to see you after your election, you promised that the Egyptian government would help rebuild churches damaged or destroyed—and you have kept your word." She promised Sisi that we would pray faithfully for him and his family.

"Thank you," Sisi replied. "I need your prayers. Egypt needs your prayers. The destruction of churches in Egypt was a disgrace for all of us, and I've worked to remove this disgrace. All of the churches that were damaged have now been repaired."

Michael Youssef, the Egyptian-born pastor of a thriving church in Atlanta, whose sermons are broadcast around the world in multiple languages on his TV program, *Leading the Way*, invited Sisi to visit Georgia. Sisi responded in English that he has loved visiting the U.S. and looked forward to future visits.

Michael Evans said, "No one has done more for Christians than you, Mr. President."

"And for Muslims and for the Jewish people, too," Sisi interjected in English.

The room erupted in applause.

Evans went on to make the case that liberating 100 million people from Islamist tyranny, protecting their right to life and security, giving Christians the freedom to build churches and practice their faith, and giving all Egyptians the right to work and start businesses was a remarkable human rights record. And though Sisi had been severely criticized in the U.S. and around the world for his crackdown on the Muslim Brotherhood, Evans said, "You are a champion of human rights."

This began an interesting dialogue that continued throughout the meeting on the importance of human rights, which mattered deeply to our group, both as Christians and as Americans.

Both in our meeting with President Sisi and in private meetings later with his advisors, we affirmed that we believed Sisi was doing much in the area of human rights, but we also encouraged him to do much more—to release prisoners and other human rights activists, particularly those with American citizenship, because it was the right thing to do and because it would help Americans see that he was a true reformer.

"Thank you for your touching words. I hope to live up to your expectations," Sisi said. "There is no superiority among Jews, Muslims, or Christians. What is known in the universe is only a little.

"O Allah, we are so poor compared to your greatness. People shouldn't exploit religion. I am speaking from an Islamic perspective. Islam has so often been cruel and harsh and used for destruction. So now I will speak about human rights.

"I am a human being," he said. "I love people. I love Egyptians, despite our diversity. It's very painful when I am attacked on human rights. These are personal attacks on my morality. I didn't return these insults with abusive language. The Muslim Brotherhood are attacking me with devilish expressions. It will take time, but we are keen on improving human rights. We have 100 million people. Income is meager. The economy is weak. The community has the right to stability. Two thousand police and security officials have been killed as martyrs in recent years, and many more were injured. Where are *their* human rights?

"At a press conference in France, I said our education is not good quality. Our health care is not good quality. We need to create more jobs. We are trying to work on all of these issues. Aren't these all considered part of human rights? We have the American University, but only rich students can go there. I don't want a penny from you, I told the Europeans. But come and build universities for more students."

TELL PEOPLE THE TRUTH ABOUT EGYPT

Pastor Mario Bramnick asked, "How can we practically help Egypt?"

Rather than ask for money, as we might have expected, Sisi asked us to go home and speak the truth.

"Communicate to your people what you have seen and heard here— not to reinforce my image but to tell the truth," he said. "Someday, I will not be here. What is written by God is the truth. We are accountable to God.

"Don't take my word for it about how the country is doing," he insisted. "Go hear from the ordinary people and convey to your own people what you see and hear."

Dela Adadevoh, who was born and raised in Ghana, shifted gears, congratulating Egypt on qualifying for the World Cup and saying he looked forward to the upcoming match between Ghana and Egypt. Sisi laughed and spoke warmly of the close relationship between Ghana and Egypt.

"The Arab Spring was a risk to all of Africa," Adadevoh said. "When you stepped in and rescued Egypt, you gave all of Africa the chance to rest." Then he raised concerns about other radical Islamist groups trying to destroy lives in Africa, from al Qaeda to ISIS to Boko Haram.

"I am pleased to meet you," Sisi replied. "And you're right. The Muslim Brotherhood, Daesh, al Qaeda, and others prey on the weak religious comprehension of younger people. All these names are one banner for ideological extremism. They are egocentric, trying to force and compel their views on others.

"Africa is the greatest continent prone to this menace," Sisi said.

Tony Perkins, a member of the U.S. Commission on International Religious Freedom, thanked Sisi for his example of protecting Christians and asked, "How can we help advance religious freedom together?"

Sisi spoke first about the depth of the problem in Egyptian education, calling for a real change in mindset in how Egypt helped its students learn to value people of different faiths and creeds. "When education is of great quality, then students will be more open," he said.

Noting that Egypt had 22 million students in kindergarten through college, he said, "You can imagine the cost. If we spent the same as you [in the U.S.] on education, our budget just for education would be 4 trillion pounds. But our entire *budget* is only one trillion pounds."

Next, he spoke about leading by example.

"I was the first president of Egypt to congratulate Christians on the occasion of Christmas," he said. "This sets an example. It means others in Egypt could begin to do this, to welcome Christians, to interact warmly with them."

But, he conceded, this was only a start.

Retired Lieutenant General Jerry Boykin, a thirty-six-year veteran of the U.S. Army and former Delta Force commander, said, "Everyone at the Army War College is bragging that they knew you when you attended there."

Sisi laughed along with the rest of us.

"Now I will go home and add my name to that list," Boykin quipped.

THE GRAVE THREAT FROM IRAN

"I wrote my thesis at the War College on the future of democracy in the Middle East," Sisi said, turning serious again. "I made two points. First, if there is a vacuum, the Islamists will usurp power. Second, I saw a potential confrontation with Iran. There will be a great danger in the Middle East between the U.S. and Iran."

Sisi warned our delegation that Iran could use "unconventional weapons" if the ayatollah and his forces acquired such weapons. He called Iran "a great menace" and insisted "we must do what we can to avoid a military confrontation" while trying to "work in the context of sanctions."

"I am speaking of a country endeavoring for forty years to build a military on religious dogma," he added.

The Iranian threat comes not from the power of their weapons but their leaders' strong religious beliefs, Sisi explained.

"Iranian leaders have a death wish," he said. "American military might is incomparable, but Iran might push you to use unconventional weapons" to stop them from doing the same.

It was a sobering moment for all of us.

THE MEDIA WAR AGAINST EGYPT

Larry Ross, the former spokesman for Billy Graham who had gone on to start a public relations firm in Dallas working for major evangelical leaders, asked the president, "What is your main message for us to take back to America?"

"We are dealing with reality versus impressions," the president replied.

He argued that he and his team were engaged in making unprecedented, historic reforms that were liberating Egyptians and building a strong foundation for all Egyptians to thrive and prosper over the long term, but he was being relentlessly and unfairly attacked by the Qatar-based Al Jazeera news network, the Iranian media, the Turkish media, and countless other Islamist media outlets. They painted him as a monster who was making life in Egypt worse than under Morsi, worse than under Mubarak, crushing everyone's human rights and suffocating everyone's freedom. Indeed, he gave special attention to Qatar and Turkey, arguing that both were huge supporters of the Muslim Brotherhood and investing enormous sums of money into media outlets attacking everything he and his team were doing to save Egypt, and attempting to divide Washington from Cairo.

"What are we supposed to do?" Sisi asked. "Are they looking for the truth? No. Turkey and Qatar wanted to undermine the U.S.-Egyptian relationship.

"The Muslim Brotherhood is the strongest Islamist organization in the world," he added, and they had effectively moved their headquarters to Turkey after he drove them out of Egypt. "They would like to usurp power in Egypt again. This will never happen—it is against the law of nature and against God's will. Erdoğan's intention is to establish a caliphate in the region and then the whole world. Erdoğan wants to turn Turkey into a theological state. What should we do with Turkey?"

Sisi left the question hanging.

He did, however, say to Larry Ross, "We can't be as influential as you." Therefore, he asked us to go home and explain to evangelical Christians and others through our media platforms and other media connections the truth about the positive reforms happening in Egypt, even if we needed to be critical, as well. He readily conceded that he was not perfect and that he and his government were making mistakes. He insisted, however, that he was leading Egypt in the right direction; and though the road ahead was going to be rocky, Egypt would prevail.

THE HOPE OF ISAIAH 19

Johnnie Moore followed up by asking, "Are you hopeful for a way forward economically, especially in creating jobs and opportunities for young people?"

"Yes," Sisi replied emphatically. He then gave several examples of economic reforms and progress that had been made over the past several years and talked about his plans for future growth. "We have created a climate of competition to draw businesses and investment," he said, even while conceding that there was much more to be done.

I asked Sisi to help us understand his approach to encouraging reconciliation between the Palestinian Authority in the West Bank and Hamas in Gaza, noting that we were aware of, and grateful for, the work that his intelligence chief Khalid Fawzi had been doing to pacify Gaza and advance Israeli-Palestinian peace.

"Gaza is not big, but unless there is change, it will explode," Sisi said. "That's why we are trying to bring about a reconciliation between the West Bank and Gaza. We are telling young people in Gaza, 'If you do not pursue peace, then you will face destructive results. There must be a peace process.'"

Finally Pastor Jim Garlow thanked the president for welcoming our delegation and reiterated my opening statement about God's love for Egypt. Then he shared with Sisi about Isaiah 19, a chapter in the Bible that speaks of God's grace and mercy toward the people of Egypt. It was, he said, a powerful prophecy about a time of great distress for Egypt, followed by an era of divine peace between Egypt, Israel, and the people of ancient Assyria, the territory that today includes Lebanon, Syria, Iraq, and Jordan. After taking a few minutes to explain the prophecy to Sisi, Garlow closed by quoting Isaiah 19:25, in which God says, "Blessed be Egypt, my people."[3]

The president seemed touched by these words from the Scriptures. He thanked the pastor for his kind message and then leaned forward, smiling, and said, "Do you hear that? Do you? If the Bible says God loves Egypt, then we need for you to stand with us."

10

THE MEDIA'S WAR AGAINST
THE MODERATES

Why our visit to Cairo became front-page news

That afternoon, to our astonishment, the palace released two official photographs from our meeting with President Sisi.

The palace also released a summary of the meeting—called a readout in diplomatic circles—in both Arabic and English. This guaranteed the story would be on most TV news programs that night and on the front page of most Egyptian newspapers the following morning. Given that Egypt is the most populous Arab country in the world, and Cairo is the Arab media capital, we were also about to become a story throughout the entire Middle East.

We had not expected this. Throughout months of planning, the Egyptians had told me this would be a quiet, off-the-record meeting. Officials at the Egyptian embassy in Washington asked us not to announce publicly that we were even going to Egypt and to keep a low profile. I had agreed because the relationship, not publicity, was our goal.

It became evident, however, that at some point during our meeting, Sisi and his team had changed their minds. The fact that our discussions had gone for two hours and forty minutes—not the one hour that had originally been scheduled—was evidence that Sisi felt he had found a group of friends who recognized the reforms he was making and were sympathetic to the media onslaught against him—even as we pressed him to make even bigger, more sweeping reforms. Now he wanted the entire Arab and Muslim world to know he had met with us and that we were newfound allies.

PUSHING BACK AGAINST THE RADICALS' NARRATIVE

The palace suddenly adopted a new strategy.

They wanted to use our visit to Egypt to model the importance of building healthy and respectful friendships and dialogue between Muslims and Christians. They also wanted to showcase our meeting with Sisi to push back against the radical Islamist narrative that Christians were the sworn enemies of Islam, that the two faiths could not be friends, and that Sisi was the enemy of Egypt, rather than its liberator.

Because this was the first time in history that an Egyptian leader had welcomed a delegation of evangelical Christians to the palace, the story got saturation coverage in Egypt and throughout the region. We were encouraged by this. But there was a price. Now that everyone knew we were in Cairo, we were potential targets for any extremists who wanted to make a statement. Egyptian intelligence decided to provide us round-the-clock armed bodyguards and police escorts wherever we went.

Evidently pleased by the initial wave of coverage, an advisor to Sisi asked me if we would consider putting out our own statement.

"Say whatever you want," he told me, "but it would be helpful for people to hear your views about yesterday's meeting and why you are here. That will also generate even more coverage."

After discussing it with the group, we agreed to issue a statement. We still had concerns about some of Sisi's policies and how he was perceived by the Egyptian Christian community and by the rest of Egyptian society. At the same time, we were disgusted by the brutal and unfair war being waged against Sisi by so many in the media.

As events in recent years have shown, Sisi was certainly not being paranoid that Qatar and Turkey were doing their best to undermine and delegitimize him. The chief culprit is Al Jazeera—the satellite TV network and affiliated websites based in Doha, Qatar, and funded by the Qatari government—which is savagely hostile toward Sisi and other moderate leaders in the region, not to mention relentlessly antagonistic toward Israel and the U.S.

According to a September 2020 report in the *New York Times*, the U.S. Justice Department ordered AJ+, "a digital news network based in the United States and owned by Al Jazeera, the media company backed by the royal family of Qatar, to register as a foreign agent." U.S. officials said that the network, which "primarily produces short videos for social media" in English, Arabic, Spanish, and French, "engages in 'political activities' on behalf of Qatar's government and should therefore be subject to the Foreign Agents Registration Act."[1]

Al Jazeera has consistently blasted Sisi, saying he has a "pharaoh illusion" (May 2016), is "destabilizing Egypt" (April 2017), has "crushed" Egyptian society (July 2018), made Egypt "more dangerous than ever" (January 2019), turned the country into "a speeding train about to crash" (February 2019), and assumed "new repressive powers" (May 2020).[2]

The Turkish newspaper *Daily Sabah* has attacked Sisi as "the new pharaoh," who shows a "complete disregard for human rights" and has turned Egypt into "an open-air prison."[3] Muslim Brotherhood TV networks based in Turkey "regularly bash and criticize" Sisi, accusing him of being an "archvillain on par with Hitler and the pharaohs."[4]

Other media outlets have called Sisi a "true monster,"[5] a "bloodthirsty dictator,"[6] and a "pharaoh" who uses "magic" and "sorcerers" to "scare the Egyptian people," impose his "tyranny," and "rule with an iron grip."[7]

SPEAKING OUT

Our delegation spoke to a wide range of Arab, Israeli, and American reporters.

We defended Sisi as a bold, if imperfect, leader who was bringing positive, demonstrable, and unprecedented change to a nation in desperate need of it. Most of the coverage was fair, even positive. But not surprisingly, perhaps, outlets such as the *Washington Post* and *New Republic* tried to spin the trip as an invention of the Trump White House.[8]

Although I briefed senior U.S. government officials on our plans and asked for their advice before we departed, I never asked the White House for permission to take a delegation to Egypt, nor were we sent by the administration. It's true that several of our delegation members served on the White House's Evangelical Advisory Board. However, I asked everyone to come as private citizens and faith leaders, representing only themselves, not the government or even their own organizations, and they all agreed. As Tony Perkins told the Christian Post, our purpose in meeting with President Sisi was "to discuss the concerns we have, as American evangelicals, for the plight of religious minorities in Egypt, especially those who are our brothers and sisters in Christ. . . . We encourage Egypt to increase public awareness of the cultural, economic, political, and national security benefits of true religious freedom."[9]

AMBASSADORS FOR CHRIST

The clearest and most well-rounded report was done by Chris Mitchell, Middle East bureau chief for the Christian Broadcasting Network (CBN).

"For the first time ever," Mitchell reported in a story published on CBN's website and aired on *The 700 Club*, "a delegation of Christian evangelicals from the United States met with Egyptian president Abdel Fattah el-Sisi. Some believe the meeting represents a landmark in evangelical relations with the Arab world's largest country."[10]

Mitchell quoted Michele Bachmann as saying, "As a former member of . . . Congress, I can tell you that President el-Sisi is the best of the best in Egypt. We can be extremely grateful—on a political and military level—that he's here." President Sisi "wants to ensure," she added, "that I as a Christian, in Egypt, am able to practice my faith without having that disrupted."[11]

In the same report, Michael Youssef spoke of the urgency of praying for the church in Egypt.

"Sometimes they feel all alone," he said. So it is important "for us to come here and say, 'You're not alone, we're with you, we pray for you.' In fact, at our church, we pray every Sunday and every Wednesday for the persecuted church—not once a year. We pray for them on a regular basis, and we support them in every way we know how. So that was a shot in the arm for the believers and Christian leaders in Egypt today. We really need to be in prayer for the Christians here."

Andrea Zaki told CBN he was grateful that our delegation had come not only to meet with the president but also to meet and pray with Egyptian Christian leaders. He described our session with the pastors as "a fantastic meeting, sharing the hopes, the dreams, the challenges facing evangelicals here [in Egypt]: how they look to the future, how they can together build a coalition for the Kingdom of God. The meeting was very prophetic and very inspiring."

I told CBN I believed our visit was "setting into motion a historic relationship between an Arab Muslim leader and the evangelical Christian movement." Speaking as a fiction writer, I said, "If President el-Sisi didn't exist, you'd have to make him up." After all, he is what we're looking for in an ally with the United States—someone who is telling us, "I want a strong, strategic alliance with America" and "I'm fighting the same people you're fighting."

I also shared with CBN that President Sisi had humbly asked for God's help.

"He asked us to pray for him. He asked the Christian community, 'Please pray for me. Please pray for Egypt, because we are in a battle.'"

DINNER ON THE NILE

On Friday, November 3, our group took a private dinner cruise down the Nile River. We needed to step away from the intensity of one high-level meeting after another and take some time to process what we had seen and heard.

There was no question that we all came away impressed by the enormous progress Egypt was making and by the gratitude so many Egyptians felt for the man they believed had saved their country. When was the last time a country has been liberated from a radical Islamist reign of terror not by the U.S. Marines but by 22 million patriotic citizens signing their names on petitions to demand that the Islamists peacefully step down?

In the summer of 2013, Egypt did not have an impeachment law on the books. The terrified masses had no legal recourse to remove Mohamed Morsi and the Muslim Brotherhood from office. When Morsi refused to respond to their grievances, the people flooded into the streets—millions of them, night after night—demanding freedom. We concluded that Sisi, who was then defense minister, deserved a Nobel Peace Prize for listening to the people and taking bold action to safeguard their rights. He did not, after all, launch a coup d'etat, seizing power for himself in the dead of night. Instead, he publicly gave Morsi forty-eight hours to submit to the will of the people and step down.

It was only when Morsi refused that Sisi ordered the military to move. Then he set about to restore order and schedule national elections. In June 2014, the people overwhelmingly elected Sisi president, giving him 96.1 percent of the vote. Morsi, by contrast, had been elected in June 2012 with 51.7 percent.

That said, we agreed with the Egyptian pastors and ministry leaders who cautioned us not to paint a rosy picture. Though positive and foundational changes had been made, enormous challenges remained. During our dinner conversation, we considered a few.

The Threat of Terrorism

Though terrorist attacks by radical Islamists had significantly declined due to dramatically improved strategies and tactics by Egyptian intelligence and security forces, the threat remained. Attacks still happened, particularly against churches in the province of Minya, against Egyptian security forces in Sinai, and occasionally against tourist sites.

The Threat of the Muslim Brotherhood

The Muslim Brotherhood's reign of terror over Egypt is over. Many Brotherhood leaders have been arrested, tried, convicted, and imprisoned or executed. But this dangerous movement has hardly been eradicated. A 2020 Egyptian public opinion poll found that 23 percent of respondents expressed a positive attitude toward the Muslim Brotherhood.[12] The good news is that represented a ten-point drop from a 2018 poll.[13] Still, 23 million people view the Brotherhood favorably. That doesn't mean, of course, they are all planning to engage in violent or revolutionary acts. But Sisi is right that Egyptian security and intelligence forces cannot lower their guard.

The Threat of Slow Economic Growth

Under Sisi, Egypt's economy has made impressive strides. But the country is still not attracting enough foreign direct investment or producing enough good jobs for its swelling population. Some of this is due to security concerns since 2011. Some is because the economy still suffers the effects of socialist policies from the Nasser era and needs far more sweeping free-market reforms. The COVID-19 pandemic certainly didn't help. Sisi is moving in the right direction, but he must do far more, lest the streets explode with protests and violence all over again.

The Threat of Being Tempted by Putin

Sisi made it crystal clear to us that he wants a close strategic alliance with the United States. But we could see that he has been hedging his bets, welcoming advances from Vladimir Putin, in case Washington decides one day to ignore him or cut him loose the way the Obama administration had. In the fall of 2014, Cairo signed a $3.5 billion arms deal with Moscow. In 2018, the two countries signed a "strategic cooperation treaty" aimed at boosting trade and military cooperation. In 2019, Cairo bought $2 billion worth of Russian fighter jets. Putin would love nothing more than to peel Egypt away from the American camp. It would be disastrous for Egypt, as it was when they let the Russians arm and train them in the 1960s and '70s, but that doesn't mean Sisi and his team won't be tempted.

The Threat of Being Seen as a Pariah on Human Rights

Sisi has a valid point when he argues that Egypt has been through multiple revolutions and near civil wars. Likewise, he is right that preventing the state from either imploding or exploding has to be the government's top priority for the foreseeable future, especially with such sizable support remaining for the Muslim Brotherhood. The question is, how to keep the country together while preserving human rights?

During the American Civil War, President Lincoln took unprecedented measures to keep the Union together, including suspending habeas corpus, curtailing civil liberties, limiting freedom of the press, and arresting upwards of fourteen thousand American citizens, charging many with treason, and trying some in military tribunals rather than civil courts. Why? Lincoln and his allies argued that the only way for the state to protect individual rights was to have a state in the first place, and that the measures necessary to hold the Union together, though not pretty, were necessary.[14]

Members of Congress, European governments, human rights groups, and foreign media outlets continue to criticize Sisi for arresting too many people, imprisoning dissidents and human rights activists, imposing too many restrictions on opposition political parties and nongovernmental organizations (NGOs), and imposing too many restrictions on the Egyptian media, on social media, and on free speech generally. Some of the criticism is unfair. But not all of it. In their efforts to maintain control, Sisi and his team are going overboard. In so doing, they risk being seen by the American people, Congress, the White House, CEOs, investors, and others as pariahs, creating an environment that Americans refuse to invest in, support, or visit.

We all agreed that Sisi must do a better job of finding the balance between preserving the state and safeguarding civil liberties.

Since our visit in 2017, there have been some signs of progress. Sisi has pardoned more than 1,600 prisoners, including 330 youth prisoners. In 2020, Egypt released 4,011 prisoners for Sinai Liberation Day, and an additional 3,000 were granted clemency for the Islamic festival of Eid al-Fitr.[15] These are positive moves, but even more needs to be done.

To be clear: The magnitude of reforms needed to turn the Egyptian ship of state and keep it headed in the right direction is staggering. The amount of money, patience, and creative thinking—and God's grace—needed to implement all the reforms necessary for Egypt's survival and success is, frankly, daunting.

Neither our first trip to meet President Sisi nor our subsequent visits and meetings convinced us that he and his team are doing everything right. When Sisi invited some of us to a follow-up session with him in Manhattan in September 2018, he was even more candid. He acknowledged that he was making mistakes, that he was likely to make more, and that he was learning as he went. But he has repeatedly asked us to pray for him, and he has sought our advice. We, in turn, have tried to be faithful in giving him both.

Like all reformers in the region, Sisi and his team must be pressed—respectfully but firmly—not to rest on their accomplishments or focus only on making life better for the elites. They must continue to set an example for the region by making big, important transformative changes that truly improve the daily lives and strengthen the human rights of all Egyptians.

They also must do a far better job of explaining to the world at large the progress they have made. Sisi has a far better story to tell than most people realize. Most of the mainstream media are not going to help him get the word out. Many, in fact, are waging war against him. We Christians have experienced some of the same. We stand ready to help the leaders of Egypt write a better story—and tell it better too.

As we left Cairo from that first trip and headed to Amman, we found ourselves encouraged and optimistic. We knew that history would not be kind to Sisi or his government if they failed to create a new, better, safer, and freer Egypt. We vowed to pray that they would not fail.

11

CROSSING THE JORDAN

Assessing the future of the eastern half of the Holy Land

On Sunday, November 5, we departed Cairo on Egypt Air flight 719 to Amman. There were twelve of us now, as scheduling challenges prevented Johnnie Moore, Jerry Boykin, Dela Adadevoh, and the Youssefs from accompanying us on the second leg of our journey. The good news was that, in Jordan, every member of our group was invited to attend every meeting, including a fascinating working lunch we had with King Abdullah II on our final day in Amman.

To give you a sense of how such a delegation worked logistically, here is a summary of our itinerary, which was patterned after the visit Lynn and I had in 2016.

SUNDAY, NOVEMBER 5

After landing in Amman at 8:40 a.m., we went by motorcade directly to the General Intelligence Directorate for an eleven o'clock meeting with Adnan al-Jundi, chief of Jordanian intelligence, who briefed us on the threats facing the kingdom.

At noon, we were whisked to the hotel for check-in, then on to the

Marka air base for a one thirty with General Mahmoud Freihat, chairman of the Joint Chiefs of Staff, and a working lunch with other officials, including the director of military intelligence and director of strategic planning.

By two thirty, we were back in our motorcade and on our way to tour the Zaatari refugee camp, near the city of Mafraq, and receive a briefing from Jordanian and U.N. officials.

At five thirty, we returned to our hotel in Amman, with time to settle in before leaving for a delicious Levantine dinner at Fakhreldin Restaurant at eight.

At nine thirty, we returned to the hotel and enjoyed a time of prayer together before turning in for the night.

MONDAY, NOVEMBER 6

After breakfast together at the hotel, we departed by motorcade for a ten o'clock meeting with Jordan's minister of foreign affairs, Ayman Safadi.

After a brief, casual lunch at noon, we were back in the cars and on our way to a two o'clock meeting with Imad Fakhoury, minister of planning and international cooperation, who told us about the economic challenges and opportunities facing the kingdom.

At four, we returned to the hotel, met privately as a delegation, and had a time of prayer.

At six, we met with Prince El Hassan bin Talal, brother of the late King Hussein, uncle of King Abdullah II, and the kingdom's former crown prince.

At seven thirty, we returned to the hotel for dinner, time to discuss the day's events, and prayer.

TUESDAY, NOVEMBER 7

At nine thirty on Tuesday morning, our motorcade departed for a meeting with a group of some three dozen Jordanian evangelical Christian pastors and ministry leaders at the Jordan Evangelical Theological Seminary (JETS) in the suburbs of Amman. There we were hosted by Imad Maayah, president of the Evangelical Synod of Jordan; Imad Shehadeh, president of JETS; and Emad Kawar, chairman of the JETS board.

Afterward, our motorcade took us to Al Husseiniya Palace for a noon working lunch with His Majesty King Abdullah II. We were joined by foreign minister Ayman Safadi, and Jafar Hassan, the king's chief of staff.

At three, we departed for a VIP tour of Mount Nebo, the mountain where Moses died after God granted him a glimpse of the Promised Land.

At six o'clock, we returned to the hotel and had some free time before a farewell dinner for the delegation at an Amman restaurant.

On Wednesday morning, we had one last breakfast together, said our goodbyes, and all flew home.

Even now, it's hard to describe how emotional it was for the group to visit the refugee camp and Mount Nebo or how moving it was to spend time with Jordanian pastors, seminary professors, and other ministry leaders. We so appreciated hearing about the challenges they face, their testimonies of God's power and faithfulness, and their candid prayer requests. We also valued the opportunity to answer many of the questions and concerns they were open enough to share with us. And what an honor it was to worship and pray together. There was so much to hear and discuss. Our only regret was that we could not spend more time with them.

A WORKING LUNCH AT THE PALACE

Certainly one of the most fascinating parts of the trip was the working lunch with King Abdullah. Whereas our meeting with President Sisi had been first on our itinerary in Egypt, this meeting with the king was the capstone of our visit to Jordan and a unique bookend to our time in the region.

King Abdullah could not have been more gracious. He greeted us one by one and chatted informally for a while, all in English. When we took our seats, he made a few brief opening remarks before dedicating the rest of the session—again, all in English—to our questions on any topic we desired. His ability to speak to us without a translator was enormously helpful and effectively doubled the length of the conversation.

To allow for candid, in-depth, and meaningful dialogue in all our meetings, while also giving our Jordanian hosts the maximum assurance that they could discuss even the most sensitive issues without fear of being quoted—much less misquoted or quoted out of context—we had agreed up front to the royal court's ground rules: All conversations would be on deep background; after leaving the kingdom, we could disclose with whom we had met and generally what we had discussed, and we could share our observations and lessons learned. This was, after all, the purpose of the trip. However, we could not quote any official by name, especially the king.

This visit would be very different from our trip to Cairo, where all our conversations with President Sisi and his advisors were 100 percent on the record. Yet we agreed to Jordan's ground rules for one simple reason: Our objective was to build long-term friendships, not make headlines.

A SENSITIVE SITUATION

Another reason that our visit to the kingdom was designed to be low-key was the particularly sensitive geopolitical and religious situation in Jordan. Well over half—and possibly upwards of 70 percent—of Jordan's population is of Palestinian descent. Queen Rania is Palestinian—and thus so are King Abdullah's children. Was it even wise for the king to invite a group of pro-Israel evangelical Christians to meet with him, let alone publicize such a visit?

The issue was not whether the king wanted to promote healthy Muslim-Christian relations. Clearly he did. Both he and his father before him had maintained good relations with Jordan's Roman Catholic and Orthodox Christian communities, as well as with the Vatican and clerics and theologians from other historic Christian denominations around the world.

Indeed, between 1964 and 2014, four Roman Catholic popes made high-profile visits to Amman and met with the Jordanian monarch. King Hussein had also met individually with various Protestant Christian leaders over the years, including Billy Graham, who visited Amman in 1960.

Likewise, since taking the throne, King Abdullah had occasionally met with evangelical Christian pastors such as Rick Warren, who led a two-day conference in Amman in 2014 to discuss violence against Arab Christians.[1] And the king had spoken at National Prayer Breakfast events in Washington, D.C., in 2006 and 2017.

Still, there are two aspects of evangelical Christianity that may have concerned the royal court.

First, most American evangelicals (though not all) believe the Old and New Testament prophecies and biblical teachings about God's special love and plan for Israel and the Jewish people.

Second, all evangelicals believe that Christians are commanded in the Bible to lovingly yet clearly share the gospel of Jesus Christ with all people in all nations. Nowhere are we told to hate or disrespect Israel's Arab neighbors. To the contrary, both the Old and New Testament teach believers to "love your neighbor."[2] We're never to coerce anyone into accepting our faith, but the Bible teaches that we are supposed to give everyone the opportunity to at least hear the gospel message so they can decide for themselves.[3]

Both issues—the theology of God's love and plan for Israel, and the biblical mandate to share our faith—are highly sensitive issues in Muslim cultures. This is certainly true in Jordan, given the kingdom's history of tension and war with its next-door neighbor, its deep love and support for the Palestinian people, and its stated determination to see a sovereign Palestinian state established in the West Bank and Gaza.

Not surprisingly, then, no formal delegation of American Christians—much less one led by a dual U.S.-Israeli citizen from a Jewish background—had ever been invited to meet with the king and other senior Jordanian officials. However, I believed these factors were actually reasons *in favor* of inviting our delegation. Evangelicals who love Israel need to understand the views of its Arab peace partners. We need to hear the perspective of leaders who love and strongly support the Palestinian people and yet want to find ways to maintain calm relations on both sides of the borders.

Who better to meet with than King Abdullah?

At the same time, the king and his advisors, in my view, could benefit from a broader network of relationships, one that would include leaders of the American evangelical community, comprising tens of millions of Americans who deeply love Israel but could also love Jordan and her people, given Jordan's immensely important role in both the Bible and the current geopolitical environment. Jordan's leaders also need more stateside advocates for a strong U.S.-Jordanian alliance and for the American and international financial assistance necessary to care for the masses of refugees that have flooded into Jordan and are not returning home anytime soon.

To be clear, the king hadn't needed to be persuaded. This was outreach he wanted to engage in. But by inviting us, he was balancing several conflicting interests. Keeping the trip quiet would likely help toward that end, which is most likely why my colleagues and I were asked not to publicize our visit.

GOING PUBLIC

Once again, however, we found ourselves surprised when, on our last day in Jordan, the royal court released a statement about our visit, along with two official photographs of our group.[4] One of the photos was of our two-hour working lunch with King Abdullah. The other was a photo of the king with our entire group, including the wives who were with us and my sons Jacob and Jonah.

The palace's statement mentioned our discussion of the peace process and efforts to relaunch negotiations for a two-state solution between Israel and the Palestinians, regional and international efforts to fight terrorism, and our delegation's desire to promote tolerance, moderation, and interfaith dialogue.

Because the statement did not provide specific information or any direct quotes from the meeting, it was within the agreed-upon ground rules. It did, however, alert the national, regional, and international media that we had met with King Abdullah, which drew a great deal of interest.

Once again, we found ourselves in the headlines, and we received calls from reporters wanting the inside scoop. Given that we were scheduled to leave in a few hours and that most of the team would be in flight for much of the following day, we quickly put out our own statement and responded to interview requests on a case-by-case basis.

"I believe God is blessing Jordan because they have been so generous to the poor and the suffering," Tony Perkins told the media. "And while I'm grateful the American people are doing more than any nation in the world to help Jordan financially during this crisis, it's critical that the rest of the world stand with the people and leaders of Jordan in their hour of need."[5]

Michele Bachmann said, "King Abdullah and President el-Sisi are to be applauded for exemplifying moderation and stability in a neighborhood scarred by intolerance and war. These men are courageously confronting the forces of terror and extremism. They're committed to their nation's peace treaties with Israel. And they want to work even more closely with the United States to advance peace in the region. These are impressive leaders, and they need America's appreciation and full support."[6]

I explained to the media how the delegation had come about and added,

"His Majesty King Abdullah II is America's most faithful Sunni Arab ally and a man of peace. . . . Nowhere in the Arab world are Christians safer than in Jordan. By God's grace, the king has created an oasis of stability amidst a sea of fire. This is a model of moderation the American people need to know more about."[7]

For the next several months, all members of the delegation spoke about what they had learned on the trip—through interviews on both Christian and mainstream media outlets, in sermons at churches and speeches at Christian conferences, as well as in private conversations with fellow evangelical leaders, members of Congress, and senior administration officials.

Further, we drafted a seven-page report summarizing our meetings in Egypt and Jordan and giving our impressions of President Sisi and King Abdullah. I delivered these to President Trump, Vice President Pence, Secretary of State Pompeo, the director of national intelligence, the National Security Council, and key members of Congress. I also sent the report through back channels to Israeli prime minister Netanyahu and Ron Dermer, Israel's ambassador in Washington. We were extremely encouraged by our visit and we wanted people to know it.

Along with the important and encouraging insights we had gained, we also came away with a clear-eyed view of some troubling trends facing Jordan.

TROUBLING TRENDS: THE ECONOMY

The massive influx of Iraqi and Syrian refugees into Jordan has strained Jordan's already-limited resources almost to the breaking point, and public frustration is real and growing. Consider a few numbers:

- In 2018, 73 percent of Jordanians described their economy as "bad" or "very bad."[8]
- In 2019, the overall unemployment rate hit 19 percent. Among people with a bachelor's degree or higher, the unemployment rate hit 25.6 percent for men and a staggering 78 percent for women. And nearly half (48.7 percent) of young people ages 15 to 19 were unemployed.[9]

And all of that was before COVID-19.

- By September 2020, the overall unemployment rate stood at 23 percent, the highest recorded level in the history of the kingdom.[10]
- Eighty percent of Jordanians blame the government for the current economic situation.[11]
- More than 90 percent say that parliament is failing "to achieve any laudable successes."[12]
- Of the 42 percent of Jordanians who said they have considered emigrating in the past few years, 94 percent cited economic reasons as their motivation.[13]
- Further, 97 percent of Jordanians say they do not earn enough money to allow for savings after covering the cost-of-living essentials.[14]

After the pandemic is contained, the Jordanian economy should have more opportunities to improve, and the confidence of Jordanians in their government along with it. But what if the resentment of some turns into anger, and anger into action?

TROUBLING TRENDS: THE ISLAMISTS

Jordanians do not want to become another Syria, Iraq, Yemen, or Libya.

They appreciate the social and geopolitical stability the king has created and maintained while violence and chaos have unfolded in other Arab states. Yet there are indicators that the population at large is not as moderate as the king is. Some are inevitably drawn to the siren song of the Islamists, believing that only a sharp pivot toward radicalism will bring the blessing of Allah to help Jordan prosper and thrive.

When asked in November 2018 about the importance of implementing more reforms that interpret Islam "in a more moderate, tolerant, and modern direction," only one-third of Jordanians (35 percent) said this was a good idea, and only 3 percent said they "strongly" supported moving in a more moderate direction.[15]

By contrast, a large majority of Jordanians (fully 60 percent) said they disagreed with the notion of promoting a more moderate approach (22 percent said they "strongly" disagreed).[16]

When asked how they viewed Hamas, the Gaza-based terrorist organization, 57 percent said they viewed the group favorably.[17]

At the same time, 23 percent of Jordanians viewed the Muslim Brotherhood favorably,[18] and 72 percent had a positive view of Turkish president Recep Erdoğan.[19]

It should be noted that though the appeal of ISIS in Jordan was small, it was not insignificant. The founder of ISIS was Jordanian, and in the early years of ISIS, around three thousand Jordanians traveled to Iraq and Syria to join the jihad, making Jordan the third largest supplier of fighters to ISIS after Russia (3,417) and Saudi Arabia (3,244).[20]

On the plus side, only 4 percent of Jordanians said that good relations with Iran were even "somewhat important" for their country in 2018. Likewise, two of Iran's terrorist proxy movements, Hezbollah and the Houthis, face 94 to 97 percent disapproval ratings in Jordan.[21]

TROUBLING TRENDS: RISING ANTI-ISRAEL SENTIMENT

Though King Abdullah remains committed to maintaining Jordan's 1994 peace treaty with Israel, he faces growing pressure to take a harder line against the Israelis.

In 2016, Speaker of the House Atef Tarawneh stated publicly that Parliament opposes the treaty.[22]

In August 2018, Jordanian legislators argued strongly against the appointment of a new ambassador to Israel. "Our fundamental stance is that the peace agreement with Israel should be abrogated and that Palestine's occupation must immediately cease," said one MP. "We seek to scrap the (peace) agreement. . . . The Palestinians are the ones who should occupy Israel and not the other way around."[23]

In October 2018, members of the Jordanian Parliament "demanded a special session be held to review the 1994 peace treaty with Israel, and some hawkish lawmakers urged King Abdullah to cancel the agreement altogether."[24]

That same month, the king announced his decision not to renew a provision in the peace treaty that had allowed Israel to lease two tracts of Jordanian territory from Jordan for twenty-five years.[25]

In March 2019, the Jordanian Parliament voted against an agreement the government made to buy 3 billion cubic meters of natural gas a year from Israel for fifteen years, a deal worth $10 billion.[26]* Though Parliament does not have the authority to change policy—such power rests in the hands of the king—the vote was perceived as a bellwether of public opinion.

THE ROAD AHEAD

Several key decisions during the Trump administration angered Jordanians and Palestinians alike:

- The December 2017 decision to move the U.S. Embassy to Jerusalem and declare the city Israel's eternal capital (albeit with final boundaries for the municipality of Jerusalem still to be negotiated).
- The January 2020 rollout of President Trump's Israeli-Palestinian peace plan.
- President Trump's role in brokering normalization agreements between the United Arab Emirates, Bahrain, and Sudan and the State of Israel in the late summer and early fall of 2020, ahead of a comprehensive peace agreement with the Palestinians.

A June 2020 poll found that only 5 percent of Jordanians had even a "somewhat" positive view of the Trump peace plan, and the same survey found that less than half (44 percent) believe that maintaining good relations with the U.S. is important. (However, that number was up from a mere 14 percent in 2018, just after Trump moved the embassy to Jerusalem.)[27]

Can King Abdullah effectively navigate such challenges? Can he continue to guide the kingdom in a moderate and peaceful direction as one of the Muslim world's leading reformers, despite significant public sentiment pulling in the opposite direction?

It will not be easy. The king and his advisors will need great wisdom. They will need to find and encourage more high-profile champions of peace and moderation within Jordanian society. They will need the military,

---

* Israel has discovered massive reserves of natural gas off its Mediterranean coast and has offered to supply both of its peace partners, Jordan and Egypt.

financial, and diplomatic support of the U.S. and the rest of the moderate Sunni Arab world, as well as the ongoing respect and thoughtful, prudent cooperation of Israeli leaders, who need to be careful not to make provocative moves that could unnecessarily enrage Jordanian citizens. Above all, they will need much prayer and the grace of God.

Are there reasons to be concerned that at some point the Jordanian volcano could blow? Yes. Yet as I have told the king, I am committed to praying daily for him, for his family, and for his people. I choose to be an optimist and to help where I can. I also pray that many others in the region and around the world will do the same. King Abdullah, after all, is a critically important leader, and the critically important Western alliance with Jordan is one worth strengthening.

12

"I AM READY TO MAKE PEACE"

Our stunning meeting with UAE Crown Prince Mohammed bin Zayed

Few leaders I have met are more intriguing, influential, or innovative than Crown Prince Sheikh Mohammed bin Zayed Al Nahyan of the United Arab Emirates.

Widely known by his initials, MBZ, he is the powerful son of the UAE's modern founder, the beloved and visionary Sheikh Zayed, who passed away in 2004. MBZ shuns the spotlight, rarely gives interviews, and almost never gives speeches. He prefers to operate behind the scenes. Though not even technically the UAE's head of state, MBZ is most definitely the man driving its reforms and its meteoric rise in the Gulf region.

Officially the UAE is led by its president, Sheikh Khalifa bin Zayed Al Nahyan, supreme leader of the armed forces and emir of Abu Dhabi. However, after suffering a stroke in January 2014, Sheikh Khalifa has been in poor health and unable to govern.[1] Thus it was that the reclusive MBZ was required to step in and govern in the sheikh's stead.

With a population just under 10 million people, the oil-rich UAE is one of the wealthiest countries in the region. Its gross domestic product in 2019 was about $420 billion. It has the largest sovereign wealth fund in the Arab world, worth upwards of $700 billion.[2] Having long recognized that its petroleum reserves are a finite asset, however, the Emirates have been systematically and quite effectively diversifying their economy away from oil dependency. Indeed, the oil and gas sectors now account for only about one-third of GDP. Still, plunging oil prices over the past decade have hit the country hard, stalling growth and forcing leadership to accelerate their diversification plans. The COVID-19 pandemic was also devastating, all but shutting down the country's thriving aviation hub and heavy tourist traffic.*

Nevertheless, MBZ—a moderate Muslim with a passion to expand freedom and opportunity for his people while vigorously opposing the Iranian regime and radical Islamism in all its forms—has worked closely with the emirs of Dubai and other regions of the country to rack up one impressive accomplishment after another.

For example, just since 2014, the UAE has become the first Arab state in the Gulf region to achieve the following milestones:

- Develop a space program and launch an unmanned mission to Mars, a probe named *Al Amal* (Arabic for *hope*).
- Build a safe, legal, nonmilitary, internationally monitored, and noncontroversial nuclear power industry.
- Open a world-class art, history, and cultural museum—the billion-dollar Louvre Abu Dhabi.
- Open a high-tech counterterrorism war room to track and counter-act violent and extremist messages on TV, radio, print, and social media in real time.
- Welcome a delegation of evangelical Christian leaders to the Gulf region, the one I was honored to lead.
- Host Pope Francis not only for a state visit but also to hold a public Mass, attended by 150,000 people.
- Sign a formal peace treaty with the State of Israel—the first Arab state to do so since Jordan in 1994.
- Purchase a squadron of F-35 stealth fighter jets, America's most advanced military aircraft.

---

* In 2015, Dubai was the world's busiest airport for international travel, serving more than 100 million passengers.

If the last point seems contradictory to the others, that is not how MBZ sees it. One evening during Ramadan several years ago, he asked his dinner guests—a variety of diplomats, intellectuals, journalists, and fellow sheikhs—"What if the UAE was attacked in its own backyard? What if Abu Dhabi is targeted by military action from a big, hostile country with regional ambitions, and at the same time the enemy moved its agents to wreak havoc inside the country, what should be our reaction? What would be the right decision?" He listened carefully to each of the answers, then bluntly gave his own assessment: "We will pound the capital of the enemy without hesitation, and we will eliminate the agents in the blink of an eye, and we will protect our homeland."[3]

This was a man I wanted to meet.

In a moment, I will share with you details of our extraordinary visit to the UAE and the vision and views of MBZ. First, let me share how we got there in the first place.

MBZ'S MAN IN WASHINGTON

I first met Yousef Al Otaiba in March 2018. The most influential Arab ambassador in Washington, D.C.—indeed, one of the most influential ambassadors to the United States of *any* country—Al Otaiba is MBZ's point man in the U.S. Rarely have I found an emissary so passionate about advancing his nation's interests and so good at it.

Born in 1974 to an Emirati father and Egyptian mother, Al Otaiba had already been serving as the UAE ambassador to the U.S. for a full decade by the time I met him. This gave him a great advantage over diplomats whose nations rotated them out of Washington every two to three years.

Bald, handsome, and fit, Al Otaiba is media savvy and fluent both in colloquial American English and in the ways of winning friends and influencing people inside the Beltway. He knows how to build connections and throw a good dinner party. He also knows how to shrewdly invest the UAE's not inconsiderable oil wealth into important American charitable causes to help boost his country's image.

Promoted in 2017 to the rank of cabinet minister in Abu Dhabi, Al Otaiba is a valued and trusted player in Washington for all these reasons—and for one more. Everyone who meets him knows he has direct access to MBZ.

Indeed, before his appointment as ambassador to the U.S., Al Otaiba served for eight years as the crown prince's director of international affairs.

It is baffling to me how many nations send ambassadors to Washington who may be accomplished diplomats and lovely people but do not have a close professional and personal relationship with the country's top leaders, can barely get them on the telephone, and thus cannot effectively speak and advocate on their behalf. This is most certainly not the case with Yousef Al Otaiba.

As it happened, the ambassador had taken notice of the largely positive media coverage our visits to Egypt and Jordan had kicked up, and he was curious. Former CIA operative Rob Richer had suggested that Ambassador Al Otaiba and I should meet. So had Dennis Ross, a former senior Middle East advisor to presidents George H. W. Bush, Barack Obama, and Bill Clinton.

On that particular March morning, I was in Washington having coffee with a senior intelligence official at the Egyptian embassy. In the middle of our conversation, he suddenly decided that Al Otaiba and I should meet each other *right then*. To my astonishment, he picked up the phone, called the ambassador, and then walked me across the street to the palatial UAE embassy and made a personal introduction. Al Otaiba happened to be heading to the White House, so we spoke for only about fifteen minutes. But he graciously invited me to visit him the next time I was in D.C.

That was in late May, and we spent an hour together in his office. He asked me many questions about my background, why I had taken groups to Egypt and Jordan, and how I felt those trips had gone. He probed, too, about why I had such an interest in the Arab world. Then he surprised me by asking if I might be interested in taking a group to Abu Dhabi in the fall, noting that the UAE had never invited a delegation of evangelical Christian leaders before.

But the time was right. The Emirates were declaring 2019 as a Year of Tolerance. They had invited Pope Francis to visit. They were also building the Abrahamic Family House, an architecturally gorgeous complex in Abu Dhabi comprising a mosque, a church, and a synagogue to encourage peaceful coexistence and acceptance of the three Abrahamic faiths.

Grateful for the invitation, I immediately agreed. But as we began sketching out the details of such a trip, Al Otaiba surprised me again.

"You know," he said, "if you really bring a group all the way over to see our crown prince and senior leadership, it would probably be good if you spent some time in Saudi Arabia and met the new crown prince there, as well."

I laughed out loud. "Well, Mr. Ambassador, I would certainly love to visit Riyadh someday. But just to be clear, I'm Jewish on my father's side and a dual U.S.-Israeli citizen. I don't really think the Saudis are ready to welcome someone like me."

"I think you're wrong," he said. "Things are changing there—and fast."

"Maybe, but *that* fast?"

Al Otaiba filled in a little more background to help me understand his reasons for optimism. Then he suggested we work together to finalize our trip to the UAE in the fall. Once that was set, if I was interested, he could discuss the idea with then-Saudi ambassador to the United States Khalid bin Salman, the younger brother of Crown Prince Mohammed bin Salman.

He had a deal.

BUILDING A NEW TEAM

To be honest, I hadn't given any thought to leading additional delegations.

The trips to Cairo and Amman had been wonderful. We had all learned a great deal and come away encouraged. In addition to writing political thrillers, I was busy following up with Egyptian and Jordanian officials to deepen those relationships. I was also working with Christian leaders in both Egypt and Jordan to find ways to encourage and support our brothers and sisters there. At the same time, the other members of our group and I were using every forum we could find to share with evangelicals about the positive reforms underway in Egypt and Jordan and the challenges that remained.

In retrospect, it made sense that the two Arab countries that had already made peace with Israel had reached out to American evangelicals to tell us their story. They could see that President Trump sought the support of the evangelical community and had surrounded himself with evangelical advisors, including the vice president, secretary of state, and U.N. ambassador, among others. They could also see that many members of Congress were evangelicals and like-minded Catholics, with whom we had a measure of influence.

What we had not expected was an invitation from an Arab country that did not have formal diplomatic ties with Israel. Some time earlier, I had committed myself to praying for all the leaders of the region by name. I was reading everything I could find about where the UAE, Saudi Arabia, Bahrain, Oman, Morocco, and other moderate-trending Sunni Arab countries were heading. I was also talking regularly with contacts in Washington and Israel to better understand the trend lines. And I had been to the UAE several times before, both as a tourist and to visit with Christian leaders there. But this was all very different—and exciting.

Once Al Otaiba and I settled on the basic framework for a trip in late October, I decided to invite several of the same leaders who had joined me before. But I also felt I should mix things up a bit by including other prominent evangelicals who might benefit from seeing firsthand the historic changes brewing in the Gulf region.

Unfortunately, among those who had scheduling conflicts were Mike Huckabee, former governor of Arkansas; Anne Graham Lotz, daughter of the late Billy Graham; and Ronnie Floyd, then-head of the Southern Baptist Convention, the largest Protestant denomination in the U.S.

Still, in short order I had a confirmed list that included Tony Perkins, Johnnie Moore, Michele Bachmann, Larry Ross, and Michael Evans from our previous trips, and five newcomers:

- **Michael Little**, then chairman of the board of the National Religious Broadcasters (NRB) and the Evangelical Council for Financial Accountability (ECFA), and president and COO of the Christian Broadcasting Network.
- **Skip Heitzig**, senior pastor of a large evangelical church in Albuquerque, New Mexico.
- **Kay Arthur**, world-renowned Bible teacher and founder of Precept Ministries International.
- **Jerry Johnson**, then president and CEO of the National Religious Broadcasters.
- **Wayne Pederson**, board member of the ECFA and the NRB, former NRB president, and member of the board of The Joshua Fund.

Two others were forced to drop out at the last minute for health reasons and other commitments, but I was glad that my son Jacob was once again able to join us as a notetaker, photographer, and my assistant. My son Jonah, however, was serving in the Israel Defense Forces and, thus, was unable to travel with us.

A GREAT PEARL IN THE GULF

The more I prepared for our trip, the more fascinated I became with the UAE.

One of the youngest of the Gulf States, the UAE received its independence from Britain in December 1971. Once a collection of sleepy fishing villages ruled by seven tribal leaders, it became a unified country through the visionary efforts and sheer grit of its founder Sheikh Zayed bin Sultan Al Nahyan.

The discovery of oil in the 1950s was a boon, but the sheikh wanted more—and he soon put the Emirates on a path to flourishing beyond anyone's wildest imagination. By the end of 2001, after thirty years under the sheikh's leadership, the UAE's economy was thirty-six times larger than it had been in 1971.[4]

In 2001, population of the UAE was 3.3 million, but 87 percent were not native Emiratis. Most were foreign workers hired to develop and run the oil industry, build cities and some of the world's tallest skyscrapers from scratch, and operate the many hotels, apartment complexes, malls, and restaurants that were popping up all over.

Along with the unique economy and demographics of the seven emirates, the sheikh capitalized on traditional values of hospitality and openness to other cultures, nationalities, and even religions to make the UAE a special place in the Gulf region.

Though Sheikh Zayed was born and raised a Muslim, he was not a radical. Unlike his Saudi neighbors, he had no interest in building a kingdom that isolated itself from the rest of the world—nor could he afford to. Both to survive and to thrive, Sheikh Zayed believed the UAE had to become known as a place of openness, tolerance, and inclusion.

And that is exactly what we found when we arrived.

Our group landed in Abu Dhabi on the evening of October 26, 2018.

Over the next four days, we met with an intriguing group of senior government officials, clergymen, and leaders in the war against violent extremism:

- **Sheikh Abdullah bin Zayed Al Nahyan (ABZ)**, younger brother of the crown prince and the UAE's minister of foreign affairs and international cooperation. He gave us a detailed briefing on UAE foreign policy.
- **Sheikh Nahayan bin Mubarak Al Nahyan**, the UAE's minister for tolerance and coexistence (the only such position we are aware of in the Muslim world), who briefed us on the rationale behind the Year of Tolerance and how the government views interfaith relations.
- **Ali Rashid Al Nuaimi**, chairman of Hedayah, the International Center of Excellence for Countering Violent Extremism, who gave us an intriguing in-depth briefing on how the UAE is working to counter the theological and ideology narratives of the Islamists.
- **Yousif Alobaidli**, director-general at the Sheikh Zayed Grand Mosque, who gave us a special tour of one of the world's largest mosques.
- **Steve Bondy**, chargé d'affaires at the U.S. Embassy, who briefed us on the history of U.S.-Emirati relations and the UAE's impressive history of economic and social reforms.
- **Canon Andrew Thompson**, until recently Anglican vicar of the UAE, pastor of St. Andrew's Church in Abu Dhabi, and author of several wonderful books, including *Jesus of Arabia: Understanding the Teachings of Christ through the Culture of the Arabian Gulf* and *Christianity in the UAE: Culture and Heritage*. Canon Thompson had dinner with us and gave us a briefing on the state of Christianity in the UAE and the Gulf region.
- **Jeramie Rinne**, then-pastor of the Evangelical Community Church in Abu Dhabi, who joined us for dinner with Canon Thompson and answered our many questions about life in the UAE for followers of Jesus.

We were also briefed by senior officials at the Sawab Center, the joint U.S.-UAE digital war room and rapid-response center, established in 2015 to counter the messaging of radicals on broadcast, print, and social media in real time. And we toured the extraordinary Louvre Abu Dhabi with the museum's senior executives.

We learned a great deal from all these meetings. But most fascinating to us was our conversation with Crown Prince Sheikh Mohammed bin Zayed Al Nahyan.

MEETING THE CROWN PRINCE

Our meeting at the royal palace with MBZ began at 1 p.m. on October 29. It was scheduled to last thirty minutes, but we talked for more than two hours.

The crown prince is a tall, lanky man with kind brown eyes, a warm smile, and a thin beard and mustache. He greeted us wearing a crisp white *thawb*—the traditional cotton robe worn by most Emirati men—black sandals, and a white headdress wrapped with a thick black cord. We expected the meeting to be held in a large, formal hall, but instead he asked us to join him in a small parlor.

MBZ sat in a gilded chair, not unlike the one President Sisi had. I was seated directly to his left, and the others were seated up close as well, on thick, maroon upholstered couches. No other leader we had met with had created so intimate a setting or sat so close to us.

Joining us were several members of the crown prince's inner circle, including Ali Rashid Al Nuaimi, chairman of the Hedayah Center, who had briefed us on the UAE's impressive efforts to wage an ideological and theological war against the extremists; Khaldoon Khalifa Al Mubarak, chairman of Abu Dhabi's Executive Affairs Authority; and Mohamed Mubarak Al Mazrouei, the undersecretary of the Crown Prince Court of Abu Dhabi.

We were served cups of steaming hot coffee and tea, and the crown prince took our questions—dozens of them—covering his views on everything from the Iranian regime and the Iran nuclear deal to the implications of the Arab Spring and the threat of radical Islamism to the future of religious freedom and pluralism not only in the UAE but throughout the

Arab Muslim world. He held court in a classic Gulf Arab tradition known as a *majlis*, in which an emir converses with his subjects or guests.

The ground rules were such that I am not at liberty to share with you the details of our conversation, more like our conversation with King Abdullah in Jordan and our talks with President Sisi in Egypt. However, the palace released a photograph to the media, along with a short video of our meeting. It also released a statement, explaining to the press that the crown prince had "received a U.S. evangelical Christian delegation led by Joel Rosenberg," and emphasizing the crown prince's determination to promote "peaceful coexistence" between religions and to "uproot the scourge of terrorism, extremism, fanaticism, and hatred."[5]

Since our return from the UAE in 2018, I have been careful not to reveal the most important part of that extraordinary meeting. But now it can be told.

Because we were meeting with the leader of an Arab country that did not yet have a peace agreement with Israel, we decided as a group ahead of time that I should make the following three points in my remarks.

First, we wanted the crown prince to know that because evangelical Christians study and believe the teachings of the entire Bible—both Old and New Testaments—we love Israel and the Jewish people and are committed to their security and prosperity. This is not a political position, I explained, but a theological one. It is, therefore, a deeply held conviction and not one from which we can be swayed.

Second, we are commanded by the Lord Jesus Christ to love our neighbors. This means that along with our love for the people of Israel, we also love the Palestinian people and all Arab and Muslim people. We wanted to make it clear that just because we love Israel does not mean we hate those who oppose her. God loves both sides, I explained, and we are commanded to do the same.

Third, I noted that, in Psalm 122:6, we are commanded to "pray for the peace of Jerusalem." Millions of Christians around the world, and certainly in America, take that verse literally and seriously. "And as we pray daily for peace," I said, "we are looking to see who will be the next Arab leader to step forward and make peace with Israel, even if the Palestinian leadership is not yet ready."

I explained that we had not come with a detailed peace plan in mind. We were not trying to lobby him to embrace a certain plan. We just wanted him to know our hearts, our desire for peace, and our biblical convictions and to take his measure on the topic.

To our astonishment, the crown prince leaned forward and said, "Joel, I am ready to make peace with Israel."

13

WHO IS MOHAMMED BIN ZAYED?

Why is he leading the way toward a new Middle East?

We were stunned by the crown prince's declaration.

MBZ had taken some steps in the years prior to our visit to warm relations between the UAE and the Jewish State, but these had been quiet, discreet, and often under the radar. Now he was signaling a major change was coming.

We pressed him to explain more of his thinking and how the road to an actual peace treaty might be forged. I even asked him if he would ever be interested in coming to Jerusalem. Though conceding that I had no political power or wealth or human ability to persuade him to come, I simply explained to him that my family and I were residents of Jerusalem and that we would love to welcome him to the Holy City.

At this, he seemed to light up, and he said, "Joel, that day is closer than you realize."

It was an exciting conversation and revealed the heart of a sincere moderate, a true man of peace. We had stumbled into a major headline, but there was just one problem: We couldn't say anything publicly. We had given the crown prince our word to keep this conversation confidential, and he was not asking us to act as some sort of go-between with the UAE and Israel. Still, we regarded it as highly significant that he trusted us and wanted us to know that he was looking for a way—charting a path, even—to a historic breakthrough in Arab-Israeli peacemaking.

"I think most Muslims and Christians don't realize how much in common we have with each other in terms of our values, priorities, and strategic objectives," I told the *National*, the UAE's English-language newspaper after the meeting. "I brought Christian leaders with me who have enormous influence back in America—who [can] go and report back to their world. We are coming away more convinced than ever that the UAE is a fantastic friend and ally to the United States—[and] more Americans definitely need to know that."[1]

THE BACKSTORY

So who is Mohammed bin Zayed, and why has he chosen to chart such a bold new course?

To answer that question, allow me to share several important stories we heard from his closest advisors that gave us insight into his character and backstory.

In the spring of 1960, for example, an American medical doctor and his wife came to Abu Dhabi and asked for a meeting with Sheikh Zayed, who was then a provincial governor. They explained that they were Christian missionaries and they wished to be allowed to set up a clinic to provide medical care for the needy. Touched by the couple's sincere faith and generosity, the sheikh explained that his wife was pregnant and that they feared losing another child after several earlier miscarriages. But if the couple could help bring the baby to term, the sheikh would give them one of his own houses to serve as the clinic.

The couple agreed, and by God's grace, a healthy baby boy was born on March 11, 1961—the future crown prince and Arab-Israeli peacemaker, Mohammed bin Zayed.

We were so blessed to hear that story upon our arrival from two very senior UAE officials. We were blessed, too, to learn that Sheikh Zayed kept his word and gave that missionary couple—Dr. Pat and Marian Kennedy— one of his homes for use as a clinic. Eventually a much larger facility, the Oasis Hospital, was built and helped to dramatically drive down the infant mortality rate. The hospital, run by evangelicals, is still operating in Abu Dhabi to this day and providing care to anyone in need, without regard to a person's nationality or religious faith.

Not coincidentally, perhaps, Sheikh Zayed looked favorably upon Christians from that point forward and allowed them to worship freely in the Emirates. Indeed, in meeting with pastors and ministry leaders throughout the Gulf, we learned of the extraordinary religious freedom granted to Christians in the UAE and the fact that more than seven hundred Christian churches operate in the UAE. No other Gulf nation even comes close.

SEPTEMBER 11, 2001: A TIME FOR CHOOSING

We also learned a great deal about the Emiratis' commitment to countering radical Islamism and how 9/11 was a pivotal moment for MBZ and his father.

Though the conversations we had with security and intelligence officials during our trip were confidential, I later asked Ambassador Al Otaiba to go on the record with me about his memories of that fateful day, as well as how the UAE views the Iranian regime and other terrorist states and organizations. He graciously agreed.

In a conversation in his office back in Washington, D.C., the ambassador told me, "I think 9/11 caught the entire world off guard. Nobody understood it, unless your sole job in the world was counterterrorism. But terrorism has been something we have been very, very focused on for a long time. I was with His Highness [MBZ] at the time. I was just twenty-seven. We were flying from Scotland to London for meetings with King Abdullah of Jordan. All three attacks happened while we were in the air. This was twenty years ago, so we didn't have Wi-Fi on the plane. But upon landing in London, someone ran up to the plane and said, 'America is burning. Someone attacked America.' And we are like 'This can't be right.' I mean, your first reaction is always skepticism. 'Fake news' wasn't an issue back then, but we thought this guy was probably exaggerating."[2]

Given that MBZ was a key military and foreign policy advisor to his father, he and Al Otaiba spent the night gathering as much information as they could before flying back to Abu Dhabi the next day. With one of the best intelligence agencies in the Arab world, the UAE quickly confirmed that al Qaeda was responsible for the attacks, and they fed the information they had to Washington.

But what were they going to do next?

"The single most profound way it changed UAE policy was when Sheikh Zayed called Sheikh Mohammed and said he wanted to deploy troops into Afghanistan," Al Otaiba said.

"That was a huge decision," I replied.

"That was a *huge* decision," Al Otaiba agreed, saying that some advisors were opposed to sending Arab Muslim troops to fight fellow Arab Muslims. "But Sheikh Zayed said, 'Either we believe in bin Laden's approach and we're *with* him, or we are against bin Laden's approach and we're *against* him. It's one or the other.' And basically he said, 'Our version of Islam is not this. This is not who we are. We are against this because this is against us.' And it was a very profound, wise moment that determined how we proceeded from that point on. If I am not mistaken, we sent the first Arab troops into Afghanistan. They were there for about twelve years and that's kind of what crystalized our approach to extremism."

Within days following the 9/11 attacks, the UAE severed ties with the Taliban. In time, they would indeed send the first Arab forces into Afghanistan to fight alongside their most important and valued ally, the United States.[3]

"We Arabs and Muslims tend to be, by far, the larger victim of terrorism," Al Otaiba continued. "More Muslims have been killed by Islamic terrorism than Christians or Jews—and our view is very clear. Whether you are Muslim Brotherhood or ISIS, it is all kind of in the same boat—your vision of the caliphate [is] this big stateless, borderless empire that is run by certain individuals' very strict interpretation of religion. The Muslim Brotherhood and ISIS have exactly the same goal. They just have two different methods of going about achieving their goal. ISIS [uses] violence, terrorism, kidnapping. Muslim Brotherhood wants to do it through the ballot box. But their ultimate goal is still a caliphate. So I think we are very clear about what terrorism is and what extremism is. And it's ironic that sometimes in the West they are a little less clear about it than we are."

Shortly after MBZ came to power in 2014, the UAE declared eighty-three Islamist groups as terrorist organizations and outlawed all of their activities. Among them were the Muslim Brotherhood, Hezbollah, and ISIS.[4]

IRAN, THE CLEAR AND PRESENT DANGER

The most serious threat in the eyes of Emirati leaders is the Iranian regime.

They could not be clearer about the urgency of building a strong strategic alliance to contain Iran or about how horrified they were to learn that the Obama administration had opened up secret negotiations with their most dangerous enemy.

"The discovery that America was negotiating with Iran without [our] being told, was the equivalent of finding out that your partner is cheating on you," Al Otaiba told me. "That's exactly how it felt: like betrayal.

"We're your partners," he added. "We're the ones who fought in six wars with you. We're the ones who trade with you and invest with you and send our students and patients to be treated there. We're the ones who buy Boeing airplanes and weapons. And you thought it was a value proposition to go behind your friends' back to make a deal with your adversary? What the hell just happened? How come our partners that we've sent our boys to fight with didn't bother telling us?"

What about Turkey? I asked. How does the UAE regard President Erdoğan and the direction Ankara is moving?

"Sultan Erdoğan?" Al Otaiba asked. "Look, the Iranians are trying to reestablish the glory days of the Persian Empire. I think that's exactly what Erdoğan is trying to do [with the Ottoman Empire] in Turkey. The only difference between Iran and Turkey is that in Iran, I think, it's the whole system, right? If something happens to the supreme leader, there is going to be another supreme leader [who is just as dangerous]. The system remains intact. [But] if something happens in Turkey, I don't think the system is trying to go where Erdoğan is trying to go. With Erdoğan, I think it's an individual direction that he has taken the country in. Anyone who works in, or is from, Turkey that I talk to is very unhappy with the direction Turkey is going.

"I think most people don't understand the link between Islamist groups," Al Otaiba added, noting that countries such as Iran, Turkey, Qatar, and others are funding, arming, supplying, and encouraging a range of terrorist organizations, including Hezbollah, Hamas, the Muslim Brotherhood, and others.

"A lot of people say, 'No, no, no, no, these [countries and leaders] are moderates and if we engage with them, they will ultimately become nice and they will talk to us.' We have a very different view, which is 'These are the same people but in disguise and you guys are falling for it hook, line, and sinker.'"

Dr. Anwar Gargash, the UAE's minister of state for foreign affairs, later invited me to his home in Dubai. As we met for over two hours, he also spoke candidly of his country's deep and growing concerns about the threats posed by Iran and Turkey.

"The last thing we want is a confrontation with Iran, okay?" Gargash said. "Because we live in a very close proximity. While we have serious issues with Iran, these issues need to be resolved politically and diplomatically."

But, he added, people must not "take the issues with Iran lightly," from Tehran's push for nuclear weapons to their support of global terrorism to their ongoing efforts to destabilize Arab regimes.

"Erdoğan is the most important Turkish leader in a hundred years," he said. And the most dangerous. "Under Erdoğan, Turkey is harkening back to old imperialist pipe dreams. The Ottoman Empire was great once, then it declined, and the Turkish people want to remember its splendor."

Gargash added that "Erdoğan is driven by political Islamism. His party are political Islamists. He is feeding his crowd red meat" by publicly attacking the UAE and other moderate Arab states, and that has helped him become "an all-powerful executive president" who is actively and aggressively pursuing neo-Ottomanism.[5]

"A TREASURE OF MODERATION"

After our meeting with MBZ, Johnnie Moore was deeply encouraged by what he had seen.

"You're seeing these Islamic leaders all across the region say, 'We're done with the terrorists, we're done with the extremists, we're going to change from the inside out, and we're going to be a more tolerant society," he told CBN News, just before we left Abu Dhabi. "The UAE is miles and miles ahead of the pack."[6]

Tony Perkins agreed. "The UAE is pursuing a path of religious tolerance and peace that I pray other countries in the region would follow."[7]

Although what is happening in the UAE is "not an American model of religious freedom," Jerry Johnson observed, the country is "moving in the 'right direction.'"[8]

"There's been a lot of persecution against Christians in this part of the world," said Michele Bachmann. "So we've come over here as advocates for Jesus Christ, but also for our fellow believers. We're really excited . . . because we've seen there are a number of churches that are already operating. There's been a real growth among believers, and there's been a tolerance in the Muslim government of the United Arab Emirates toward Christians."[9]

I concurred.

"What we found here in our meetings with the crown prince . . . is an extraordinary story that's almost a hidden treasure of moderation, of resistance to radical Islamism, of wanting a close relationship with the United States, and of freedom of worship for Christians. . . . I think Americans should be encouraged. . . . While there are serious threats in this region, there are also real allies that many of us didn't know existed."[10]

AN OPEN LETTER TO THE CROWN PRINCE

Upon returning home to Jerusalem, I wondered if there was a way to signal the UAE's deep and growing commitment to advancing peace in the region, without violating our commitment to the crown prince.

After studying the reforms the crown prince and his team were making, I wrote an open letter to MBZ, which was published in the *Jerusalem Post* on February 6, 2019.[11]

> *Greetings from the holy city of Jerusalem, beloved and venerated by the world's 15 million Jews, 2 billion Christians, and 1.8 billion Muslims, and by you.*
>
> *I write this letter first and foremost to commend you, your fellow sheikhs, and the people of the United Arab Emirates on declaring 2019 as the Year of Tolerance. From the moment your father, the widely respected Sheikh Zayed, led his nation to independence and admittance into the United Nations in December of 1971, the UAE has endeavored to chart a path of social, religious, and political moderation, as well as economic innovation, growth, and progress. The results to date have been impressive.*
>
> *Recently, however, you have taken even more dramatic and courageous steps. You have sought to demonstrate in both symbolic*

and practical ways that Muslims, Christians, and Jews can live
together in peace and mutual respect . . . even while holding
different (and deeply held) theological and political views on a range
of significant issues.

I went on to applaud the crown prince for making history by welcoming Pope Francis to the UAE, the first ever papal visit to a Sunni Arab Gulf country; for giving the pope a wonderful gift—the deed to the first Catholic church ever built in the UAE, in 1962—and for not only permitting but encouraging the pope to hold an open-air Mass in the country's largest stadium, an event that became the largest Christian worship service ever held on the Arabian Peninsula, with upwards of 150,000 Catholics in attendance.

I also highlighted a two-day conference hosted by MBZ for Muslim, Christian, and Jewish leaders, to advance the cause of peaceful coexistence. At the conference, Pope Francis and Sheikh Ahmed al-Tayeb, grand imam of Egypt's al-Azhar mosque and university, were awarded the first-ever Human Fraternity Award for their outspoken efforts to oppose religious violence and extremism and promote tolerance and cooperation between peoples of different faiths.

The imam made headlines throughout the region, including on the front page of newspapers in Saudi Arabia, by urging Muslims to "continue to embrace your brothers the Christian citizens everywhere, for they are our partners in our nation."

Next, I expressed my gratitude for MBZ's gracious invitation to me to bring the first-ever delegation of evangelical Christian leaders to visit the UAE.

We were deeply encouraged . . . to learn that you and your
government happily permit more than 700 Christian church
congregations to meet and operate openly and safely in the
UAE and that nearly one million followers of Jesus live in the
UAE, approximately 10 percent of the population. We were also
encouraged that there is a small but thriving Jewish community in
your country that, because of your leadership, is feeling increasingly
comfortable to come out of the shadows.

I closed the letter by inviting the crown prince to visit the holy city of Jerusalem and bring a delegation of Muslim, Christian, and Jewish leaders with him. Obviously I was not writing in an official capacity—"simply as a Jew, an evangelical, and a resident of Jerusalem."

> *Come meet with Israeli and Palestinian government, business, civic, and religious leaders. Come meet with Israeli and Palestinian young people. Share with us your much-needed message of peace, mutual respect, and tolerance. Share with us lessons you have learned from your father, and lessons you are teaching your children.*
>
> *I have every reason to believe you would be welcomed warmly by the people of both sides. Indeed, I pray that God would use your visit to help bring a fresh breeze of healing and hope to a land much in need of both.*

Everywhere I looked at the time, prominent diplomats, respected columnists, and renowned Middle East analysts were saying there was absolutely no chance of a major breakthrough in Arab-Israeli peacemaking anytime soon. They were likewise dismissing everything the Trump White House was doing at the time to lay the groundwork for such a breakthrough. But my colleagues and I knew something they didn't, and we prayed for peace more faithfully than we ever had before.

14

THE ROAD TO RIYADH

The rise of a new king, a new crown prince,
and a new president

It had long been known as the Forbidden Kingdom.

Unless you were a diplomat, an oil executive, or a Muslim on pilgrimage to Mecca—the *hajj*—there was very little chance a Westerner was ever going to travel into Saudi Arabia. The Saudis simply didn't want you to come. Until 2004, non-Muslims could not receive a tourist visa. If you were Jewish or Israeli—or simply had an Israeli stamp in your passport—forget it. You could not enter even for business purposes.[1]

Not many Westerners *wanted* to visit. Certainly most Americans did not. They remembered all too well the oil embargo imposed by the Saudis against the United States for standing with Israel during the Yom Kippur War in 1973. They remembered the long lines to buy gasoline, with prices that seemed to rise from one day to the next. They knew that fifteen of the nineteen hijackers on 9/11 were Saudi nationals. And that Osama bin Laden was a Saudi.

Still, I had long been intrigued by this Forbidden Kingdom. I had been praying for some time for its people and leaders. I had been praying, too, for an open door, hoping that one day I might actually be able to go.

In a moment, I will share with you how the eventual invitation came about and take you inside the Saudi royal palace along with the first Christian delegation ever allowed into the kingdom. But first it's important to lay the foundation for the road to Riyadh.

A MODERATE MONARCH TAKES THE THRONE

The tectonic shift began on January 23, 2015, when King Abdullah bin Abdulaziz Al Saud passed away at the age of ninety—and Salman bin Abdulaziz Al Saud, governor of Riyadh, ascended to the throne.

Though few realized it at first, the new monarch was not like his predecessors.

First, believing the kingdom faced existential threats, King Salman came to power with a sense of urgency to counter those threats.

Second, he believed the only way forward was to pursue rapid and unprecedented economic and social reforms. These included forging an airtight strategic alliance with the United States, rather than keeping Washington at arm's length, buying American weapons and selling the U.S. oil, but never getting too close.

Third, like any smart corporate executive leading an effective restructuring effort, he believed he needed to get the right people on his team and in the right positions. To me, it was as if he had torn a page out of Jim Collins's legendary business book *Good to Great*.

> The executives who ignited the transformations from good to great did not first figure out where to drive the bus and then get people to take it there. No, they *first* got the right people on the bus (and the wrong people off the bus) and *then* figured out where to drive it. . . .
>
> If you have the wrong people, it doesn't matter whether you discover the right direction; you *still* won't have a great company.[2]

Upon ascending the throne, King Salman appointed his fifty-five-year-old nephew, Mohammed bin Nayef (aka MBN), as the new crown prince. This was seen by American officials as a positive, if mixed, development. MBN was well-known in the U.S. intelligence and counterterrorism communities as a moderate. He was also known as the man responsible for tearing up the underground al Qaeda network in the kingdom, imprisoning Osama bin Laden's operatives, and cutting off their ability to move money. He was not, however, regarded as a reformer. One Mideast analyst at the time dubbed MBN "Washington's favorite Saudi," calling him "the scourge of al Qaeda and Iran but no friend of those who want to see major reforms in the kingdom."[3]

Less noticed at the time was that the king appointed as defense minister his twenty-nine-year-old son, Mohammed bin Salman (known as MBS). MBS soon made his mark by sending air strikes against pro-Iranian Houthi rebels in Yemen.[4]

By April 2016, having solidified his hold on power, King Salman took the next step in his reform plans, authorizing MBS to unveil a sweeping agenda for the kingdom, known as Vision 2030. It suddenly became clear that the king had tasked MBS not only with combatting radical Islamist threats to the kingdom but also with running the country's oil industry and developing a plan to shift the kingdom's dependency on oil to something far more dynamic and entrepreneurial for the twenty-first century.

In June 2017, the king made even bigger headlines—stunning the world by removing MBN as crown prince and installing MBS in the role.[5]

Step by step, the new Saudi monarch was turning the ship of state in a very different direction.

Such course corrections caught my eye, but there were even more interesting developments afoot. I soon found myself tracking growing signs that relations were gradually warming between the Saudis and the Israelis.

THE TRUMP PIVOT

The rise of King Salman and MBS were major turning points for the Kingdom of Saudi Arabia.

So was the election of Donald Trump as president of the United States.

Whereas the Obama-Biden administration had angered the Saudis (and America's other regional allies) by initiating secret talks with Iran without informing them, and later signing a dangerous nuclear deal with Tehran, the new Trump administration took the opposite approach. Trump vowed to scrap the Iran nuclear deal and reengaged with Israel and the Sunni Arabs—particularly the Saudis.

I began alerting American evangelical Christians to the importance of what the new commander in chief was doing in the Arab world.[6]

"President Trump is sending a signal," I told the Christian Broadcasting Network during an April 2017 interview. "We want to work with leaders like [President] el-Sisi and King Abdullah and the Saudi deputy crown prince and the Gulf States, and of course Israel, to build an Israeli-American-Sunni alliance against Iran and against ISIS and against the horrific situation going on in Syria."[7]

Immediately I was seeing a warm reaction from Arab leaders to the Trump pivot, as I told CBN News. "I think there is a different environment than we've had, because leaders in the region who were our traditional allies see in President Trump a true ally, a friend, who wants to work *with* them against radicals and isn't abandoning the region."[8]

In May 2017, President Trump announced he was going to make Saudi Arabia the first stop on his first foreign trip, followed immediately by a visit to Israel. This was a hugely positive move. "The president's decision to visit Israel on his first foreign trip keeps a campaign pledge," I wrote at the time. "[It is also] a sharp contrast to the last eight years. President Obama skipped Israel on his first visit to the Mideast in June of 2009."

I also praised Trump's decision to visit Saudi Arabia. During the 2016 campaign, I had been critical of his call for a "Muslim ban" and welcomed his change of policy and tone. "Mr. Trump has been intentionally—and rightly—reaching out to Arab Muslim leaders in recent months to forge a working alliance against Iran and ISIS," I noted, adding that to his credit, he had already met in Washington with the Saudi deputy crown prince, along with Jordanian, Egyptian, Iraqi, and Palestinian leaders.[9]

THE SAUDIS TAKE CENTER STAGE

Trump's visit to Riyadh was a game changer.

First, it put the Saudis on center stage, and the royals made it clear they were deeply grateful for a change of leadership and perspective in the White House. King Salman rolled out the red carpet, met Trump at the airport when Air Force One landed, and greeted him warmly, something he had pointedly refused to do when Obama visited in 2016.[10]

Second, the summit not only shifted U.S.-Saudi relations in a dramatically positive direction, it helped reset U.S.-Muslim relations, as well. Trump did not use the visit simply to sign more than $300 billion in trade and defense deals with Riyadh. He also held a face-to-face summit with the leaders of more than fifty Arab and Muslim countries. And in his address, he provided moral clarity in the war against radical Islamism that had been much lacking during the Obama years.

> Here at this summit we will discuss many interests we share together. But above all we must be united in pursuing the one goal that transcends every other consideration. That goal is to meet history's great test—to conquer extremism and vanquish the forces of terrorism. . . .
>
> In sheer numbers, the deadliest toll has been exacted on the innocent people of Arab, Muslim, and Middle Eastern nations. They have borne the brunt of the killings and the worst of the destruction in this wave of fanatical violence.
>
> Some estimates hold that more than 95 percent of the victims of terrorism are themselves Muslim. . . .
>
> This is not a battle between different faiths, different sects, or different civilizations.
>
> This is a battle between barbaric criminals who seek to obliterate human life, and decent people of all religions who seek to protect it.
>
> This is a battle between Good and Evil. . . .
>
> America is prepared to stand with you—in pursuit of shared interests and common security.
>
> But the nations of the Middle East cannot wait for American power to crush this enemy for them. The nations of the Middle East will have to decide what kind of future they want for themselves, for their countries, and for their children.
>
> It is a choice between two futures—and it is a choice America CANNOT make for you.
>
> A better future is only possible if your nations drive out the terrorists and extremists. Drive. Them. Out. DRIVE THEM OUT of your places of worship. DRIVE THEM OUT of your

communities. DRIVE THEM OUT of your holy land, and
DRIVE THEM OUT OF THIS EARTH.[11]

Third, Trump singled out the Iranian regime and rallied the Muslim
world to join a reassertive American effort to contain Tehran's aggression.

From Lebanon to Iraq to Yemen, Iran funds, arms, and trains
terrorists, militias, and other extremist groups that spread
destruction and chaos across the region. . . .
　　It is a government that speaks openly of mass murder, vowing
the destruction of Israel, death to America, and ruin for many
leaders and nations in this room. . . .
　　The Iranian regime's longest-suffering victims are its own
people. . . . Until the Iranian regime is willing to be a partner for
peace, all nations of conscience must work together to isolate Iran,
deny it funding for terrorism, and pray for the day when the Iranian
people have the just and righteous government they deserve.[12]

Fourth, in a bold move, Trump told Muslim leaders that he was going
to press them to make peace with Israel.

For many centuries, the Middle East has been home to
Christians, Muslims, and Jews living side by side. We must
practice tolerance and respect for each other once again—and
make this region a place where every man and woman, no matter
their faith or ethnicity, can enjoy a life of dignity and hope.
　　In that spirit, after concluding my visit in Riyadh, I will travel
to Jerusalem and Bethlehem and then to the Vatican—visiting
many of the holiest places in the three Abrahamic Faiths. If
these three faiths can join together in cooperation, then peace
in this world is possible—including peace between Israelis and
Palestinians.[13]

There was no shortage of critics in response to Trump's speech. The
Iranian regime and the Islamist media especially hated it. But Trump

received praise from many in the Muslim world and from regional analysts who understood exactly what he was saying and wholeheartedly agreed.

"Bravo President Trump," tweeted Anwar Gargash, the UAE's state minister for foreign affairs. "Effective and historic speech defining approach toward extremism and terrorism with candid respect and friendship."[14]

The government of Indonesia—the world's largest Muslim country—hailed the speech and the summit, saying that "it is the first time a meeting between the new American government and Islamic countries [is] addressing issues that are of concern to us all, especially regarding the fight against radicalism and terrorism."[15]

"President Trump gave an effective speech focusing on one of the major challenges facing the Middle East and the world: terrorism and extremism," observed Zalmay Khalilzad, former U.S. ambassador to Afghanistan, Iraq, and the United Nations. "His call on Muslim leaders at the summit to do more to take on extremists and terrorists was important."[16]

A REFORMER RISING IN RIYADH

Saudi Arabia's reform efforts were not just talk.

By the summer of 2018, Riyadh's promises were turning into action.

Most Americans were not paying close attention, so I decided to write a column explaining what the new crown prince was doing and why it was significant. As it happened, Fox News published the article on MBS's birthday with this headline: "Mohammed bin Salman Is 33—Here Are 21 Impressive Reforms Already Underway."[17] Here are some excerpts, with a few updates included.

Amidst so much war and terrorism in the Middle East, there is actually remarkably good news coming out of Saudi Arabia.

A reformer is rising, pursuing the most dramatic economic, social, and foreign policy changes in the history of the kingdom.

His name is Mohammed bin Salman. Widely known simply as "MBS," he's young [born August 31, 1985]. Yet he has already amassed tremendous power. . . . In June 2017, he was named crown prince, and thus heir to the throne.

With the blessing of his father, King Salman, he's moving quickly to expand women's rights, diversify the country's oil-based economy, confront violent Islamism, and even advance peace between the Israelis and Palestinians.

"What happened in the region in the last thirty years is not the Middle East," MBS told the *Guardian* in October 2017. "After the Iranian revolution in 1979, people wanted to copy this model in different countries, [and] one of them [was] Saudi Arabia. We didn't know how to deal with it. And the problem spread all over the world. Now is the time to get rid of it. . . .

"We are simply reverting to what we [once] followed—a moderate Islam open to the world and all religions. Seventy percent of the Saudis are younger than thirty, [and] honestly, we won't waste [the next] thirty years of our [lives] combating extremist thoughts. We will destroy them now and immediately."[18]

Radical Islamists such as the late Hamza bin Laden, son of Osama bin Laden, accused MBS of being too moderate and working too closely with Washington, I noted.

At the other end of the spectrum, liberals were attacking MBS for not being moderate enough. Human rights advocates blasted him for repressing dissent, jailing dissidents, and resisting international accountability. When Canadian officials, for example, expressed concern in 2018 about the arrest of human rights activists in the kingdom, MBS responded by expelling Canadian diplomats and cutting off diplomatic relations with Ottawa. Many saw the move as a reckless overreaction by MBS, who was developing a reputation among some Middle East analysts for being "thin-skinned" and "heavy-handed."[19] Palace insiders said the crown prince was simply sending a message to the kingdom's friends that criticism was one thing, but demands from foreign governments were not welcome.

There was no question in my mind that Saudi Arabia had a long way to go in the area of human rights, but I argued that it was still worth considering the significant reforms that MBS had already advanced.

Since he had come to power, women's rights had begun to move in a positive direction. Women were no longer required to wear the long black cloak known as the abaya. The much-feared religious police had been reined in. In 2018, it became legal for women to drive in the kingdom, and within a year more than 70,000 licenses had been issued. Saudi women could now attend soccer matches and other sporting events. Women's sports teams were forming in the kingdom. And Saudi women could now join the military and intelligence services.

At the same time, MBS had launched his Vision 2030 campaign to dramatically diversify the private economy and wean the kingdom off what he calls its "dangerous addiction to oil." He and his father announced a $500 billion plan to build a futuristic new province called NEOM, along the Red Sea, that would link Saudi Arabia with Egypt and Jordan and create high-tech businesses and thousands of new jobs. Financial reforms were being made to attract international investors into Saudi companies and foreign companies operating—or wanting to operate—in the kingdom. MBS had also launched an anti-corruption campaign and recovered $100 billion from officials allegedly bilking the government.

The crown prince was also increasingly outspoken that the most serious threat to peace in the Mideast was Iran, not Israel, and he urged other world leaders to join forces to neutralize the Iranian threat. In an April 2018 interview with the *Atlantic*, MBS bluntly warned, "The supreme leader [Ayatollah Khamenei] is trying to conquer the world. . . . He is the Hitler of the Middle East. In the 1920s and 1930s, no one saw Hitler as a danger. Only a few people. Until it happened. We don't want to see what happened in Europe happen in the Middle East. We want to stop this through political moves, economic moves, intelligence moves. We want to avoid war."[20]

What's more, during a March 2018 visit to the United States, the crown prince held a rare meeting with Jewish and Catholic leaders, emphasizing "the common bond among all people, particularly people of faith, which stresses the importance of tolerance, coexistence, and working together for a better future for all of humanity."[21] Soon after, he stunned observers by declaring that Israel "has a right to live in their peaceful nation" and "the right to have their own land."[22] Further, the crown prince had taken an active, if behind-the-scenes, role in urging the Palestinian leadership to end their seven-plus-decade stalemate with Israel and forge a comprehensive peace treaty. Intelligence and security cooperation between Saudi and Israeli officials was also underway and increasing.

Meanwhile, MBS held unprecedented meetings in early 2018 with Christian leaders, including Archbishop of Canterbury Justin Welby and Pope Tawadros II of Egypt. He even visited a Coptic Church in Cairo, publicly declaring that Christians were welcome to visit Saudi Arabia and calling for interfaith tolerance and dialogue between Christians and Muslims.

Were far more reforms needed? Absolutely. Yet clearly something historic was underway in Saudi Arabia. In a region of radicals, a reformer was on the rise. Mohammed bin Salman and his team should be lauded for the progress they had made, I argued, even as the world encouraged them to make far more sweeping positive changes.

15

AN INVITATION TO
THE FORBIDDEN KINGDOM

---

*Our decision to go to Saudi Arabia
and the firestorm that followed*

On September 6, 2018, I received an email from the chief of staff for
Khalid bin Salman.

KBS was a son of the king, younger brother of the crown prince, and (at
the time) the Saudi ambassador to the United States. The following day,
I called the official at his office in Riyadh from my home in Jerusalem. I
wasn't sure the call would even go through, but I had to smile as I imagined
every intelligence agency in the world perking up their ears. After all, how
many calls could there be between Israel and Saudi Arabia?

The conversation could not have been more encouraging. Yousef
Al Otaiba's prediction was coming true. The Saudi royal family was actually inviting a delegation of Christians to the kingdom. Specifically, they
were proposing that our delegation to the UAE go on directly to Riyadh.

I immediately contacted every delegation member with the news and
asked them to confirm that they could add Saudi Arabia to their itinerary.
Unfortunately, Tony Perkins and Kay Arthur had other commitments after
the UAE portion of the trip, but everyone else said yes. I briefed the group
on the initial details and emphasized the need for confidentiality.

"Tell only your closest colleagues on a need-to-know basis," I said in my email. "Eventually the trip will be public knowledge, but we're not there yet. . . . This is a very sensitive trip at a very sensitive time. For now, we need much prayer."

I had no idea how true that caution would prove to be.

PREPARATIONS

A few weeks later, I flew from Israel to Washington, D.C.

On September 21, I spoke at the Values Voter Summit—hosted by Tony Perkins and the Family Research Council—briefing them on the tectonic changes underway in the Arab Muslim world and on the delegations I had led to Egypt and Jordan. I did not mention the upcoming trip to the UAE and Saudi Arabia.

The next day, Tony and I met with Vice President Mike Pence to get his counsel about our proposed trip. He was enormously helpful and arranged for us to meet with members of the National Security Council who could answer our many questions in more depth.

I met with U.S. Ambassador at Large for International Religious Freedom Sam Brownback, a friend since 1994, to get his take on the latest conditions in Saudi Arabia for all religious minorities but especially for Christians. I also headed over to the Washington Institute for Near East Policy, a bipartisan think tank, to get the input of two regional experts whose counsel I trusted: executive director Rob Satloff and Ambassador Dennis Ross, former senior Middle East policy advisor to presidents George H. W. Bush, Bill Clinton, and Barack Obama. Both had far more experience in the region than I did. Both had also met with MBS and thus could give me real insights into what to expect.

From there, I took the Delta Shuttle up to New York, where the U.N. General Assembly's fall session was about to begin. There, several members of our delegation and I participated in a small follow-up meeting with Egyptian president Abdel el-Sisi. I also met with Sheikh Abdullah bin Zayed Al Nahyan, who was the UAE foreign minister and younger brother of the crown prince of Abu Dhabi. The occasion was a reception the Emiratis were holding for about three hundred diplomats, CEOs, and other international guests at an art museum in Manhattan. Sheikh Abdullah told me how enthusiastic he was about our upcoming visit.

He and I discussed the details of the visit, and he asked me to pray for him and his country. I said I would be honored—before realizing he meant right then and there. In the middle of this lovely reception, with hundreds of guests milling about, he took my hands and bowed his head. I bowed my own and prayed for the sheikh, for the crown prince, for the people of the Emirates, and for the Lord Jesus to bless and guide our upcoming trip.

It was then that Sheikh Abdullah and Ambassador Al Otaiba introduced me to Adel al-Jubeir, the soft-spoken Saudi foreign minister, who was helping to plan our visit and who would accompany us to our meeting with the crown prince. Though I had often seen al-Jubeir on television, this was my first opportunity to meet him in person. Indeed, it was the first time I had met *any* Saudi official face-to-face, much less one this senior. The whole notion was still surreal to me, given my faith, citizenship, and Jewish roots.

As we conversed about the upcoming trip, now just over a month away, al-Jubeir took me aside from the crowd and informed me that we were the first group of Christian leaders ever invited to the palace in the three hundred years that the Al-Saud family had governed much of the Arabian Peninsula.

When our conversation was done, I shook al-Jubeir's hand, thanked him for his time, and told him I looked forward to seeing him in Riyadh. The magnitude of what we were heading into was only beginning to sink in.

The next day, I had a private, one-on-one meeting with Secretary of State Mike Pompeo in the State Department's suite at the Lotte New York Palace hotel. In addition to giving him an advance copy of my latest political thriller, *The Persian Gamble,* I asked the secretary for his thoughts on U.S.-Saudi relations, how he saw the tensions between the Saudis and Iran, and the progress of the Vision 2030 reforms. I also asked him to assess MBS's performance thus far and for advice on how we should interact with him. Pompeo was incredibly gracious with his time and candid with his insights.

We were not asking the U.S. government for permission to go to Saudi Arabia. Nor were we acting in any official capacity. However, given the unique nature of the trip, I knew I needed wise counsel. I remembered that whenever Billy Graham traveled to meet world leaders in sensitive countries, he made it a point to receive briefings from his friends in Washington, D.C., be they presidents, vice presidents, secretaries of state, members of Congress, or other experts. This seemed like a good model to follow.

THE FIRESTORM

In early October came the bombshell headlines regarding Jamal Khashoggi.[*]

The Saudi-born journalist, a columnist for the *Washington Post* and fierce critic of the royal family, with some 1.7 million Twitter followers, was missing and presumed dead. He was last seen entering the Saudi consulate in Turkey on October 2.

Stories began appearing in the Turkish media that Khashoggi had been murdered by Saudi operatives, and the allegations created a global firestorm of anger against MBS, who was accused of masterminding the murder.

At first, the Saudis denied it, but global interest in their reform efforts came to a screeching halt. CEOs and investors canceled plans to visit the kingdom, including the glitzy investment conference dubbed "Davos in the Desert."

The Turkish media was filled with macabre tales about the Saudis murdering Khashoggi and dismembering his body with a bone saw. Anonymous sources claimed to have all kinds of hard, factual evidence proving the most sinister of actions by the Saudis, but nothing concrete or compelling had been released.

The Trump administration, along with members of Congress, called for a full and transparent investigation by both countries. If Khashoggi was alive, then where was he? If not, what happened to him? The world was asking for answers. We needed to know.

In the end, it turned out the Turks were telling the truth about Khashoggi's murder. Turkish intelligence had bugged the Saudi consulate and their listening devices had never been detected. Now Erdoğan and his spy chiefs had gruesome evidence, audio recordings of the heated confrontation between Khashoggi and Saudi operatives that ended in his death.

By October 20, after weeks of wild rumors and unsourced allegations about his disappearance, the tragic truth had become known: Jamal Khashoggi was dead. The Saudi government said their intelligence officials

---

[*] Khashoggi is pronounced *ka-SHOW-gee*.

had only been directed to interrogate Khashoggi at the consulate and then bring him back to Saudi Arabia. Khashoggi was killed when he resisted, they said, but the team wrote a false report for their superiors saying they had allowed Khashoggi to leave the consulate. These false reports were fed to senior Saudi officials, Riyadh claimed, and formed the basis of their public statements. Once their agents were found to be lying, the Saudi government finally admitted responsibility.

As I kept my readers up to speed on the unfolding story, I reported that "eighteen Saudi intelligence officials have been arrested for participating in Khashoggi's death" and that "five senior Saudi officials have been fired in the affair."[1]

I then raised two critical questions.

First, did Crown Prince Mohammed bin Salman directly authorize the capture and killing of Khashoggi?

Second, how does all this affect the U.S.-Saudi alliance?

Saudi officials, speaking on condition of anonymity, told reporters that the crown prince had authorized Saudi intelligence to bring dissidents back to the kingdom, but there were no orders to kill Khashoggi or even specifically to kidnap him.

Nevertheless, many human rights activists, journalists, members of Congress, and Mideast experts were demanding that the Saudi government be punished. Some were calling for the cancellation of military sales. Others called for sweeping economic sanctions and targeted sanctions against individual Saudi officials, under the Global Magnitsky Act, which would have barred them from entering the United States.

Other experts, while acknowledging the need for the Trump administration to deal forthrightly with the situation and not soft-pedal it, also cautioned the White House not to overreact or take steps that might fundamentally undermine the U.S.-Saudi alliance. The U.S. and Saudi Arabia, they said, share vital national interests, from thwarting radical Islamism in the region to establishing peace between Israel and her Arab neighbors. Throwing the Saudis under the bus would be shortsighted and imprudent, they argued.

Further, it was not as if the Turks had clean hands, having arrested, jailed, and killed scores of dissidents, journalists, and other innocents during the regime of President Erdoğan. The Iranians, meanwhile, were the worst terrorist state on the planet, yet the very same Obama administration officials who were now demanding severe punishment for the Saudis were the ones who had removed sanctions against Iran—effectively handing tens of billions of dollars to the tyrants in Tehran.

WHO WAS JAMAL KHASHOGGI?

Most Americans had never heard of Jamal Khashoggi.

Now he was a household word.

But who was he really? And why might the Saudis have wanted him silenced?

As I searched for answers, I found allegations that Khashoggi was a wolf in sheep's clothing, a radical Islamist trying to portray himself as a voice of moderation and reason. Some reports indicated that Khashoggi was more than a mere critic of the Saudi government but someone long connected to the jihadist movement, increasingly close to the Turkish and Qatari regimes, using his role as a columnist to attack and weaken the Saudi government.

If such reports were true, they might provide a motive for the Saudis wanting to bring Khashoggi back to the kingdom for questioning. They were certainly no justification for an inexcusable and ghastly murder. But were they true?

Curiously, it was a widely respected *Washington Post* columnist—David Ignatius—who confirmed Khashoggi's long history with radical Islamists. In an opinion column under the headline "Jamal Khashoggi's Long Road to the Doors of the Saudi Consulate," Ignatius reported the following facts about Khashoggi:

- "He was friendly with Osama bin Laden in his militant youth."
- He "criticized Prince Salman, then governor of Riyadh."
- He was photographed in Afghanistan, "standing among the Arab fighters, cradling a rocket-propelled grenade launcher in his hands."
- He was "a passionate member of the Muslim Brotherhood," which he joined about the same time Osama bin Laden did, in the late 1970s.

- He "shared a passion [with bin Laden] for the mujahideen's war in Afghanistan, first against the Soviet Union and later for power in Kabul. He covered the war "as a journalist, but he was clearly sympathetic to the [jihadists'] cause."
- He was close friends with a woman named Maggie Mitchell Salem, the head of the Qatar Foundation International, an organization "partially funded by Qatar," home to the bitterly anti-Saudi Al Jazeera TV network.
- He told Lawrence Wright, author of *The Looming Tower*—a Pulitzer Prize–winning book detailing the birth, rise, and history of al Qaeda leading up to the 9/11 attacks—why he was drawn to the Muslim Brotherhood: "We were hoping to establish an Islamic state anywhere. We believed that the first one would lead to another, and that would have a domino effect which could reverse the history of mankind." Wright used the quote in his book.[2]

Ignatius went on in his column to state that "Khashoggi's friends say he had become wary of the extremism of bin Laden and other jihadists. He was moving toward his mature belief that democracy and freedom were the Arabs' best hope of purging the corruption and misrule he despised."

Not everyone, however, believed Khashoggi had changed. Other journalists confirmed Khashoggi's close and continuing ties to the Muslim Brotherhood, and his critics pointed to the fact that he had strongly defended the Muslim Brotherhood's rise to power in Egypt in 2012, was critical of the Egyptian military's decision to remove the Brotherhood from power in 2013, and was adamantly opposed to congressional efforts to declare the Muslim Brotherhood a foreign terrorist organization.[3]

Two writers for the *New York Times* reported that Khashoggi's "attraction to political Islam helped him forge a personal bond with President Recep Tayyip Erdoğan of Turkey." And though he "stopped attending meetings of the [Muslim] Brotherhood, he remained conversant in its conservative, Islamist, and often anti-Western rhetoric, which he could deploy or hide depending on whom he was seeking to befriend." He also "hid his personal leanings in favor of both electoral democracy and Muslim Brotherhood–style political Islam."[4]

In one of his last columns for the *Washington Post*, headlined, "The U.S. Is Wrong about the Muslim Brotherhood—and the Arab World Is Suffering for It," Khashoggi voiced strong support for the Brotherhood and blasted Saudi and UAE leaders for their "intolerant hatred for any form of political Islam."[5]

Was he doing this solely on his own, some asked, or was Khashoggi being assisted—possibly even paid—by enemies of Saudi Arabia?

"In the conspiracy-driven climate of Middle East politics, Khashoggi came under mounting suspicion because of his writing as well as associations he cultivated over many years with perceived enemies of Riyadh," the *Washington Post* later reported. "Among Khashoggi's friends in the United States were individuals with real or imagined affiliations with the Islamist group the Muslim Brotherhood, and an Islamic advocacy organization, the Council on American-Islamic Relations, regarded warily for its support of the public uprisings of the Arab Spring. Khashoggi cultivated ties with senior officials in the Turkish government, also viewed with deep distrust by the rulers in Saudi Arabia. . . .

"Perhaps most problematic for Khashoggi were his connections to an organization funded by Saudi Arabia's regional nemesis, Qatar," the *Post* report continued. "Text messages between Khashoggi and an executive at Qatar Foundation International show that . . . Maggie Mitchell Salem at times shaped the columns he submitted to the *Washington Post*, proposing topics, drafting material, and prodding him to take a harder line against the Saudi government."[6]

TO GO OR NOT TO GO?

Amid all the turmoil in the news, I had a decision to make: Should we proceed with our trip to Saudi Arabia or cancel?

Few people knew of our plans, which were still a closely guarded secret. From those who did know, I received conflicting advice. Meanwhile, my contacts in Riyadh and at the Saudi embassy in Washington had gone into blackout mode, no longer responding to any of my calls, emails, or text messages.

As the date of our departure to the UAE approached, all I knew for certain was that I felt sympathy for Khashoggi's family and friends for all the grief they were going through. I was sickened by this disgusting, unconscionable crime. Maybe it had been an arrest gone wrong. Maybe it was a planned execution. Either way, it was reprehensible.

"Please pray for the Khashoggi family, for comfort at this very hard time," I wrote on October 21. "Please pray for more facts to be revealed in a timely way and a complete picture to emerge. Please pray for U.S. leaders to have the wisdom to know how best to handle the situation. Please pray for the leaders of Saudi Arabia to know how best to deal with this tragic injustice and make sure it never happens again. Please pray, too, for the people of Saudi Arabia who have been very much in favor of the economic and social reforms that MBS has been implementing, and surely want to see these reforms continue and expand, not to see the kingdom suddenly isolated and potentially destabilized."[7]

In the end, after much prayer and discussion, our delegation decided to go to Riyadh as planned—that is, if we were still invited. We weighed the fact that we were the first Christian leaders invited to meet with the senior leadership of the Saudi royal family in three hundred years. We had prayed for months for an open door, and now here it was. If we canceled the trip, were we slamming the door on the opportunity for other Christians to visit Saudi Arabia in the future? Would we not also be acting as judge and jury, condemning the crown prince as guilty when we had not seen any direct evidence proving he had ordered the murder? The story was still so new and details still so scarce.

We also weighed our biblical mandate toward the king, the crown prince, the rest of the royal family, and the people of the Kingdom of Saudi Arabia. In the New Testament, Jesus met with and healed Roman military officials who were occupying the nation of Israel. The apostle Paul met with controversial, even brutal, Roman leaders—including Nero—to be a faithful witness and ambassador of Christ. Indeed, writing in the power of the Holy Spirit, through the direct revelation of God, Paul commanded followers of Jesus to pray for all those in high positions of government.

> First of all, then, I urge that requests, prayers, intercession, and thanksgiving be made in behalf of all people, for kings and all who are in authority, so that we may lead a tranquil and quiet life in all

godliness and dignity. This is good and acceptable in the sight of
God our Savior.

1 TIMOTHY 2:1-3

One thing was certain: We were unified in our belief that if the door
remained open to us, this was going to be a visit unlike the others.

A DEATH IN THE FAMILY

We had made our decision, but the question still remained.

Was our invitation from the Saudis still valid?

We had no idea. The royal court was not responding to any of my efforts
to contact them.

On Monday, October 22, Lynn and I drove to Ben Gurion International
Airport near Tel Aviv to welcome home our son Jacob, who had spent the
past few weeks visiting friends in the U.S. We had no sooner parked the
car when Lynn received devastating news. Her father had just passed away
at a nursing home in New Jersey. He had been ill for some time, so his
passing was not a complete surprise, and because he was a Christian, we
had the assurance that he was now in heaven, released from his suffering
on earth. Nonetheless, we were heartbroken.

The next day, Lynn and Noah boarded the day's first flight to Newark.
Jacob and I followed on United's evening flight. Jonah was able to get a
pass to leave his IDF base, and he took yet another flight back to the States.
Meanwhile, our eldest son, Caleb, and his wife, Rachel, flew in from their
home near Los Angeles. Landing in Newark in stages on Wednesday, we
spent the day with family and friends, sharing memories of Lynn's father.
At the memorial service on Thursday afternoon, Lynn's brother, a pastor
in Virginia, preached a beautiful eulogy. Then, with Lynn's blessing, Jacob
and I caught a ride to JFK and boarded a late-night flight to Abu Dhabi.

It was Jacob's third transatlantic flight in four days, and my second. As
we settled into our seats and prayed for the rest of our team, who were taking off from airports all across the U.S., we still had no idea what lay ahead.

16

MEETING MBS

*Two hours on the record with the most controversial
leader in the Arab world*

Our visit to the UAE was well underway, but we still had not heard a word from the Saudis.

On Sunday evening, October 28, I finally told the team that we had to be realistic and pull the plug. We were not going to Saudi Arabia, but we should be praying for the kingdom more than ever. I called my executive assistant back in the States and asked her to cancel our flights to Riyadh. That done, I collapsed into bed around midnight, exhausted but grateful for all we were seeing in Abu Dhabi.

Around three in the morning, however, my American mobile phone rang.

That cannot be good news, I thought as I grasped in the darkness to find the light switch. I didn't recognize the number, but I knew the area code: 202.

That's Washington.

A jolt of adrenaline rocketed through my system and I was instantly wide-awake.

THE CALL

"Hello, Mr. Rosenberg?" said a man with an Arab accent.

"Yes, this is Joel," I replied, unsuccessfully trying to place the voice.

"Yes, hello, I'm calling from the office of the ambassador and wondered if you had a moment to chat."

"Ambassador? What ambassador?"

"His Excellency Khalid bin Salman. He wanted me to go over the final details of your upcoming visit."

"Visit?" I asked. "What visit?"

"Your visit to Riyadh, of course."

"I'm sorry; I'm not following—there is no visit to Riyadh."

"What do you mean?"

"What do *I* mean?" I replied. "With respect, we have not heard from your office in nearly a month. We understand why, of course, but nevertheless—we have no plans to come to Riyadh and we have canceled our tickets."

"Oh no," came the reply. "This will not do. Everything is set. The crown prince is looking forward to meeting you. You simply must come."

For a moment, I was not sure what to say. But the young staffer was nearly pleading with me. Then he asked if I could at least come to the embassy so that we could discuss this in person.

"I'm sorry; that's impossible—I'm not in Washington."

"Where are you?"

"Abu Dhabi."

"Oh, my, then it is very late there."

"It is—listen, we are willing to come. Some of us, anyway. In a few hours, we will all have breakfast together. I can discuss this with everyone and then get back to you."

THE PLAN

At 4:37 a.m., my new contact sent the following email:

> Joel,
>   Thank you for connecting us.
>
> Meetings have been scheduled with the following:

    HRH Crown Prince, Deputy Prime Minister, and Minister
of Defense
      H.E. Minister of Foreign Affairs
      H.E. Minister of Islamic Affairs, Dawah, and Guidance
      H.E. Minister of Education
      H.E. Secretary-General of the Muslim World League
      ETIDAL (Global Center for Combating Extremist Ideology)
      Ideological Warfare Center

I was also politely informed that "for this trip, we kindly request that it not be covered by the media."

At breakfast, I broke the news to the group. They were as stunned as I was, but as I walked them through the details, every single one was willing to come to Riyadh with me (aside from those who had prior commitments back in the States). It was a difficult, sobering moment. We spent time in prayer together, then informed the Saudis we were coming and rebooked our tickets.

THE MOTORCADE

Wednesday was our first day in Riyadh.

The meetings went well. We were learning a great deal, and each senior official could not have been more hospitable. Still, I woke up on Thursday morning feeling anxious. I wasn't really worried about our physical safety or the prospect of meeting the most controversial leader in the Arab world, but there was a heightened spiritual battle raging over the kingdom and its future, and I could feel it.

At 11:30 a.m., a long line of glistening black Mercedes luxury sedans and SUVs pulled up in front of the Four Seasons, each with the royal symbol of the kingdom—a single palm tree in the center and two crossed swords at the base—emblazoned on its doors. Police cars and motorcycles, with lights flashing, marked the beginning and the end of the motorcade.

The chief protocol officer directed Jacob and me to the back seat of the lead Mercedes. Everyone else was ushered to their assigned vehicles. We buckled up, literally and figuratively, and were off. The moment we cleared the hotel grounds, the driver hit the accelerator. Soon we were racing down city streets and onto major superhighways at breakneck speeds, swerving in and out of traffic as the police officers in the lead cars used loudspeakers to order other drivers to get out of the way. The experience was singularly different from any other country we had visited. The cars were newer and faster, the aides more hurried and intense, and the palace far grander than in any other Arab country we had been to. And the stakes were so much higher.

Still, as we drove up the palm-lined driveway to the Irqah Palace, a sense of peace finally settled over me. Nothing visible had changed. I had no new information. The questions I was about to ask were still going to be uncomfortable. All I can say is, whatever was about to happen, I had a sense of calm assurance that, at that moment, we were where God was asking us to be.

THE MEETING

We were led to a small, intimate wood-paneled meeting room with cream-colored carpeting.

Set high on the wall at the far end of the room was a Saudi royal emblem that appeared to be made of gold, above a large, golden abstract work of art. Up against this wall were two large, modern, beige upholstered chairs, flanked by wooden end tables, each of which held a lamp and a decorative ceramic plate. Behind the chair on the left—that of the crown prince—stood the distinctive green Saudi flag on a brass pole.

Directly to its left was a similar beige chair against the left side wall. That is where the protocol officer led me. The rest of our delegation were directed to their assigned seats on several couches along the side walls. Two sets of wooden coffee tables were positioned in front of the couches, with vases of yellow flowers, gold-plated tissue boxes, and—very soon—steaming cups of Arabic coffee and sweet mint tea.

The first official to meet with us was foreign minister Adel al-Jubeir. He entered the room wearing a beige robe and a red- and white-checkered kaffiyeh wrapped by a double black cord. After introductions, we asked him to respond to charges that the Saudi war in Yemen had created a humanitarian disaster and horrible human rights abuses. For the next twenty minutes, in his soft-spoken manner, he made the case that the

Iranians and their terrorist proxies—the Houthi rebels—were responsible for the war and the disaster that had ensued. He said that efforts by Riyadh to bring about a diplomatic resolution to the crisis had been repeatedly rejected by the Houthis. He also noted that the Houthis had fired almost two hundred ballistic missiles at Saudi cities—including Riyadh—over the past three years. The Saudis had intercepted some of the missiles, but the strikes had killed at least 112 Saudi civilians and wounded hundreds of others.[1] America, he said, should not allow an Iranian-backed terror force to attack one of its allies with impunity.

Without notice, the doors swung open and Crown Prince Mohammed bin Salman entered the room with a gust of energy and a cadre of palace photographers snapping away. We all stood.

Beaming, his dark-brown eyes filled with what struck me as eager determination, MBS greeted each member of our delegation in idiomatic American English, beginning with my son Jacob, who had been seated by the door. He shook each person's hand, including that of former congress-woman Michele Bachmann, the only woman in our group.

A bear of a man, large of frame and over six feet tall, MBS sported a full black beard and mustache. He was wearing a gold-and-beige *bisht*—a traditional outer cloak worn by Arab men, particularly by royals, on special occasions—over a crisp, clean white *thawb* and sandals. Like the foreign minister, he wore a red- and white-checkered kaffiyeh wrapped by a double black cord.

Right behind MBS, and also greeting each one of us with a handshake, were Prince Khalid bin Salman, then the Saudi ambassador to the U.S.; and Mohammad Al-Issa, secretary-general of the Muslim World League, the world's largest Islamic religious organization. Each introduced himself in English and asked our names.

The crown prince sat directly to my left. Prince Khalid sat directly across the room from me. Sheikh Al-Issa took his place on one of the couches on the right side of the room, next to the foreign minister.

Shifting forward to the edge of his seat, MBS welcomed us to the king-dom. He had no prepared remarks. He was there, he said, to listen and to answer whatever questions we had. He would speak without a translator, he said, though he noted that he might need to turn to his brother for help with a word or phrase from time to time, and he asked us to be patient with his English.

He told us he was in no hurry, that our conversation could go as long as we wanted. In the end, the meeting lasted for more than two hours.

"I want you to report what you see," he told us. "You need to describe Saudi Arabia as it is, not as we want it to be."

The first ninety minutes were on the record. The last thirty minutes, when we talked specifically about Israel and the peace process, he asked to be kept private. Though we were not permitted to record the conversation—and had to leave our mobile phones in the cars—we had designated two of our group as notetakers on our team. One was Larry Ross, longtime spokesman for Billy Graham. The other was my son Jacob. The rest of us took notes, as well, and we later combined and cross-checked everything to compile a detailed "transcript."

While we had been in Abu Dhabi, each member of the delegation had prepared a question for MBS, all of which were written down, discussed, and approved in advance by group consensus. Because of the highly sensitive nature of our meeting with MBS, we wanted to be as precise as possible in the wording and nature of our questions.

The group also encouraged me, as the head of the delegation, to ask unscripted follow-up questions when necessary, which I did several times.

THE ELEPHANT IN THE ROOM

After thanking the crown prince for inviting us to meet with him and giving him an overview of the topics we hoped to cover, I asked the first few questions, all of which dealt with the most current and controversial event.

"Your Royal Highness, I must begin with the question to which everyone in the world wants an answer. How did the murder of Jamal Khashoggi happen, who was responsible, and what is going to be done about it?"

"You have come a long way; I want to be as accessible as I can to answer all of your questions," the crown prince replied. "A terrible mistake happened. We are holding accountable those responsible. We are waiting for and want all the information from Turkey. Then they [who have been arrested] will be taken to court soon, probably in a few weeks, for trial. I can promise that the people responsible will be held accountable, and any problem we have in the system will be addressed."

He told us that eighteen Saudis had been arrested in connection with Khashoggi's death. Five more had been fired from government service.

"I want to make sure that the investigation will have credibility. We are trying to resolve this as soon as possible. We want a thorough investigation. Once we get a report of the facts, there are three options. First, we believe the report and take the perpetrators to court. Second, we don't believe it and demand the prosecutors get us more evidence. Third, if the Turks don't give us all their information, we have to move to court with knowledge that the world knows we have done all we could, and we will continue working with our allies, including the U.S."

Then he added, "But what about other countries when they do what they do and make mistakes? Do they have consequences? Are they holding people accountable and taking them to court?"

We mentioned that a number of theories were floating around about how the murder had occurred, and we pressed the crown prince to address the fact that many people—including many in the United States and in Congress—believed he was personally responsible for the crime.

"Look, sure, I may bear some guilt," he replied. "But not because I authorized the heinous act, because I did not, but because I may have caused some of our people to love our kingdom too much and delegated authority in a way that made it too easy for them to think they would be pleasing us by taking matters into their own hands."

He insisted, "We will prosecute whoever did this crime. Those responsible need to pay for their mistakes, and we have to fix it. But we also have to keep the rest of our people moving in the right direction to stay focused on our reforms."

How was that possible? I asked. How was he going to navigate forward? I noted that a global media firestorm had erupted, business leaders were dropping out of the Davos in the Desert event, and he and his government were facing withering criticism from all directions for what he had publicly admitted was a "heinous crime that cannot be justified."[2]

"It's a completely unacceptable mistake," MBS replied, "and it comes at a time that threatens all the reforms we are trying to get done—it's a disaster. But this is life. Surprises come. Some of them bad surprises. This came at a very bad time, and my enemies are, of course, exploiting it to their advantage. I get it."

Reflecting for a moment, he added, "In their shoes, I would probably do the same."

Then he pivoted, returning to the question of double standards.

"But how about Iran? How about Russia? Are they being held accountable for their actions?" he argued, referring to the scores of journalists, dissidents, and others arrested and even murdered by the regimes in Tehran and Moscow. "And America has made mistakes. When we saw pictures of American soldiers doing terrible things to Iraqis [at Abu Ghraib], does this mean America is bad? Does this mean we won't work with America any longer? No, of course not."

I was sickened by the grotesque, revolting murder of Jamal Khashoggi and grieving for his family. Everyone in our delegation was. The more we learned from Western media about the background, history, and ideology of the Saudi journalist-turned-dissident, the more we could imagine why some Saudi officials saw Khashoggi as an ally-turned-enemy. Nevertheless, there was no justification for murdering him. None. It was an indefensible and unconscionable act.

Now here we were, sitting with the Saudi crown prince. He was calling Khashoggi's death a "crime," a "heinous act," a "terrible mistake," and a "completely unacceptable mistake." He was conceding to us something he had not said publicly anywhere else: that he "may bear some guilt" in the affair. He was also vowing to prosecute those involved and promising to fix Saudi systems to prevent anything like this from happening again.

Was he telling the truth? Was he saying enough? What else should we ask him? We felt a great weight of responsibility. Still, we weren't there to interrogate or investigate him. And we had come to discuss other vital matters that few Christians—and no private citizens—ever got to ask him.

So I made the decision to change the topic.

ON IRAN AND HIS OTHER ENEMIES

The Saudi view of the Iranian regime was one of our top concerns.

We pointed out that the crown prince had denounced Iran's supreme leader, Ayatollah Ali Khamenei, as "the new Hitler." He confirmed that he had said it and meant it.

We asked MBS if he viewed Khamenei as "a crazy person" or simply "a hard-liner."

"He is a little bit of both," MBS replied.

He spoke at some length about the history of Iranian aggression in the region, the Iranian Revolution of 1979, and the horrors inflicted by Ayatollah Ruhollah Khomeini, and compared these to the immense damage caused in the region several decades earlier by Egyptian president Gamal Abdel Nasser.

MBS added that the Iranian regime wanted to take over the Saudi Kingdom and destroy Yemen.

"We have spent $13 billion to save people in Yemen. It is a high cost and low return for Saudis."

On the Iranian threat in Yemen, he said, "We started working with the Obama administration. They worked with us for a few weeks, then got cold feet. They started leaking rumors that the Saudis don't know what we are doing."

He emphasized how serious a threat Iran poses to the kingdom and to the rest of the Gulf Cooperation Council countries and that Riyadh could not simply ignore the threat coming from Yemen when hundreds of Iranian missiles have been fired at Saudi Arabia from there.

"Have you noticed that Iran is the only country *not* attacked by al Qaeda or ISIS?" he asked. "Why? Because they are aiding both."

Next, the crown prince excoriated the Iran nuclear deal negotiated by the Obama administration, which he called "lousy" for many reasons but especially because of the "sunset clause" that would allow the restrictions on Tehran's nuclear program to soon expire.

"This is a tough neighborhood," he said. "We have a lot of enemies— Iran, the Muslim Brotherhood, Hezbollah, Hamas, al Qaeda, Daesh [ISIS], and others. The Iranians are extremists. The Muslim Brotherhood are extremists. There are many extremists, but we will not let them win.

"The extremists are trying to destroy us daily," he continued. "They want to regain the dignity of the Muslim community and restore its power and glory. But they want to do it by force, by terrorism. That is not true

Islam. The Iranians are trying to export their revolution. We will not accept this. We need to live as peaceful nations, within our nations."

Then he talked about how grateful he was for the long-term friendship and alliance between the Saudis and the United States.

"We are grateful for America," MBS said. "They helped us build our country. We will stand with America against the enemies of this region. What we must do is work with America to build an alliance in this region of strong allies—an economic alliance, a security alliance—to make everyone, all the people, more prosperous and to make sure we are all safe against our enemies."

ON COUNTERING VIOLENT EXTREMISM

We pressed him further on how the Saudis are countering violent extremism.

We told him we had toured—and were impressed by—the high-tech ETIDAL (Global Center for Combating Extremist Ideology), where the kingdom tracks and counters extremist messaging on TV, radio, print, and social media in real time, just as the UAE has been doing for several years. But we also took note of the fact that the Saudis had been funding a radical Wahhabi vision of Islam for many years.

"The duty of Islam is the spread of the word all over the world," he replied. "Now the message has been completed. You can find the Qur'an all over the world. You can find Muslims everywhere. The problems come from people who don't have hope for their lives that enable them to push in a positive direction, or don't have a good education.

"In 2015, according to our polling, 30 percent of Saudis were extremists, 10 percent were open-minded, and 60 percent were in between," he told us. "We have been working very hard through our reforms to change attitudes and perceptions and morals—and we see our efforts working. Now, in 2018, we find that only 5 percent of Saudis are extremists, between 30 and 40 percent are open-minded, and the rest are in between. So we're making progress, but we have a lot of work to do. We have to work together with other countries to make sure we are all putting pressure on terror and extremist groups.

"We are fighting extremists in the ideological war, and we are fighting terrorists in a physical war. At every stage, we encounter obstacles, but we have to keep pushing forward. Over the last two years, on three different occasions, my security guards have been killed by terrorists trying to get to me. The head of Egyptian intelligence just came to visit me. He told me they caught a terrorist cell in the northern Sinai that had Saudis in it. The cell was planning to assassinate me.

"We must fight the extremists and defeat them, or they will stop us and the reforms we are making to make life better for the people of Saudi Arabia. So that's what we're doing, and it's working. The terrorists and extremists are on the run. This is not easy. There are many risks. But don't worry—we're not doing it for you. We're doing it for us."

ON EXTREMIST RHETORIC IN SAUDI MOSQUES AND TEXTBOOKS

It was one thing to crack down on dangerous social media rhetoric. But what was the crown prince doing about what was taught in mosques and state school systems?

"I am having problems with the mosques in Saudi Arabia going on autopilot," he said. "The country was hijacked years ago by a lot of extremist groups, and we are working hard to change that. We have a new minister of Islamic affairs. The man is fearless. He has already fired a thousand imams."

Sheikh Al-Issa gently corrected the crown prince, saying that the number of imams the crown prince had fired was more than 3,500.

"Oh, wow, really!" MBS exclaimed. "Okay, there you go—more than 3,500!"

Turning to the question about the state schools, he said, "About the textbooks: It is absolutely indefensible—really, totally crazy. They showed me some of the stuff that was written in there, and I couldn't believe it. So we're changing the whole system. Did you meet with the minister of education?"

"Yes," we replied.

"Good. Because he is changing all the textbooks and retraining the teachers. Our schools need to be open to new ideas. We need to educate people as to other points of view, allowing outside sources to inform. We want to turn to a competency-based education rather than a content-based one. We are wanting to meet an international benchmark for performance.

We are giving more autonomy to the universities. Our challenge is that the system is slow and centralized. We need to put an emphasis on good education with good values—but we also need to go about change in the right way because the extremist groups are watching, and they will say we are being influenced by the West."

ON THE HISTORIC MEETING WITH EVANGELICAL LEADERS

"Your Royal Highness, we notice that you are reaching out to Christians," I said. "In March, you traveled to Cairo for several days and met personally with Coptic Orthodox Pope Tawadros at St. Mark's Cathedral, in front of a beautiful painting of our Lord Jesus Christ," I noted. "We don't recall any Saudi leader ever doing that before."

"Welcome to the new Saudi Arabia," he said.

"Then we noticed that you traveled to London and met with the Archbishop of Canterbury. And when you visited the U.S., we noticed that you met with Jewish leaders. Again, we cannot recall any modern Saudi leader having such meetings in the past."

MBS smiled and said, "I believe it is important for Muslims to reach out to people of other faiths."

"We agree," I said, "and we want to thank you for inviting us to come to visit you here—it is historic for evangelical Christians to meet with the crown prince of the Kingdom of Saudi Arabia. And I understand from speaking with Foreign Minister al-Jubeir when we met in New York a few weeks ago that this is the first time the kingdom has invited a delegation of Christian leaders. Thank you for welcoming us to your home for this important conversation."

"Thank you for coming," MBS replied. "It is good for the Kingdom of Saudi Arabia and for relations between our two nations. We want to engage with people from many countries and many religions. You have to engage if you want to spread what you believe is right. We believe our religion is positive preparation. The prophet Muhammad, peace be upon him, had good relations with Christians and Jews. He had a Christian wife and a Jewish wife."

Then he quipped, "I can't do this."

Everyone laughed. The mood was gradually becoming more relaxed, even warm, as the conversation continued.

"And Christians were part of the establishment of the third Saudi kingdom," he added.

"Still, I'm guessing that the term *evangelical Christian* is not one that is used much here in the kingdom. Is that a fair assessment?" I asked.

Now he laughed. "Yes, I guess that's fair."

"Well, Your Royal Highness, since you have invited us to come all this way, I wanted you to know that we have with us an ordained pastor from Albuquerque, New Mexico, in our group, and I was wondering—would it be all right for him to take a few minutes to define the term so that you and your colleagues might have a better understanding of who we are and what we believe?"

"Of course, yes, that would be wonderful," the crown prince replied.

I introduced Skip Heitzig again and turned the floor over to him. Skip thanked the crown prince for the opportunity to come to the kingdom and, in this case, to explain evangelicalism. He also mentioned that he had a son of his own who was just slightly younger than MBS.

None of us took precise notes on what Skip said next, in part because as evangelicals ourselves we knew essentially what he would say, but also because it was so striking to hear him addressing it to a Muslim leader of such prominence. When I was writing this chapter, I asked Skip to email me his recollection of exactly what he had said.

"Your Royal Highness, it is our delight to be here, to celebrate what we have in common, and to share with you what we believe," he began. "The term *evangelical* refers to 'the evangel,' which comes from the Greek word meaning 'good news,' or what we call 'the gospel.' As evangelical Christians, we believe in God's revelation as given in the Scriptures, the Bible. We believe the Bible is God's Word. It reveals that sin has separated us from God. But the good news is that God sent his only Son, Jesus, into the world to redeem it, to die on the cross to pay for our sins and then rise from the dead. And whoever places his trust in Jesus will be forgiven of his sins and live with him forever. We believe that doing this brings us into a personal relationship with God and transforms us—and that we can then be a redeeming and transforming presence in our culture and communities.

"This emphasis on having a *personal* relationship with God through faith in Jesus Christ—a deep commitment to careful study of, and obedience to, the Bible, along with a commitment to sharing this good news of God's love, mercy, and forgiveness with others—is what makes evangelical Christianity distinct."

The crown prince thanked Skip and said that he had recently finished reading a book about evangelical Christians and was very interested in who we are and what we believe. Unfortunately, we did not think to ask him the name of the book—perhaps because MBS then made two comments that intrigued us a great deal:

- "Each nation should allow its people to believe in what they want to believe."
- "We believe in Jesus as the Savior of the whole world—he is in our book as he is in yours. When he comes back, Jesus will judge the entire earth and lead us in the right direction."

ON BUILDING CHURCHES IN SAUDI ARABIA

One of the main reasons we went to Riyadh was to raise our concern that not a single Christian church facility had ever been allowed to be built, or allowed to operate freely, in the modern Saudi kingdom.

This, we noted, stood in sharp contrast to the United Arab Emirates, where there are more than seven hundred Christian church congregations operating freely. We asked the crown prince to reconsider this policy and to allow the first church building to be built—perhaps in the Diplomatic Quarter, at first, where there would be plenty of security.

"Look, we're moving in that direction, but it's not at the top of my list," he said.

Wouldn't it send a very positive signal to the rest of the world that you are willing to allow Christians here to begin meeting in churches?

"I'm not going to do that now, and you should not want me to do that now, and I'll tell you why," he said.

He certainly was not trying to tell us what we wanted to hear.

Why not? we asked.

"We have a *hadith*[*] that says there should not be two religions together in the 'Arabian island,' just Islam," MBS explained. "Now, there is a question as to what defines the 'Arabian island.' Does that mean just Mecca and Medina? Does it mean all of the Arabian Peninsula? Something in between? So we have scholars looking at that. And maybe there is a scenario where it is doable [to build churches]. We'll see.

"But again, it's not on the top of my list," he quickly added, "because building a church in Saudi Arabia right now is exactly what al Qaeda and the extremists would love. If that would happen, bombs would fall [on those churches] and there would be terrorist activity. I am sorry, but I have to keep in mind the safety of my people. And this would not make life better for my people."

We were disappointed, but the crown prince went further to explain his approach to advancing change.

"Look, when I announce a reform, like letting women drive, all the extremists go crazy. They say everything is going to be a disaster, that women would be raped, the country is going to blow up. But when women drove, there were no terrorist attacks. People liked it. And everything was fine.

"The same with women attending soccer matches in stadiums. Nothing bad happened. In fact, good things happened. Attendance at soccer matches doubled. So the sports teams were happy. They were making more money. The restaurants near the stadiums were happy. They were making more money.

"My point is, as each obstacle is overcome and people see that their lives get better when we do the reforms, it gets easier to do the next reform. People have more confidence. But I'm not sure that would be the case if we built a church at this time."

---

[*] A *hadith* is part of "a narrative record of the sayings or customs of Muhammad" (Merriam-Webster).

17

READING MBS

*Processing and explaining our visit
to the new Saudi Arabia*

We had covered many controversial topics—yet we still wanted to understand the crown prince's crown jewel: his Vision 2030 plan and dreams for a dramatically new future for Saudi Arabia.

Observing that the kingdom of 34 million has such a young population, we asked, "When you see a twenty-year-old Saudi, what is your vision of his or her future?"

"Our dream is to be a normal country, helping our people lead normal lives, with security, health care, and so forth," MBS replied. "We want to create jobs, reduce our dependency on oil, and empower our citizens. People say, 'Vision 2030 is so ambitious.' But I say, 'If you want to get to the mountaintop—aim for the moon.'

"More than 70 percent of our population is under the age of thirty," he said. "That means 70 percent of our country is younger than I am. And over 50 percent are under the age of twenty. I want to provide them with a good future, but we need to change the focus, change the direction of the country.

"What is a young person's value in this country? What does he want to do? I want to ensure he has all the elements he needs for success. I want to make sure that young person is not hanging around and just having a job, but that he is dreaming dreams.

"Google some pictures of Saudi Arabia before 1979. Women didn't wear abayas. We had theaters. We respected other faiths. We had a moderate country. . . .

"We see huge potential in Saudi Arabia, but we need to make changes. I need people to think big. I want dreamers in Saudi Arabia. How can I convince people to come invest here if Saudis themselves go vacationing in Europe? It used to be that people couldn't go to a movie in Saudi Arabia. Couldn't go to a concert. Couldn't do many things. For that, they had to go to Europe or Dubai. But we're changing all that. We want people to enjoy their life here. And we want our people to spend their money here.

"We need to think big. And I believe in numbers. So I look at numbers. Saudi Arabia uses only 10 percent of its capacity. We're not using all of our oil reserves. We can do more. We're only using 2 percent of our minerals. We have opportunities in transportation—land, sea, and air. There are so many international flights that fly *over* Saudi Arabia, but very few flights land here. We need them to land here. We need to become a transportation hub. A destination.

"And tourism," he added. "Seven years ago, Saudi Arabia had 8 million tourists. This year, we had 12 million tourists. That's projected to rise to 30 million tourists in ten years.

"We spend a lot on military equipment. But we need to start building some of those weapons and systems here in the kingdom.

"We need to sell off part of Aramco [the state oil company] and turn those funds into a sovereign wealth fund. We expect to have $2 trillion dollars in the fund by 2030.

"We need to be competitive economically. We also have to be globally competitive in all social standards. How do you get people to invest when there are Saudis leaving because there is nothing for them to spend their money on? My view is 'Happy Saudis, happy country. Happy Middle East, happy world.' Now the extremists won't agree on any of this, and they'll use their movement to spread their hate. But we'll stop them."

When MBS had finished his discourse and was ready for another question, I said, "Your Royal Highness, you are a millennial, and thus you're thinking about the future of your country in a very different way than the older generation. I have a millennial with me—my son Jacob. Would it be all right if he asked a question?"

"Of course," the crown prince said, turning his attention to the back of the room, where my son was seated. "What is your question, Jacob?"

Jacob's question was completely different from all the others, and the crown prince's response gave us a unique insight into his interest in technology and the future.

Noting that the kingdom had recently granted citizenship to a robot, Jacob asked MBS about his views regarding artificial intelligence (AI) and whether the future monarch saw AI as a potential threat.

MBS lit up at the question. He spoke of the exponential growth of technology. He conceded that there could be a point at which AI would be out of human control, but it was impossible to know what will happen exactly. He noted that some fear AI will take over and perhaps humanity will become extinct. Others say we will merge with AI and become cyborgs. He said that he is excited about the potential of AI and the notion that the younger generations will continue to witness such rapid and exponential technological change, adding that he wants Saudi Arabia to be part of it. And though he agreed that AI presents both "military and ideological" challenges, MBS emphasized that "we as young people need to make sure we're going on a good path."

Afterward, Prince Khalid told Jacob that if MBS could have spared the time, he would have wanted to talk about AI and the future for hours.

ISRAEL, THE SAUDIS, AND THE ROAD TO PEACE

The crown prince was astonishingly candid with us on his views regarding Israel.

However, he specifically asked that his comments on this subject—which occupied the last thirty minutes of our two-hour meeting—not be published or shared publicly. We gave him our word and have honored his request.

That said, what we told the crown prince regarding our views of the Arab-Israeli conflict is public and on the record, and I will share it with you here.

Speaking on behalf of our delegation, I asked MBS and his inner circle to take three key points into consideration as they developed the kingdom's approach to peacemaking.

First, I told him that the vast majority of the 60 million evangelical Christians in the United States love and strongly support the State of Israel and the Jewish people. I wanted him to know how deeply we care about Israel and why this was a deeply held theological—not political—conviction of ours that would never change.

Second, I explained that, as followers of Jesus Christ, we are compelled to obey Jesus' command to "love your neighbor as yourself."[1] We consider the Palestinian people our neighbors, and thus we are committed to loving them. We grieve for the suffering they have endured. We want a better life for them. Some people think that Christians who love Israel don't care about the plight of the Palestinians. This, sadly, may be true of some evangelicals, I conceded, but it is not true of most. Nor should it be.

Third, we wanted him to know that many of the 600 million evangelicals around the world "pray for the peace of Jerusalem," as we are commanded to in Psalm 122:6. And as we pray, we are looking to see who the next Arab leader will be to make peace with Israel. Whoever it is will be deeply appreciated by the evangelical Christian community and remembered forever.

Continuing my remarks, I added a fourth point that I had not felt necessary to make in Abu Dhabi to MBZ. "Your Royal Highness, I was born in 1967, into a world in which Egypt's Gamal Abdel Nasser was the leader of the Arab world and was threatening to destroy Israel and 'throw the Jews into the sea.' I'm now fifty-one years old, and I never imagined ever setting foot in the Kingdom of Saudi Arabia or visiting Riyadh in my lifetime. I am Jewish on my father's side. I am a follower of Jesus Christ. I was born and raised in the United States, and I am an American citizen. But four and a half years ago, my family and I moved to Israel, and we are now dual U.S.-Israeli citizens. With all that, it never occurred to me that I might be invited to the royal palace or have a conversation with the crown prince of Saudi Arabia. Thank you for inviting me to bring this delegation and for being willing to have this conversation with us on a wide range of issues, even quite sensitive issues."

Then I added, "You know, with 60 million evangelical Christians in the

U.S., you could have thrown a dart out the window and found another leader to bring the first delegation to your country. You didn't have to choose a Jewish-Israeli-American with a son in the Israeli army. But you did, and I'm grateful. And I hope this is one small step on the way to Saudi Arabia and the State of Israel making peace and becoming friends."

With all that as preamble, I then asked the crown prince the specific question that the group and I had crafted together back in Abu Dhabi.

"Your Royal Highness, the Bible describes Jesus as the Prince of Peace. As I noted, the Bible commands us to 'pray for the peace of Jerusalem.' And Jesus told his followers, 'Blessed are the peacemakers.' So we want to see peace between Israel and the Palestinians and between Israel and her Arab neighbors. We have heard a great number of rumors and leaks and unsourced stories about quiet contacts between Saudi Arabia and the State of Israel. And we've read about President Trump and his team and the peace plan they are working on. But we tend to be skeptical of what we read in the media. So I'd like to ask you directly: What is your vision of getting to the point of signing a peace treaty with Israel? What is the path forward? And if the Palestinians continue to refuse to come to the nego-tiating table, can you envision a scenario in which the Kingdom of Saudi Arabia would decide, in its own national interests, to go ahead and make peace with Israel—and hope the Palestinians come along soon thereafter?"

PRAYING FOR THE PRINCE

As we reached the two-hour point, I felt it was time to wrap up. No one at the palace—including the crown prince—had ever specified an ending time for the meeting. Still, we did not want to overstay our welcome.

We asked MBS if we could close the meeting in prayer and asked if he had any specific prayer requests. He welcomed this, and we bowed our heads and prayed for King Salman, for MBS and his family, for Prince Khalid and the other officials in the room. We prayed for safety and secu-rity and prosperity for all the people of Saudi Arabia. We prayed for peace and for wisdom, for all leaders of goodwill in the region. And we closed in the name of our Lord and Savior Jesus Christ.

The crown prince rose to his feet, and we immediately followed suit. He thanked us for coming to the kingdom and told us how much he appreciated our questions and our comments. Then he shook our hands and left the room, followed by the foreign minister and the head of the Muslim World League.

Prince Khalid stayed behind, and for nearly half an hour, we processed the meeting together and discussed next steps toward building a working relationship. Then he surprised us by saying that the palace had decided to go public with our visit. They would release pictures and a statement very shortly. We talked this through and agreed that we would put out a statement as well. Then the prince walked us out to where the motorcade was waiting, thanked us again for coming, and said he looked forward to seeing us again soon.

GOING PUBLIC

Back at the hotel, we regrouped to draft a press release.

As always, Larry Ross and Johnnie Moore provided wise counsel. We wanted to provide the media with the basic facts of our trip, and we wanted to strike the right tone in our statement.

We had not come to Riyadh to become apologists for Saudi Arabia. We were in no position to know at that moment whether the crown prince's explanation of his innocence in the Khashoggi affair was true or not. Nor could we independently evaluate the many economic and social reforms that MBS and his team had briefed us on. Still, we had done a great deal of research in the months leading up to the trip, and we were encouraged by the new direction the kingdom was taking. We had heard things that no Saudi leader had ever said before. What's more, we'd had an opportunity to say things directly to the nation's leaders that few others in the world had—or would have—the opportunity to say.

In the end, we kept our statement brief. We listed the names and titles of the officials we had met with. We listed the names and affiliations of everyone in our group. We included the two photos released by the palace and this short statement:

> We were pleased by the invitation extended to us more than two
> months ago by the Kingdom of Saudi Arabia. It was a historic
> moment for the Saudi crown prince to openly welcome evangelical
> Christian leaders to the palace. We were encouraged by the

candor of the two-hour conversation with him today. We discussed his Vision 2030 plan, the region, Islam, and Christianity. Without question, this is a season of tremendous change in the Middle East, and therefore we have been grateful for the opportunity to meet in person with key Arab leaders to understand their goals and to ask direct questions. We look forward to building upon these relationships and continuing the dialogue.[2]

Given the firestorm of controversy swirling about the kingdom, word of our visit was a far bigger story than any of our previous trips to Arab countries—and quickly went viral. The following morning, the story and palace photos were on the front page of every Saudi newspaper, both Arabic and English editions, as well as on the front page of many newspapers throughout the region.

"Saudi Arabia's Crown Prince Mohammed bin Salman held a rare meeting with American evangelical Christians on Thursday, as the ultra-conservative Muslim kingdom seeks to open up more to the world and repair an image of religious intolerance," the Reuters wire service reported. "A visit by such prominent non-Muslim leaders . . . is a rare act of religious openness for Saudi Arabia, which hosts the holiest sites in Islam and bans the practice of other religions. Some of the [delegation members'] support for Israel, which the kingdom does not recognize, is also striking."[3]

In the days that followed, the story was published throughout the Middle East, and as far away as Europe, Asia, and North America.

"In Historic First, Saudi Crown Prince Meets Israeli Evangelical Christian," read the lead headline in the *Jerusalem Post*.

In a story headlined "Israeli in Saudi," Israel's Channel 10 News broadcast an interview with me by Barak Ravid, one of the nation's leading diplomatic correspondents, during its prime-time 8 p.m. broadcast.

Back in the U.S., the *Washington Post* was the first to publish a major story, which began:

A group of prominent U.S. evangelical figures, including several of President Trump's evangelical advisers, met Thursday with Saudi crown prince Mohammed bin Salman, whose role in the killing of *Washington Post* contributing columnist Jamal Khashoggi remains unclear. In a statement that included photos of those present smiling, a member of the group said "it is our desire to lift up the name of Jesus whenever we are asked and wherever we go." . . .

Group spokesman Johnnie Moore, who also serves as the White House's unofficial liaison to a group of well-known conservative evangelicals, said Khashoggi's killing and other human rights issues were "discussed" Thursday with the Saudi prince. . . .

"The Kingdom of Saudi Arabia is among the wealthiest, most powerful, and most important nations in the Middle East, in all of history," Moore said. "It also has enormous influence on the Islamic theology taught throughout the entire globe. While the kingdom is restrictive and controversial in various and serious respects, it has under the crown prince begun to undergo reform and professed the desire to change in profound ways. Precisely for these reasons, we thought it was wise to accept the invitation we received from the kingdom, issued more than two months ago, to come as evangelicals to engage in a dialogue."[4]

"I think it would have been immoral not to accept this invitation, because of the potential implications of it in the long run," Johnnie Moore later told the *Atlantic* magazine. He said our group had taken the trip "to advocate for the religious rights of the 1.4 million Christians who are estimated to live in Saudi Arabia."[5]

Did you ask MBS about the murder of Jamal Khashoggi? the writer from the *Atlantic* asked him.

"It was the first question we asked," Moore replied. "We knew we were going in this context . . . so we weren't going to dodge it. We just asked it outright. He was totally consistent with us with what he'd said publicly before— he said this is a terrible and heinous act and they were going to find and prosecute everyone involved with it. He emphatically denied involvement."[6]

The reporter pressed Moore on whether we were sacrificing concerns about human rights in order to elevate our push for religious freedom. While acknowledging such criticism, Moore observed that human rights activists often tend to downplay or ignore issues of religious freedom, yet both are vitally important.

"You can choose to take the long view or the short view," he said. "If you take the long view, you engage when these people are ready to engage."[7]

Michele Bachmann echoed this view in an interview with the Christian Broadcasting Network. "We aren't here for a short-term purpose. We are not here for a photo op. We could care less about that. We're here to build long-term relations and to benefit our brothers and sisters that are here in this region."[8]

WHAT I TOLD THE MEDIA

Going public is always a risk.

There's no guarantee of being quoted accurately or in context—or quoted at all.

We certainly received a great deal of blowback from Islamist media outlets, left-wing commentators, and others who hated—or simply wanted to mischaracterize—what we had done and why we had done it.

A headline in a British tabloid comes to mind: "Saudi Arabia MURDER: Crown Prince Bursts into FURIOUS RANT after Khashoggi Death."[9] The article, in the *Express*, said I had told people that MBS launched into an angry "outburst." The White House even contacted me to find out if this was true. But nothing could have been further from the truth. The conversation about Khashoggi had been calm and respectful, even though we pressed the matter a number of times and from a number of angles. But the tabloid didn't care. The reporter didn't contact me or anyone in our delegation. Instead, the paper reported what MBS was "thought to have ranted" and what he was "alleged to have angrily said"—whatever fit the publisher's biases and preconceptions.[10]

The Salon website—citing Al Jazeera, the world's leading Islamist media outlet—ran this memorable headline: "Michele Bachmann and Other End-Times Evangelicals Turn Up in Saudi Arabia." In the article, the writer said, "The delegation to Riyadh was led by Bachmann and communications strategist Joel Rosenberg, who are each known for pushing an apocalyptic worldview relating to events in the Middle East, and the heads of other Israel-tied evangelical organizations."[11]

In a report on National Public Radio's *Morning Edition*—and published on NPR's website under the headline "Evangelicals Seek Détente with Mideast Muslim Leaders as Critics Doubt Motives"—correspondent Jerome Socolovsky never quite said why he thought seeking a peaceful détente with Muslim leaders was a bad idea. But he was clever enough to track down a professor at a Christian college who was willing to attack my colleagues and me for somehow being driven to advance Middle East peace because of our beliefs in "end-times prophecy" and for failing to "challenge the Saudi crown prince about the war in Yemen and other human rights abuses."[12]

An Iranian newspaper noted that MBS "hosted a delegation of evangelical Christians . . . led by a prominent pro-Israel advocate who lives in occupied Palestine."[13]

The attacks were expected, and these were not the last of them. Nevertheless, the team and I believed then, and believe today, the risks were worth taking. We had not expected our trip to be made public. We had not gone looking for publicity, and we had readily agreed with the Saudis' initial ground rules. But if MBS was willing to go public, we saw it as an opportunity to explain why we went, what we saw and heard, and why it mattered.

"There's a lot of people who would say this is the wrong time to go to Saudi Arabia and meet with the leadership there," I told CBN News. "I understand that criticism, but I disagree.

"Given the fact that we care about the people of Saudi Arabia [and] Christianity in the Arabian Peninsula, the desire to see more freedom of worship, even Christian churches being allowed to be built, this all seemed important for us to do. . . . We're under no illusions about the challenges that [remain] in Saudi Arabia. . . . But I think it's respectful to go and listen to leaders who have the opportunity to make life better for Christians and Muslims, and potentially for Israel as well, and who are against the crazies in Iran and the Muslim Brotherhood."

As the Saudis continue their efforts to advance economic, social, and religious reforms, I ask you to pray. Pray for the king. Pray for the crown prince. Pray for the people of Saudi Arabia. Given the high stakes—the lives and futures of 34 million people—I believe that's the right thing to do.

18

LUNCH AT THE WHITE HOUSE

---

*Briefing the president and vice president on
my observations in the Middle East*

On February 20, 2019, I received an email from an official at the White
House:

The VP wants to see you.

I was already planning a return trip to the U.S. to release my latest
political thriller *The Persian Gamble*, so I accepted the invitation and
immediately made plans to include a stop in Washington, D.C.

At the time, the Trump administration was designing a counterintuitive
and controversial strategy to advance peace and security in the Middle
East. They were quietly seeking input from outside the usual "peace industry," the wide array of former officials, ambassadors, experts, and consultants whose views of how to forge a détente between Arabs and Israelis
had long been sacrosanct in D.C. but, more often than not, had proved
ineffective or had done more harm than good.

Was it possible to make peace in the Middle East after decades of
terror, war, and genocide? I believed that the answer was yes, and I was
heading to the White House to explain why.

MEETING MIKE PENCE

As I boarded United flight 91 in Tel Aviv for the journey across the Atlantic, I thought back to the first time I had met Mike and Karen Pence.

At the time, June 2012, Pence was a congressman from Indiana and the third highest-ranking official in the Republican House leadership. Earlier that month, the Pences were having dinner at the home of some close friends and noticed a copy of one of my novels on the coffee table. When Mike and Karen mentioned they were readers of my books, their hosts said they were friends with Lynn and me and that they served on the board of our nonprofit organization, The Joshua Fund, which mobilizes Christians to bless Israel and her neighbors in the name of Jesus. The Pences asked if it might be possible to meet me.

"Absolutely," said our mutual friends. "I'll shoot Joel a message right now."

Of course, I immediately said yes. I had been an admirer of Mike's for many years.

When we got together on June 28, 2012, I addressed him as "Congressman," but he insisted I call him Mike.

We had lunch at the Capitol Hill Club, and Karen was able to join us partway through our conversation. For several hours, we covered a lot of ground, from the writing of political thrillers about the threats of radical Islamism for the U.S., Israel, and our Arab allies to the direction of the American economy and society; and from our shared Christian faith to what we were each reading in the Bible as part of our daily study of the Scriptures. When I got home, I told Lynn how much I enjoyed the Pences and how I wished she'd been able to join us rather than homeschooling our children that day. Then I sent Mike an email to thank him and Karen for a lovely time.

"Thanks for the kind note," he wrote back a few days later. "Karen and I were both delighted to have some time with you. Though we tried to mask it, we are both fans . . . and it is a privilege to now say we are friends. We have so much in common—our Christian faith, talk radio backgrounds, Kemp, Bennett, and the think tank world. I can't help but think we will be friends for a long time. . . . Thanks again for the time and kind encouragement. Your pen is an important one and I will be praying for your safe travels, energy, and wisdom."

In the years that followed, we stayed in close contact and visited when we could. When Mike was elected governor of Indiana, he and Karen invited Lynn and me to come for a visit. We spent a wonderful week-end with them, even staying at the governor's mansion. When Lynn and I "made aliyah" to become dual U.S.-Israeli citizens and moved with our sons to Israel in August 2014, we invited the Pences for a visit. They came between Christmas and New Year's that year, bringing a trade delegation, giving a few speeches, meeting with Netanyahu, and then spending an encouraging, and at time hilarious, evening with us in their suite at the David Citadel hotel. For much of that year, we had been encouraging Mike to run for president. But that night, he and Karen told us that they did not sense it was the Lord's will for them.

When Donald Trump won the Republican nomination and chose Mike to be his running mate—and then, against all odds, won—we could hardly believe it. Now Mike Pence was vice president of the United States.

THE DEAL OF THE CENTURY

On March 7, 2019, I arrived at the White House.

After being cleared by the Secret Service, I entered the lobby of the West Wing for my scheduled coffee with Vice President Pence. An aide greeted me and explained that several critical matters had come up at the last minute, requiring the VP's attention. I expected her to say that the meeting was canceled or would have to be rescheduled. Instead, she asked if I was free to have lunch with the VP in a few hours—and in the meantime, would I like to join a briefing that was about to begin on the president's Middle East peace plan?

Delighted, I accepted the offer and we walked over to the Eisenhower Executive Office Building, which is part of the White House campus, to meet with Jason Greenblatt, assistant to the president and special repre-sentative for international negotiations. Greenblatt was one of the chief architects—along with Jared Kushner and David Friedman—of the admin-istration's Mideast peace plan. He and I first met in Jerusalem while dining at adjacent tables at the King David hotel. We had now known each other for several years and were in regular contact about the ongoing develop-ment of the plan that President Sisi had dubbed the "deal of the century."

Greenblatt described the state of the plan's development to a group of fifteen prominent evangelical leaders and sketched out a possible time frame for its release. Then he asked us for our views and any concerns we might have that should be factored into the president's thinking as he finalized the plan. One by one, the pastors made an impassioned case for the president not to divide Jerusalem and not to say yes to a sovereign Palestinian state.

When it was my turn, I made a somewhat different case.

As both an evangelical Christian and an Israeli citizen—with one son having completed his service in the Israel Defense Forces and another son then serving in an IDF special forces unit—I echoed that I, too, was deeply committed to Israel's security and to Jerusalem remaining the eternal and undivided capital of the Jewish people. That said, I added that as I prayed for the peace of Jerusalem, I was coming to believe that peace treaties between Israel and several Gulf Arab states were not only possible but were coming soon and that we needed to look very closely at how to help those deals come to pass and be careful not to inadvertently place new obstacles in the way. Though I explained I was not at liberty to share everything I had heard from senior Arab leaders, I was encouraged by the tectonic changes underway in Arab thinking toward Israel.

"We need to allow the president freedom of movement—and latitude— to present a plan that would allow those Arab states which are more willing than ever to make peace with Israel to move forward," I urged. "We need to give the Arab states the ability to support [the president's plan]. If the Saudis, the Egyptians, and others can say that this plan is credible, it will open the door for them—after the Palestinians say no—to talk about how to move forward with Israel."[1]

I encouraged the evangelical leaders to support the president in putting into writing in his plan two specific things he had already said repeatedly and publicly.

First, that he was open to the possibility of a Palestinian state, so long as it could not threaten Israeli security.

Second, though Trump had recognized Jerusalem as the capital of Israel and moved the U.S. Embassy from Tel Aviv to Jerusalem, he still considered the final boundaries of the municipality of Jerusalem open to negotiation.

BRIEFING THE VICE PRESIDENT

I then met the vice president for lunch in the White House Mess.

Joining us was Pence's senior advisor Tom Rose, a conservative Jewish businessman from Indiana who had previously served as publisher of the *Jerusalem Post*. The VP and I first caught up on news of our families and shared our prayer requests with each other. We had a long-standing practice of praying with and for one another, and this time was no exception.

When we got down to business, the subject, of course, was the Middle East. The vice president said he had been reading the trip reports I had sent regarding our various delegations, but he wanted to hear more of the nuances of the conversations and my thoughts on how best to craft the final draft of the peace plan.

I began by recounting the conversation I had just had with Jason Greenblatt and my evangelical colleagues and shared my recommendations. Then I explained how stunned I had been by Mohammed bin Zayed's insistence that he was ready to make peace between the UAE and Israel. Not only was I convinced MBZ was telling the truth, I said, but I believed he was actively looking for a way to thread the needle.

I told Pence and Rose how astonished I was by the public statements and signals coming out of Saudi Arabia about Israel's right to exist, and the frustration they were expressing publicly about ongoing Palestinian intransigence toward any direct negotiations with Israel. Then I gave them a detailed briefing on the meeting with Mohammed bin Salman in Riyadh.

Though I certainly did not want to overstate the importance of our delegation, I told them I thought it was not insignificant that the Saudis had invited such a strongly pro-Israel group of evangelical Christians—led by an Israeli. Pence agreed.

I also explained that, just the day before, UAE ambassador Yousef Al Otaiba had invited me to have lunch with him and the Bahraini ambassador to the U.S., Sheikh Abdulla bin Rashid Al Khalifa. Though it had been my first opportunity to meet the Bahraini ambassador, I told Pence I already liked him. He was young. Smart. Moderate. Deeply pro-American. And every indication I was getting suggested that Bahrain, like the UAE, was increasingly ready to make peace with Israel.

"I believe you guys are on the verge of making history," I said.

"Joel," Pence asked suddenly, "have you ever met the president?"

Caught off guard, I replied, "No, Mr. Vice President. I've never even been in the Oval Office."

"Come with me," he said.

INTO THE OVAL OFFICE

The next thing I knew, the vice president of the United States was leading me into the historic room that I have written so many fictional scenes about but had never seen for myself.

The first person I saw was Mike Pompeo. He greeted me warmly, as did then-National Security Advisor John Bolton, whom I had known much longer than Pence and Pompeo, though not as well. Then President Trump entered from a side room.

"Mr. President, I'd like to introduce you to a friend of mine," Pence said. "This is Joel Rosenberg. He's a bestselling author with some 5 million copies of his books in print. He's also an evangelical and lives in Israel."

Trump smiled broadly and shook my hand. "Great to meet you, Joel. Welcome to the White House."

"It's my honor, Mr. President."

Pence briefly explained what we had discussed over lunch, and Trump motioned for me to sit down.

"Let's talk," he said, taking his chair behind the *Resolute* desk.

Pence interjected, "Sir, I know that time is short, and we have that meeting coming up with the Czech prime minister, but I just wanted you and Joel to meet, as he's on the campus today and is usually in Israel."

"No, no, it's fine—we have plenty of time," Trump replied. "Come, Joel, have a seat and let's chat for a few minutes."

It was a surreal moment.

As I sat down directly across from the president, the vice president was to my right. To my left were the secretary of state and the national security advisor. I would love to tell you I had something profound to say at that moment, but to be honest, all I could think of was a line from a *Sesame Street* song I had grown up with: "One of these things is not like the others; one of these things doesn't belong."

"So tell me about yourself, Joel," the president said.

Before I could figure out something to say, Trump turned back to Pence. "Wait—Mike, I'm sorry, but did you just say that Joel is an evangelical Christian?"

"Yes, sir."

Trump turned back to me. "Is that true, Joel? Are you an evangelical?"

"Yes, sir, Mr. President. I'm a follower of Jesus."

Trump looked quizzical. "But isn't your name Rosenberg? Isn't that Jewish?"

"Yes, sir. My father's side is Jewish. My mom's side is not."

"I don't understand—how can you be Jewish and believe in Jesus?"

I smiled. It's a question I get asked all over the world and one I'm happy to answer. But I never expected it to come up in my first visit to the Oval Office.

I briefly explained that I believe Jesus of Nazareth is the Jewish Messiah, and I believe the New Testament Gospel accounts that he died and rose again. In fact, I said, there are actually more Jewish followers of Jesus today than at any other time in history.

The president leaned forward in his seat and said, "Doesn't that confuse your Jewish friends?"

I laughed. "It does. And my Muslim friends too. But it's always been the basis for an interesting conversation."

"I bet," Trump said. "Okay, tell me something else about yourself."

Not knowing how much time we had left, I briefly told him that my wife and I had bought an apartment in Jerusalem and had become dual citizens of the U.S. and Israel.

"I don't know how many Israeli citizens, beyond the prime minister and the ambassador, get to sit with you and personally thank you for moving the American embassy to Jerusalem, but I would certainly like to thank you. No other American president has been willing to do that, and I'm deeply grateful."

That lit him up. He mentioned how much resistance he had gotten from world leaders and even from some members of his own cabinet. But he was proud that it had cost so little to make the move—far less than the State Department had estimated.

"Great, what else?" he asked. "You're an author, right? What's your latest book about?"

"Well, sir, I brought you and the VP copies. It's called *The Persian Gamble*."

"Give me the elevator pitch."

"Sure thing, sir," I said, determined to make it quick. "What if the Iranian regime took the $150 billion that the Obama administration gave them for that insane nuclear deal, secretly went to North Korea to buy a half-dozen fully operational nuclear warheads off the shelf, and then quietly tried to ship those warheads back to Iran?"

At this, the president sat back in his chair.

"Wow—that's pretty scary," he said, turning to look out the window.

After a moment, he turned back to me and said, "How do you know they're not trying to do that in real life?"

"Well, sir," I said, looking at Pence, Pompeo, and Bolton, then back at the president, "I'm counting on you and the men in this room to make sure *The Persian Gamble* never comes true."

They laughed and I thanked the president for withdrawing the U.S. from the Iran nuclear deal. We talked about the seriousness of the Iran threat and Iran's growing alliances with Russia and North Korea. To my regret, I didn't think quickly enough to raise my concerns about the direction Turkey was heading or my concerns that Trump was being too soft on Erdoğan, aside from the excellent work he had done to get pastor Andrew Brunson released from a Turkish prison and returned to the United States.

As the conversation continued, the president kept pressing me to share more about myself. I can't explain why he was asking me so much about my background and my views on the Middle East, but I appreciated his questions. I saw none of the bluster for which he was so routinely attacked in the media. Nor was he trying to command the floor.

I told him that though I had been a Never Trumper in 2016, I had voted for him at the last moment, in part because Pence was on the ticket. I had been skeptical of his conservative campaign promises, but now I wanted to thank him for keeping so many of them. I listed ten or twelve specific examples, from ways he had strengthened Israel to the work he was doing to defeat radical Islamists, to his tax cuts and his stellar appointments to the Supreme Court and federal courts.

"Sir, if you accomplish nothing else for the rest of your term, you will go down in history as the most pro-life and pro-Israel president in the history of the country. And I just want to say thank you for all the promises you've kept."

The president thanked me for my words and asked if I wanted to have a picture with him. I did. As we waited for the official photographer to arrive and set up, I said, "I want you to know, sir, that I have prayed for you and your family every day since you took the oath of office."

"Thank you, Joel. That means a lot to me."

A moment later, the photographer took our picture. I thanked the president for his time and walked out of the Oval Office with Vice President Pence.

When we got back to Pence's office, we returned to the issue of Arab-Israeli peacemaking. I mentioned the growing chorus of cynics who were declaring the still-unfinished White House plan "dead on arrival." Tragically, I said, Mahmoud Abbas was risking going to his grave as the man who deprived generations of Palestinian men, women, and children of the freedom, opportunity, and economic prosperity they craved and rightly deserved. But given the seriousness of the Iran threat and the rise of a new generation of Arab leaders who were thinking very differently than their predecessors, it was no longer difficult to envision a scenario in which Abbas's rejection of a reasonably structured peace plan could actually breathe new life into a regional peace process. Indeed, I argued, it could create the very conditions that Gulf Arab leaders needed to negotiate their own peace treaties, thereby hyper-accelerating regional trade, investment, and economic growth.[2]

I thanked the VP for taking the time to listen to my case, we prayed together, and I wished him well as he advised the president and they charted their next steps.

19

9/11 IN SAUDI ARABIA

Why I brought a second delegation to the kingdom

Do you recall where you were on September 11, 2001?

On that gorgeous Tuesday morning, I was in our town house in northern Virginia, fifteen minutes from Washington Dulles International Airport. I was finishing work on my first political thriller, *The Last Jihad*, and did not have the radio or TV on.

The first page of *The Last Jihad* puts you inside the cockpit of a jet that has been hijacked by radical Islamist terrorists who are flying a kamikaze mission into an American city. The target happens to be Denver, not New York or Washington, D.C., and the weapon is a Gulfstream IV business jet, not a commercial airliner. But when Lynn burst into the house after dropping our kids off at school and told me what she had just heard on the radio, my blood went cold. The details might have been different, but the fictional scenario I had created seemed to be coming to pass.

We switched on the television in time to see the second plane fly into the World Trade Center. Soon, both towers collapsed. The threat I had feared, the one I had spent nine months writing about, was now a chilling reality. And just like in my novel, America was about to head into a long, brutal series of wars.

When we asked Mohammed bin Salman where he was on that fateful Tuesday, he told us he remembered it vividly. He was sixteen years old and his father was governor of Riyadh. He was in his room that afternoon when his mother suddenly called him and told him to come quickly. He reached the TV just in time to see the second plane fly into the World Trade Center. He remembered thinking, *The reputation of Islam is over. It's been destroyed.*

MBS said he felt especially angry because he and his family had been in Manhattan just a month earlier, where his mother received medical care. He and his family felt close to the U.S. and were grateful for the long-standing U.S.-Saudi alliance.

He also told us that he and cousins felt a sense of humiliation. They now feared that, whenever Saudis traveled abroad, they would have to hide their nationality or risk being branded as terrorists, connected forever with Osama bin Laden.

"It created a will for revenge" in the younger generation of Saudis, he said.

"Did you say *revenge?*" we asked.

"Yes," he said. "Revenge against the terrorists."

Then he added, "As cousins, we made a promise to one another. 'One day we're going to kick these people's asses.' And that's what we're doing."

Having met with MBS and his most trusted advisors, I believe 9/11 has shaped—and even drives—the way they think. And I believe it fuels their determination to fundamentally transform not only the way the kingdom is perceived in the U.S. and around the globe but also the way it actually is.

Let me explain why.

AN INVITATION TO RETURN

On March 24, 2019, I received an email from the Saudi embassy:

Vice Minister Khalid bin Salman will be in D.C. this week, March 25-29. He has requested to meet with you.

I was certainly interested in catching up with Prince Khalid. He and I had stayed in contact since my visit to Riyadh, but this would be the first opportunity to see him since he had been promoted from ambassador to vice minister of defense.

But this was very last-minute notice. I was in California on a cross-country book tour promoting *The Persian Gamble*. I was scheduled to speak that week at the Reagan Library in Simi Valley. Still, I had told the Saudis I was interested in building a long-term friendship. If I meant it, I needed to say yes.

I called Nancy, my intrepid executive assistant, and said, "You know I'm always trying to keep life interesting for you . . ."

I have no idea how she did it—I never do—but she really came through. Within a few hours, she had figured out how to get me to Washington by Wednesday morning, so I could have lunch with the prince, and then straight back to the airport to take a red-eye flight back to California.

Forty years to the week since Egypt and Israel signed a permanent peace agreement at the White House, Prince Khalid and I spent ninety minutes discussing the growing Iran nuclear, missile, and terror threats and the prospects for new peace treaties in the Middle East. The prince was intrigued to learn the premise of *The Persian Gamble* and that, in the novel, Saudi intelligence works closely with the Americans and the Israelis to thwart an Iranian operation to buy nuclear warheads from Pyongyang. He was also interested in my Oval Office meeting. When I gave him signed copies of the novel for his brother and him, he asked why I had not brought one for his father.

"I never imagined His Majesty the king would be interested in a political thriller."

"He loves them," the prince said.

"All right then, I'll have my colleague FedEx a copy to the embassy."

"Why don't you bring a copy and deliver it in person?"

"I'm sorry?"

"The crown prince has asked me to invite you to bring a second delegation to the kingdom," he said. "There is much more to show you and much more to discuss. Would you be open to doing that, Joel?"

I agreed. When the prince asked if November would work, however, I had to inform him that Johnnie Moore and I were in the early stages of planning trips to Bahrain and Azerbaijan during that time. Though I had only just met the Bahraini ambassador to Washington, Johnnie had already developed a wonderful working relationship with the king of Bahrain, Hamad bin Isa Al Khalifa, and had helped draft the landmark Bahrain Declaration protecting religious freedom. Likewise, we both were developing relationships with officials in Azerbaijan, the one Shia Muslim government that had established diplomatic ties with Israel (in 1992). The Azerbaijanis had forged close economic and security ties with the Jewish State and had welcomed Netanyahu to Baku in December 2016. Both governments were watching what Johnnie and I were doing in the region and had expressed interest in us bringing evangelical leaders to visit their leaders as well.*

How about October? Prince Khalid asked.

Unfortunately, that month, too, was booked with other events.

"How about the week of September 11?" I countered.

The prince just looked at me.

"No, really, I'm serious," I said quickly. "Imagine what a signal that would send of the kingdom's commitment to counterterrorism and many other kinds of reform if you hosted an American delegation during the week of 9/11."

He took the idea to his brother, and I received the following email from the Saudi embassy.

Dear Joel,

Hope this finds you well.

It was a great pleasure to have hosted you and your esteemed delegation last year in Riyadh. The delegation's meeting with His Royal Highness the crown prince was an important and historic one.

To build upon last year's constructive visit and to continue the important dialogue, the embassy has the pleasure of extending an invitation to host you in a trip to the kingdom.

We suggest the following tentative time frame for the visit— September 8 to 12, 2019. Please let us know of your availability and we look forward to your response.

---

* Unfortunately, the delegations to Bahrain and Azerbaijan—planned for November 1-8, 2019—had to be postponed due to scheduling conflicts in Manama and Baku. Attempts to reschedule them for 2020 were scuttled by the COVID-19 crisis.

On June 1, I received a formal invitation. I immediately accepted and soon sent back a confirmed guest list with six members of our first trip to Saudi Arabia—Johnnie Moore, Larry Ross, Michael Little, Skip Heitzig, Wayne Pederson, and me—plus three newcomers: Ken Blackwell, former U.S. ambassador to the U.N. Human Rights Commission; Skip's wife, Lenya; and my wife, Lynn.

The Saudis gave the green light to Chris Mitchell, CBN's Middle East bureau chief, to cover the visit, along with his cameraman, Jonathan Goff. At the last minute, my son Jacob was also able to join us as a notetaker and photographer.

OUR SECOND MEETING WITH THE CROWN PRINCE

On our first day back in the kingdom—this time, in Jeddah, the summer capital—Lynn and I were given a tour of the Old City with a Saudi historian, followed by dinner with Princess Reema bint Bandar Al Saud, the new Saudi ambassador to the United States, and four young Saudi business, civic, and government leaders.

The following day, Sunday, the rest of the delegation arrived from the U.S. and checked in to the Jeddah Royal Hotel. We met with everyone for an opening time of prayer.

After breakfast on Monday, we met with retired General John Abizaid, the U.S. ambassador to Saudi Arabia; and U.S. Consul General Ryan Gliha, followed by a meeting with Sheikh Mohammad Al-Issa, secretary-general of the Muslim World League.

That afternoon, we had a working lunch with Sheikh Al-Issa and Mohamed Al Jaber, the Saudi ambassador to Yemen, followed by a meeting with Ambassador Al Jaber and several Saudi military officials who gave us a detailed briefing on the war in Yemen.

After a quick stop at our hotel, we traveled to the Ministry of Foreign Affairs for a briefing with Faisal bin Muaammar, secretary-general of the King Abdullah International Dialogue Centre in Vienna, Austria, and advisor to His Majesty King Salman. That briefing was followed by another—this time with senior staff of ETIDAL, Saudi Arabia's center for countering extremist ideology.

After a very full day, we returned to the hotel for a late dinner.

On Tuesday morning, we had extended time to meet as a delegation, pray, and debrief together before the motorcade took us to the royal palace. We first met with Princess Reema. Then, at two o'clock, we met with Crown Prince Mohammed bin Salman; Prince Khalid, the vice defense minister; Adel al-Jubeir, minister of state for foreign affairs; Sheikh Mohammad Al-Issa; and Princess Reema.

With no need for introductions, we plunged into two hours of questions and answers. We asked for an update on the investigation of the Khashoggi murder and the prosecution of those involved. We spent a great deal of time asking about human rights issues, including the importance of expanding religious freedom in the kingdom and allowing the first churches to be built. We returned to the Iran threat and asked MBS more about his thoughts on making peace with Israel. We also asked him for a detailed update on his Vision 2030 plan.

We also presented him with several gifts, including a signed copy of *The Persian Gamble* for His Majesty the king, as promised. The crown prince and Prince Khalid were very grateful and said the novel would be immediately translated into Arabic and set on the nightstand by their father's bed.

The ground rules for our discussion this time were different. MBS initially asked that his comments not be made public. We were free to share our general impressions of the meeting and what *we* said to MBS. We were allowed to take detailed notes, as before, and we could provide information from the meeting to senior officials in Washington and even Jerusalem. But the crown prince felt it would be a more interesting and candid conversation if he could speak completely openly with us without having to measure his words for public consumption. Later, however, the Saudis allowed me to put some of MBS's comments on the record for this book, including his reflections on 9/11.

Wayne Pederson opened our conversation with the crown prince with an interesting question.

"Your Royal Highness, there have of course been some very rocky periods in the long history of the U.S.-Saudi relationship. Yet in the Bible, we read the words of the Hebrew prophet Isaiah: 'Forget the former things; do not dwell on the past. See, I am doing a new thing! Now it springs up;

do you not perceive it? I am making a way in the wilderness and streams in the wasteland."[1]

"This passage of Scripture does not mean that we are not to learn from history. It means we are not to be paralyzed by past sins and failures. With God's help, there is always a way forward."

Though Pederson's point could apply to any number of areas, he chose to focus on 9/11.

"These words come to mind because, by God's providence, we are in Saudi Arabia on the anniversary of the attacks by al Qaeda on New York and Washington. So I would like to ask you: Do you remember what you were doing on September 11, 2001? What are your memories of that day? And looking back at this from a broader perspective, what lessons would you say you have learned from the rise of a Saudi like Osama bin Laden and his al Qaeda terrorist network, and how do these lessons shape your thinking about the future of the kingdom?"

I have already relayed the crown prince's illuminating answer. But MBS also took the opportunity to talk about the threat posed by the ayatollahs in Iran, where the supreme leader and his inner circle are pursuing a dangerous, revolutionary, apocalyptic ideology that threatens everyone in the region, including the Iranian people.

"The leaders of Iran are driven by ideology," he said. "They don't care about the nation. If their mission is accomplished, we're going to have a huge, huge problem—twenty times bigger than Afghanistan. It's a nightmare."

To that end, MBS expressed gratitude that President Trump understood the severity of the Iran threat and was pursuing a "maximum pressure" campaign of tough economic sanctions and a new regional security alliance—a Middle East NATO, of sorts—to counter the terror masters in Tehran.

"We believe what Trump is doing to pressure Iran is right," he said. "We support sanctions until they [Iran's leaders] come to the table."

MBS said more world leaders needed to join the U.S. effort to force the mullahs to give up their nuclear and terror ambitions and pursue peace instead. If not, Iran will get the Bomb and the consequences will be catastrophic.

"You're going to pay for it," he said to leaders who showed weakness toward the Iranian regime. "And you're going to destabilize Arab nations and Israel."

MBS made clear he doesn't want war. Rather, he wants to pursue Vision 2030, create a roaring Saudi economy, and make major social reforms. But, he vowed, "we'll use all the defensive measures we need" to protect the kingdom and its allies.

Among the many other questions we asked the crown prince—including why only two U.S. senators had come to visit him over the previous year, how he had answered these senators' questions regarding the blistering criticism being leveled at him back in Washington, and how he was going to get his Vision 2030 reforms back on track—there are two subjects in particular that I want to mention here: improving human rights and making peace with Israel.

RAIF BADAWI AND THE QUESTION OF HUMAN RIGHTS

We certainly discussed at length with MBS the issue of expanding religious freedom in the kingdom, including allowing the building of the first churches in the kingdom, just as we had during our previous visit. But this time we spent even more time asking him about other troubling human rights issues within the kingdom.

"There are cases that are very difficult for your friends in Congress and elsewhere—those who see the importance of your reforms and support them—to explain or defend," I said. I mentioned that Vice President Pence had raised one case in particular: that of Raif Badawi, a Saudi blogger arrested in June 2012.

By way of context, here is a quick summary of Badawi's situation, as reported by the U.S. Commission on International Religious Freedom:

> In July 2013, a Saudi court sentenced Badawi to six hundred
> lashes and seven years in prison for insulting Islam and breaking
> the anti-cybercrime law by founding a liberal website. Following
> an appeal of the sentence, a criminal court resentenced him
> in May 2014 to ten years in prison, one thousand lashes, a
> one million riyal fine, and a ten-year travel and media ban

following release. Badawi received the first fifty lashes in January 2015 in front of Al Juffali Mosque in Jeddah. Following an international outcry and a medical doctor's finding that Badawi could not physically endure more lashings, no further lashings have yet been carried out. However, in June 2015 and March 2017, Saudi Arabia's Supreme Court upheld the sentence of ten years in prison and one thousand lashes.[2]

On July 18, 2019, the vice president publicly asked the Saudis to release Badawi. Now, on September 10, 2019, we were asking for this as well, explaining that the Bible commands followers of Jesus to "remember those in prison as if you were together with them in prison, and those who are mistreated as if you yourselves were suffering."[3]

Seeking to be faithful to the teachings of Jesus, we explained that we felt it was our responsibility to ask for clemency for Mr. Badawi; for Badawi's sister, Samar, a women's rights activist; for other women who were arrested after advocating for the right to drive and other women's rights; and for several dual U.S.-Saudi citizens who have been imprisoned on a range of charges. We did not take a position on whether any of these individuals or other controversial detainees were guilty of violating Saudi laws. We simply asked for compassion.

"We are not here to demand anything," I said. "We recognize that you are a sovereign government and have every right to make your own decisions. But we humbly ask that you and your father, His Majesty, show mercy to these prisoners, pardon them, and release them."

We explained that we believed this was the right thing to do and that we saw no way for the Saudi government to ever convince the American people or government, or the rest of the world, of the sincerity of its reforms without releasing these and other prisoners and doing far more to protect human rights, including religious freedom.

THE QUEEN OF SHEBA AND THE KING OF ISRAEL

We also asked MBS whether he was ready to make peace with Israel.

Lenya Heitzig made the historical case.

"Your Royal Highness, thank you for the incredible honor to visit your beautiful country," she began. "Your generosity has made it possible for a humble pastor's wife from America to journey across the world to view the kingdom, and I am honored.

"This experience reminds me of my favorite woman in the Bible. We know her as the queen of Sheba. It is believed she traveled a long distance from her home on the Arabian Peninsula, with a great caravan of camels and riches, to meet with and present gifts to King Solomon, the great monarch of ancient Israel, because she had heard of his incredible wisdom and leadership.[†]

"When she arrived, she was overcome with the vastness of Solomon's kingdom. She understood that only a very wise king could build such an incredible country. In 1 Kings chapter 6, we learn that she told King Solomon, 'The report I heard in my own country about your achievements and your wisdom is true. But I did not believe these things until I came and saw with my own eyes. Indeed, not even half was told me; in wisdom and wealth you have far exceeded the report I heard. How happy your people must be! How happy your officials, who continually stand before you and hear your wisdom! Praise be to the LORD your God, who has delighted in you and placed you on the throne of Israel. Because of the LORD's eternal love for Israel, he has made you king to maintain justice and righteousness.'[4]

"This great woman of Arabia recognized that only God could enable a king to govern wisely and prosper. The Bible tells us that God puts rulers in place, and he has put you and your father in place to facilitate reform, 'for such a time as this,'"[5] Lenya said, referencing both the book of Daniel and the biblical account of Esther, another prominent woman in the Bible who had influence on a regional monarch.

"My question, then, is really a follow-up to a question Lynn asked earlier, but let me phrase it this way: What can I tell the women in the United States about your heart toward women and the future that you see for them in the kingdom?"

Lynn and I have long appreciated Lenya's heart. As the author of books and Bible studies for women, Lenya has a deep love for the Scriptures and for strengthening and empowering women to fulfill their God-given

[†] Some believe the queen of Sheba was from Ethiopia, and surely the Ethiopians claim her. But many scholars and archaeologists believe the queen was from the kingdom of Saba (also spelled Sheba or Sabea), located on the Arabian Peninsula.

potential. She had also, I thought, taken a very interesting approach to raise the prospect of a future peaceful friendship between the people of Arabia and the people of Israel by sharing the biblical story of a special friendship between an Arab queen and an Israelite king.

The following day, the crown prince sent us a beautiful framed piece of art depicting the queen of Sheba meeting King Solomon in Jerusalem. It is now hanging on the living room wall of our apartment in Jerusalem and reminds us to pray every day for Israel and the Saudis to make peace.

"BLESSED ARE THE PEACEMAKERS"

Michael Little took a different angle on the question of peace with Israel.

"Your Royal Highness, as the former president of the Christian Broadcasting Network, I want to thank you for permitting a CBN News crew to come into the kingdom to cover our visit and other news stories," he began. "I also want to ask you more about the prospect of peace between Saudi Arabia and Israel.

"As Bible-believing Christians, we care a great deal about peace. In the Old Testament, in Psalm 122:6, God commands us to 'pray for the peace of Jerusalem.' In Psalm 34:14, we are commanded to 'seek peace and pursue it.' In the New Testament, the Lord Jesus says in Matthew 5:9, 'Blessed are the peacemakers.' And the apostle Paul commands us in Romans 12:18, 'If possible, so far as it depends on you, be at peace with all people.'

"Toward this end, I wanted to pick up the fascinating conversation we had with you last year about your views regarding the prospects of peace between Saudi Arabia and Israel. We see that your team participated in the Peace to Prosperity economic conference that Jared Kushner recently held in Bahrain. We see that you recently allowed a Saudi blogger to visit and tour Israel and even to meet with Israeli prime minister Netanyahu, though we were sorry to see how disrespectfully your citizen was treated by Palestinians outside the Dome of the Rock and the Al-Aqsa Mosque. Would you give us an update on your thinking about peace with Israel? And can you envision a scenario in which you would invite the prime minister of Israel to come visit you and His Majesty the king and begin discussions on a peace treaty, or even that you would be willing to travel to Jerusalem to do the same?"

When it was my turn, I picked up on this theme.

I explained that I was writing a novel called *The Jerusalem Assassin* and said, "In it, the fictional American president wants to release his Middle East peace plan in a big speech in Jerusalem. However, the Palestinian leadership publicly rejects the plan before it is formally released, and several senior U.S. officials involved in drafting the plan are assassinated. The American president is just about to decide not to publicly release his plan when he receives a message from the Saudi crown prince that he is ready to come to Jerusalem to engage in direct peace talks, but only if the American president personally invites him. Obviously this is going to be a work of fiction, but it explores the possibility of a path toward peace between Saudi Arabia and Israel, as well as those enemies who might emerge to try to blow up such a peace deal."

I recalled that on November 20, 1977, Egyptian president Anwar Sadat made his historic visit to Israel and addressed the Israeli nation and its leaders in a speech to the Knesset in Jerusalem, all of which set into motion the Egyptian-Israeli peace accords negotiated at Camp David. I also recalled that, on October 26, 1994, Jordan's beloved King Hussein signed a peace treaty with Israeli prime minister Yitzhak Rabin.

"In both cases, Your Royal Highness, President Sadat and King Hussein chose to make peace with Israel *before* there was a full and final resolution of the conflict with the Palestinians, and both leaders did so because they believe that peace with Israel was in their own national interests. They did not make peace for public relations but because it was the right thing to do and the time was right."

I then encouraged the crown prince and his father to seriously consider making a similar bold move toward full peace with Israel. We urged the crown prince not to wait for Mahmoud Abbas, whom we have painfully and reluctantly concluded is likely never going to make peace. We also made the case that, in addition to being good for Saudi Arabia—building a stronger alliance against Iran and opening the door to Israeli technology and Jewish venture capital—normalizing relations with Israel would be seen very favorably by millions of Christians in the U.S. and many other Americans, as well.

"Before 1977, Anwar Sadat was one of the most hated men in the world by the millions of Jews and Christians in the U.S. who loved Israel," I said. "But after his visit to Jerusalem, and after he signed the Camp David Accords, there were few world leaders more beloved than Sadat. Obviously the Egyptian president did not make peace to make Americans happy. But that was one of the wonderful results. You and your father, His Majesty, need to make your own assessment, of course. But if you come to the point where you truly believe that making peace with Israel is in the supreme national interests of the kingdom, then we would encourage you to act sooner rather than later."

Thus far, the crown prince's reply remains off-the-record.

After the meeting ended, we were taken to the airport—at MBS's insistence—for a flight on one of the royal jets to the Medina region of the kingdom. We toured the ancient Nabataean city of Al-Ula, the first UNESCO World Heritage site in the kingdom, with VIP guides and Saudi historians, followed by dinner with a group of tourism experts, who discussed Saudi plans to open up the region to guests from all over the world.

The next morning, we got an early start, beginning with a visit to the house in the Old City where King Abdulaziz Al Saud (widely known as Ibn Saud), the founder of the modern Saudi kingdom, once lived. Later we met with Saud bin Saleh Al-Sarhan, secretary-general of the King Faisal Center for Research and Islamic Studies, and some of the center's senior researchers. They briefed us on peaceful relations between the prophet Muhammad and Christians and Jews during the seventh century and the significance of the recently signed Charter of Mecca.

Next, we flew on a royal jet to the northwestern province for a tour of the NEOM region, where the Saudis and others are planning to invest some $500 billion to build cities (and tourist sites) of the future. We returned to Jeddah in time for a farewell dinner before the rest of the delegation left for the airport for the long flight home.

Lynn and I had one last morning in the kingdom, meeting with senior officials at the U.S. Embassy and consulate before catching our flight to Israel.

20

SITTING WITH
SHEIKH MOHAMMAD AL-ISSA

Are the Saudi reforms real or merely cosmetic?

After the terrifying morning of September 11, 2001, I never imagined meeting a man like Sheikh Mohammad Al-Issa.

A loyal Saudi citizen who, because of 9/11, made it his life's mission to combat radical and violent extremists and advance moderate Islam.

A devout Sunni Muslim who teaches hundreds of millions of Muslims around the world to reject violence and embrace Jews and Christians as both neighbors and friends.

A Muslim cleric and a scholar who actively opposes anti-Semitism and Holocaust denial and who led the first delegation of Muslim leaders to visit the Auschwitz-Birkenau death camp in southern Poland.

Once the kingdom's justice minister, the sheikh was elected in 2016 to serve as secretary-general of the Muslim World League, the world's largest nongovernmental Muslim organization. Based in Mecca, the MWL has offices in Riyadh and Jeddah and in 139 countries. The sheikh is thus one of the most influential Sunni Muslims on the planet. In recent years, he and I have become the unlikeliest of friends.

I first met Sheikh Al-Issa at the royal palace in Riyadh when we had an audience with the crown prince in 2018. After that meeting, the sheikh spent many hours with us, discussing a wide range of issues. When we met with MBS in Jeddah in 2019, the sheikh was again in the room. We also had a working lunch with him and his colleagues, followed by a much longer meeting, where we discussed areas of mutual concern between devout Christians and Muslims.

Despite our profound theological differences, I asked Sheikh Al-Issa if he would become a founding member of the advisory board of All Arab News. He immediately said yes. Indeed, he was the first advisor to join.

Since then, he has been helping me and our team of Palestinian, Lebanese, and other journalists, editors, and web designers as we have worked hard to build a platform for a wide range of peaceful and moderate voices, be they Muslim, Christian, Jewish, or other.

In an exclusive interview published on September 1, 2020, our first day of live operations at All Arab News, Sheikh Al-Issa shared his memories of 9/11 and how it shaped his life's mission.

JOEL ROSENBERG: Given that we are about to mark the tragic anniversary of the horrific terrorist attacks of September 11, 2001, I would like to ask where you were on that day. What do you remember about that day? How did you first hear about the attacks? What were you doing when you heard? And what was your immediate reaction?

SHEIKH AL-ISSA: I was at home when the news broke of the terrorist attack on the World Trade Center. It left me, like the whole world, in a state of bewilderment.

The attack was ghastly and shocking, and I remember those around me were astonished and could not believe what they saw or heard. . . . Every year, we all relive this painful tragedy, and I think back to that day. It is a terrorist crime like no other in human history.

ROSENBERG: In the months and years that followed, how did the 9/11 attacks—and the tremendous blow they had, both on

U.S.-Saudi relations and the perception of people in the West and all over the world toward Islam—impact you personally, as a Saudi and as a Muslim? Did it change you in any way—your views, your personal mission—and if so, how?

AL-ISSA: As a human being, I felt an indescribable sense of pain and sadness for those innocent people who lost their lives on that horrible day. And as a Muslim leader, I was angered by those terrorists that purported to commit such an abominable crime in the name of Allah. True Islam does not promote hatred and violence. It does not teach intolerance and injustice. In fact, it teaches us the exact opposite. Islam instructs us to advance peace and coexistence, as well as embrace people of other faiths and beliefs.

From that day forth, I vowed to speak out against those who seek to hijack Islam to commit violence and advance hate. This is what I do every day at the Muslim World League. My objective is to advance the true, moderate values of Islam, build coexistence among all faiths and peoples, and confront the extremist rhetoric and expose its flaws, particularly as they pertain to the misinterpretation of religious ideas. The extremists avoid engaging with us, knowing too well the truth is on our side, yet they continue to deceive and spread their lies. We will not rest until we uproot their ideology.

ROSENBERG: What makes the Muslim Brotherhood theology and ideology so dangerous?

AL-ISSA: The Muslim Brotherhood poses a serious threat to the very fabric of our society because it seeks to exploit Islam by deceiving and encouraging Muslims, especially our youth, to commit egregious and deplorable acts. There is no room for the Muslim Brotherhood—or any form of political Islam—in our religion. It does not abide by the true, moderate values of Islam.

The ideology of the Muslim Brotherhood has no respect for the constitution or laws of any country, and it actually alienates

Muslims from the nations and societies they live in. And in doing so, it succeeds in sowing division and promulgating hatred. We have seen repeatedly how such a process leads to hatred, extremism, violence, and terrorism. We must do all in our power to prevent the spread of this warped ideology.

ROSENBERG: In January [2020], you led the first-ever delegation of Muslim leaders to visit the Auschwitz-Birkenau death camp in Poland, working closely with the leadership of the American Jewish Committee. Why did you decide it was time to go?

AL-ISSA: Since taking over the Muslim World League, I have made it my mission to work with my Jewish brothers and sisters to rebuild our storied relationship that dates back many centuries to the time of the prophet Muhammad (peace be upon him), all of which is vividly documented in the Charter of Medina.*

I began by acknowledging the atrocities of the Holocaust, deeming it a crime against humanity, and I called for Muslims around the world to do the same. I made a concerted effort to expand my outreach and vowed to stand shoulder to shoulder with the Jewish community in our fight against hatred.

I felt I had a sacred duty to personally bear witness to the unconscionable crimes committed against those poor souls at Auschwitz.

With attacks against worshipers of all faiths regularly happening around the world, and the risks of genocide remaining with us today, my timely visit to the Nazi death camp not only helped preserve the memories of the victims. It also demonstrated our solidarity in the face of those who seek to divide us, and our unmistakable resolve: "Never Again."

---

* Though it is not well-known among Jews and Christians today, the Charter of Medina—also known as the Constitution of Medina—was a document written by the prophet Muhammad in 622. It declares that Muslims should live in peace with the Jewish people, physically protect the Jews, and allow Jews freedom of religion. Article 2.5 reads, "To the Jew who follows us belong help and equity. He shall not be wronged nor shall his enemies be aided." Article 8.5 reads, "Everyone shall have his portion from the side to which he belongs; the Jews . . . have the same standing with the people of this document" (i.e., the Muslims).

ROSENBERG: You were in both of our meetings with the crown prince, and you know His Royal Highness very well. Why did the crown prince invite the first evangelical Christian delegation in the history of the Kingdom of Saudi Arabia to visit him? And why did he invite us to come back?

AL-ISSA: All around the world, we are faced with the constant challenge of building bridges of communication, understanding, and friendship. But at a time when threats have become more complex, from terrorist attacks to global pandemics, our partnerships are more important than ever.

This is why the kingdom welcomed [your] delegation to Saudi Arabia. And we are proud to have partners like you to help us in our efforts to spread the virtues of understanding, tolerance, empathy, and most importantly, a deep love for one another. These values are grounded in the scriptures of Islam, as much as they may be in the doctrine of your religion too.

The Qur'an teaches [us] to treat all people justly, regardless of their faith or creed. And it calls on us to renounce hatred and extremism in all its forms. Your visit to Saudi Arabia demonstrates that the Saudi authorities are committed to these principles in action, and not just words.

As you witnessed on your recent visit to the kingdom, Saudi Arabia is forging ahead with its transformation agenda, Vision 2030, and a big component of this vision is embracing a more moderate Islam. We call this true Islam. These transformations aim to return the moderate Islam that was the very basis on which the Kingdom of Saudi Arabia was founded by King Abdulaziz.

Unfortunately, after 1979, extremist groups tried to penetrate and corrupt our ideology, and they managed to manipulate some of these principles. But today, thanks to our reformist course, we see these extremist ideologies fading at a rapid pace. Today, the kingdom has built the most powerful international platforms to face extremist ideologies.

And while the Muslim World League is a nongovernmental organization, I have a responsibility as a Muslim leader and Saudi citizen to help, in any way I can, drive this change in the kingdom and around the world.

We at the Muslim World League have been leaders in this larger effort by cultivating new relationships with other faith communities. . . . And no one has been a bigger champion of this effort, with its purely humane objectives, than the king and the crown prince of Saudi Arabia. For that, they should be applauded.[1]

THE CENTRAL QUESTION

The fact that Sheikh Al-Issa is such an outspoken moderate is encouraging.

That fact that he is close to the crown prince is also encouraging, providing more clues as to where MBS is taking the kingdom.

When it comes to the crown prince himself, however, cynics and skeptics abound—and not just among his enemies. Let's be honest: The crown prince has lost some people forever. No matter what he does in the future, they will never forgive him for things he has done, things he has not done, and things they think he has done. With these people, there will be no second chances.

Others, however, believe the crown prince is doing the right things overall. They acknowledge that he has made mistakes but say he is learning from those mistakes and we ought to work closely with him.

MBS is unquestionably a conundrum. Indeed, he is a Rorschach test of sorts. Some look at him and see a dangerous enemy. Others look at him and see a flawed but important ally. Who is right? Which analysis is closer to the truth?

Over the last several years, as I have built my own relationship with MBS and his inner circle, I have also sought the views of a wide range of senior U.S. diplomatic and intelligence officials and respected Middle East analysts—both Republicans and Democrats—who have carefully studied MBS's life and career. Some have spent time with MBS and spoken with him at length. They break in both directions. But there is certainly an influential group who argue that MBS is pursuing worthy and historic reforms, that the future of Saudi Arabia depends largely on whether he succeeds, and that a good deal of the future of peace and security in the Middle East will also be significantly influenced by whether he succeeds. They further maintain that while the U.S. and other Western nations absolutely need to help MBS move away from his darker, rasher impulses—arguably the *old* way of doing business in the kingdom—we also must help him to advance his Vision 2030 plan, the *new* way, with far more vigor and discipline.

Such officials note that King Salman chose MBS to be his crown prince and has not removed him, despite his mistakes. All evidence suggests the king is directing MBS to make these bold reforms and has no interest in removing him from the line of succession. Given MBS's young age, they add, he will likely take the throne and could conceivably reign for fifty years or more. For those who hate him, that prospect seems horrifying. Yet for those who believe he can make critical course corrections, this seems heartening. And what, these advocates ask, is the alternative?

These officials readily concede that MBS is not interested in turning the kingdom into a democracy. He and his father run an absolute monarchy, and they intend to keep it that way. But they see themselves as benign rulers determined to turn Saudi Arabia into the crown jewel of moderation in the Middle East—technologically advanced, economically robust, militarily potent, and the West's most important strategic ally in the Arab world. Thus, the argument goes, MBS should not be cut loose or ostracized; rather, he should be actively engaged.

What's more, observers directly contrast MBS with Turkish president Recep Erdoğan. They note that Washington considers both men allies, even though both have used harsh, authoritarian measures. But even if one argues that both are ruthless dictators, they say MBS is trying to move himself and his country in a more positive, inclusive, and pro-Western direction. Erdoğan, on the other hand, is taking Turkey—a once-moderate and friendly Muslim country and a key Western ally—down a dark and dangerous path toward radical Islamism and increasingly allying himself with our most serious enemies, men like Vladimir Putin in Russia and Supreme Leader Ali Khamenei in Iran. Yet few in Washington, London, or Brussels advocate completely cutting off the West's relationship with Erdoğan. At the very least, it is a double standard that is difficult to explain.

The central question, then, is this: Does MBS have any chance of reestablishing trust with leaders in the U.S., with the American people, with other world leaders, and with investors, tourists, Christians, and Jews around the world?

Yes, but he has an enormous amount of work ahead of him.

RESOLVING THE KHASHOGGI CRIME

Step one in Riyadh's road to recovery, of course, must be resolving the grisly and unconscionable murder of Jamal Khashoggi.

The crown prince privately and publicly denounced the killing and said that the ultimate responsibility for making it right falls on his shoulders. He said this to me personally and in his only TV interview on the subject.

In September 2019, Norah O'Donnell of *60 Minutes* asked MBS directly, "Did you order the murder of Jamal Khashoggi?"

MBS replied, "Absolutely not. This was a heinous crime. But I take full responsibility as a leader in Saudi Arabia, especially since it was committed by individuals working for the Saudi government."[2]

The Saudis began providing financial compensation to Khashoggi's four children, in the form of homes and significant monthly payments that reportedly will ultimately amount to several million dollars.[3] The *Washington Post* cited a Saudi official who said the payments were "consistent with the country's long-standing practice of providing financial support to victims of violent crime or even natural disasters." The official also "rejected the suggestion that the Khashoggi family would be obligated to remain silent."[4]

The criminal investigation and trials of those accused of the murder and initial cover-up have been completed. Five senior Saudi officials were fired over the affair and King Salman ordered the restructuring of the intelligence services to prevent such things from happening again. Eighteen Saudi officials were arrested. Seven were released for lack of evidence. Eleven suspects were eventually put on trial.

In December 2019, charges were dismissed against three defendants, and they were released.[5]

In September 2020, a Saudi court found eight defendants guilty. Five were convicted of murder and sentenced to death. But after the Khashoggi family—who still live in Saudi Arabia—reportedly forgave the men, the death sentences were commuted. All five are now serving twenty-year prison terms. One Saudi official was sentenced to ten years in prison. Two more were sentenced to seven years each. The lawyer for the Khashoggi family told reporters that "the family welcomes the 'fair and deterrent' ruling and is satisfied by it."[6]

Khashoggi's Turkish fiancée called the trials "a complete mockery of justice."[7] Other groups and individuals have been highly critical of the trials, as well.

Though numerous accusations have been made, as of this writing, no definitive proof has been publicly reported confirming that MBS ordered or approved of Khashoggi's murder. Critics and enemies insist that a confidential CIA report definitively confirmed the crown prince's guilt, but that was not the case. The *Wall Street Journal* reported on December 1, 2018, that excerpts of the report reviewed by its correspondents stated that the CIA had "medium-to-high confidence" that MBS "personally targeted" Khashoggi to be brought back to the kingdom and "probably ordered his death."[8] Enemies of MBS emphasize the "high confidence." Allies cite the "medium confidence" and point to this line in the CIA report: "To be clear, we lack direct reporting of the crown prince issuing a kill order."[9]

Secretary of State and former CIA director Mike Pompeo told senators and reporters in December 2018 that he had read every piece of U.S. intelligence regarding the Khashoggi killing and that "there is no direct reporting connecting the crown prince to the order to murder Jamal Khashoggi."[10]

In June 2019, Agnes Callamard, the U.N. special rapporteur, issued a ninety-nine-page report on the Khashoggi murder based on her six-month investigation. She argued that "every expert consulted finds it inconceivable that an operation of this scale could be implemented without the crown prince being aware, at a minimum, that some sort of mission of a criminal nature, directed at Mr. Khashoggi, was being launched."[11] Yet Callamard also specifically stated, with regard to MBS, that "no conclusion is made as to guilt," though she urged "further investigation."[12]

On February 25, 2021, the Biden administration—at the insistence of Congress—released a declassified report on the U.S. intelligence community's conclusions in the Khashoggi murder. The report made headlines around the world, particularly because of this sentence: "We assess that Saudi Arabia's Crown Prince Muhammad bin Salman approved an operation in Istanbul, Turkey, to capture or kill Saudi journalist Jamal Khashoggi."[13]

Yet those who actually read the four-page report found no new facts. There was no smoking gun. Indeed, no proof at all was offered that MBS ordered or approved the murder, or even that he knew of it in advance. Instead, words and phrases such as "probably," "this suggests that," and "we do not know" were peppered throughout the report.

The strangest section of the report reads, "We have high confidence that the following individuals participated in, ordered, or were otherwise complicit in or responsible for the death of Jamal Khashoggi on behalf of Muhammad bin Salman. We do not know whether these individuals knew in advance that the operation would result in Khashoggi's death."[14]

The report then listed eighteen Saudi officials by name. One of the names was that of Saud al-Qahtani, an advisor to MBS who was not prosecuted.

MBS, however, was not one of the eighteen named.

What's more, the logic of the case against MBS broke down when making a careful reading of the text. The report states that U.S. intelligence officials *"do not know* whether [the eighteen] *knew in advance* that the operation would result in Khashoggi's *death."*[15]

How, then, could the U.S. intelligence community "assess" and "judge" that MBS absolutely knew in advance, much less approved of or ordered the eighteen to murder the journalist?

To be clear, it is certainly possible that the report's assessments are correct and that MBS is 100 percent guilty of ordering the murder. However, the report—published by the Office of the Director of National Intelligence—did not come close to proving the case. Rather, it was full of conjecture.

This raises troubling questions. Why publicly accuse a key American ally of murder if the case cannot be proven? If there is proof, doesn't the public need to know it? Why not present it in the report? And if there isn't definitive proof, is it not irresponsible to so strongly imply that there is?

Indeed, at least two other scenarios are possible based on the same set of facts and similar conjecture. One scenario is that perhaps officials close to MBS *assumed* they were supposed to "take care of the Khashoggi problem," thought MBS would be pleased by their actions in killing the journalist, had no idea that Turkish intelligence had bugged the Saudi consulate and would therefore catch them, setting into motion a disaster that MBS never imagined, much less ordered. The other scenario is that perhaps MBS told people close to him to "take care of the Khashoggi problem"—or some equivalent phrasing—but meant *bring him back to the kingdom for questioning*, never imagining that his subordinates would botch a rendition operation so badly, much less that they might commit murder or even premeditated murder.

I don't have a theory of my own. And it is beyond the scope of this book to provide a comprehensive examination of every detail in this sordid case. What I do know for certain is this: The killing of Jamal Khashoggi should never have happened. It was cruel and stomach turning and utterly unjustifiable. *Period.* Yes, other regimes have committed similar horrifying crimes. Yes, those regimes must also be held to account. But in this case, the Saudi government—and the Saudi government alone—was responsible for this extrajudicial killing. A group of Saudi officials set into motion a dark and deeply disturbing episode, and ultimately the Saudi king himself must make it right—and make sure it is never again repeated.

PRESSING FORWARD WITH REFORMS

The past cannot be undone, so the Saudis must move forward. And that must include advancing far more vigorous and far-reaching reforms.

Despite the global coronavirus pandemic that caused oil prices to plunge and hit the Saudis' GDP and state budget hard, the crown prince, in fact, has continued implementing one reform after another. Most media outlets have given these moves scant attention, but fairness requires that they be noted. Let's walk through the most important ones chronologically.

On February 23, 2019, MBS appointed Princess Reema bint Bandar— an entrepreneur, CEO, and women's rights champion, who is also divorced and the mother of two—as the first Saudi woman ever to serve as an ambassador. And he posted her to the United States. She is the daughter of the famed Prince Bandar, former head of Saudi intelligence and the most influential ambassador to the U.S. in the history of the kingdom (serving from 1983 to 2005). Lynn and I and our colleagues have gotten to know Princess Reema over the last several years, and we have been impressed by her commitment both to moderation and peace and to a sweeping transformation of the kingdom's economic and social policies.

In May 2019, the Charter of Makkah (Mecca) was signed by King Salman and 1,200 of the world's leading Muslim scholars—from 139 countries, representing twenty-seven sects of Islam. The signatories unanimously endorsed the principle that moderate Islam is the only legitimate form of Islam that should be taught and practiced around the globe.

This conference and document received virtually no coverage in the mainstream media in the U.S. or Europe, but it was immensely significant. Here you had the most influential Islamic experts—in the most sacred city in the Islamic world—pledging themselves once and for all to "combat terrorism and injustice"; oppose all attacks on places of worship; advance "the Islamic values of tolerance, peace, and harmonious coexistence"; protect human rights; and advance the "empowerment of women."[16]

The document stipulates that "all people, regardless of their different ethnicities, races, and nationalities, are equal under God." It also asserts that "responsible educational institutions form the social safeguard of Muslim communities [and] require effective curricula and teaching tools . . . [for] "promoting centrism and moderation, especially among youth."[17]

With the signing of the charter, King Salman declared that "Saudi Arabia has strongly condemned and fought all forms of extremism, violence, and terrorism with ideology, determination, and decisiveness, and has opposed any identification with them."[18]

In August 2019, the kingdom announced the following reforms:

- Women are entitled to equal pay for equal work under Saudi law and are protected from employment discrimination.
- Women may register as a "head of household," which means they can apply for their own identity cards and family papers, their name can appear on property documents, and they may register the births of their children, even if they are single or divorced.
- The retirement age for women is now the same as for men (sixty).
- Women may not be fired for becoming pregnant.

- Women over the age of twenty-one may obtain a passport and travel abroad without the permission of a male relative.[19]

In September 2019, the kingdom announced a new, one-year, multiple-entry visa for foreign tourists. Before COVID-19, the kingdom received around 41 million tourists annually. By 2030, Kingdom projects it will welcome 100 million tourists annually.

Among the other reforms accomplished by the end of 2019 were these:

- Two thousand prisoners had been released.
- Seventy thousand driver's licenses had been issued to women.
- Seven new driving schools designed for women opened across the country.
- Uber was operating in the kingdom and hiring women drivers.
- The minister of media was approving licenses for movie theaters.
- AMC Theatres opened its first cinema in the kingdom in thirty-five years.
- The movie theater industry is expecting to hire 160,000 employees by 2030, contributing more than $24 billion to the annual economy.[20]

Heading into 2020, the U.S. State Department reported on the investment climate in Saudi Arabia:

In December 2019, the kingdom fulfilled its long-standing objective to publicly list shares of its crown jewel—Saudi Aramco, the most profitable company in the world. The initial public offering (IPO) of 1.5 percent of Aramco's shares on the Saudi Tadawul stock market on December 11, 2019, was a cornerstone of Crown Prince Mohammed bin Salman's Vision 2030 program. The largest-ever IPO valued Aramco at $1.7 trillion, the highest market capitalization of any company, and generated $25.6 billion in proceeds, exceeding the $25 billion Alibaba raised in 2014 in the largest previous IPO in history.[21]

In February 2020, Sarah Al-Suhaimi became the first Saudi woman ever reappointed chairman of the Saudi stock exchange, having first been named to that role in 2017.

In March 2020, the kingdom released 250 foreign prisoners "for eventual repatriation" in an effort to contain the spread of COVID-19.[22]

On April 26, 2020, the kingdom announced the end of flogging as a form of criminal punishment and abolished the death penalty for individuals convicted of crimes when they were minors.

In October 2020, Amal Al-Moallimi became the second Saudi woman appointed to serve as an ambassador—this time to Norway.

In January 2021, the Saudis announced they would soon be appointing women judges.

Also that month, the *Washington Post* reported on a new study indicating that MBS was making good on his vow to reform Saudi textbooks.

> Saudi Arabia has been sharply criticized over the decades for school textbooks that preach women's subservience to men, anti-Semitism, and a general enmity toward religions other than Islam. But those textbooks have been slowly scrubbed of much of this objectionable content, with particularly significant revisions made in the fall. . . .
>
> Anti-Semitic references and calls to "fight Jews" are now far fewer, with the latest edition of a tenth-grade textbook having removed a passage quoting the prophet Muhammad as saying, "The [Day of Judgment] will not come until Muslims fight the Jews, and the Muslims will kill them [all]."[23]

Though there is certainly more to be done, this was a big deal. As David Weinberg, Washington director for international affairs at the Anti-Defamation League, told the *Post*, "Some of the most demonizing passages about Christians, about Jews, and about Shiite Muslims have in some places been removed or toned down."[24]

That same month, Saudi Arabia, the UAE, Bahrain, and Egypt announced they were moving to reconcile with Qatar, a rapprochement brokered by Jared Kushner in the waning days of the Trump administration. Though all four countries, and especially the Saudis, remain deeply concerned by the Qataris' support for radical Islamist leaders and organizations—and the extremism and anti-Western propaganda spewing out of Al Jazeera in Doha—they decided to end their boycott that began in 2017 and resume diplomatic, commercial, and travel ties in the hopes of shoring up the alliance of Gulf countries in the face of the rising threat from Tehran.[25]

In February 2021, the Saudis released three political prisoners, including two dual U.S.-Saudi citizens and a woman who had spent more than a thousand days in a Saudi jail after publicly urging Riyadh to lift the ban denying women the right to drive.

"I have some welcome news that the Saudi government has released a prominent human rights activist, Loujain al-Hathloul, from prison," said President Joe Biden. "She was a powerful advocate for women's rights and releasing her was the right thing to do."[26]

THE TICKING CLOCK

If the crown prince is truly innocent of the Khashoggi murder, then history will judge him by the scale and scope of his reforms.

He cannot stop or slow down. Rather, he needs to accelerate the pace of change. Making peace with Israel would capture the most attention and fundamentally reshape the global conversation about him. But even that would not be enough.

Transforming Saudi Arabia by 2030 is the standard MBS has set for himself. By then, the kingdom must be viewed as one of the safest, most prosperous, most tolerant, most innovative, most intriguing, and most compelling countries in the Middle East. Pro-American. Pro-Western. Anti-extremist. Not perfect, mind you, but a place you would absolutely want to visit and take your kids. A place you would absolutely have to invest in.

Can MBS do it? Only time will tell. And the clock is ticking.

SEVEN TRUTHS ABOUT THE FUTURE OF SAUDI ARABIA

Since returning from our second trip to Saudi Arabia, I have had time to analyze what I've seen and have come to seven conclusions.

First, the Kingdom of Saudi Arabia is the most important and influential country in the Arab world today.

If MBS's reform agenda fails there, the results could have a catastrophic ripple effect across the region and the world, discouraging other Arab leaders from embracing bold reform initiatives. Conversely, if the kingdom emerges as a truly moderate, modern, open, economically vibrant, diversified country, that is close to the U.S. and Israel and a bulwark against radical Islamism, many in the Arab world will be inspired to go down the same path.

Second, the future of reform in the kingdom is directly tied to MBS.

If he implodes—or is removed from power—it is difficult to imagine another Saudi reformer emerging to take his place anytime soon.

Third, MBS should be challenged when he makes mistakes— the question is how to challenge him so that he will listen.

There is a time and place for public criticism. But the U.S. should also place a high value on engaging with MBS directly, in person, behind closed doors. Publicly and privately, give him credit for what he is doing right. Call him out on his mistakes. But always suggest a pathway forward. Driving an ally into a corner is rarely productive.

Fourth, reforming Saudi Arabia is not easy—and we should not be naive about how many people in the kingdom want MBS and his reforms to fail.

This is why MBS is cracking down so hard on dissenters. Is he overdoing it? Yes. Should he be releasing more prisoners? Yes. That said, does he face real threats? He does, indeed.

MBS needs the public's buy-in so another Arab Spring does not erupt. But the most important reforms can and must be made by fiat. Seventy percent of Saudis are under the age of thirty-five. Most are not looking for democracy. They are yearning for changes that will make their daily lives better and give them more opportunity to live their dreams. Overall, they strongly support where MBS is going. The other 30 percent is the establishment—the "deep state," if you will. This is the clerical class, the government class, the business class, and the academics. Some of them want change and are cheering MBS on. But many prefer the old system, which gave them money, power, and perks. They are not reformers; they are resisters—and precisely because of them, MBS has to watch his back.

Fifth, I believe MBS wakes up every morning asking himself three critical questions:

- How do I not die or get overthrown today?
- How do I protect the kingdom today from the threats posed by Iran and other external forces?
- What do I do today to leverage our enormous oil wealth and fundamentally transform and diversify our economy before the oil runs out or becomes irrelevant due to alternative energy sources?

Sixth, MBS wants the closest possible alliance with the United States.

He knows he needs the U.S. to help him answer his three critical questions. But he is also flirting with Russia and the Chinese. If the U.S. cuts MBS loose, either Moscow or Beijing—or both—will win, and the U.S. and Western alliance will lose. That is not an outcome we should welcome.

Seventh, the key to ensuring that MBS and his team truly learn from their mistakes lies in their passion for making Vision 2030 a success.

Some say the crown prince is a gambler. If that is true, then he has put all his chips on 2030. If the plan succeeds, the country succeeds. If the country succeeds, he succeeds.

What will it take for the plan to succeed? Saudi Arabia must attract enormous flows of foreign direct investment, acquire cutting-edge foreign technologies, dramatically increase trade with the rest of the world, and welcome tens of millions of new foreign tourists each year.

None of this can happen—not on a sustained basis, anyway—if the kingdom and its leaders are perceived as being ruthless, cutthroat, backward, or repressive people. A few CEOs might be able to jet into Riyadh, sign a billion-dollar deal, and then jet back to New York, London, or Singapore. But if their board members are horrified by having anything to do with Saudi Arabia—or if the spouses and friends of those CEOs are horrified—those deals will not be locked in, much less repeated.

Thus, the only way for the Saudi reforms to succeed is for MBS and his team to focus and become more disciplined. While they cannot undo the past, they had better learn from it so they can chart a far different future. There is simply no other path forward. I believe that American and other world leaders would be wise to understand and heed these principles and engage MBS and his inner circle accordingly.

21

THE ABRAHAM ACCORDS

*Witnessing the historic signing of the first Arab-Israeli
peace deals in nearly twenty-six years*

On Thursday, August 13, 2020, at 4:56 p.m., I received an urgent text
message.

Watch the news in the next hour, came the cryptic message.

What's happening? In a meeting, I texted back.

A breakthrough in the region, came the reply.

Good or bad?

Very good.

When news breaks in the Middle East, we tend to brace ourselves for
disaster.

But when I saw the words *breakthrough* and *very good*, I knew instantly
what was about to happen. The message, after all, came from Ali Rashid
Al Nuaimi, the senior UAE official who was close to Crown Prince
Mohammed bin Zayed.

Since that time, Al Nuaimi and I had become good friends. He had
even joined the advisory board for our All Arab News site. Indeed, he was
actively involved in helping us get ready for the September 1, 2020, launch
of All Arab News and its sister website, All Israel News.

This news, however, was not going to wait for our sites to go live.

The United Arab Emirates and the State of Israel were about to make history.

A GAME-CHANGING MOMENT

As the news broke, my phone blew up.

I was inundated with text messages and calls from reporters looking for details and comment. Over the next twenty-four hours, I did a dozen interviews. That night, I spoke live from Jerusalem with Shannon Bream of Fox News.

"Now, Joel, I know, because of conversations that we've had, you have been in communications with a number of key players and people connected to this," Bream said. "Would you give us some context about what it could mean for the rest of the Middle East as this comes together?"

"Well, I think this is historic," I replied. "It's a game changer. We haven't had an Arab-Israeli peace deal in twenty-six years, almost, since the king of Jordan in 1994. This is huge. I'm talking to you from Jerusalem. This is a country that's electrified by this decision. And I will tell you that the UAE crown prince, Mohammed bin Zayed, invited me to bring a delegation of evangelical Christians to meet with him a little more than eighteen months ago. We sat in the palace in Abu Dhabi and he said directly—it was a two-hour, off-the-record conversation, but I can tell you now—he said, 'I am ready to make peace.'

"We were stunned, and we talked through what the process would be like. And I said to him, 'Look, I have no political power. I'm a novelist. I'm a political analyst. But I live in Jerusalem. I'm an Israeli-American citizen. I want to invite you to come to Jerusalem.' And he leaned forward, and he said to me, 'Joel, that day is coming sooner than you realize.'

"So this is just an extraordinary set of developments. And also, kudos to Prime Minister Netanyahu, who has decided to set aside the issue of annexation to focus on regional peace. This is a huge, huge development."[1]

More on the annexation issue in the next chapter.

WHO WOULD BE NEXT?

On September 1, All Israel News and All Arab News went live.

The timing could not have been better. The region was undergoing monumental changes, and we hit the ground running. My exclusive interview with former governor and presidential candidate Mike Huckabee on the significance of the Israel-UAE peace deal was our lead story on All Israel News. Huckabee immediately tweeted the story to his 1.6 million followers.

On All Arab News, we led with an exclusive interview with Sheikh Mohammad Al-Issa on how the events of 9/11 changed the course of his life and why moderate Islam was now reshaping the region. The Muslim World League immediately tweeted the story out to its 2.1 million followers.

The next day, I wrote an analysis for All Israel News under the headline "Who Will Be Next to Make Peace with Israel?" I identified the leading contenders as Saudi Arabia, Oman, Bahrain, Sudan, and Morocco but explained that "the tea leaves seem to be pointing to Bahrain."[2]

Why did I think so? As far back as 2009, Prince Salman bin Hamad Al Khalifa, Bahrain's crown prince, had written an op-ed for the *Washington Post* in which he called for "fresh thinking" to advance Arab-Israeli peacemaking.

"Peace will bring prosperity," the crown prince wrote. "Already, the six oil and gas nations of the Gulf Cooperation Council have grown into a powerful trillion-dollar market. Removing the ongoing threat of death and destruction would open the road to an era of enterprise, partnership, and development on an even greater scale for the region at large."[3]

In June 2019, events really began to pick up speed. Bahrain hosted a critically important meeting in its capital, Manama, where a delegation from the Trump administration unveiled the economic component of their Israeli-Palestinian peace plan.

Led by Jared Kushner, the Peace to Prosperity event included senior diplomats and financial experts from most of the Gulf countries.

Kushner laid out a plan to invest $50 billion of Gulf, U.S., and other international resources in the Palestinian economy over ten years to build factories, infrastructure, water desalinization plants, and so forth, thereby creating one million new jobs and dramatically lowering Palestinian unemployment.

Palestinian president Mahmoud Abbas rejected the entire concept out of hand; but the fact that the Bahrainis, Emiratis, Saudis, and others were involved sent an important signal.

The following month, Johnnie Moore introduced me to then-Bahraini foreign minister Khalid bin Ahmed Al Khalifa. We met at the Four Seasons Hotel in Washington and spent ninety minutes together. Joining us was Bahrain's ambassador to the U.S., Sheikh Abdulla bin Rashid Al Khalifa. They could not have been more warm or more enthusiastic about discussing the importance of making peace—and soon. I came away convinced the Bahrainis were totally ready now and looking for the right window of opportunity.

A few days later, at a State Department conference on religious freedom, the Bahraini foreign minister met for a few minutes with Israel Katz, then Israel's foreign minister. The two men snapped a picture together and tweeted it out. Most media outlets ignored it.

When I was back in Washington, D.C., in December 2019, Ambassador Al Khalifa and I decided to tour the Museum of the Bible together. It was my first time there and the ambassador's first official visit, though he had been there previously with friends. Over lunch afterward, I was encouraged that he brought up the prospect of rescheduling our delegation to Bahrain, since our previous plans had been postponed.

Also in December, Jerusalem's chief rabbi, Shlomo Amar, made history in Bahrain by attending a religious forum in Manama alongside Muslim clerics from all over the Arab world.

In January 2020, when President Trump finally and formally unveiled his peace plan—"Peace to Prosperity: A Vision to Improve the Lives of the Palestinian and Israeli People"—at the White House, with Prime Minister Netanyahu at his side, the ambassadors of Bahrain, the UAE, and Oman were all in attendance.

When I returned to Washington in July 2020, I had lunch again with Ambassador Al Khalifa. I told him I believed the UAE was considering a major move if Netanyahu could be dissuaded from applying Israeli sovereignty to large swaths of the West Bank. I encouraged Bahrain to do the same and came away confident they would.

As soon as the Emiratis made their announcement on August 13, I began reporting that more was coming.

In a tweet on August 13, I wrote, "Last month, I had lunch in Washington with my friend, Bahraini Ambassador @AbdullaRAK. At the moment,

I'm not at liberty to say more, but I am convinced that Bahrain's king and senior leadership are serious about also making peace with Israel at the proper time."

Sure enough, the Bahrain bombshell dropped on September 11, of all days.

EYEWITNESS TO HISTORY

On Saturday, September 12, I received an email from the White House:

> The president requests the pleasure of your company at the Abraham Accords Signing Ceremony to be held at the White House on Tuesday, September 15, 2020, at twelve o'clock.

I immediately accepted and flew to Washington.

On that remarkable day, Skip Heitzig and I met for a time of prayer at a nearby hotel and then headed to the White House. Skip is not only a dear friend who had traveled with several of our delegations, he was also now a member of the board of directors of Near East Media, the nonprofit organization we had established to run our new websites. From the South Lawn, he and I fed live updates of the ceremony to our team in Jerusalem for them to post along with video of interviews we conducted with major Jewish, Christian, and congressional leaders in attendance.

After welcoming Prime Minister Netanyahu and his wife, Sara; Emirati foreign minister Sheikh Abdullah bin Zayed; and Bahraini foreign minister Abdullatif bin Rashid Al Zayani, President Trump said:

> We're here this afternoon to change the course of history. After decades of division and conflict, we mark the dawn of a new Middle East. Thanks to the great courage of the leaders of these three countries, we take a major stride toward a future in which people of all faiths and backgrounds live together in peace and prosperity. . . .
>
> In Israel's entire history, there have previously been only two such agreements. Now we have achieved two in a single month, and there are more to follow. . . .

Together, these agreements will serve as the foundation for a comprehensive peace across the entire region—something which nobody thought was possible, certainly not in this day and age.[4]

The president thanked his Middle East peace team: Vice President Pence, Secretary Pompeo, National Security Advisor Robert O'Brien, Jared Kushner, U.S. special representative for Iran Brian Hook, Avi Berkowitz, and U.S. ambassador to Israel David Friedman.[*]

"This day is a pivot of history," said Prime Minister Netanyahu. "It heralds a new dawn of peace. For thousands of years, the Jewish people have prayed for peace. For decades, the Jewish State has prayed for peace. And this is why, today, we're filled with such profound gratitude."

Thanking President Trump, he added, "This is not only a peace between leaders, it's a peace between peoples. Israelis, Emiratis, and Bahrainis are already embracing one another. . . . This [was] unimaginable a few years ago."[5]

Speaking in Arabic to the entire Arab world, UAE foreign minister Sheikh Abdullah bin Zayed, who is also the crown prince's brother, said, "We are already witnessing a change in the heart of the Middle East, a change that will send hope around the world."

Addressing Prime Minister Netanyahu, he said, "Thank you for choosing peace and for halting the annexation of Palestinian territories, a decision that reinforces our shared will to achieve a better future for generations to come."

Continuing his remarks, he added, "For us in the United Arab Emirates, this accord will enable us to continue to stand by the Palestinian people and realize their hopes for an independent state within a stable and prosperous region. This accord builds upon previous peace agreements signed by Arab nations with the State of Israel. The aim of all these treaties is to work toward stability and sustainable development."[6]

Abdullatif Al Zayani, the new Bahraini foreign minister, echoed these same sentiments.

"Today is a truly historic occasion," he said, "a moment of hope and

---

[*] Another key architect of the president's Arab-Israeli peace strategy was Jason Greenblatt, who announced his return to private life on September 5, 2019.

opportunity for all the peoples of the Middle East and, in particular, for the millions in our younger generations.

"The declaration supporting peace between the Kingdom of Bahrain and the State of Israel is a historic step on the road to genuine and lasting peace, security, and prosperity across the region and for all who live there regardless of religion, sect, ethnicity, or ideology.

"For too long, the Middle East has been set back by conflict and mistrust, causing untold destruction and thwarting the potential of generations of our best and brightest young people. Now I'm convinced we have the opportunity to change that. . . .

"It is now incumbent on us to work urgently and actively to bring about the lasting peace and security our peoples deserve. A just, comprehensive, and enduring two-state solution to the Palestinian-Israeli conflict will be the foundation, bedrock of such peace.

"We have shown today that such a path is possible, even realistic. . . . We can see before us a golden opportunity for peace, security, and prosperity for our region.

"Let us together, and with our international partners, waste no time in seizing it."[7]

Sadly, during the event, Palestinian terrorists in Gaza fired rockets at southern Israel.

As I fed material back to our team in Jerusalem and live-tweeted from the South Lawn, I interviewed a range of Jewish leaders, including Malcolm Hoenlein, vice chairman of the Conference of Presidents of Major American Jewish Organizations, who has led dozens of faith diplomacy missions to meet with Arab and Muslim leaders; and the conference's CEO, William Daroff. Both were deeply moved by the moment.

Daroff told me we were witnessing "a new tide, a new path . . . of peace in the Middle East, with countries all over the Arab world, the Gulf States coming together and recognizing Israel's place to be as a legitimate member in the family of nations and as a country that they want to call a friend and partner."[8]

Pastor John Hagee, founder of Christians United for Israel—the leading pro-Israel political organization in the U.S., with some 9 million members—told me, "This is a day that people six months ago would have said, 'This could not possibly happen.' But because of the efforts of our president and Benjamin Netanyahu, the sons of Abraham are coming together for the first time in thousands of years. This is nothing short of a literal miracle, and if they don't give the president the Nobel Peace Prize for this, they should stop giving it away. . . . It is [also] a day that puts Iran on the defensive, because Israel just shuffled the deck and they've got the trump cards now."[9]

INTERVIEWING VICE PRESIDENT PENCE

Jewish people have a Hebrew expression we use on Passover.

"*Dayenu.*"

It means "this alone would be enough."

That's the word that kept echoing in my heart that day. Just knowing that the Lord had dramatically answered the prayers of millions around the world for peace would have been a *dayenu*. Getting invited to the White House to witness not just one but two Gulf Arab states sign peace treaties with Israel would have been a double *dayenu*. But I had also been invited to meet with and interview my old friend Vice President Mike Pence immediately following the ceremony to discuss the historic moment and his reaction to it.

Better yet, I was joined by two Christian journalist friends: David Brody, chief Washington correspondent and political analyst for CBN News; and Erick Stakelbeck, a Middle East reporter and host of a program on the TBN network.

We were scheduled to meet with the vice president in his ceremonial office, but first we had to undergo a COVID-19 test. It was the first time for me. Both of my nostrils were swabbed three times by a member of the White House Medical Unit. Then the swab was inserted into a high-speed medical analyzer. Only when it was confirmed that none of us had the virus did the VP enter the room, coming directly from a private luncheon with the president, the prime minister, and the two foreign ministers.

Pence told us that the signing ceremony for the peace treaties and the Abraham Accords was "deeply moving" to him, both as a national leader and as an evangelical Christian. He called Israel "our most cherished ally" and said the president had decided from the very beginning of his administration that he was going to do everything he could to strengthen the U.S.-Israel alliance and try to advance peace.

Pence acknowledged there were a host of critics who had been saying that the administration had no idea how to make peace and might worsen the situation in the Middle East. But the Abraham Accords were hard evidence, he said, that dramatic progress was being made. Moreover, he told us, "There are more Arab nations that are preparing to make peace with Israel."

The vice president noted the strong bipartisan support for Israel in the U.S. over the past seven decades. He specifically noted that it was a Democrat, President Harry Truman, who recognized the State of Israel just minutes after David Ben Gurion declared independence on May 14, 1948. Pence said that President Trump was continuing that bipartisan tradition of strengthening Israel and securing peace.[10]

THROWING OUT THE OLD PLAYBOOK

I asked the vice president why Trump was succeeding where his recent predecessors had failed at peacemaking in the region.

Pence told me the reason was that Trump had chosen to throw out the old playbook.

"The president made a decision from the moment he came into office that he wasn't going to do things the same old way," Pence said. "He wasn't going to keep rewarding Palestinian refusals to negotiate. He wasn't going to keep giving them financial support for that."

After trying to build trust with Palestinian Authority president Mahmoud Abbas but being repeatedly rebuffed on a range of important matters, Trump moved the U.S. Embassy to Jerusalem. He cut U.S. aid to the PA. He recognized Israeli sovereignty over the Golan Heights. And he laid out a vision for peace that called for the creation of a Palestinian state—with even more land than it currently controls—so long as the PA implemented a wide range of serious internal reforms and the state was demilitarized and could not endanger Israel.

Pence noted that Trump's first trip overseas was to Saudi Arabia, where he met with the leaders of fifty Arab and Muslim countries, after which he went to Jerusalem to meet with the leadership there. These moves made it clear, Pence said, that advancing Middle East peace was a top priority for the administration right from the beginning.

"I call Israel our most cherished ally, and I believe that, literally from the founding of this nation, the desire to see the Jewish people restored to their historic homeland was sown into the hearts of the American people," Pence told us.

"They prayed for that day to come, labored for that day to come, and in 1948 it came. And from this White House, it would be President Harry Truman who made the United States the first nation on earth to recognize the Jewish state of Israel.†

"But I have to tell you, as a strong supporter of Israel, I couldn't be more proud of the leadership President Donald Trump has provided that has brought us to this day. I mean, first he made it clear that if the world understands nothing else, they need to understand this: America stands with Israel. . . .

"We've reaffirmed our strong commitment to Israel, as perhaps no other administration in my lifetime. But at the same time, President Trump made his very first trip overseas to go to a capital of the Arab world. He brought together more than fifty [Arab and Muslim] nations to form a new alliance to counter radical Islamic terrorism. And we began to forge relationships within the Arab world."

Pence explained that Trump's decision to isolate and pressure the Iranian regime—rather than trying to placate Tehran as Obama had done—had been a key to rebuilding trust with Arab leaders.

"President Trump demonstrated that as we stand strongly with Israel, but also stand for peace, then we can see history unfold," he said. "What happened today . . . is the beginning of a new era of peace for Israel and for the wider Arab world. And it's very humbling for me to be some small part of it."[11]

"DEEPLY MOVING"

That night, I was interviewed on Fox News.

"Joel, this is an area where you have lived and worked for years and years," anchor Shannon Bream began. "What does it mean today to see

---

† "Truman granted de facto recognition eleven minutes after the proclamation of independence." De jure recognition was extended on January 31, 1949, once "a permanent government was elected in Israel" (jewishvirtuallibrary .org/international-recognition-of-israel).

this come together, as critics say, 'Listen, these entities—Bahrain and the UAE—were not at war with Israel. They already had some trade and commerce'? They're downplaying this and saying the president shouldn't get credit. What do you say?"

"Oh, goodness, well, if you can't get credit for making the first Arab-Israeli peace deals—and two of them, I might add—in twenty-five years, I don't know what you get credit for," I told her.

"Look, for me, it was an emotional moment. . . . To sit there, on the lawn—as a novelist, as a Middle East analyst, starting this new website, All Israel News, but also having two sons that have served in the Israeli army—I want this peace. And to see two Arab leaders and the prime minister of Israel and the president of the United States making these deals, it was deeply moving to me personally."[12]

NOBEL PRIZE OR NO BIG DEAL?

The titanic battle to define the significance
of the Abraham Accords

It never let up throughout the four years of the Trump presidency.

Ridicule. Dismissal. Mockery. Outrage.

Almost no one in the peace industry in Washington, and very few in the media, believed that a businessman and his team of geopolitical "novices" could broker a single Arab-Israeli peace deal, much less several. Before we consider the lasting significance of the Abraham Accords, then, it is worth taking a moment to understand the partisan political context in which they were achieved—and how they almost never came to be.

"NO, NO, NO, AND NO"

Even before Trump took office, the reigning experts insisted he was living in fantasyland.

No one made the case more clearly than John Kerry, who served as secretary of state during the Obama administration.

Less than a month after the 2016 election, Kerry spoke at a conference at the Brookings Institution and made two things clear: Trump was never going to get a single Arab country to make peace with Israel ahead of the Palestinians, and he was a fool for trying.

"I have talked to Bibi Netanyahu more than 375 times in this term," Kerry told the audience. "That's only the public recording, because I was in the habit of picking up the phone and calling him at home or calling him here and there. . . . I've talked to him in those public transactions more than 130 hours. My wife accused me of having talked to him more than I've talked to her in these four years. . . .

"So the question for all of us is not the road we've traveled for the last one hundred years. The question is, 'What are the next one hundred years going to look like—where are we going?' And let me tell you a few things that I've learned for sure in the last few years. There will be no separate peace between Israel and the Arab world. I want to make that very clear to all of you. I've heard several prominent politicians in Israel sometimes saying, well, the Arab world is in a different place now, we just have to reach out to them, and we can work some things with the Arab world, and [then] we'll deal with the Palestinians. No, no, no, and no."[1]

"ABSURD" OR "DANGEROUS"?

Trump's approach to the Middle East peace process was routinely denigrated.

Yet the critics could not get their stories straight. Were "the most inexperienced president in American history"[2] and his team simply wasting everyone's time on an absurd errand? Or was he going to make things much, much worse?

Iran's Ayatollah Khamenei called Trump's approach to the region "foolish" and "stupid," and his plan so "satanic," it would "never bear fruit."[3]

Of all the peace plans ever proposed, a New York Times editorial quipped, "the one President Trump announced [is] the hardest to take seriously."[4]

"The Trump administration's new Mideast 'peace' plan is absurd," declared the Washington Post.[5]

On the other hand, Senator Bernie Sanders said Trump's approach to the Middle East "will only perpetuate the conflict."[6]

Aaron David Miller, a former State Department official, published an op-ed for the Jewish Telegraphic Agency, headlined, "I'm a Veteran Middle East Peace Negotiator. Trump's Plan Is the Most Dangerous I've Ever Seen."[7]

Then-candidate Joe Biden called Trump's approach "a political stunt" that could "set back peace even more," and added, "I've spent a lifetime working to advance the security and survival of a Jewish and democratic Israel. This is not the way."[8]

THE "GEORGE COSTANZA DOCTRINE"

The Trump team began by carefully analyzing past American peace plans and strategies.

Senior White House officials told me that, at the beginning of the previous administration, Barack Obama had been advised by Malcolm Hoenlein of the Conference of Presidents of Major Jewish Organization that "peace progress was likelier when there was 'no daylight' between Israel and the United States." Obama had rejected that advice, telling Hoenlein that, during the eight years of the Bush administration, "there was no daylight and no progress."[9] Obama felt he needed to show the Arab world he was willing to get tough on Israel to make peace—yet that strategy had proved disastrous.

What's more, multiple senior officials in the Trump administration told me that while they wanted to create the most detailed and realistic plan to make peace between the Palestinians and the Israelis, they came to the conclusion that the Palestinian leadership simply had no interest in a final deal. Thus, they eventually made a significant pivot. If the ultimate goal of their Peace to Prosperity plan was to get the Palestinians to say yes, then it really would be "dead on arrival." But if one of their goals was to expose Mahmoud Abbas and his inner circle as perennial rejectionists of all peace proposals, then their plan could pave the way to a normalization deal with at least one, and possibly several, Arab states.

In the end, Trump and his team pursued what has been called the George Costanza Doctrine. In the fifth season of the hit TV series *Seinfeld*, Jerry advises George: "If every instinct you have is wrong, then the opposite would have to be right."[10] Taking the thought to heart, George begins doing the exact opposite of his natural instincts, and his life takes a sudden and dramatic turn for the better.

Similarly, Trump and his Middle East strategy team decided to do the opposite of whatever Obama had done in the region. Rather than accepting the conventional wisdom of the "peace industry" in Washington, they would chart a different path.

This is what Pence meant when he told me that Trump threw out the old playbook.[11] This is what Secretary Pompeo meant when he told me that Trump chose to "flip the switch" and take an entirely new direction in the Mideast from Obama.[12]

This is also what White House peace negotiator Jason Greenblatt meant when he told me Trump wanted his team to be "willing to think outside the box" and be able to persuade other leaders in the region to do the same.

"I don't think we could have jumped from nothing to the Abraham Accords," Greenblatt told me. "I think that putting out an [Israeli-Palestinian peace] plan that we deemed realistic and implementable—despite the criticism from many—was an essential step. . . . These were essential building blocks. . . . I think we were earning a level of trust [with Gulf Arab leaders] by trying in good faith to reach a peace deal with the Palestinians." In fact, he added, "the Palestinians' rejection of the [Trump] plan was one of the biggest things that [led to] the Abraham Accords" because it finally "removed the veto card" from the Palestinian leadership and cleared the way for Arab countries to make their own decisions with regards to Israel.[13]

In the end, the Trump approach worked.

AMERICAN MEDIA REACTION: IGNORE AND DISMISS

The signing of the Abraham Accords was, therefore, huge news in the Middle East.

Not so much in the U.S.

A few prominent observers saw the magnitude of the moment. Most notable was *New York Times* columnist Thomas Friedman, who openly said, "I pray each night that Trump is defeated in November," yet he heralded the accords as a major breakthrough.

"The Trump-Kushner peace plan may be the most consequential peace plan ever put on the table," Friedman wrote in the *Times* on September 15. "They are guilty of a thousand sins—but this deal isn't one of them."[14]

That said, few other American reporters or networks seemed to care. Most of those who covered the story downplayed its significance.

The day after the signing, for example, White House press secretary Kayleigh McEnany did not receive a single question on the Abraham Accords.[15]

A columnist for the *Washington Post* said it was "a big step—in the wrong direction."[16]

Even Meghan McCain—cohost of *The View* and a sharp critic of President Trump—called out the media for downplaying what she called "a really big day" and "an amazing step forward for peace in the Middle East."[17]

ISLAMIST MEDIA REACTION: ATTACK AND THREATEN

Iranian, Turkish, Palestinian, and Qatari leaders and media outlets were furious.

Tehran bitterly denounced the deal, calling the UAE "a traitor to the Islamic ummah [religious community] and to Palestine," threatening the leaders of the UAE and Bahrain and any Muslim leader who made peace with Israel, calling Bahrain "a province belonging to the Iranian people," and vowing once again to destroy Israel.[18]

A senior advisor to Ayatollah Khamenei vowed that "the stupidity of Trump, Netanyahu, and Pompeo ignited this fire [and now] the infidels will burn in its flames and the world will be rid of the Arrogance [i.e., the U.S.] and the Zionists."[19]

Turkish president Recep Erdoğan blasted the Trump plan for Arab-Israeli peace as "a document of surrender" and the decision by the Gulf states to normalize relations with Israel "not a step that can be stomached."[20] The Turkish foreign ministry also said, "History and the conscience of the region's peoples will not forget and never forgive this hypocritical behavior."[21]

Hypocritical behavior?

For all his bluster, Erdoğan has already normalized relations with Israel. Turkey has robust bilateral trade with the Jewish State. Indeed, Turkey has become Israel's sixth-largest trade partner under Erdoğan's rule.[22]

Palestinian leaders angrily decried the moves by the UAE and Bahrain as a "betrayal" and a "stab in the back" and a "complete sellout," claiming "we were blindsided" by the decisions of the Gulf States to normalize.[23]

The Qatari media, led by Al Jazeera, blasted the deal as "appeasement" of the enemy, Israel.[24] They also dismissed Trump's desire to advance Arab-Israeli peace as a "farce" driven by "blatant lies" and "offensive deceit" that would lead to "disastrous consequences."[25]

THEN CAME SUDAN

On October 22, 2020, our All Arab News site broke the story: Sudan was going to make peace with Israel and join the Abraham Accords.[26]

On October 23, President Trump made the official announcement.

This was no small development. Sudan, after all, was the country which had hosted the Arab League Summit in 1967 that issued the famous Three Nos declaration: no peace with Israel, no recognition of Israel, no negotiations with Israel. Sudan was once home to Osama bin Laden and al Qaeda. It had been an ally of Iran, close to Moscow, led by radical Islamists, and engaged in genocide until its government was dramatically replaced in August 2019 and its radical president, Omar al-Bashir, put in prison. Sudan was now suddenly declaring Three Yeses: yes to negotiations with Israel, yes to recognizing Israel, and yes to making peace with Israel. It was also paying $335 million to compensate American victims of Sudanese terrorist attacks and their families.[27] And the U.S. was removing Sudan from its list of terrorist nations.

On December 10 came more dramatic news. President Trump announced that the Kingdom of Morocco was ready to normalize relations with Israel. I got the heads-up from our All Israel News staff while I was in Dubai and had the joy of reporting the story on social media while dining with friends from Morocco at a restaurant at the top of the Burj Khalifa, the tallest building in the world.[28]

Four Arab-Israeli peace deals in three months.

All without the Palestinians ever accepting—much less offering—a comprehensive peace deal of their own.

Shortly before leaving office, Trump received not just one but three separate nominations for the 2021 Nobel Peace Prize. Members of Trump's negotiating team—Jared Kushner, Ambassador David Friedman, and Avi Berkowitz—were also nominated. Separately, Prime Minister Netanyahu and UAE crown prince Mohammed bin Zayed were also nominated, as was Ron Dermer, Israel's ambassador to the U.S. for seven years and Netanyahu's closest foreign policy advisor. Yet relentless attacks against all of these leaders intensified. Indeed, a titanic battle had been joined over the long-term significance of what these men had accomplished.

HOW ANNEXATION ALMOST KILLED NORMALIZATION

Were the Abraham Accords worthy of a Nobel Prize or no big deal?

They were certainly not inevitable. And what few people know is that all three peace deals were nearly scuttled.

Almost immediately after Trump unveiled his Peace to Prosperity plan in January 2020, Netanyahu began talking publicly about applying Israeli sovereignty to 30 percent of the West Bank. In the Trump plan, Israel would receive this territory in the heartland of Judea and Samaria, much of which includes places of deep significance in Jewish and biblical history. The Palestinians, however, would be compensated. In addition to the remaining 70 percent of the West Bank and all of Gaza, Trump was offering to give them enormous tracts of territory in southern Israel that would end up creating a demilitarized Palestinian state significantly larger than the current footprint of the Palestinian Authority.

As written, the Trump plan gave the Palestinians up to four years to make a series of internal reforms, negotiate with Israel, conclude a final agreement, and then receive their own sovereign state. Only then would Israel receive the 30 percent of Judea and Samaria. Netanyahu, however, believed he had been given the green light by the White House to incorporate the land, beginning on July 1.

The Palestinians were furious. But so were the Emiratis, the Bahrainis, the Egyptians, and especially the Jordanians, not to mention the rest of the Arab world.

AN EVANGELICAL PERSPECTIVE

Critics said Trump and Netanyahu were doing this to please evangelical Christians.

As that charge gained traction in the spring of 2020, I felt the need to counter it. We had not yet launched All Israel News or All Arab News, so in early June, I began writing columns for the *Jerusalem Post* and other publications; giving interviews to U.S., Israeli, and Arab journalists; and briefing senior U.S. and Israeli officials.[29]

This was my case:

First, would most evangelicals like to see Israel peacefully incorporate more of the biblical heartland of Judea and Samaria into the current, modern, sovereign State of Israel, so long as it did not infringe on the ability of Palestinians to live in safety and security and be able to build a more prosperous future for themselves? Absolutely.

Second, do evangelicals want to see an explosion of tension, or even new violence, with Palestinians that could be sparked by Israeli annexation? Absolutely not.

Third, do evangelicals want to see Jordan withdraw its ambassador and suspend its peace treaty with Israel, or see the Hashemite monarchy rocked by riots and violence as the result of such an Israeli move? By no means.

Fourth, do evangelicals want to see Israel hit with international condemnation, boycotts, and sanctions that could result from annexation? No.

Fifth, if Israel were to forgo any immediate annexation and focus on securing a historic new peace treaty with an Arab state such as the United Arab Emirates, Bahrain, Oman, Saudi Arabia, Morocco, and others—and do so with the active diplomatic assistance of the Trump administration— might evangelicals prefer this to all the troubles and complications that annexation could bring? I believe they would.

Evangelicals, I argued, wanted Israel to be safer, stronger, and more peaceful, not necessarily bigger. Yes, most evangelicals believe that Bible prophecy indicates that one day Israel will have all the land that was promised to Abraham, Isaac, and Jacob, which is far more territory than Israel has today. However, nowhere in Scripture, certainly not in the New Testament, are individual believers commanded to focus on expanding Israel's territory. Rather, the emphasis time and again is on praying for and working for peace.

Sixth, would evangelicals turn out to vote for President Trump in larger numbers if he gave Israel the green light to annex large swaths of Judea and Samaria? I did not believe so. Most evangelicals already believed that Trump was the most pro-Israel president in American history.

Indeed, most evangelicals in the U.S. had not even heard of the annexation debate that summer. Over the months that the debate had been raging in the Middle East, I had not received a single email, text, or phone call from an American evangelical about it. Why? Because they were, understandably, concentrating on far more pressing domestic matters—including COVID-19, lockdowns, massive unemployment, how to reboot the economy, when to reopen their churches, and how to deal with the fallout of the George Floyd murder and reestablish safety in American cities beset by riots and looting.

WHAT THE POLLS WERE TELLING US

Beyond my personal analysis, I marshaled some number to press my case.

In March, just before the release of my latest political thriller *The Jerusalem Assassin*—about an American president hosting a peace summit in Jerusalem between Israel and Saudi Arabia—I commissioned a national survey of one thousand likely American voters to better understand how Americans viewed the Middle East peace process. The firm I used was McLaughlin & Associates, whose founder, John McLaughlin, conducted polling for both Trump and Netanyahu.

We found that 49 percent of Americans approved of President Trump's "Deal of the Century" and the administration's ongoing efforts to help the Israelis and Palestinians make peace. Only 27 percent disapproved, while 24 percent said they didn't know enough about the president's plan to answer. However, among evangelical Christians, the numbers were significantly higher. Fully 65 percent said they approved of the Trump peace plan. Only 15 percent disapproved. The rest were not sure.

In March, I had not asked about annexation. It hadn't seemed an imminent issue. (How quickly things had changed.) I had, however, asked two other questions relevant to this discussion.

If Palestinian leaders are not ready or willing to make peace with Israel, what should Gulf Arab states like Saudi Arabia, the United Arab Emirates, Bahrain, and Oman do?

Only 18 percent of Americans—and 17 percent of evangelicals—said "the Gulf Arab states should continue to stand in solidarity with the Palestinian leadership and refuse to negotiate and sign their own separate peace treaties with Israel."

By contrast, 45 percent of Americans—and 55 percent of evangelicals—said "the Gulf Arab states should no longer wait for the Palestinian leadership but should instead move forward immediately with negotiating and signing their own separate peace treaties with Israel."

In 1979, Egypt signed a peace treaty with Israel. In 1994, Jordan signed a peace treaty with Israel. Yet these were more than twenty-five years ago. If another Arab Muslim leader were to genuinely make peace with Israel soon— even visiting Jerusalem and speaking honestly and warmly to the Israel people and their parliament—would that change your view of that Arab leader and his nation?

The results were intriguing.

Some 51 percent of Americans—and 53 percent of evangelicals—said they would view such an Arab Muslim leader more positively.[30]

CRITICAL DECISION POINTS

There were three men whose courage and counterintuitive leadership fundamentally turned the tide of history: Sheikh Mohammed bin Zayed, President Trump, and Prime Minister Netanyahu.

Based on extensive and detailed conversations with senior players in all three countries, it became clear that MBZ made the first set of critical strategic decisions. The time had finally come, he believed, to normalize relations with Israel because this was in the Emiratis' supreme national interests.

First, solidarity among the UAE, Israel, and the U.S. against the threats from Iran were vital to the security of each nation and the region.

Second, Emirati investments and Israeli technology would be a match made in heaven, unleashing enormous creative potential and untold prosperity in both countries.

Third, by being the first to make peace with Israel, the UAE would reap tremendous goodwill from the American people, from Congress, and from both major American political parties. If Trump won reelection, the UAE would be well positioned for good relations during his second term. If Biden won, the UAE would be positioned to interact with the new administration as a significantly enhanced asset and perceived as an increasingly helpful and constructive ally to Washington, whose voice would be even more respected and valued.

Fourth, the UAE would dramatically reinforce a global image it was carefully and consciously crafting: one of the "good guys"—a faithful, trustworthy ally against the forces of radical Islamism; an economic, cultural, and security partner that other peaceful, productive nations could appreciate and depend on.

What's more, MBZ believed that by breaking the mold and making peace with Israel without giving the Palestinian leadership a veto over his freedom of movement, he could open the door for other Arab countries to see the benefits of normalization and follow suit. Bahrain, he knew, was ready; but it was too small a country to take the lead. However, if MBZ made peace with the Israelis, the Bahrainis would almost certainly follow. In time, so would others in the Gulf Cooperation Council and the Arab League.

As more Arab states normalized relations with Israel, MBZ and his team believed it could create the conditions under which the Palestinians could finally say yes to a comprehensive peace plan of their own with Israel. In the meantime, the UAE—together with Egypt and Jordan— would have far more influence and leverage to urge Israel's government to refrain from making provocative moves against the Palestinians and, thus, keep the two-state solution viable.

MBZ'S STRATEGIES

MBZ could see, however, that Netanyahu was being severely tempted to acquire more of the biblical territory that every member of his Likud political party considered precious.

If that happened, MBZ believed the door for the UAE to normalize relations with Israel would slam shut.

At the same time, MBZ knew that Netanyahu had another dream. For more than a decade, the Israeli leader had been passionately making the case that the only way to make peace with the Palestinians was to take an "outside-in" approach. That is, if Israel could make peace with several Arab states first, this would create enormous prosperity, and Arab-Israeli tourism, and foster a climate that might finally persuade the Palestinian people and their leaders that it was time to end the conflict once and for all.

Both were "legacy options." If Netanyahu could significantly enlarge the boundaries of the sovereign State of Israel without a new war, this would be something for which he would be remembered by the Israeli people forever. On the other hand, if Netanyahu could sign the first peace treaty with a Gulf Arab state—and maybe several treaties—this would be a huge breakthrough and would also seal his historic legacy in Israeli eyes.

The only way to stop Netanyahu from grabbing what the Emiratis saw as Palestinian land was to go full *Godfather* and make Bibi an offer he couldn't refuse.

The question was *how?*

In December 2019, the White House had asked the UAE and several other Arab countries to consider signing a nonaggression and nonbelligerency pact with Israel. Not a full treaty but a stepping-stone. MBZ was open to the idea, but he now realized it would not be enough to pull Netanyahu away from his desire to annex large swaths of the West Bank. The only way to get what he wanted, MBZ recognized, was to give Netanyahu what he wanted most—full peace, full recognition, full normalization. But MBZ would have to move fast.

He quickly crafted two strategies.

First, he would take his proposal directly to Trump and get Trump to sell it to Netanyahu. There would be no haggling with Bibi in the souk—the traditional Arab bazaar—over this line item or that. All the negotiations would be done through the White House, not with Israel directly. After all, the White House was looking for a big breakthrough. So let them do the heavy lifting. They knew Netanyahu best. They had his trust. They had all the leverage. If it was possible to persuade Netanyahu to abandon annexation and instead embrace his dream of making peace with the Arabs "outside in," Trump and his team were the only ones who could get it done.

MBZ was ready. But was Bibi?

Second, MBZ would take his case directly to the Israeli people. He dispatched Yousef Al Otaiba to write the UAE's first op-ed for an Israeli newspaper, making the case in a friendly but firm manner (and in Hebrew) that this was not a pipe dream: The UAE was really ready to make peace with Israel—a real peace, a warm peace—and the deal could be sealed immediately, so long as Israel set aside all talk of annexation.

Trump loved the idea. So did Kushner, Pompeo, and the rest of the team. The seeds they had been planting, watering, cultivating for nearly four years were finally bearing fruit. Their work was paying off, and ahead of the elections.

They immediately brought the deal to Netanyahu and Ron Dermer, Israel's ambassador in Washington. This was it, they told the Israelis. This was real, and it was now or never. Applying Israeli sovereignty over more of Judea and Samaria would come in due time. But front-loading annexation would be a serious strategic mistake. It would enrage the Arab world. It would enrage the Europeans. It could spark a Third Intifada, a violent uprising in the West Bank. But make peace with MBZ and Americans will cheer, and the world will cheer, and hopefully other Arab countries will come on board too.

To his credit, Bibi had the courage to say yes.

The world did not see it coming. Indeed, it almost did not happen. But by the grace of God, the prayers of millions, and the leadership of three men and their closest advisors, it came to pass. For me, each absolutely deserved the Nobel Peace Prize. They made historic decisions that will be remembered and cherished forever, and they opened extraordinary new opportunities for real peace and immense prosperity.

NOW WHAT?

What I saw among Gulf Arab leaders in the months following the signing of the Abraham Accords was tremendous optimism for the future.

"The Abraham Accords have the potential to change the region strategically with goals of peace, prosperity, and stability," Anwar Gargash, the UAE's minister of state for foreign affairs told me at his home in Dubai. "We're very excited. It really represents the seed for us to work for a new region, for a new Middle East. Hopefully, together we will be successful."[31]

In December 2020 alone, 40,000 Israelis traveled to the UAE, intrigued with their new peace partner and looking for new tourism and trade options.[32] Gargash expects trade between the two countries to surge to $5 billion in the next few years. Yet the UAE wants more than a "transactional" relationship with Israel, he said.

The success of the Abraham Accords will be "a 360-degree success, one that goes beyond trade and investment," Gargash told me. It will improve religious tolerance between Jews, Muslims, and Christians. It will create warm people-to-people interactions. It will convince Muslims that Israel has a rightful place in the Middle East. And "it will help reignite the peace process and will [help] Israelis and Palestinians address the issues and arrive also at an equitable, just, and acceptable peace to both. If we can achieve all that, it would be great."

In the fall of 2020, my friend Sheikh Abdulla bin Rashid Al Khalifa, Bahrain's ambassador to the U.S., hosted me and a small group of evangelical leaders for lunch at his home in northern Virginia to brief us on how his country's leaders came to their decision to make peace.

He said they want to rapidly codify the "fullest and warmest peace with Israel"—not just an exchange of ambassadors and embassies but robust trade, tourism, investment, sports, and cultural exchanges. In fact, he told us that Bahrain does not even think of this as "normalization." They prefer the term *formalization* since they have been working steadily, if quietly, for years to make peace with Israel.[33]

In December, at the ambassador's invitation, I traveled to the Kingdom of Bahrain for the first time, meeting with senior officials, touring the capital of Manama, and experiencing for myself the palpable sense of excitement over the Abraham Accords. One of the most special moments was when Sheikh Khalid bin Ahmed Al Khalifa, diplomatic advisor to the king (and former foreign minister), invited me to his home for lunch on National Day, the celebration of Bahrain's independence from the British in 1971.

It was crystal clear that Sheikh Khalid was immensely proud of King Hamad's decision to join the Abraham Accords and to announce it on September 11, of all days.

"Notice that we did not *declare peace* with Israel," he told me. "We declared *support of peace*—because we never had a war with Israel. We never had . . . belligerence or animosity. So peace was there between us, but it was a quiet one. So now we support it [openly]. We are not sending our armies back to camp. We're not turning our rockets around."[34]

Bahrain, he said, wants "a warm peace," not a cold one. "Cold peace does not work," he said. That's why the king is working at "a fast pace" to create a robust and dynamic relationship with Israel.

"Jews have been here for millennia," he insisted. "And [Israel] is *their* land. They have been living in those towns and cities as their own since before our religion. They belong here. Who says they don't? They belong here and . . . the people of Israel should now have a good feeling about the future in the region."

Will more Arab countries normalize—or formalize—relations with Israel in the years ahead? I am praying the answer is yes, and the country

I am watching most closely is the Kingdom of Saudi Arabia. That's what made the events of November 23, 2020, so interesting.

"All Israel News can now confirm that Israeli prime minister Benjamin Netanyahu and Mossad chief Yossi Cohen secretly flew to the north-western province of Saudi Arabia on Sunday and met with Saudi Crown Prince Mohammed bin Salman and U.S. Secretary of State Mike Pompeo," I reported. "The prime minister made the clandestine trip and met with senior American and Saudi officials in a region known as NEOM."[35]

We were the first to confirm the rumors through multiple senior diplomatic sources.

Though such a meeting between an Israeli prime minister and a Saudi crown prince—brokered by an American secretary of state—was a big story, I found it not surprising, but inevitable. After all, Americans overwhelmingly want Saudi Arabia to be the next country to make peace with Israel. What's more, they want the American president to make it happen. And it's not just Republicans. The vast majority of Democrats say a Saudi-Israeli peace deal is important to them and should be a top foreign policy priority for the White House. Given the intense partisan rancor over the future of U.S.-Saudi relations in the past several years, that was the surprising finding of an exclusive poll I commissioned in November 2020 (before the Morocco deal was announced).

Using the McLaughlin & Associates polling firm, we asked one thousand Americans to evaluate the following statement: *"Now that the U.S. has helped the United Arab Emirates, the Kingdom of Bahrain, and the Republic of Sudan sign full peace treaties and normalization agreements with the State of Israel, I believe that the Kingdom of Saudi Arabia should be the next Arab country to make peace with Israel. The next president, whoever it is, should make brokering an Israeli-Saudi peace treaty one of his top foreign policy priorities."*

Nearly eight-in-ten Americans (78.4 percent) said they agreed, 21.2 percent disagreed, and only 0.5 percent said they did not know. Interestingly, 84.6 percent of Trump voters agreed with the statement. Yet 72.5 percent of Biden voters also said they wanted to see an Israeli-Saudi peace deal and wanted the next president to give it a big push.[36]

Part Three

THE FUTURE

23

WHAT IS THE FUTURE OF FAITH IN THE MIDDLE EAST?

My remarks at the State Department's conference on religious freedom

We have examined the serious threats in the Middle East two decades after 9/11.

We have also considered the steadily changing attitudes and extraordinary opportunities that are emerging in the Arab Muslim world.

In this final section, let us consider what the future may hold for religious freedom, security, prosperity, and peace in the Middle East—and why this should matter to you and me.

In this chapter, I would like to share some of my observations about the challenges facing Christians, Jews, Muslims, and other people of faith in the region. It will by no means be comprehensive. Consider it, instead, both a call to prayer and a call to action to advance religious freedom throughout the region.

THE WORLD'S LARGEST RELIGIOUS FREEDOM CONFERENCE

I first met Sam Brownback in December 1994.

The conservative Republican with an evangelical Christian faith, who also loves and has embraced the traditions of the Roman Catholic Church, had just been elected to Congress from Kansas's Second District. Two years later, he was elected to the United States Senate.

An outspoken champion of religious liberty, he became a strong supporter of the International Religious Freedom Act of 1998, which was passed overwhelmingly in the House, by a vote of 375-41, and unanimously in the Senate, and was then signed into law by President Bill Clinton. The two central provisions of the legislation were to make it the policy of the United States

(1) To condemn violations of religious freedom, and to promote, and to assist other governments in the promotion of, the fundamental right to freedom of religion.

(2) To seek to channel United States security and development assistance to governments other than those found to be engaged in gross violations of the right to freedom of religion.[1]

The bill also created a new executive branch position—ambassador at large for international religious freedom—and a new congressional organization, the U.S. Commission on International Religious Freedom (USCIRF).

In 2010, Brownback was elected governor of Kansas. Then, in 2018, President Trump appointed him to serve in the very position the Religious Freedom Act had created.

Throughout the more than twenty-five years Sam and I have been friends, I have so appreciated his—and his wife, Mary's—heart for the underdog, for minorities, for the down-and-out, the persecuted, and the forgotten. To see him confirmed as U.S. ambassador for international religious freedom at a time when Christians and many other people of faith around the world were suffering so terribly was a great encouragement.

Ambassador Brownback and Secretary of State Pompeo, a fellow Kansan, quickly set out to advance the Trump administration's mandate to raise religious freedom to a much higher priority on the U.S. foreign policy agenda. One way they did this was to host a series of high-profile conferences on the issue.

In 2019, given the evangelical delegations I was leading throughout the Arab Muslim world, Brownback invited me to be a keynote speaker at the State Department's second Ministerial to Advance Religious Freedom, a gathering of more than one thousand civil society and spiritual leaders, foreign ministers, and clerics from around the globe, in what became the largest-ever religious freedom gathering of its kind.[2]

The following is the text of the address I delivered on July 17, 2019.

"Speak up for those who cannot speak for themselves, for the rights of all who are destitute" (Proverbs 31:8-9, NIV).

In an age of horrific attacks against Jews, Christians, Muslims, and those of other religions, these words from the book of Proverbs *must* be our mission.

I want to thank the president, the vice president, Secretary of State Pompeo, and of course, Ambassador Brownback . . . for making the advancement of religious freedom a top global priority . . . and for holding this conference to let us speak for those who cannot speak for themselves.

I have titled my remarks this morning "Advancing Religious Freedom in the Middle East: An Israeli Evangelical's Perspective," and I would like to share a few thoughts in two areas:

- The state of religious freedom in Israel.
- The state of religious freedom in the Arab Muslim world.

First, some context.

I am the grandson of Orthodox Jews who escaped out of Russia in the early years of the twentieth century, when Jews were being beaten, raped, and murdered in the pogroms. By God's grace, my grandparents and great-grandparents came to America, and it was here . . . that they were free to pray, to keep kosher, and to study Torah.

It was here that my father was raised Orthodox Jewish. And it was here that my father was free not only to study the Hebrew Scriptures, but the New Testament, as well.

Free to study and explore.

Free to ask hard and sometimes unpopular questions.

Free to come to his own conclusion that Jesus of Nazareth is the Messiah that our prophets spoke of and our people have longed for.

So, in 1973, my father became a follower of Jesus.

And a few years later, I became a follower of Jesus, as well, and for this, I am deeply grateful.

Five years ago, my wife and sons and I were free to make another choice: We went through a process known as "making aliyah." That is, we became citizens of the State of Israel. Specifically, we became *dual* citizens of the United States and Israel. We sold our home, we sold our possessions or gave them away, and we moved to Israel to start a new life.

Today, we live in Jerusalem. Two of our sons serve in the Israeli army. Slowly but surely, we are putting our roots down in ancient soil. It has been the hardest but the most exciting journey that our family has ever been on, and it has given us a unique perspective on what's happening in Israel and the region.

The State of Religious Freedom in Israel

Now, the State of Israel is certainly far from perfect, but it is a modern miracle.

- Born out of the ashes of the Holocaust. . . .
- The fulfillment of ancient prophecies.
- Thriving, despite repeated wars and enemies who are hell-bent for our annihilation.
- A booming economy.
- And a robust and, I would say, raucous democracy—the only [one] in our region.

What's more, Israel is a magnificent model of religious freedom. A safe harbor for Jews from all over the world, regardless of how religious or nonreligious they are. And the safest, freest country in the Middle East for people of all faiths and no faith.

- 75 percent of Israel's population of 9 million people are Jews.
- 20 percent are Muslims or Druze—full citizens, absolutely equal rights, free to attend mosque, build mosques, read the Qur'an, and raise their children in the faith.
- Only about 2 percent of Israel's population are Christians, or followers of Jesus—Catholics, Orthodox, evangelicals, and messianic Jews. We are admittedly a small minority, but we are *free*; we are free to practice our faith and to preach it.

Do religious minorities in Israel face a variety of governmental and societal challenges? We do, including an inordinate and, I would say, unhealthy control by one faith stream—ultra-Orthodox Judaism, a relatively small minority—but who has quite an outsize control over the daily lives of others . . . whether it deals with rules governing marriage or burial or divorce or immigration or other issues.

There is much that the Israeli government can and should do to make reforms and improve the quality of life for religious minorities of all kinds—and the sooner the better.

That said, when you hear from our critics that Muslims and Christians face enormous persecution from the government, that is not accurate. Certainly not by the standards of the rest of our region. And there is no apartheid.

- Muslim, Druze, and Christian Arabs have served as members of the Knesset, Israel's parliament, since the founding of the state. In fact, eighty-one of them have served as members of parliament—including twelve at this very moment.
- Muslims, Druze, and Christians serve with distinction in Israel's military, police, academia, media, and businesses. Just this past week, a wonderful, brilliant Israeli Arab Muslim was named chairman of [one of] Israel's largest banks.
- Arab Christians and Muslims also have and do continue to serve as justices on Israel's Supreme Court. . . .

Challenges remain, including, and maybe especially, the wrenching conflict that we have with our Palestinian neighbors and for which we must continue to work and pray very hard for peace and reconciliation. Still, I want to say as I begin that I am deeply encouraged by the state of religious freedom in Israel today.

The State of Religious Freedom in the Arab World

I am also pleased to report that something very hopeful is happening with regards to the safety and freedom of Christians in the Sunni Arab Muslim world.

Not long ago, radical Islamists were beheading Christians in Libya, burning down churches in Egypt, waging genocide against Christians in Iraq and Syria . . . and vowing to exterminate Christianity throughout our region.

Today, the situation is vastly different.

- Arab Muslim leaders have been valiantly fighting to defeat the forces of radical Islamism, which, after all, represents a very, very small percentage of the Muslim world.
- Tens of millions of Muslims, Christians, Yazidis, and others have been liberated, finally, from the forces of barbarism and savagery.
- A growing number of Arab governments are waging an ideological and theological battle against radical Islamists in their mosques, in their schools, on social media, and [are] training a new generation of clerics to preach moderation and mutual respect. . . .
- Some Arab kings and crown princes, presidents and prime ministers, are calling for a new era of peaceful coexistence with Christians and with Jews. And some are even inviting Christians to meet with them to improve religious freedom and the quality of life for Christians in their countries.

Such trends are not receiving nearly enough attention. . . . But these changes are real and they are historic. And they do deserve more attention.

Over the last few decades, I have had the opportunity to travel extensively throughout North Africa and the Middle East, from Morocco to Afghanistan, building friendships with Muslims and with Christians.

Recently, I've had the opportunity, over the last several years, to lead five different delegations of American evangelical leaders to Sunni Arab countries—twice to Egypt, once to Jordan, and once to the United Arab Emirates and Saudi Arabia. We met with Christian leaders and with Muslim leaders at the highest levels.*

In Amman, King Abdullah II—winner of last year's Templeton Prize for his historic and extraordinary efforts to promote interfaith dialogue and religious freedom—he invited our delegation to come and have a wonderful working lunch at his palace.

In Cairo, we were supposed to spend an hour with President el-Sisi and ended up spending three hours almost. This was the first time an Egyptian president had ever invited a group of evangelical Christians to come and sit with him. . . .

In Abu Dhabi, Crown Prince Mohammed bin Zayed spent two hours with our delegation in his home—also the first time that leaders of the United Arab Emirates had ever invited evangelicals for such dialogue and such meetings.

In Riyadh, Crown Prince Mohammed bin Salman also spent two full hours with us—and we were told that this was the first time evangelical Christian leaders had ever been invited to meet with senior members of the Saudi royal family in three hundred years.

In each country, we made it clear that we were not coming for a photo op, but we wanted to build long-term strategic friendships. And in each country, our talks were not only friendly—I would say they were *warm*. We listened to each leader's vision of reform and to their accomplishments, their record of accomplishments. We also asked candid, sometimes

---

* Our second delegation to Saudi Arabia—my sixth overall—took place in September 2019, two months after this address.

very direct questions about the challenges facing Christians in their countries, about other human rights issues, about the plans that these leaders have for improving religious freedom and human rights for Christians and for all religious minorities.

Signs of Progress

I wish I had time to go into all that we learned, but I want to report a few things, very encouraging things, that we came away with.

In Saudi Arabia, admittedly, no churches have been yet built, but I pray this will change soon. Still, there are important signs of progress. Thousands of extremist preachers who refuse to change their teaching of extremism have been fired from the mosques. Christian foreign nationals are increasingly allowed to gather in private homes and businesses for worship and for Bible study without government interference. And the crown prince is beginning to reach out to leaders of other faiths, not only meeting with us as evangelicals, but with Coptic Orthodox Pope Tawadros in Cairo and the archbishop of Canterbury in London and Jewish leaders in New York.

In the United Arab Emirates, some seven hundred Christian churches now operate freely without fear of government persecution. New houses of worship are being built. And in February, the United Arab Emirates welcomed Pope Francis for several days of high-level talks, as well as to lead a Mass in their largest stadium with 185,000 people attending. This was the first time a Roman Catholic pontiff had ever stepped foot on the Arabian Peninsula in the 1,400 years of Islam. . . .

In Jordan, King Abdullah II has granted land along the Jordan River so that thirteen Christian denominations were able to build churches and now baptize Christians. Through documents like "The Amman Message" and "A Common Word," the king has taken the lead in promoting religious moderation, tolerance, and respect for Christians. Indeed, I would argue that under the wise leadership of His Majesty, Jordan has emerged as the safest and freest country for Christians in the entire Arab world, though I believe there are other countries that are competing for that title. And I'm glad for that.

That said, perhaps the most dramatic progress in recent years is being made in Egypt. Under the leadership of President el-Sisi, every church that was burned down, destroyed, or damaged during the Muslim Brotherhood's reign of terror has been rebuilt at government expense. Some 6,500 new churches have applied for permission to legally operate in Egypt and more than a thousand have already received their permission. The rest, meanwhile, are operating freely . . . while their applications are being reviewed, since the new church-building law states that the government has no right to close churches that have filed formal applications.

In January, President el-Sisi invited me to bring a second evangelical delegation and we attended the dedication of the gorgeous Nativity of the Christ Cathedral not far from Cairo. I was honored to be part of that delegation, much less lead it. And then I visited the cathedral again a few days later with my friend Secretary of State Mike Pompeo. . . . Think about it: When was the last time a devout Muslim president, leader of the world's largest Arab country, built a church—the largest in the Middle East—and gave it as a gift to the Christians of his country on Christmas Eve?

This is extraordinary. This was a game-changing moment in the history of Muslim-Christian relations. It sent a powerful message not only to all Egyptians, but to all Muslims and Christians everywhere, that Muslims and Christians can really live [together] in peace, despite our real and profound differences.

There is so much more that I would love to share about all of this. . . .

Just yesterday, I met with Bahrain's foreign minister and their ambassador. I told them how encouraged I am by King Hamad's commitment to tolerance and moderation and by the landmark Bahrain Declaration that His Majesty issued last year to further advance religious freedom.

And today I'm happy to announce that my colleague the Reverend Johnnie Moore . . . and I have accepted Bahrain's gracious invitation to bring an evangelical delegation to Manama this fall. We look forward to that.

Significant Challenges Remain

I don't want to paint a rosy or naive picture.

Enormous challenges remain for Christians and other religious minorities in the Arab world. Deep change must occur in education, in culture, and in government.

But, as a dual U.S.-Israeli citizen, a Jewish evangelical, building friendships with leaders throughout Israel and the Muslim world, I want to tell you that I see signs of hope. And I believe that when leaders of any country advance real reforms and make real progress—especially in the area of religious freedom—they should be publicly praised, even as we encourage them to do more.

Allow me to close with a quote from the Universal Declaration of Human Rights. I want to point your attention specifically to Article 18, which was approved by the U.N. General Assembly in December of 1948: "Everyone has the right of freedom of thought, conscience, and religion; and this right includes the freedom to change his religion or belief."

Perhaps the most uncomfortable element for some when it comes to discussing matters of religious freedom is the right of every person not only to choose his faith but to change it. Yet we must not shy away from this topic, sensitive though it is. . . . For having the freedom to decide what we believe about God—and having the freedom to change our mind—is a sacred human right, granted to us by God himself. Government's job is not to grant rights; it's to guard them. And no human right—none—is more important than the right to seek the truth about who God is, how to know him personally, and how our soul can spend eternity with him.

This is the freedom my father found here in the United States. *This* is the freedom that changed his life and mine.

I want to thank you, each of you, for all that you do to preserve, protect, and defend that right and for speaking up for those who cannot speak for themselves.

God bless you, and may your tribe increase.[3]

CHRISTMAS IN CAIRO

No Arab country has more professing followers of Jesus than Egypt.

Leaders there tell us there are upwards of 17 million Christians—15 million Coptic Orthodox and about 2 million Protestants plus about 250,000 Roman Catholics.

During our first delegation's meeting with President Sisi in November 2017, he told us he was in the process of building a large Coptic Orthodox cathedral in Egypt's new administrative capital.

When several evangelical leaders and I met privately with Sisi for a ninety-minute follow-up in Manhattan in September 2018, he told us the cathedral was almost completed and asked if we would bring a delegation to Cairo in January 2019 to participate in the dedication.[4]

The group that traveled with me on the second trip to Cairo included nine from previous delegations: Tony Perkins, Johnnie Moore, Jerry Johnson, Larry Ross, Wayne Pederson, Ken Blackwell, and Skip Heitzig, as well as CBN News correspondent Chris Mitchell and cameraman Jonathan Goff.

To these we added Nadine Maenza of the United States Commission on International Religious Freedom; Mark Yarbrough and Darrell Bock of Dallas Theological Seminary; Tim Tomlinson and Rick Segal of Bethlehem College and Seminary; Mark Rodgers of the Clapham Group, a consulting firm in the arena of social justice reform; and his wife, Leanne.

Here's a brief itinerary of our visit:

- Attend the Protestant evangelicals' official Christmas celebration at Kasr El Dobara, a large church in Cairo. Andrea Zaki, head of the Protestant Churches of Egypt, and I both addressed the gathering, which was broadcast on nationwide television.
- Meet with Pope Tawadros II to discuss the challenges facing 15 million Coptic Orthodox Christians in Egypt.

- Meet with several dozen evangelical leaders.
- Participate in a roundtable discussion with Muslim and Christian leaders, members of the Egyptian Parliament, policy makers, and civil society leaders.
- Travel to the new administrative capital for a special presentation on the future of religious freedom in Egypt, hosted by President Sisi and attended by some two thousand Egyptian and foreign VIP guests.
- Attend the inauguration of the largest mosque ever built in Egypt, with President Sisi, Palestinian president Mahmoud Abbas, Egypt's top Muslim leaders, top Coptic Orthodox and Protestant leaders, and Muslim leaders from throughout the Arab world. The event was broadcast live on Egyptian TV.
- Attend the inauguration of the Nativity of the Christ Cathedral, the largest Christian church ever built in the Middle East, with senior Christian and Muslim leaders; and attended the Orthodox Christmas mass led by Pope Tawadros II, all broadcast live on Egyptian TV.
- Sightseeing tour on Egypt's national Christmas holiday to the pyramids and other historic sites.

One of the most special elements of the trip for me was our private meeting with Egyptian Christian leaders—listening to their hearts, praying with them, trying to understand the hardships they have endured, and hearing their optimism for the future.

It is also impossible to overstate how moving it was to attend the inauguration of the Nativity of the Christ Cathedral. Imagine a pious Sunni Muslim Arab president of the world's largest Arab country building the largest church in the history of the Middle East and giving it as a present to the Christians of his country on Christmas Eve. Nothing close to this has ever happened in the fourteen centuries of Islam. Yet this is precisely what our group was privileged to witness.

And because these events were broadcast live on TV, tens of millions of Egyptians were able to watch Muslims and Christians singing together, laughing and talking together, visiting each other's holy places, and demonstrating what religious freedom and tolerance for different views really means.

What a beautiful picture of what people in Egypt want the new Egypt to be. Just a few years ago, the Muslim Brotherhood was burning down churches and killing Christians. Now Egyptian Muslims were building churches and celebrating with Christians.

"There is a verse in the Bible that says, 'What the enemy meant for evil, God uses for good,'" Johnnie Moore told the Christian Broadcasting Network. "The horrific terrorism of the last decade . . . has created fertile ground for a new spirit of tolerance to rise across the region; and you have leaders who are facilitating that."[5]

"I think Egypt is moving," Andrea Zaki told CBN News. "Change is not like a computer—click, you have a new screen in a second. Culture, customs, nations, economy, all of these are taking [a] long time. But you can feel and see and touch the changes. Egypt is changing."[6]

My colleagues and I have been sharply criticized by some in the Coptic Orthodox diaspora community in the U.S. who practically dismiss the enormous reforms that Sisi is making and believe we are whitewashing the many problems for Christians that still remain in Egypt. Though I don't believe this criticism is valid, there is certainly a great deal more to do. I applaud their determination to keep pushing for deeper and wider reforms in Egypt. We intend to keep pushing as well.

POMPEO COMES TO CAIRO

In our September 2018 meeting in New York, President Sisi asked for something else.

Not only did he want us to bring a delegation to celebrate the opening of the new cathedral and mosque, he also wanted us to encourage a senior U.S. government official to come, as well, and to publicly acknowledge the significance of these moves.

I immediately reached out to Vice President Pence, Secretary of State Pompeo, and Ambassador Brownback to see if any of them would be available. In the end, Secretary Pompeo took the lead. Though his tight schedule would not allow him to be in Cairo on the Eastern Christmas Eve, he told me he could come a few days later.

I asked if he would visit the new cathedral and do an interview with the Christian Broadcasting Network. He promised he would.

In addition to meeting with President Sisi and Foreign Minister Shoukry, Pompeo delivered a major address at the American University of Cairo on January 10, 2019.

> This trip is especially meaningful for me as an evangelical Christian, coming so soon after the Coptic Church's Christmas celebrations. This is an important time. We're all children of Abraham: Christians, Muslims, Jews. In my office, I keep a Bible open on my desk to remind me of God and his Word and the Truth. . . .
>
> The United States under President Trump has reasserted its traditional role as a force for good in this region. We've learned from our mistakes. We've rediscovered our voice. We've rebuilt our relationships. We've rejected false overtures from our enemies. . . .
>
> President Sisi joined us. He joined us in denouncing the twisted ideology [of radical Islamism] which has brought death and suffering on so many. I thank President Sisi for his courage. . . .
>
> I also applaud President Sisi's efforts to promote religious freedom, which stands as an example for all leaders and all peoples of the Middle East. I was happy to see our citizens, wrongly convicted of improperly operating NGOs here, finally be acquitted. And we strongly support President Sisi's initiative to amend Egyptian law so that this does not happen again. More work certainly needs to be done to maximize the potential of the Egyptian nation and its people. I'm glad that America will be a partner in those efforts.[7]

I was honored to attend this excellent speech—the polar opposite of the address President Obama gave in Cairo in 2009—and to travel to the cathedral in Pompeo's motorcade. After the secretary toured the gorgeous facility, I thanked him for making this a priority in his very busy schedule.

Then I introduced him to Chris Mitchell of CBN, who conducted an exclusive interview.

Pompeo's most important point was vowing that the U.S. would continue to stand with persecuted Christians across the Middle East to ensure that they are not vanquished by radical Islamists.

"America is with them," he told CBN. "Christianity is at the heart of the history of this place here in the Middle East. All you have to do is grab a Bible and read the places and the names. Christians have been central to the Middle East. We want to make sure that they continue to have opportunities and freedom, and for Christian churches to grow alongside [places of worship] of other faiths, as well. Our message is simple. We stand for religious freedom every place American diplomacy is at work."[8]

24

WHAT IS THE FUTURE ROLE OF EVANGELICAL CHRISTIANITY IN THE MIDDLE EAST?

After two decades of genocide and terror,
what Christians see coming next

On October 7, 2016, the Turkish government arrested an evangelical Christian pastor.

His name was Andrew Brunson, and he was the pastor of the Izmir Diriliş (Resurrection) Church, a small Presbyterian congregation in the city of Izmir, nestled on the Aegean Sea south of Istanbul.

Having lived in Turkey with his wife for twenty-three years, Brunson was not famous. He was not political. But to his shock, he was about to become the most well-known evangelical Christian in the Middle East.

With no evidence whatsoever, the Turkish government charged him with "membership in an armed terrorist organization," and later with "support of a terrorist organization and political or military espionage."[1] He was denied access to a lawyer and was transferred to a maximum-security prison.

Ambassador Sam Brownback, members of the U.S. Commission on International Religious Freedom, and Secretary of State Pompeo advocated for Brunson's immediate release, but Turkish officials told them no. Vice President Pence then called for Brunson's release. Again, the Turks said no. Eventually President Trump intervened personally, demanding that Turkish president Recep Erdoğan release Brunson and giving an already-big story global prominence.

On August 1, 2018, after Erdoğan repeatedly refused to release Brunson, Trump hit Turkey with economic sanctions and target tariffs in what *Time* magazine called "an unprecedented escalation against Turkey, a NATO ally that hosts America's largest foreign stockpile of nuclear weapons."[2] The Turkish economy, already struggling, began tanking even further. Its currency lost 20 percent in ten days.[3]

For two more months, Erdoğan dug in his heels, publicly accusing Brunson of having "dark connections to a terrorist group," but providing no evidence.[4] Yet, as Turkey's economic crisis worsened, and with the lira in freefall, Erdoğan finally relented, releasing Brunson on October 12, 2018, after two years of prison and house arrest.

RISING PERSECUTION, RISING PRAYER

Brunson explained the harrowing journey in his 2019 book, *God's Hostage: A True Story of Persecution, Imprisonment, and Perseverance.*

I listened to the audio version—a powerful, personal, and painfully candid account read by Brunson himself—and was deeply moved by how much he suffered in prison, as well as by how God proved himself faithful to his servant.

In an interview for this book, I asked Pastor Brunson, "Why do you believe President Erdoğan and his forces decided to arrest you and hold you for so long?"

He said he believes part of the answer is that the Bible indicates that persecution of Christians will intensify in the last days of history. He also believes the Lord is in the process of mobilizing millions of evangelicals around the world to pray for Turkey and the broader Muslim world.

"Following the attempted coup in the summer of 2016," Brunson told me, "Erdoğan was using that as an opportunity to consolidate his power—which is, at this point, near total in the country. He needed to rule as an authoritarian and as a dictator. There was an anti-Christian animus in Turkish culture, history, and also in him. As he tries to restore more of an Islamist bent to the country and reestablish the influence that Turkey had in the Ottoman Empire, he wants to get rid of missionaries, which they are doing at an accelerated rate. . . .

"I think [he] wanted to make an example of a missionary so that that would lead other missionaries to self-deport and have an exodus of missionaries. Another thing was to intimidate the Turkish [evangelical] leaders, church leaders, and to intimidate Turkish believers [in Christ]. *'If we could hold an American, if we can do this to an American, we can do it to anybody.'* . . . I think that was the original impetus of this."[5]

However, after seventy-eight members of Congress signed a letter to Erdoğan demanding Brunson's release, and Secretary of State Pompeo got involved, Erdoğan saw an opportunity to hold Brunson longer, signaling to Islamists in Turkey and throughout the region that he was their champion.

Still, Brunson came to believe that God had a higher purpose for his suffering.

"I do not believe God put me in prison," he told me. "I think that was a satanic attack that God was fruitful in using for his purposes."[6]

Brunson believes the Lord spoke to him directly and personally in 2009, during a time of prayer—something, he said, that has not happened often in his life.

"He spoke to me specifically and said, 'Prepare for harvest,' meaning a powerful move of God in Turkey. . . . And I think that God was raising up this prayer movement and I was the magnet to draw that prayer into Turkey. God was doing other things, because he works in multiple levels at the same time, but that was one of the main things he was achieving. And so I began to think that I was serving my original assignment, which was to prepare for harvest—just by being in prison."[7]

After his release, Brunson and his wife, Norine, started asking, "Why Turkey?"

"Why would God raise up an unprecedented amount of prayer that poured into that country, rather than Egypt or Syria or anywhere else?" he asked. "I think the reason is because Turkey is a spiritual key to the area. . . . I believe it is a spiritual key because of Turkey's role as the head of Islam for centuries leading the Ottoman Empire. . . . I believe the reason for this targeted prayer is that, when that spiritual power breaks to some degree in Turkey, it will lead to a movement of God there; but this is also going to bring a greater degree of spiritual freedom in the area that Turkey ruled in the name of Islam."[8]

HOW DO EVANGELICALS SEE THE FUTURE OF FAITH IN THE MIDDLE EAST?

Since 9/11, Christians in the Middle East have experienced terrorism and genocide.

Today the situation is significantly better.

But will this last, or are we seeing only a temporary respite?

Government can play a role for good or evil. As Americans, we believe the government is supposed to ensure people's God-given rights to life, liberty, and the pursuit of happiness. This includes protecting every person's right to full religious freedom—the right to practice one's faith, the right to change one's faith, and the right to be wrong.

Governments should never mandate what people can and cannot believe nor persecute people for their religious beliefs. Governments that abuse or deny people their God-given human rights must be pressed to change. Sometimes the most effective way is to engage them quietly and respectfully, behind the scenes. Other times, they need to be challenged publicly—at the grassroots level, in the media, and government-to-government. Often it takes a combination of both approaches.

Followers of every faith have the right and responsibility to preach and teach what they believe to be true and to persuade others to embrace those beliefs without being coerced or deceived. At the same time, religious leaders should educate their disciples to show love and respect to people of different faiths and to those who profess no faith at all.

Given that there are an estimated 600 million evangelical Christians worldwide, my colleagues and I are often asked what we believe and how we see the future of faith in the Middle East. Let me address these questions in this chapter.

1. What exactly is an evangelical?

Here is what the National Association of Evangelicals (NAE) says:

> Evangelicals take the Bible seriously and believe in Jesus Christ as Savior and Lord. The term *evangelical* comes from the Greek word *euangelion*, meaning "the good news" or the "gospel." Thus,

the evangelical faith focuses on the "good news" of salvation brought to sinners by Jesus Christ. . . .

These distinctives and theological convictions define us—not political, social, or cultural trends. In fact, many evangelicals rarely use the term *evangelical* to describe themselves, focusing simply on the core convictions of the triune God, the Bible, faith, Jesus, salvation, evangelism, and discipleship.[9]

When polling to understand the views of evangelical Christians, the NAE and Lifeway Research include "four statements to which respondents must strongly agree in order to be categorized as evangelical."

1. The Bible is the highest authority for what I believe.
2. It is very important for me personally to encourage non-Christians to trust Jesus Christ as their Savior.
3. Jesus Christ's death on the cross is the only sacrifice that could remove the penalty of my sin.
4. Only those who trust in Jesus Christ alone as their Savior receive God's free gift of eternal salvation.[10]

2. *What do evangelicals believe about the future of faith in the Middle East?*

Throughout the Bible, God asserts that he knows and will explain what the future holds.

In Isaiah 46:10, for example, he declares: "I make known the end from the beginning, from ancient times, what is still to come."[11]

This doctrine of God's omniscience is stated in the Scriptures time and again.

Fully 27 percent of the verses in the Bible are prophecy.[12] About half of those prophecies have already been fulfilled, including more than one hundred prophecies about the Messiah coming to earth the first time. The remaining passages describe events that will happen leading up to the return of the Messiah to Jerusalem.

Let's briefly consider several things that evangelicals believe about the future of the Middle East.

THE SECOND COMING OF JESUS CHRIST

While devout and sincere evangelicals disagree on the interpretation of some prophetic passages, all believe the doctrine that Jesus will physically and literally return to earth.

Most believe he will also literally establish the throne of his global kingdom in Jerusalem.

Mark Hitchcock, a leading evangelical expert on eschatology, notes:

- Of 333 prophecies concerning Christ, 109 were fulfilled by his incarnation, leaving 224 yet to be fulfilled in the Second Coming.
- There are more than three hundred references to the Lord's Second Coming in the 260 chapters of the New Testament—one out of every thirty verses.
- Twenty-three of the twenty-seven New Testament books mention the Lord's coming.
- Jesus refers to his Second Coming at least twenty-one times.
- For every time the Bible mentions Christ's incarnation, the Second Coming is mentioned eight times.
- We are exhorted more than fifty times to be ready for the return of Jesus Christ.[13]

Consider just one passage:

And I [John] saw the holy city, new Jerusalem, coming down out of heaven from God, prepared as a bride adorned for her husband. And I heard a loud voice from the throne, saying, "Behold, the tabernacle of God is among the people, and He will dwell among them, and they shall be His people, and God Himself will be among them, and He will wipe away every tear from their eyes; and there will no longer be any death; there will no longer be any mourning, or crying, or pain; the first things have passed away."

And He who sits on the throne said, "Behold, I am making all things new." And He said, "Write, for these words are faithful and true." Then He said to me, "It is done. I am the Alpha and the Omega, the beginning and end. I will give water to the one who thirsts from the spring of the water of life, without cost. The one who overcomes will inherit these things, and I will be his God and he will be My son.

REVELATION 21:2-7

THE COMING APOSTASY AND GREAT AWAKENING

The Lord Jesus explains in Matthew 24 that the world will experience "birth pains" as the time of his return approaches.

The metaphor suggests there will be times of *contraction*—severe pain and suffering—and times of *release*. As the specific (yet unknown) day of Christ's return draws nearer, the contractions will become more severe and the times of release will become shorter.

Jesus and his apostles also repeatedly indicated that there would be two contradictory trends in motion in the last days.

On the one hand, many will turn away from faith in God the Father and the Lord Jesus Christ.[14] At the same time, many others will repent and turn to Jesus.[15]

They also made it clear that believers will face ever-increasing persecution as the return of Christ approaches.

- "Then you will be handed over to be persecuted and put to death, and you will be hated by all nations because of me" (Matthew 24:9, NIV).
- "Everyone who wants to live a godly life in Christ Jesus will be persecuted" (2 Timothy 3:12, NIV).

Pastor Brunson and his family and friends experienced these truths all too painfully. But they are by no means alone.

"Every day, eight Christians worldwide are killed because of their faith," reports *Christianity Today*. "Every week, 182 churches or Christian buildings are attacked. And every month, 309 Christians are imprisoned unjustly."[16]

"There is more persecution of Christians now, arguably, than any [other] time in the history of the world, and the Christian faith is the most persecuted faith in the world by far," says Ambassador Brownback.[17]

THE COMING WAR OF GOG AND MAGOG

Though the ancient biblical prophets did not describe all future events in every country, they wrote extensively about specific events that will happen in specific countries that are uniquely part of God's plan for mankind. Most of these countries are in the Middle East.

In Ezekiel 38–39, the Hebrew prophet describes an eschatological conflict in the Middle East known as the war of Gog and Magog. As I wrote about extensively in my 2006 nonfiction book, *Epicenter: Why the Current Rumblings in the Middle East Will Change Your Future*, some evangelical Bible scholars (though by no means all) believe Ezekiel 38–39 describes a coalition of armies led by Russia (referred to in the prophecy as the ancient regions of Magog, Rosh, and Meshech), Iran (ancient Persia), Turkey (ancient Gomer), and other powers who will come against Israel to attack her in the last days.[18]

The text does not indicate that Israel or any of her allies will fight or defeat the enemy coalition. Rather, the prophet states that God himself will supernaturally intervene, rescue Israel, defeat her enemies, and bring judgment to those enemies in order to draw humankind to himself.

> "It will come about on that day, when Gog comes against the land of Israel," declares the Lord GOD, "that My fury will mount up in My anger. In My zeal and in My blazing wrath I declare that on that day there will certainly be a great earthquake in the land of Israel. . . .
>
> "With plague and with blood I will enter into judgment with him; and I will rain on him and on his troops, and on the many peoples who are with him, a torrential rain, hailstones, fire, and brimstone. So I will prove Myself great, show Myself holy, and make Myself known in the sight of many nations; and they will know that I am the LORD."
>
> EZEKIEL 38:18-19

What is particularly interesting about Ezekiel 36–39 is that there are five prerequisites for the war of Gog and Magog to come to pass:

- After centuries in exile, the Jewish people must be returning to the land of Israel en masse: "But you, mountains of Israel, will produce branches and fruit for my people Israel, for they will soon come home. . . . I will cause people, my people Israel, to live on you. They will possess you" (Ezekiel 36:8, 12, NIV).
- The Jewish people must be rebuilding the ruins of their ancient homeland: "The towns will be inhabited, and the ruins rebuilt" (Ezekiel 36:10, NIV).
- The sovereign State of Israel must be prophetically reborn and become militarily strong, having "an exceedingly great army" (Ezekiel 37:10).
- After years of conflict and strife, the people of Israel enter a season where they feel that "they are living securely" and "are at rest" (Ezekiel 37:8, 11).
- Israel is experiencing a remarkable season of prosperity, causing their enemies to desire "to capture spoils and to seize plunder" (Ezekiel 37:12).

Though a good number of prophecies from Ezekiel 36–37 have come to pass over the past century, it is too soon to draw any conclusions as to whether the prophecies from Ezekiel 38–39 will also come to pass soon, or even in our lifetime. Still, the emerging alliance between Russia, Iran, and Turkey is understandably drawing increasing attention among evangelicals.

It is also drawing the attention of a growing number of rabbis and Jewish scholars who believe that the war of Gog and Magog will occur before the coming of the Messiah.[19] What's more, it is simultaneously attracting the increased attention of Muslims because the Qur'an also mentions a future war of Gog and Magog (known as *Yajuj wa Majuj*), and many Islamic scholars believe it will take place before the coming of the Mahdi to rule the world.[20]

THE COMING PEACE BETWEEN ISRAEL, EGYPT, AND ASSYRIA
Isaiah 19 conveys another prophecy that is drawing growing attention from evangelicals.

The ancient Hebrew prophet describes a violent, painful, and economically disastrous period for Egypt in the last days, followed by a time of great hope and redemption. Yet Isaiah also speaks of God's divine love for Egypt. God promises to bless the people of Egypt and create a future of true and lasting peace between Egypt, Israel, and the region once known as Assyria (which now encompasses the countries of Lebanon, Syria, Jordan, and Iraq). This is the prophecy that one of our delegation members raised with President Sisi on our first trip to Cairo.

> The LORD will make Himself known to Egypt, and the Egyptians will know the LORD on that day. . . . And the LORD will strike Egypt, striking but healing; so they will return to the LORD, and He will respond to their pleas and heal them.
>
> On that day there will be a road from Egypt to Assyria, and the Assyrians will come into Egypt and the Egyptians into Assyria; and the Egyptians will worship with the Assyrians.
>
> On that day Israel will be the third party to Egypt and Assyria, a blessing in the midst of the earth, whom the Lord of armies has blessed, saying, "Blessed is Egypt My people, and Assyria the work of My hands, and Israel My inheritance."
>
> ISAIAH 19:21-25

Evangelicals who take seriously these and other Mideast prophecies— including the future judgment and liberation of Iran (Jeremiah 49:34-39) and the future judgment and destruction of Damascus (Isaiah 17 and Jeremiah 49:23-27)—do not know *when* these events will occur. We do not believe we can prevent them or accelerate them. Rather, we believe that these events are foreordained and trust that they are part of God's sovereign plan for humanity.

3. How should evangelicals interact with the people of the Middle East?

Here are six biblical principles that should govern our approach as Christians toward the people of the Middle East:

We are called to love Israel *and* her neighbors—not just one or the other.

> "At that time," declares the LORD, "I will be the God of all the families of Israel, and they shall be My people." This is what the LORD says . . . [to Israel]: "I have loved you with an everlasting love; therefore I have drawn you out with kindness."
> JEREMIAH 31:1-3

> I say then, God has not rejected His [the Jewish] people, has He? Far from it! For I too am an Israelite, a descendant of Abraham, of the tribe of Benjamin. God has not rejected His people whom He foreknew.
> ROMANS 11:1-2

> Love your neighbor as yourself.
> LEVITICUS 19:18; MARK 12:31

Jesus commanded his disciples to love their neighbors *and* love their enemies.[21] His call to love left no one out.

We are called to be peacemakers.

> In Psalm 122:6, we are told to "pray for the peace of Jerusalem. May they prosper who love you."

> In Psalm 34:14, we are admonished to "seek peace and pursue it."

> Jesus said, "Blessed are the peacemakers, for they will be called children of God" (Matthew 5:9, NIV).

> The apostle Paul added, "If it is possible, as far as it depends on you, live at peace with everyone" (Romans 12:18, NIV).

We are called to oppose injustice and care for those who are suffering.

Micah 6:8 says, "He has shown you . . . what is good. And what does the LORD require of you? To act justly and to love mercy and to walk humbly with your God."[22]

Proverbs 31:8-9 says, "Speak up for those who cannot speak for themselves. . . . Defend the rights of the poor and needy."[23]

Jesus inaugurated his public ministry by citing the prophet Isaiah: "The Spirit of the Lord is on me, because he has anointed me to proclaim good news to the poor. He has sent me to proclaim freedom for the prisoners and recovery of sight for the blind, to set the oppressed free, to proclaim the year of the Lord's favor."[24] Then Jesus practiced what he preached—feeding the hungry, healing the sick, honoring women, denouncing religious extremism and hypocrisy, and preaching a message of forgiveness and hope, not only to those in the land of Israel but in Lebanon, Syria, and Jordan, as well.

We are called to strengthen our Gentile Christian and messianic Jewish brothers and sisters, including providing financial support when the Lord directs.

Be constantly alert, and strengthen the things that remain, which were about to die.
REVELATION 3:2

All the believers were together and had everything in common. They sold property and possessions to give to anyone who had need.
ACTS 2:44-45, NIV

I am on my way to Jerusalem in the service of the Lord's people there. For Macedonia and Achaia were pleased to make a contribution for the poor among the Lord's people in Jerusalem. They were pleased to do it, and indeed they owe it to them. For if the Gentiles have shared in the Jews' spiritual blessings, they owe it to the Jews to share with them their material blessings. So after I have completed this task and have made sure that they have received this contribution, I will go to Spain and visit you on the way.

ROMANS 15:25-28, NIV

We are called to give everyone, everywhere, the opportunity to hear the gospel of Jesus Christ, understand it, and make a definitive decision either to receive Jesus as Savior and Lord or reject him.

Jesus came to them and said, "All authority in heaven and on earth has been given to me. Therefore go and make disciples of all nations, baptizing them in the name of the Father and of the Son and of the Holy Spirit, and teaching them to obey everything I have commanded you. And surely I am with you always, to the very end of the age."

MATTHEW 28:18-20, NIV

The Lord said to Ananias, "Go! This man [the apostle Paul] is my chosen instrument to proclaim my name to the Gentiles and their kings and to the people of Israel."

ACTS 9:15, NIV

If you declare with your mouth, "Jesus is Lord," and believe in your heart that God raised him from the dead, you will be saved. For it is with your heart that you believe and are justified, and it is with your mouth that you profess your faith and are saved. As Scripture says, "Anyone who believes in him will never be put to shame." For there is no difference between Jew and Gentile—the same Lord is Lord of all and richly blesses all who call on him, for, "Everyone who calls on the name of the Lord will be saved."

How, then, can they call on the one they have not believed in? And how can they believe in the one of whom they have not heard? And how can they hear without someone preaching to them? And how can anyone preach unless they are sent? As it is written: "How beautiful are the feet of those who bring good news!"

ROMANS 10:9-15, NIV

We are called to never stop praying.

Be joyful in hope, patient in affliction, faithful in prayer.

ROMANS 12:12, NIV

Rejoice always, pray without ceasing, in everything give thanks; for this is the will of God for you in Christ Jesus.

1 THESSALONIANS 5:16-18

I tell you, love your enemies and pray for those who persecute you.

MATTHEW 5:44, NIV

MAKING IT PRACTICAL

Aside from caring for my own family and friends and being a writer, investing in the people of the Middle East—and strengthening the church in this region—is one of the great passions of my life.

In 2006, Lynn and I founded The Joshua Fund, a nonprofit organization dedicated to educating and mobilizing Christians to bless Israel and her neighbors in the name of Jesus, according to Genesis 12:1-3. This famous passage is known as the Abrahamic Covenant.

Now the LORD said to Abram,
    "Go from your country,
    And from your relatives
    And from your father's house,
    To the land which I will show you;
    And I will make you into a great nation,

And I will bless you,
And make your name great;
And you shall be a blessing;
And I will bless those who bless you,
And the one who curses you I will curse.
And in you all the families of the earth will be blessed."

Thus, The Joshua Fund has hosted conferences and seminars all over the world to help evangelicals better understand what the Bible teaches about God's love for both Israel and her Arab and Muslim neighbors, and to encourage Christians to "learn, pray, give, and go" to the work of the Lord in the Middle East. The Joshua Fund has also invested more than $50 million toward caring for Holocaust survivors, Syrian and Iraqi refugees, widows, orphans, and other vulnerable people in the region, and toward strengthening the church in Israel, the Palestinian Authority, Lebanon, Syria, Jordan, Iraq, and Egypt; equipping and encouraging pastors, distributing Bibles, and helping to build the first Christian radio station in the history of Iraq, among many other projects.

Given the enormous pressures against Christians—and the current and coming wars and traumas in the region—is it enough? Not nearly. But with an amazing board and staff and regional allies, we do what we can in the power of the Holy Spirit and ask God "to do immeasurably more than all we ask or imagine."[25]

WHAT IS THE FUTURE OF SECURITY AND PROSPERITY IN THE MIDDLE EAST?

The Biden administration and the road ahead

With the election of Joe Biden in 2020, the world changed yet again.

As the nations of the Middle East experience unprecedented tectonic changes, an entirely different team began overseeing the American economy, national security, and foreign policy—and new questions arose.

How would the new administration approach the threats rising in the Middle East and North Africa? How would they approach the extraordinary new opportunities presenting themselves in the region? At the same time, how would they handle matters of religious freedom and other human rights in the Middle East and around the world?

WHO ARE JOE BIDEN AND KAMALA HARRIS?

These were not the only questions, of course.

As I completed this chapter in February 2021, a deeply divided American electorate was trying to get to know its new president and vice president. So was the rest of the world. And two specific issues had risen to the fore that had never before been true of a new presidential administration.

The first was this: Having turned seventy-eight on November 20, 2020,

Joe Biden was the oldest person ever elected president of the United States. For many Americans, this raised serious questions about his physical health and stamina, his memory and analytical acuity, and his ability to serve out his full term.

It was not only his political opponents who were raising these issues. So were some of his friends and allies. During the Democratic primaries, the *New York Times* published an editorial column headlined "Are Biden and Sanders Too Old to Be President?"[1] In August 2019, Jack Shafer, a senior media writer at *Politico*, noted that "the *New York Times*, the *Washington Post*, *Politico*, CNN, the *Atlantic*, the Associated Press, *Slate*, and just about every other premium and low-rent outlet you can name has crossed the ageism line to ask the 'too old' question in recent articles about Joe Biden."[2]

During the 2020 campaign, Biden himself raised the issue. "People have a right to question all of our ages," he said. "That's [a] totally legitimate thing. But like I say, 'Watch me. Just watch me.'"[3]

This question created a unique focus on Kamala Harris. In addition to making history as the first woman, first African American, and first Indian American ever elected to serve as vice president of the United States—and one with a Jewish husband—she also was twenty-two years younger than her boss. However, she had precious little experience on the national or international stage, having been a U.S. senator, representing California, for only four years before becoming the second most powerful official in the country. Would she be up for the task to step in if something happened and Biden could not complete his term? If so, how would she approach matters in the Middle East? She traveled to Israel as a freshman senator in November 2017, met with Netanyahu, and is considered more moderate on Israel issues than some in her party.[4] Still, with a record so thin, it was impossible to know for certain.

From the inauguration, I committed myself to pray daily for Joe and Jill Biden, Kamala Harris and her husband, Doug Emhoff, and the members of their team—just as I prayed daily for the Trumps, Pences, and their team. I hope that millions of others are doing the same, whether they voted for them or not. Like all leaders, America's president and vice president need the Lord's protection, wisdom, and grace.

NEEDED:
FRESH EYES ON A RAPIDLY CHANGING REGION

A second issue that had never been raised about a new presidential administration was this:

Joe Biden was first elected to the U.S. Senate in 1972. He entered the White House in January 2021 after serving in Washington, D.C., in one capacity or another, for nearly half a century. This was something that no other incoming president could say.

Was this an asset or a liability? Would Biden be stuck in old ways of seeing things, or would he be able to assess with fresh eyes the rapidly changing trend lines in the Middle East and adapt his policies to meet the new realities? Biden's allies insisted that his thirty-six years in the Senate and eight years as vice president would make him the most experienced commander in chief ever. Others who have served with him, however, harbored significant doubts about his approach to foreign policy generally and to the Middle East in particular.

THE GOOD NEWS

President Biden sees himself as a loyal and longtime friend of Israel.

"I am a Zionist," he says. "You don't have to be a Jew to be a Zionist." Indeed, he insists, Israel is "part of my soul."[5]

As I interviewed for this book senior Democrats who are experts on the Mideast and have worked closely with Biden, they repeatedly emphasized that, throughout his political career, Biden vigorously fought against anti-Semitism, traveled to Israel many times, and had been far warmer in his personal relations with Israeli leaders than Obama ever was—even when disagreeing with them.

An old-fashioned Irish pol raised in blue-collar towns in Pennsylvania and Delaware, Biden has a down-to-earth ease with people and a likability factor that is part of his political charm and success, they argued.

Further, "We've been friends, our families have been friends, for years," Biden said of Netanyahu.[6] Indeed, he once signed a photo to the prime minister with these words, "Bibi, I don't agree with a damn thing you say, but I love you."[7]

Biden has spoken regularly at AIPAC conferences, consistently voted for generous U.S. military aid for Israel, and has refused to condition American aid on Israeli knuckling under to White House demands on controversial policy matters.

What's more, Biden strongly backed U.S. financial support for creating Israel's Iron Dome anti-rocket system. For example, over a four-year span during the Obama administration, the U.S. provided Israel with more than $929.3 million for the Iron Dome program, creating a state-of-the-art system—unduplicated anywhere in the world—that has shot down more than 90 percent of the rockets fired at Israel by terrorists in Gaza and saved countless Israeli lives (including my own).[8]

While it is true—and in my view, unfortunate—that Biden opposed Trump's decision to move the U.S. Embassy to Jerusalem (especially given that Biden voted for the authorizing legislation back in 1995), to his credit, Biden later promised not to reverse it. "The move shouldn't have happened in the context as it did," he said. "But now that [it] is done, I would not move the embassy back to Tel Aviv."[9]

Though Biden initially dismissed the Trump approach to Arab-Israeli peacemaking, he later praised the Abraham Accords and offered to build on them.

"I welcome the United Arab Emirates and Bahrain taking steps to normalize ties with Israel," Biden said. "It is good to see others in the Middle East recognizing Israel and even welcoming it as a partner. A Biden-Harris administration will build on these steps, challenge other nations to keep pace, and work to leverage these growing ties into progress toward a two-state solution and a more stable, peaceful region."[10]

If he chooses to make it a priority, Biden could certainly build on the Trump legacy, helping numerous other countries normalize relations with Israel—chief among them Saudi Arabia—while potentially coaxing the Palestinians back into direct talks with Israel.

Likewise, Biden's reservations about President Erdoğan of Turkey could prove significant. During the campaign, the *New York Times* asked, "Do you feel comfortable with the United States still having nuclear weapons in Turkey given Erdoğan's behavior?"

Biden replied, "The answer is my comfort level is diminished a great deal. I've spent a lot of time with Erdoğan. . . . What I think we should be doing is taking a very different approach to him now. . . . We have to speak out about what we, in fact, think is wrong. He has to pay a price. He has to pay a price for whether or not we're going to continue to sell certain weapons to him."[11]

Biden also expressed concern over how close Erdoğan is with Russia.

"At the end of the day, Turkey doesn't want to have to rely on Russia," he said. "But they've got to understand that we're not going to continue to play with them the way we have."[12]

I believe it is high time for the U.S. to get tough with Erdoğan. Trump was right to impose sanctions on Turkey to force Erdoğan to release pastor Andrew Brunson. Trump was also right to refuse to sell F-35 stealth fighters to Erdoğan after Turkey purchased Russia's S-400 air defense system. Overall, however, I believe Trump was far too soft on Erdoğan. Will Biden take a different path?

Another critical question: Will Biden and his team prove tougher on Vladimir Putin than Obama was? In 2011, Biden told the Russian leader to his face, "I'm looking into your eyes, and I don't think you have a soul." Putin smiled and replied, "We understand one another."[13]

In 2018, Biden warned that the West is "navigating a new relationship with the rise in China, and declining, but aggressive, Russia." Under Putin, he said, the Kremlin was "using every tool at its disposal to destabilize and sow discord," through propaganda and sophisticated disinformation campaigns, manipulation of energy markets, undermining public confidence in democratic elections, blackmail, assassination, and even military invasion. "Putin's ultimate goal," Biden said, "is the dissolution of NATO and the European Union, rather than reestablishing the Soviet Union. He'd rather deal with individual nations he can try to strong-arm than a unified, democratic West."[14]

Will Biden and his team rally the Western alliance—and our allies in the Middle East—to demonstrate a muscular, unified, and sustained response to Kremlin aggression and the alliances Putin is building with anti-American nations? If so, he will likely find strong bipartisan consensus in Congress for a get-tougher-on-Russia campaign.

THE BAD NEWS

Saying the right things is not enough, however.

Strong American leadership requires more than mere rhetoric. It requires clear thinking, strategic discernment, and decisive action.

Unfortunately, some officials who have worked closely with Biden have expressed significant reservations about his foreign policy judgment. Most notable has been Robert Gates, who served as secretary of defense during the Obama-Biden administration.

"Joe is simply impossible not to like," Gates writes in his memoir. "Joe is a man of integrity, incapable of hiding what he really thinks, and one of those rare people you know you could turn to for help in a personal crisis. Still, I think he has been wrong on nearly every major foreign policy and national security issue over the past four decades."[15]

To be fair, I don't believe that Biden has been wrong on *everything*. But I find a good deal of his record on the Middle East troubling.

COLD WAR

Biden opposed President Reagan's arms buildup and missile defense programs in the 1980s that helped win the Cold War and prevented the Soviet Union from dominating the Middle East.

FIRST GULF WAR

Biden voted against President George H. W. Bush's decision to go to war in 1991 to remove Saddam Hussein's forces from Kuwait after Saddam had illegally invaded and pillaged the Gulf state and threatened to attack U.S. allies, including Israel and Saudi Arabia.

SECOND GULF WAR

Biden voted to remove Saddam Hussein from power in 2003 but quickly turned against the war and opposed "the surge" in 2007—the critical decision by President George W. Bush to increase the number of U.S. forces in Iraq, a move that turned the tide of the war and allowed the U.S. and our allies to crush the violent insurrection led by former Saddam loyalists, Iranian proxy forces, and al Qaeda.

PULLOUT FROM IRAQ

Biden has boasted that he led the charge to remove all U.S. military forces from Iraq by the end of 2011. During a Democratic presidential candidate debate in 2019, he said, "I made sure the president turned to me and said, 'Joe, get our combat troops out of Iraq.' I was responsible for getting 150,000 combat troops out of Iraq."[16] Yet this move created the

very vacuum that allowed for the rise of ISIS and its campaign of genocide to slaughter Muslims, Christians, and Yazidis across Iraq and Syria.
At the time, senior Democrats warned Obama and Biden against pulling
out prematurely. For example, Leon Panetta, who served as CIA director
from 2009 to 2011 and as defense secretary from 2011 to 2013, vigorously opposed the pullout. "It was clear to me—and many others—that
withdrawing all our forces would endanger the fragile stability then barely
holding Iraq together," Panetta wrote in his memoir.[17]

KILLING BIN LADEN
Though Biden supported going into Afghanistan in 2001 to remove the Taliban
from power and crush al Qaeda, he incredibly opposed the 2011 decision by
President Obama to send U.S. special forces into Pakistan to kill Osama bin
Laden. By his own account, Biden told Obama, "Mr. President, my suggestion
is, don't go."[18] Even Hillary Clinton supported taking out bin Laden.

DIVIDING ISRAEL
Biden supported President Obama's 2011 decision to pressure Israel to
retreat to the 1967 armistice lines, a move that would force the Israelis to
divide Jerusalem.[19]

Most Israeli leaders—even those who support a two-state solution—
agree that the 1967 borders are indefensible and cannot serve as the basis
for a secure and stable peace. Yet President Biden appears to be heading
that direction again. During the 2020 primary campaign, the *New York
Times* asked all the Democratic candidates, "Do you support the establishment of a Palestinian state that includes West Bank land as demar-
cated by pre-1967 borders, except for longtime Israeli settlements?" Biden
replied, "Yes, except for longtime Israeli settlements or other land swaps
and arrangements negotiated by the parties."[20]

TAKING OUT SOLEIMANI
Biden opposed the U.S. drone strike in 2019 that took out Iranian terror
mastermind Qassem Soleimani.

IRAN NUCLEAR DEAL
Most problematic of all, Biden fully supported President Obama's 2015
decision to make a deeply flawed nuclear deal with Iran (the Joint

Comprehensive Plan of Action), including giving the regime in Tehran upwards of $100 billion to $150 billion.[21] He vigorously opposed President Trump's 2018 decision to take the U.S. out of the JCPOA. During the 2020 campaign, Biden repeatedly said he intends to rejoin the JCPOA.

"The recent killing of Quds Force commander Qassem Soleimani takes a dangerous actor off the board," Biden told the *New York Times*, "but also raises the prospect of an ever-escalating cycle of violence in the region and has prompted Tehran to jettison the nuclear limits established under the Iran deal. Tehran must return to strict compliance with the deal. But if they do so, I would rejoin the agreement and use our renewed commitment to diplomacy to work with our allies to strengthen and extend it, while more effectively pushing back against Iran's other destabilizing activities."[22]

Immediately upon taking office, Biden formally offered to restart talks with Iran. In turn, the Israelis, Emiratis, Bahrainis, and Saudis openly began pressing Biden and his team to consult with them closely before rushing back into negotiations with Tehran. Some warned Biden not to try to strike a new deal with Iran at all.

"With the changing of the administration in the United States, the Iranians have said they want to return to the previous agreement," IDF chief of staff Aviv Kochavi said in a speech on January 26, 2021. "I want to state my position, the position that I give to all my colleagues when I meet them around the world: Returning to the 2015 nuclear agreement, or even to an agreement that is similar but with a few improvements, is a bad thing and it is not the right thing to do."[23]

On February 5, I spoke at length with Benny Gantz, Israel's defense minister and former chief of staff of the IDF (2011–2015). It quickly became clear to me that he regarded the apocalyptic Iranian regime—and its growing alliance with Russia, Turkey, North Korea, and China—as the number one threat facing Israel for the foreseeable future. And he was worried that the U.S. might rush into another flawed and dangerous nuclear deal with Iran. He was not, however, happy with Kochavi for getting into a public spat with the new administration over how to deal with Tehran, believing such discussions are best held behind closed doors. So I pressed him to explain how he sees the regime in Tehran and how he hopes Washington will, as well.

"While I'm very respectful of the Iranian culture and the Iranian people, I'm very much worried about the Iranian regime," Gantz told me, referring specifically to their determination to build, buy, or steal fully operational nuclear warheads. "But it's not only the nuclear aspect; it's also the launcher capabilities, the missile capabilities, the regional aggression—that we see them [supporting] different militias in Iraq and Syria, supporting the Houthis in Yemen. It all comes from this octopus—the Iranian octopus, I would say—which sends out its arms [in many directions]."[24]

"When the supreme leader says he wants to annihilate the State of Israel, or when Mahmoud Ahmadinejad used to say, 'We're going to wipe Israel off the map,' and the supreme leader didn't oppose that—even seemed to support it—do you think he really means that?" I asked Gantz.

I also asked, "Does the ayatollah want to bring about a second Holocaust, or is that just rhetoric, in your view?"

"I cannot allow myself to think it's just rhetoric," Gantz, the son of a Holocaust survivor, told me. "He [the supreme leader] said it, and he's trying to build measures to be able to do it."

I noted that former Iranian president Akbar Hashemi Rafsanjani famously suggested that Israel is a "one-bomb country." "So if Tehran ever gets to the point of having nuclear weapons, there is really no margin for error, is there?"

"That's right," Gantz said. "Therefore, we are adamant about it."

He then raised his concerns about the end-times theology of Iran's supreme leader and his inner circle and how those beliefs might affect Tehran's first-strike doctrine.

"I cannot ignore that there is the factor of religious belief or perspective," he told me. "It's very hard to measure it, but it would be wrong to assume it's not there. So we will have to take our measures, our precautions, our capabilities, and make sure that we are not undefended under those circumstances."

Gantz then showed me a map of the Middle East that he keeps on his desk. On it he has drawn a thick black line dividing the region into two parts. To the north and east lie Russia, Turkey, Lebanon, Syria, Iraq, and Iran. These countries, he told me, form a "radical axis"—countries that Israel needs to view as enemies or potential enemies. To the south and the west of the line lie Israel, Jordan, Egypt, Saudi Arabia, Bahrain, the

United Arab Emirates, and Qatar. These, he said, form the "camp of the moderates"—countries that Israel can view as allies or potential allies, all of whom are supported by the United States.

What worried Gantz most is that more and more countries are aligning themselves with the regime in Tehran, despite its continuing pursuit of nuclear weapons and long-range missiles, genocidal rhetoric, and apocalyptic religious doctrine.

"The [Iranian] regime is fundamentalist and radical," Gantz told an Egyptian TV correspondent that same month. "[That's why] Israel has a clear objective: that Iran not be nuclear. It is not just an Israeli interest. It is first and foremost a global and regional interest."[25]

If the U.S. and international community do not move quickly and decisively to intensify pressure on Tehran to give up its nuclear ambitions, might Israel have to take unilateral action?

"Yes," Gantz said ominously. "The IDF and Israel's defense establishment are holding on to the option of taking action against Iran's nuclear project if that is what has to be done. I hope it doesn't come to that."[26]

THE ROAD AHEAD

What is the biggest fear in the Middle East today?

That America will lose interest in the region, act naively, or pull out.

Tired of war, consumed with domestic problems and deep internal divisions, burdened with massive and growing debt, what if the United States cannot or will not stay engaged in the most volatile and dangerous region in the world? Yes, Trump accomplished many good things in the region during his four years. Yes, his desire to wrap up the wars in Afghanistan and Iraq two decades after 9/11 was among them. And yes, the Abraham Accords were a triumph of diplomacy. But what if the Biden administration turns inward or becomes distracted by other countries and other issues or makes unwise and irresponsible decisions? What if a future administration in Washington does? What then?

Many Arabs and Israelis worry they are witnessing a slow but steady American retreat from the Middle East. Knowing that nature abhors a vacuum, they fear a reduction of American participation in the Middle East because they believe that only a robust American–Israeli–Sunni Arab alliance can counter the rising threats posed by Russia, Iran, and Turkey, combined with the growing ambitions of China and North Korea. Such fears are responsible, in part, for driving Israelis and Arabs to work more closely together. Yet people here worry that all the good that has been accomplished in recent years could be erased if America refuses to play a major constructive role in the region or makes foolish concessions to Iran and other enemies.

That is why there was so much concern about Biden as he entered office. Despite having been in or near the center of power in Washington for half a century, Biden was not actually a known quantity to most Americans. How exactly would he lead? No one was quite sure. And what if, for whatever reason, he could not lead? How well prepared was Kamala Harris to step in if she had to? What path would she chart? Even fewer had any clear idea.

Here's a word of encouragement to my evangelical friends in the United States: Though we will strongly disagree with Biden and Harris on many domestic and economic policy issues, we should nevertheless build bridges to the administration, on matters related to Israel, Iran, and the broader Arab and Muslim world. Let us support the White House if and when we can. Let us criticize when we must. But let us always do so with civility and respect. May we remember the wisdom of Proverbs:

A gentle answer turns away wrath, but a harsh word stirs
up anger.
PROVERBS 15:1

The heart of the righteous ponders how to answer.
PROVERBS 15:28

Do you see a person who is hasty with his words? There is more
hope for a fool than for him.
PROVERBS 29:20

Let us also pray, in particular, that the Biden-Harris team navigates wisely in the Middle East. Specifically, let us pray that they would stand firm against the regime in Tehran and play a uniquely helpful role with regard to the Saudis, the Israelis, and the Palestinians. After all, the opening weeks of Biden's administration were not particularly promising on these fronts.

In February 2021, Biden took the Houthi rebels in Yemen off the official U.S. list of foreign terrorist organizations and removed sanctions that the Trump administration had placed on the Houthis—despite even the *New York Times* conceding that "the Houthis' main patron is Iran."[27] Next, Biden announced that the U.S. would no longer assist the Saudis in their ongoing war with the Houthi forces in Yemen. He banned the sale of offensive weapons to Riyadh for use in the war, held up all arms sales to the kingdom pending a review, and demanded, "This war has to end."[28]

Biden is certainly right that this tragic and costly war must end. But he is wrong to blame the conflict on the Saudis. Has Riyadh made errors in prosecuting the fight? Yes. But let's not kid ourselves: The war is being driven by the Houthis, radical Islamists who want to take over Yemen and make the country a base camp for terror operations against the Saudis and other moderate Middle Eastern countries. The Houthis are not only backed and funded by Tehran, they have launched more than one thousand Iranian-made rockets and drones at Saudi cities in recent years, including the Saudi capital.[29] Though the Saudis have intercepted at least 872 of them, no American ally should simply have to play defense in such a situation. The Houthi terrorists must be neutralized and the firing upon the Kingdom of Saudi Arabia must end. The Saudis have invested hundreds of millions of dollars in humanitarian relief for suffering civilians in Yemen. They have also repeatedly tried diplomatic initiatives to end the war. But the Houthis alternatively refuse to negotiate or to keep their word when they do make agreements.

What kind of message does it send to Iran—and the rest of the world—for Biden to blame an ally for a war, rather than the enemy?

Also in February, Biden imposed a ban on seventy-six Saudi nationals he concluded were complicit in the murder of Jamal Khashoggi, preventing them from entering the U.S. He also imposed sanctions on two aides close to MBS who he said were also complicit, including Saud al-Qahtani. Biden did not impose sanctions on MBS directly, however. He simply decided not to interact with MBS, only with King Salman.[30]

I fully support pressing the Saudi monarch to bring everyone to justice who is guilty in that murder. Nothing less will suffice. Yet releasing a declassified intelligence report—which provided the public with no new facts, no concrete proof, and certainly no smoking gun backing up the bombshell assertion of MBS's guilt—was a mistake.

Why, then, did Biden release the document? What, exactly, is the point of accusing a major American ally of murder without providing proof?

If Biden was trying to placate his liberal friends and allies, he failed. Many were livid with Biden for not throwing the book at MBS.

"Biden has done nothing to punish MBS. Absolutely nothing—to the astonishment of human-rights groups, foreign-policy experts, Saudi activists, and even some on his own staff," wrote Robin Wright in a column in *The New Yorker* headlined "The Sweeping Impact of a Broken Biden Campaign Promise."[31]

Few of Biden's allies were as appalled as Fred Ryan, publisher of the *Washington Post*, who accused the president of "weakness and surrender" on human rights. "The world has waited for more than two years to see how the United States would ultimately respond to the brutal killing of *Post* journalist Jamal Khashoggi at the hands of a Saudi Arabian assassination team," Ryan wrote. "Candidate Biden was firm and unequivocal in assuring American voters that, if elected president, he would make the regime 'pay the price and make them, in fact, the pariah that they are.' . . . [Instead] the Biden administration now seems ready to move on while proposing some sanctions falling far short of honoring Biden's campaign promise. . . . It appears as though under the Biden administration, despots who offer momentarily strategic value to the United States might be given a 'one free murder' pass."[32]

The Biden team insisted they were trying to "recalibrate"[33] the U.S. relationship with the kingdom, not "rupture"[34] it. They said they wanted to send the Saudis a strong message of disapproval, while also signaling their willingness to work together on common objectives, so long as the Saudis make significant changes in policy, tactics, and strategy. But could that not have been done with a series of carefully crafted policy moves rather than the release of an unsubstantiated allegation?

Only time will tell whether President Biden's opening moves will bear positive fruit. They may, but accusing an ally of cold-blooded murder without either having or presenting proof could very well backfire. As I wrote for All Arab News at the time, "Given growing Iranian aggression in the region—including more missile attacks by Iranian-backed Houthi terrorists in Yemen—Biden would be foolish to set into motion a train wreck of the U.S.-Saudi alliance."[35]

I would encourage the president and his team to consider the seven points I made in chapter 20 about the future of Saudi Arabia and how to interact with its leadership and chart their path accordingly.

I would also add an eighth point about Saudi Arabia's future: I have little doubt the Saudis are going to normalize relations with Israel. As I see it, the question is not *if*, but *when*. That said, I suspect the Saudis would much prefer to make peace believing they are a strategic American ally—not a "pariah state"—as well as in such a manner that allows them to play a useful role in encouraging the Palestinian leadership to also make peace with Israel and achieve a level of security and prosperity that thus far has eluded them.

If Biden can help the Saudis defend themselves against Iran and its terror proxies, improve their human rights record, advance their Vision 2030 agenda, normalize relations with Israel, and provide the Palestinians a realistic pathway to peace that in no way endangers Israel, he and his administration will have made a significant and lasting difference in the Middle East. And earn Nobel Peace Prizes of their own.

The keys to success in the region for Biden, however, are making certain there is no daylight between Washington and its Israeli allies, ensuring that he does not "go wobbly" on Iran (to cite an old Margaret Thatcher phrase), accepting the "outside-in" premise of Arab-Israeli peacemaking, and exercising strategic patience.

These last two points are critical. Deeply divided internally, the Palestinian leadership has shown little evidence thus far they are ready to make peace. That could change, but until it does, Washington should focus its attention first on helping more Arab countries normalize relations with Israel, starting with the Saudis. As the Palestinians see the positive, prosperous fruit of such normalization deals, and the futility of remaining perennial rejectionists, they may become more ready to make the necessary compromises with the Jewish State that they have been unwilling to make before now. Likewise, with the establishment of more full and warm peace treaties with Arab states, the Israelis may also become more willing to make difficult compromises of their own.

After all, if a comprehensive peace treaty between the Israelis and the Palestinians is really possible—I am not entirely sure that it is, but *if* it is—it will likely only happen when the post-Abbas, post-Netanyahu era begins. For years, both Abbas and Netanyahu have dug in their heels and built political constituencies around not making any significant compromises. Washington, therefore, should not hold its breath—or push too hard—for new breakthroughs, unless and until new leaders with new approaches emerge on both sides.

THE COMING MIDDLE EAST GOLD RUSH?

As I close this chapter, let's consider what the future could look like in the Middle East.

Imagine more dramatic breakthroughs in Arab-Israeli peacemaking, involving more and more Arab and Muslim countries, including a game-changing normalization agreement between Israel and Saudi Arabia.

Imagine a sustained and enhanced "maximum pressure" campaign against the regime in Tehran, combined with a vibrant U.S.–Israeli–Sunni Arab alliance standing together militarily, diplomatically, and economically against Iranian hegemony.

Imagine the passing of Supreme Leader Ali Khamenei and the rise of a new supreme leader—infused with Persian nationalism, perhaps, but not apocalyptic Islamism—and ready to end the nation's bid for nuclear weapons and end its support for terror and subversion.

Imagine Putin and Erdoğan on their heels, chastened by a revived and far more robust American-led alliance in Europe, Asia, and the Middle East.

Imagine, too, a new era of Palestinian and Israeli leadership coming to power that is ready, willing, and able to hold direct talks, make necessary compromises, say yes to the tens of billions of dollars that the U.S. and Gulf countries have put on the table to build a vibrant, private Palestinian economy with a million new jobs, and work together to build a secure and prosperous future for both sides, not just one.

Imagine the economic boom that could result.

A pipe dream? Perhaps. A desert mirage? Maybe.

In 1993, when Shimon Peres wrote his book *The New Middle East*, he was widely ridiculed for suggesting that if Arabs and Israelis chose peace over war, a massive economic boom—fueled by high technology, trade, and tourism—could result. On September 11, 2001, the prospect of a new Middle East seemed further away than ever. But today, many in the region believe it is not only conceivable but actually achievable.

Don't get me wrong. I am not predicting it will come to pass. Or if it does, that it will happen soon. Or even if it does, that it will last. What I am saying is that for the first time in two thousand years, people in the vortex of the Middle East suddenly think such a new way forward is possible. That alone is extraordinary. Indeed, business leaders, entrepreneurs, CEO, investors, and venture capitalists I have spoken to throughout the region believe a new gold rush is being set into motion.

"What was a trickle of contact and contracts before is now growing into a tsunami of ultimately billions of dollars of bilateral investment, joint ventures, and joint venture creation and research," says Jon Medved, a leading Israeli investment strategist for a firm called OurCrowd. "When two entrepreneurial countries like the UAE and Israel get together, just watch the sparks fly and real value get created."[36]

Jason Greenblatt, who left the White House peace team to advise companies and investors interested in working with both Israel and the Sunni Arab world, is also seeing a massive surge of business opportunities in the region.

"What I'm trying to do now is create what I call a Middle East 2.0," he told me in an interview for this book and All Israel News. "What I found at the beginning—long before the Abraham Accords were announced—was that there was strong interest [by Arab businessmen in doing deals with Israel], but also a slight trepidation. Less so in the security space [where] they've been dealing with each other for a long time. . . . However, as soon as the Abraham Accords were announced, it really did become a gold rush.

"I spent most of the week in Saudi Arabia at the FII [Future Investment Initiative] conference, [with] the sovereign wealth funds who hosted that conference. And I would say that the excitement is deeply palpable—not just at the conference itself, but while visiting with friends in restaurants, at their homes, and just talking to them about the Abraham Accords, about Israel, about the region."

Greenblatt said he has "high hopes" for an Israeli-Saudi peace deal, and he believes the economic potential of such a treaty is staggering.

"There is so much opportunity in that region," he added. "There's so much undeveloped land in Saudi Arabia," especially in the northwest quadrant known as NEOM, where the Saudis want to invest $500 billion in developing the cities of the future. "This is a particularly pristine and beautiful area of land. [The Saudis] are ready to pump a real fortune in there. And I think we should all watch it closely, because how often do you get to see something like that created out of nothing?

"People are excited about the possibilities. Look, in particular, they're excited about His Royal Highness, the Crown Prince MBS's vision—and not just Vision 2030. He just unveiled some great plans on the coast of the Red Sea and his plans for Riyadh. People are excited about the region. I think that filters through everywhere—the United Arab Emirates, Bahrain, Qatar, certainly Morocco. I think we are about to see sort of a dawn of a new economic powerhouse among this group of countries—and, where possible, in partnership with Israel."[37]

Indeed—consider a few numbers:

ISRAEL
- Population: 9.29 million
- Annual GDP: $357.9 billion
- Third most companies listed on the NASDAQ, behind only the U.S. and China[38]

UAE
- Population: 9.8 million
- Annual GDP: $421 billion
- Sovereign wealth funds:
    - Abu Dhabi Investment Authority, UAE: $696.7 billion
    - Investment Corporation of Dubai, UAE: $239.4 billion
    - Mubadala Investment Company, UAE: $228.9 billion
    - Emirates Investment Authority, UAE: $45 billion

BAHRAIN

- Population: 1.6 million
- Annual GDP: $38.6 billion
- Sovereign wealth fund:
  - Mumtalakat: $18.9 billion

SAUDI ARABIA

- Population: 34.7 million
- Annual GDP: $793 billion
- Sovereign wealth funds:
  - SAMA Foreign Holdings, Saudi Arabia: $505.76 billion
  - Public Investment Fund, Saudi Arabia: $320 billion

What if these oil-rich Arab countries—who urgently want to diversify their economies away from dependency on oil—began investing in Israeli health care, cybersecurity, water desalinization, and other technologies of the future? What if Israeli scientists and entrepreneurs were free to work hand in glove with their Arab counterparts? Wouldn't the sky be the limit?

Would new threats arise? Of course. Would new dangers appear? They always do. Indeed, they are prophesied. But what if there first came an astonishing season of security and prosperity? It has happened before. Recall the ancient Hebrew prophecy in 1 Chronicles 22:9: "You will have a son who will be a man of peace and rest, and I will give him rest from all his enemies on every side. His name will be Solomon, and I will grant Israel peace and quiet during his reign."[39]

That prophecy was fulfilled.

A new leader arose in Israel.

A new era of peace and prosperity transpired.

It didn't last—but while it did, it was something to behold.

26

WHAT IS THE FUTURE OF PEACE IN THE MIDDLE EAST?

My conversation with Israeli president Reuven Rivlin,
the ninth-generation Jerusalemite who loves the Arabs

Three days before Bill Clinton left office in 2001, he received a phone call.

It was from Yasser Arafat, bidding him farewell.

"You are a great man," Arafat told him.

"The hell I am," Clinton shot back. "I'm a colossal failure, and you made me one."[1]

Clinton proceeded to read Arafat the riot act. In the summer of 2000, he had invited the Palestinian leader to Camp David, where Ehud Barak would make the most significant offer of peace ever presented by an Israeli prime minister. It included provisions for

- A sovereign Palestinian state.
- Palestinian control of the entire Gaza Strip, plus additional territory in Gaza.
- Israel to withdraw from 97 percent of the West Bank.
- East Jerusalem to be the Palestinian capital.
- Palestinian control of the Muslim and Christian quarters in the Old City.

- Palestinian control of the Haram al-Sharif, known to Israelis as the Temple Mount.[2]

Yet not only did Arafat turn down the offer, he returned to his home in Ramallah and presided over the eruption of the Second Intifada, a horrific wave of suicide bombings and other terror attacks against the Jewish State that left one thousand Israelis dead and thousands more wounded and forced Israel to build the security fence that now separates Israel from the Palestinian people.

"Arafat's rejection of my proposal," Clinton would later write in his memoir, "was an error of historic proportions."[3]

What made Arafat's rejection particularly astonishing was that these were the final status negotiations to conclude the Oslo Accords, the agreements of 1993 and 1995 that had created the Palestinian Authority and laid out the path to a sovereign Palestinian state. The same interim agreements for which Arafat had won a Nobel Peace Prize. The only peace deals with Israel to which the Palestinians had ever said yes.

A PAINFUL TRAGEDY THAT MUST NOT BE IGNORED

In a moment, I will share my conversation with the most interesting Israeli leader I have ever met. A Jewish president who deeply loves the Arab people.

First, however, I want to share a few thoughts about my friends and neighbors, the Palestinian people, who are enduring a painful tragedy that must not be ignored.

It is true that I am excited about the hope offered to the region by the Abraham Accords. Yet let me be clear: It is a fallacy—and a dangerous one—to believe that peace between Israel and the Arab states is enough. Anyone who truly cares about peace in the Middle East must care about finding a compassionate, practical, and workable answer to the conflict between Israel and the Palestinian people.

Not enough evangelicals say this, but I will: God loves the Palestinian people. He cares about their plight. He cares about their future. And so must we. To turn a blind eye to the Palestinian people is morally wrong. To discount their hopes and dreams and fears and struggles is cold and inhumane. Two million Palestinians live in the Gaza Strip. Three million live in the West Bank. Their lives and souls and fortunes and children and grandchildren matter.

I do not have a secret plan, a secret map, a secret set of parameters that will solve this wrenching problem or heal the bitter wounds that both sides have suffered. I have crisscrossed the Holy Land for three decades, getting to know Israelis and Palestinians, having coffee and baklava together, trying to understand their perspectives and how they would solve the conflict. I have met with kings and crown princes, presidents and prime ministers. I've heard many ideas along the way, but no one has ever shared a perfect plan with me. And there is a reason for this. Apart from the return of the Messiah to establish his Kingdom of peace on earth, such a plan does not exist.

That does not mean, however, that in this lifetime we should allow the perfect to be the enemy of the good. David Ben Gurion and his advisors were not completely satisfied with the Partition Plan in 1947. It did not give them all the land they wanted to build the state of their dreams. Yet they said yes anyway, and today Israel is one of the most powerful and prosperous countries in the region.

Why, then, do the Palestinian leaders continue to say no to a final agreement again and again and again? Why are they unwilling to present their own credible, creative, sensible proposal that might become the basis for the end of this conflict? I've seen American proposals. I've seen international proposals. I've seen Israeli proposals. What I have not seen is a serious Palestinian proposal that incorporates the realities of the twenty-first century. How can that be?

On November 29, 1947, the United Nations passed Resolution 181—the Partition Plan that authorized the creation of both a Jewish State and a Palestinian Arab state living side by side on the west side of the Jordan River. The Jews said yes and founded their state on May 14, 1948. The Arabs said no and went to war instead.

In June 1967, after Egyptian president Gamal Abdel Nasser threatened to "throw the Jews into the sea," Israel won the Six-Day War, tripling the size of its territory and reunifying Jerusalem, its ancient capital. Still, Israel immediately offered the Palestinians and the Arab world "land for peace." Israeli foreign minister Abba Eban declared "everything is negotiable," and defense minister Moshe Dayan concurred, famously saying, "Israel is wait-ing for a phone call from the Arabs."[4] Yet again the Arabs said no. Indeed, on September 1, 1967, they issued the famous Three Nos declaration at the Arab League summit in Khartoum, Sudan—no peace with Israel, no recognition of Israel, no negotiations with Israel.

On March 26, 1979, Israel and Egypt signed the historic peace treaty negotiated by Menachem Begin and Anwar Sadat at Camp David. Yet Palestinian leaders bitterly denounced the agreement, rather than negoti-ate one of their own. This was yet another tragic missed opportunity for the Palestinians.

So was the rejection of the Clinton-Barak offer at Camp David in 2000.

So was the handover of the entire Gaza Strip by Ariel Sharon in 2005 that gave Palestinians in Gaza total freedom, no "Israeli occupation," miles of beachfront property on the Mediterranean, and massive reserves of nat-ural gas just off the coast—none of which was ever pursued and developed.

So was the rejection of an even more generous offer by Ehud Olmert to Mahmoud Abbas in 2008 for a sovereign Palestinian state.

So was the Palestinians' rejection of the Netanyahu offer in 2009, which was less generous than Olmert's but marked the first time a right-wing Israeli leader had offered a sovereign Palestinian state.

So was the Palestinians' rejection of Netanyahu's decision to suspend all settlement construction in the West Bank for ten months to help jump-start final peace talks.

So was the rejection of the Trump Peace to Prosperity plan in 2020.

None of those offers was perfect. Yet the Palestinian leaders never took any of them seriously. Nor have they presented their own plan. Why not?

THE SAUDI PEACE PLAN

Two decades ago, Saudi Arabia put forward a peace plan.

In March 2002, the entire Arab League adopted an agreement known as the Arab Peace Initiative at a summit in Beirut. It required three things of Israel:[5]

1. Withdraw from all disputed territories, including the Golan
   Heights, to return Israel's borders to the June 4, 1967, lines.

2. Reach a just solution to the Palestinian refugee problem, as prescribed by U.N. Resolution 194.
3. Accept the establishment of a sovereign Palestinian state composed of the West Bank and Gaza Strip, with East Jerusalem as its capital.

If Israel agreed, the initiative required two things of the Arab and Muslim world:

1. All fifty-seven countries of the Organization of the Islamic Conference (including the twenty-two members of the Arab League) would deem the Arab-Israeli conflict over for good, and commit to peaceful relations with Israel, guaranteeing her security.
2. All fifty-seven Arab and Muslim countries would establish normal diplomatic relations with Israel, establish embassies, exchange ambassadors, and open bilateral trade relations.[6]

On paper, it sounded good. However, there were two problems.

First, Israeli military and intelligence officials consider the 1967 lines indefensible. Those borders simply do not provide enough of a buffer zone to effectively repel regional attacks. At its narrowest point, Israel would be just nine miles wide. What's more, if the 1967 borders could magically establish true peace and stability, why was there no peace and stability in 1967? The reason was that the Arab states and Palestinians still wanted to destroy Israel and seize it for themselves, as evidenced by the 1973 Yom Kippur War.

Second, when the Saudis made their offer, no one in Israel believed that Riyadh, much less the Arab League, much less Yasser Arafat, really wanted peace. Palestinian leaders were openly calling for 100 percent of the land, not just the West Bank and Gaza. Radical Islamism was on the rise. Al Qaeda had just launched devastating terror attacks against the United States. The U.S. and her NATO allies were now at war in Afghanistan. Saddam Hussein was rattling his saber again. And the vilest forms of anti-Semitism were being preached in mosques and taught in schools in Saudi Arabia and most of the Arab world.

There was one other feature embedded in the Arab Peace Initiative worth noting: the principle that no Arab or Muslim country would make peace with Israel until the Palestinians had done so. Thus, as Palestinian leaders continued to reject every offer Israel made, the initiative went nowhere for nearly two decades.

TURNING POINT

Now, however, some Arab countries are saying enough is enough.

While saying they still support the Palestinian people and cause, a growing number of Arab leaders are no longer willing to give Ramallah a veto over the entire Arab-Israeli peace process ad infinitum. None agreed with all the details in Trump's Peace to Prosperity plan. Indeed, they formally rejected it at an Arab League Summit in Cairo in February 2020. Yet they have grown increasingly exhausted by, and angry with, perennial Palestinian rejectionism.

Few have expressed it on the record more clearly or poignantly than Prince Bandar bin Sultan, who served as Saudi Arabia's ambassador to the U.S. during the 1980s and 1990s, as chief of Saudi intelligence from 2012 to 2014, and as head of the Saudi National Security Council from 2005 to 2015. Prince Bandar spent decades of his life trying to advance the Palestinian cause on behalf of Riyadh. Yet when he saw Abbas and others so viciously attack Emirati, Bahraini, and Sudanese leaders for normalizing relations with Israel, he agreed to a three-part interview with the Al Arabiya satellite news network based in Dubai in October 2020 to express both his sadness and disgust. The interview was seen by millions and was the clearest public signal yet that Riyadh's level of exasperation with Abbas has reached the tipping point.[7]

The decision by some Arab countries to make peace with Israel without waiting any longer for Ramallah was a political earthquake that shook Abbas and Palestinian officials to the core. They became angry and bitter. Their people felt more alone and abandoned. Polls reflected the utter despondency, and it was painful to watch.

Over the last several decades, Lynn and I have made many Palestinian friends here in the region and abroad. Generally, we avoid talking politics. These friendships are too precious to us to turn into sharp disagreements over matters that none of us are in positions to solve. While no Israeli can truly understand the pain that the Palestinian people are going through today, Lynn and I empathize and pray faithfully for a way forward. After all, these brave, proud, remarkable, beautiful people have suffered so much in the past century. They deserve something vastly better, as do their children and grandchildren.

NEW VOICES, NEW HOPE

Today, I see something new happening.

A growing number of Palestinians are calling out their leaders for so many past mistakes and missed opportunities. They are urging Ramallah to embrace the Abraham Accords and to leverage the moment to negotiate the best possible deal for the future of the Palestinian people, before it is too late. I have had the honor to interview some of them and let their voices be heard on All Arab News.

On September 14, 2020, for example, we published an exclusive interview with Ghaith al-Omari, a former negotiator for the Palestinians, who had called the Emirati and Bahraini peace deals with Israel "a diplomatic win-win-win in the Middle East."[8] But he said the Palestinians would need a major change of strategy if they wanted to capitalize on these gains and seek their own peace with Israel.

Al-Omari was born in Jordan, served as the executive director for the American Task Force on Palestine, before joining the Washington Institute for Near East Policy as a senior fellow. From 1999 to 2001, he served as an advisor to the Palestinian negotiating team during the permanent status talks and was at the Camp David summit in 2000 with Yasser Arafat, Ehud Barak, and Bill Clinton.

Al-Omari told me he believes the Barak offer represented "some very significant breakthroughs" and "defined . . . what we see as the contours of a solution." Indeed, he lauded Barak for being willing to take big risks for peace.

"What Arafat should have done was come up with a counteroffer," he said, noting that their negotiating team had developed a range of counteroffer scenarios, none of which Arafat deployed. "It was a tactical approach by Arafat to simply say no and demand for more," al-Omari said, calling this a "strategic mistake" because both Israelis and Americans concluded that the Palestinians "were not serious [about making peace], and they only could say no." And, he said, "we continue to pay the price until today."[9]

Al-Omari was even more critical of Abbas for rejecting the 2008 offer by Ehud Olmert. "That was the main missed opportunity," he told me, conceding that while perhaps the moment had not been "ripe" for peace in 2000, it was definitely "ripe" in 2008. "That was a moment that called for leadership, for taking risks, and Abbas simply did not rise up to the moment," he said.[10]

I asked al-Omari if history will record that the 2008 offer was the "high-water mark." Prime Minister Olmert believed it was. Indeed, he pressed Abbas at the time, saying, "Remember my words—it will be fifty years before there will be another Israeli prime minister that will offer you what I am offering you now. Don't miss this opportunity."[11] Yet Abbas again said no.

Al-Omari agreed this was a devastating moment. Olmert's offer was "the most that any Israeli leader could offer" and "ultimately what a [final] deal would look like."[12]

Looking forward, he told me he believes that the Abraham Accords are "something to be celebrated," not denounced. He called the accords "a reality that the Palestinians either accept, and try to make the best of, or they will be left behind." He also noted that Arab countries that already have peace with Israel—Egypt and Jordan—had been the most effective at advancing the Palestinian cause and interceding on their behalf with Israeli officials to defuse tensions. More Arab countries making peace will be even more helpful, he said, noting that trying to isolate Israel internationally had not worked and that Ramallah should stop trying.[13]

Al-Omari particularly praised the UAE for insisting that Israel halt all movement toward annexation in return for full peace, saying this demonstrated precisely how normalization can help not hinder the Palestinian cause.

"The challenge right now is to seize the moment and to take initiative, because otherwise I think what could be a promising moment could end up being a wasted opportunity."[14]

He concluded our conversation by saying, "I don't think that Abbas is capable, politically, right now to reach a peace deal." Part of that, he said, was a failure of legitimacy. "When 80 percent of the Palestinians tell you that their government is corrupt and is incapable of delivering, it is hard to see legitimacy there to make the huge concessions that we need." And yet, he said, he has not lost hope. "It's always fascinating to see how leaders change when they are leaders. To my mind, Ariel Sharon was maybe the poster boy for this—someone who came as the father of the whole settlement enterprise, someone who in Palestinian perception was as close to evil as you can get, ends up being the Israeli prime minister who actually evacuates Gaza," pulls all Israeli settlers out of the Gaza Strip, and gives the entire thing to the Palestinian people. "So I think leaders change. Leaders change when reality changes."[15]

Other Palestinian businessmen and political analysts that I interviewed for this book—usually on condition of anonymity—told me very similar things to what I heard from Ghaith al-Omari. I cannot say such views represent the majority, by any means. But in some sectors of Palestinian society, new thinking seems to be stirring.

MY CONVERSATION WITH PRESIDENT RIVLIN

On September 11, 2001, Reuven Rivlin was Israel's minister of communications.

Seven hours ahead of the American East Coast, it was about 4:30 in the afternoon in Israel and Rivlin was touring a major Israel telecommunications company when he learned about the attacks. At first, he was in shock. He knew instantly it was al Qaeda. But how in the world had they pulled it off?

"I could hardly believe that al Qaeda had succeeded to hit in the heart of America—in New York, the creative and economic center of America, and in Washington, in the Pentagon."[16]

As a member of the security cabinet under Prime Minister Sharon, Rivlin began asking his colleagues how Israel needed to prepare for possible similar strikes on Tel Aviv and Jerusalem. He knew that most terror attacks in the past had been near the borders of Israel. What had happened in America, however, raised the sobering possibility of airborne attacks on major Israeli population centers. If al Qaeda could pull off such stunning attacks in the U.S., Israel had to fundamentally rethink how to protect its citizens.

The world, Rivlin knew, was going to war. Radical Islamism was no longer a threat that the Israelis faced alone. The jihadists had found a way to cross the planet. They had found a way to do untold damage to the world's only superpower. But a day of reckoning was coming. The Americans were going to battle stations, and everyone in the Middle East had to brace for impact.

Nearly two decades later, I sat down with Rivlin—whom friends and colleagues call Ruvi—at the official residence of the Israeli president in the heart of Jerusalem. We had met several times before over the years, but this would be our first in-depth conversation and our first on-the-record interview. I wanted to hear how 9/11 had affected him as an Israeli Jew; but even more I wanted to understand why, as an Israeli president from the Likud Party—on the center-right of the political spectrum—he clearly loved the Arabs so much.

Ever since making aliyah in March 2014—and moving as a family to Israel on August 15 that year—Lynn and I had been watching Rivlin closely. Elected by his Knesset colleagues as the state's tenth president that summer, he had immediately begun reaching out to Israeli Arabs, Christians, Druze, and other minorities, making the case that we were all members of the same national family.

I remember reading in the Israeli media that, in one of his first major moves, Rivlin had spoken at "a memorial ceremony to mark the fifty-eighth anniversary of the Kfar Kassem massacre, during which Israeli border police shot to death forty-nine Arab Israelis, among them several women and many children." The story noted that "Rivlin was the first Israeli president to attend the annual memorial ceremony at the town." He called the massacre "a terrible crime" and "another stain in the history of the tragedy of the Israeli-Palestinian conflict. . . .

"We must look directly at what happened," Rivlin told his fellow Jews. "It is our duty to teach this difficult incident and to draw lessons. . . .

"The Arab population in Israel is not a marginal group," he said. "We are destined to live side by side and we share the same fate."[17]

That was not the message put forth by all right-wing Israeli leaders. Indeed, some had proved very divisive over the years. But the views were vintage Rivlin. Why? What made him such a deeply committed Zionist and a security hawk who loved the Jewish people so passionately and also had such respect for—indeed, such a love for—Israel's minorities and her neighbors? Was it possible that Rivlin's heart, his words, his tone offered a model that could help expand and deepen Israel's circle of peace?

RIVLIN'S ROOTS

Reuven Rivlin does not suffer from an identity crisis.

His Jewish and Zionist credentials are firmly intact.

He is a ninth-generation Jerusalemite, from a family that emigrated to the Promised Land from Lithuania 212 years ago because their rabbis told them the Messiah was coming soon and they had to greet him in Jerusalem. There were only about 10,000 people living inside the walls of the Old City at the time, and the Rivlin family was warmly welcomed, finding Jerusalem a microcosm of Jewish philosophy and learning.

"Jerusalem was not considered politically important to the world at that time," Rivlin told me. "It was considered a holy city, but not politically important."

Still, his family came to see firsthand how deeply important the mythology of the city was, not only to Jews but also to Christians and Muslims. They could see that Jerusalem was central to the story of Christianity, for it was here that Jesus preached, was crucified by the Romans, was buried, and where Christians believed he rose again. The Rivlins knew, too, that though the Qur'an does not explicitly mention the city, it is where Muslims believe that the prophet Muhammad was taken up to heaven on the creature known as *Buraq*, and of course where the Dome of the Rock and the Al-Aqsa Mosque were built, making it the third holiest city to the world's 1.8 billion Muslims.

LEARNING ARABIC

Rivlin's father, Yosef Yoel, was a scholar and a professor at Hebrew University.

He grew up at a time when relations with the Arabs of the Old City and surrounding areas were peaceful and friendly, and he had many Arab friends. When Eliezer Ben-Yehuda—the father of modern Hebrew—was collecting new words for Hebrew to expand the national vocabulary, he believed the best approach was to draw from Arabic, another Semitic language. So he asked a group of young scholars to learn the language, and Rivlin's father was one of them. Not only did Yosef Yoel master the language, he later translated the entire Qur'an into Hebrew.

Ruvi was born in Jerusalem on September 9, 1939. He grew up not only learning Hebrew and English, but also Arabic, which he can speak and read. Despite mounting tensions between the Jewish and Arab communities of Mandatory Palestine—followed soon by the outbreak of World War II, and then Israel's War of Independence—Rivlin fondly recalled his father instilling into him a great love and respect for the Arab people.

He told me a story about a time during World War II when the Rivlins' Arab neighbors came to his father and said, "Look, [Nazi General Erwin] Rommel is about to win in North Africa, and then he is coming here to conquer Jerusalem. But you, the Rivlin family, have nothing to worry about. You are our friends, and we will protect you."

Rivlin's father replied, "Well, thank you, but actually [British General] Montgomery is going to win, and the Jews are going to fulfill the dream of two thousand years and build a Jewish State. But you don't have to worry. You will be safe and full citizens of the Jewish State."

Those Arab neighbors did not necessarily believe their Jewish friend, but they appreciated his heart and remained friends through many traumas.

"I have always believed that Israel must be a Jewish and a democratic state," President Rivlin told me, explaining that Israel was the only Jewish State in the world and had to remain distinctly Jewish to be a safe haven for other Jews coming from around the world; yet it also had to be a democratic state that protected and honored its minorities.

"My father believed that we need to build an iron wall to protect ourselves from attacks," Rivlin told me. "But we need a window in that wall to see when the Arabs are adjusting themselves to our being here."

FINDING BRIDGES AND BUILDING OTHERS

Ruvi was just a child during the 1948 war.

But eventually he became a soldier and served in many of Israel's next battles.

After the 1967 war, he became a member of the Jerusalem Council and worked closely with Mayor Teddy Kollek.

"I urged Kollek to take care of *all* the citizens of Jerusalem," he told me. "In order to bring peace, we need to find and build bridges to the Arabs."

Kollek agreed and worked hard to create a sense of unity and respect between Jews, Muslims, and Christians.

"We have never been at war with Islam or with Muslims," Rivlin insists. "We have always respected Islam. Israel's fight has been only with people who refuse to let Jews live in peace in their biblical homeland. It is not a religious war."

He noted that, in 1948, both David Ben Gurion and Menachem Begin— men from polar opposites on the political dial—agreed that Israel should not capture "the holy mountain," because they did not want to make the war about the Islamic holy sites of the Dome of the Rock and the Al-Aqsa Mosque, even though the mount is revered by Jews and Christians as the site of both the first and second Jewish Temples. Many disagreed with that decision, he said, but that was the rationale. In 1967, of course, the decision was made to take the Temple Mount, but also to preserve the Islamic holy places, not raze them to clear the way for the building of a third Temple.

"We need to find bridges to the Arab people," Rivlin insists.

It is not just a catchphrase; it's a life mission.

"I have always believed that the Israeli Arabs are a bridge to the rest of the Arab world. The Palestinians are also a bridge."

Yet he underscores again that "we cannot find understanding with our neighbors unless we are both a Jewish State and a democratic state."

The Camp David Accords in 1978, the full Israeli-Egyptian peace treaty in 1979, and King Hussein's peace treaty with Israel in 1994 were solid agreements that have been severely tested. Though they have held up well over the decades, he said, they have not created warm relations, tourism, and robust trade—nowhere near the levels he would like to see.

"We tried to find a way to bring peace between two peoples, but we failed. We don't actually have peace with the people of Egypt and Jordan, though we want to. We have peace between governments, between armies. That is good. But it is not a peace that is deep down in the hearts of the peoples."

He has spoken often on this point to American presidents and to various

Israeli prime ministers, as well, insisting that we must find a better way to "build confidence" between the people on both sides.

Complicating the situation is that "Islamists will always reject Israel's right to exist, because to them we are heretics, and it is not possible from an Islamist point of view to make peace with heretics." This is true, he believes, of both Sunni and Shia Islamists. That is why Rivlin believes Israel, the U.S., and especially the Arab countries need to work much harder to counter the theological and ideological narratives of the Islamists, not simply think of counterterrorism as a military objective.

Under Prime Minister Sharon, Rivlin was appointed, along with Shimon Peres, to serve on a negotiating team with Palestinian leaders such as Mahmoud Abbas, then Arafat's deputy, and Salam Fayyad, the centrist, pragmatic economist who won acclaim in the West for the reforms he made as finance minister and later prime minister of the Palestinian Authority before being driven out of office by Abbas.

Rivlin enjoyed meeting with Fayyad and Abbas.

"I met them; I understood them. They understood Hebrew. I understood Arabic. We could also speak in English."

They worked on many difficult and sensitive issues together and won each other's respect, he said, and Rivlin was not afraid to be blunt.

"I would tell them, as long as you don't control your people [the jihadists] and we have no confidence in your ability to stop terrorism and really make peace, then there is no chance of a treaty."

Fayyad and Abbas—who was far more of a moderate at the time—did not always like what they heard and often pushed back, but they listened.

"They would say to me, 'You are not patronizing us. If you disagree with us, we know it. You say so. But you treat us with respect.'"

Today, he insists, Israeli leaders in Jerusalem need to do a far better job of strengthening the economies and building the communities of Israel's Arab citizens, both Muslims and Christians, who after all make up close to one-quarter of the population.

"The attitude of Israelis toward Israeli Arabs could really show the Arab people [throughout the region] how we can all live together."

He is especially interested in Israel and the Arabs partnering on high-tech projects.

"Young Arab Israelis are studying at Israeli schools, graduating, and developing skills, and they come to me and say, 'Give us a chance to succeed.'"

In the post-COVID world, he looks forward to the day that Arab citizens will be leaders in Israel's technology sector, just as a growing number of Arabs are now serving in high positions in business, finance, the policy forces, and even as justices on Israel's Supreme Court.

THE ABRAHAM ACCORDS

Were you surprised by the dramatic diplomatic breakthroughs of 2020? I asked.

Not at all, Rivlin replied without missing a beat. "I thought this was possible eighty years ago."

He has always believed that true peace, mutual respect, and cooperation between Jews and Arabs was possible because he had seen it with his own eyes growing up. We sat together just days after he welcomed the first-ever delegation of Bahraini diplomats to Jerusalem to discuss how to accelerate commercial, cultural, and tourism ties, and Rivlin was enthusiastic about the Abraham Accords because they validated his view of how Arab-Israeli relations should be.

"I believe the Abraham Accords are very important," he told me. "I know that the people of the Emirates, and the people ruling the Emirates and ruling Bahrain and ruling Saudi Arabia, they are people who have never had a war with Israel. They are very open. They are very successful in the business world and they believe in the power of free markets. So it is easier to make peace with them.

"These countries are very important to us, and peace with them shows that we have no war with Islam, that we have no war with Arab nations. We have only war with people who are trying to reject our right to exist and who are trying to destroy us."

JESUS THE PEACEMAKER?

There is one other topic that has animated Rivlin as much or more than any other.

The president of Israel was passionate about honoring—indeed, celebrating—the place where Jesus of Nazareth was baptized in the Jordan River.

That may sound surprising. I was certainly surprised. But this was a project he was investing a great deal of time on, especially in his final year or so in office. Specifically, he was working together with the kingdom of Jordan and the Palestinian Authority to restore the historic baptism site of Jesus and make it a must-see destination for millions upon millions of Christians, Jews, and Muslims.

Upon becoming president in 2014, Rivlin began noticing that Christians wanted to see the place where Jesus was baptized by John the Baptist; yet, because so many land mines remain from past Arab-Israeli wars, and the area lacked developed facilities, the site known as Qasr al-Yahud—Castle of the Jews—was receiving only about one thousand Christian tourists a year. He also noticed that there was only one church in the area, an ancient monastery built around AD 400, which was also one of the first churches built after the Romans adopted Christianity as their official religion.

Upon the advice of then–Major General Yoav Mordechai, who served as the Israeli military's coordinator of government activities in the territories (COGAT) from 2014 to 2018, Rivlin became intrigued with the idea of bringing millions of Christian tourists, among others—so long as the initiative would benefit not only Israel but also the Palestinians and the Jordanians. He found funds to begin clearing the Jordan Valley of mines and worked to improve access to the site and draw attention to it. By 2019, before the coronavirus pandemic hit, nearly one million tourists visited Qasr al-Yahud.

As Lynn and I had seen on our visits to Jordan, King Abdullah has already created a national park on the east side of the river to honor the baptism of Jesus. He also invited thirteen historic Christian denominations to build churches and cathedrals there and directed archaeologists to excavate the site known in the New Testament as Bethany beyond the Jordan, where John the Baptist lived and ministered for a time.

So Rivlin began thinking: What if Israel could work with the Jordanians to create a unique international park that linked the two baptism sites, that would have bridges allowing tourists on Israel's side to cross over and see the Jordanian churches and Bethany beyond the Jordan and that allowed tourists on the Jordanian side to cross over and visit the Israeli side, all within a jointly operated "security bubble" that would keep everyone safe?

"I want to allow people to fulfill their wishes to be baptized," he told me.

To get the buy-in of Roman Catholics, Rivlin went to the Vatican and explained the potential of the project to encourage cooperation between Christians, Jews, and Muslims—and asked for the pope's blessing for the project.

Pope Francis loved the idea and told Rivlin, "If you manage to do this, you could bring peace to the region."

Rivlin then went back to the Jordanians and found the idea received favorably by King Abdullah and Prince Ghazi, the king's special representative for interfaith religious matters. Rivlin went back to the Vatican and gave the pope an update. Pope Francis said he would love to come to the site once such a project was ready to be implemented.

Then the controversy over Netanyahu's annexation proposal for the Jordan River Valley brought all talks to a halt. Now, however, because the Israeli government opted for the Abraham Accords rather than annexation, the negotiations are getting back on track. Rivlin says Palestinian leaders have been cautiously supportive, so long as Israel does not change the status of the baptism site. They do not want the site to be annexed into Israel. For now, they want the Israeli commander of the territories to oversee the area until a final status agreement is reached defining borders.

Rivlin agreed.

He even found funding to create mechanisms to clean the water flowing through the Jordan so that it will not be so murky—so that those being baptized will have the optimal experience.

"This is going to be very good for the Palestinians and specifically for Jericho," he told me with excitement in his voice. "Millions of Christians are going to come to Israel, visit the Church of the Nativity in Bethlehem, visit the Via Dolorosa and Church of the Holy Sepulchre in Jerusalem, then go up to Nazareth and visit the Church of the Annunciation. Then they will visit the Sea of Galilee and come down the Jordan Valley and visit Qasr al-Yahud and get baptized in the Jordan River, and then cross over the river and visit the national park of the churches in Jordan, and then come back into Israel."

Jericho, he insisted, will become "one of the most interesting cities" for Jews and Christians who know their Bibles, and "tens of thousands of new jobs will be created in hotels, restaurants, and other tourist sites."

Jesus told his disciples, "Blessed are the peacemakers."

How remarkable would it be if a Jewish president and a Muslim monarch found a way to advance peace by honoring the life and ministry of Jesus and welcoming millions of his followers to come and step into the story for themselves?

I love Rivlin's vision and told him I stood ready to help advance this project in any way I can, particularly with evangelicals in the U.S. and around the world for whom the biblical accounts of Jesus' life have so powerfully transformed their own.

During his years as Speaker of the Knesset, Rivlin met with many Christian leaders from all over the world and developed a fondness for evangelicals. Indeed, he told me that while he and his fellow Jewish members of Parliament do not believe that Jesus is the Messiah, they have been touched by how deeply and unapologetically evangelicals love Israel and the Jewish people.

Years ago, Rivlin shared, "I was a partner with [Menachem] Begin and Yitzhak Rabin and we met a prominent Christian leader. Rabin asked the minister, who was praising the Jewish people, 'Tell me, why do you love us so much?' And the Christian man said, 'We believe in the Redemption, and we believe the Redemption will only come when all of the Jews get to the land of Israel, and then they will really recognize that he—Yeshua—is the Son of God. There is no possibility to get to the Redemption unless we bring all the Jews to the land of Israel and let them find by themselves that they were wrong two thousand years ago.' So Rabin said to him, 'As long as we agree to the first step—that all the Jews will return to Israel—we have no problem. We are partners. Absolute partners. One hundred percent. But about the second step, when he will return, we will ask him . . .'"

Rivlin's voice trailed off. He did not finish the sentence, but he did not need to. Many Israelis and other Jewish leaders around the world have said this to me before, so I knew where he was heading.

"When the Messiah comes, we will ask him," the line typically goes, "'Have you been here before?'"

A FINAL WORD

I cannot fully explain why doors to such intriguing leaders have opened for me.

A Jewish follower of Jesus discussing matters of war and peace and religious freedom and economic prosperity with the most powerful men and women in the world is not normal. But it has been fascinating, and I have been humbled by the opportunities that God has given me.

Two decades after those horrific attacks of 9/11, the Middle East and North Africa are in the throes of sweeping, stunning, nearly unfathomable change. We have seen wars and heard rumors of war. We have seen terror and revolution, jihad and genocide. But we have also seen moments of breathtaking statesmanship and courage, seasons of game-changing peace-making, and a thousand small acts of kindness and generosity.

With so much swirling about in the vortex of the Middle East, so much of the future remains as murky as the waters of the Jordan River. Yet one thing is clear: What is needed more than ever are leaders at every level of government, business, the media, academia, and the church who can clearly see the threats, understand the opportunities, and have the wisdom to know how best to navigate forward.

The Bible speaks of the ancient tribe of Issachar, "men who understood the times and knew what Israel should do."[18]

May every state and kingdom in this region—and those affecting the region—find, honor, and elevate men and women who understand our times and know what their nation should do.

Acknowledgments

Working on *Enemies and Allies* has been one of the most fascinating journeys on which I have ever been fortunate enough to embark—not just the writing, but also the traveling, reporting, researching, and editing.

Best of all, it was not a journey I had to take on my own.

Every step of the way, I have been blessed with an extraordinarily smart, professional, and dedicated team willing to help me in a wide variety of ways. In a moment, I will thank them by name. But first let me thank all of the royal, political, military, intelligence, business, and religious leaders in Israel and the Arab and Muslim world who have invited me to spend time with them, shared their stories and perspectives with me, and let my colleagues and me ask our questions.

Most of those I have listed here spoke on the record. Some chose not to be quoted but provided enormously important context and guidance to help me better understand the complex and fast-moving changes underway in their countries and throughout the region. Many more (especially Palestinians) spoke to me on the condition that they would not be mentioned or quoted at all—so concerned were they for their freedom, and even some for their safety. To all, I am deeply grateful.

BAHRAIN

- Khalid bin Ahmed Al Khalifa, diplomatic advisor to the king and former foreign minister

- Abdulla bin Rashid Al Khalifa, ambassador to the United States
- Thomas Bezas, chief of staff to the ambassador to the U.S.
- Zayed bin Rashid Alzayani, minister of industry, commerce, and tourism
- Tariq Al Hasan, chief of public security
- Ahdeya Ahmed Al-Sayed, president of the Bahraini Journalists Association

EGYPT

- Abdel Fattah el-Sisi, president
- Abbas Kamel, chief of intelligence
- Mohamed Mokhtar Gomaa, minister of religious affairs
- Shawki Ibrahim Abdel-Karim Allam, Grand Mufti
- Yasser Reda, ambassador to the United States
- Ashraf Mamdouh, minister at the Egyptian embassy in Washington
- Ahmed Helmi, counselor at the Egyptian embassy in Washington
- Pope Tawadros II of Alexandria, head of the Coptic Orthodox churches of Egypt
- Andrea Zaki, president of the Protestant Churches of Egypt
- Shafik Gabr, founder of the East-West: The Art of the Dialogue initiative
- Thomas Goldberger, chargé d'affaires at the U.S. Embassy in Cairo

ISRAEL

- Reuven Rivlin, president
- Benjamin Netanyahu, prime minister
- Benny Gantz, defense minister, alternate PM and former IDF chief of staff
- Ofir Akunis, minister for regional cooperation
- Yair Lapid, member of Knesset and leader of the opposition
- David Friedman, U.S. ambassador to Israel during the Trump administration
- Aryeh Lightstone, counselor to Ambassador Friedman
- Major General Aharon Ze'evi Farkash, IDF, retired, former head of military intelligence
- Gadi Eisenkot, former IDF chief of staff

- Ron Dermer, ambassador to the United States
- Fleur Hassan-Nahoum, deputy mayor of Jerusalem
- Shuli Davidovich, foreign policy advisor to President Rivlin
- Reuven Azar, foreign policy advisor to Prime Minister Netanyahu
- Yarden Avriel Lato, foreign policy advisor to Defense Minister Gantz
- David Aaronson, foreign policy advisor to Minister for Regional Cooperation Akunis
- Mordechai (Moti) Zaken, advisor to the minister of public security
- Oded Revivi, mayor of Efrat and international liaison of the Council of Jewish Communities in Judea and Samaria
- Nitzan Chen, director of the Government Press Office
- Barak Ravid, diplomatic correspondent for Axios
- Yaakov Katz, editor in chief of the *Jerusalem Post*
- Calev Ben-David, anchor for i24 News
- Nurit Ben, former anchor for i24 News
- Amir Tibon, diplomatic correspondent for Haaretz
- Chris Mitchell, bureau chief for CBN News
- Calev Myers, president of ARISE (Alliance to Reinforce Israel's Security and Economy)

JORDAN

- King Abdullah II
- Prince El Hassan bin Talal, former crown prince and brother of the late King Hussein
- Lieutenant General Mahmoud Friehat, chairman of the Joint Chiefs of Staff
- Abdullah Ensour, former prime minister
- Ayman Safadi, foreign minister
- Nasser Judeh, former foreign minister
- Prince Ghazi bin Muhammad, personal envoy and special advisor to the king
- Rob Richer, former CIA station chief in Jordan, former CIA associate deputy director for operations, and former chief of the CIA's Near East and South Asia division

- Manar Dabbas, chief of staff of the king's office
- Jafar Hassan, former deputy prime minister and former chief of staff for King Abdullah II
- Dina Kawar, ambassador to the United States
- Dana Zureikat Daoud, director of the Jordan Information Bureau
- Henry Wooster, U.S. ambassador to Jordan
- Imad Maayah, president of the Evangelical Synod of Jordan
- Imad Shehadeh, president of the Jordan Evangelical Theological Seminary (JETS)
- Captain Emad Kawar, Royal Jordanian Airline executive and JETS board vice-chairman

PALESTINIANS

- Ghaith al-Omari, former advisor to the Palestinian negotiating team during the permanent status talks (1999–2001) and former executive director of the American Task Force on Palestine
- Khalil Sayegh, member of the All Arab News advisory board, senior correspondent for All Arab News, advocacy fellow with the Philos Project
- Bassem Eid, founder and former director of the Palestinian Human Rights Monitoring Group
- Numerous others who requested anonymity

SAUDI ARABIA

- Mohammed bin Salman, crown prince and defense minister
- Khalid bin Salman, vice defense minister and former ambassador to the United States
- Adel al-Jubeir, foreign minister
- Ahmed Al-Issa, former education minister
- Sheikh Abdullatif bin Abdulaziz Al-Sheikh, minister of Islamic affairs, da'wah, and guidance
- Reema bint Bandar, ambassador to the United States
- Ryan Gliha, U.S. representative to the Organization of Islamic Cooperation and consul general at the U.S. Consulate General in Jeddah

UNITED ARAB EMIRATES

- Mohammed bin Zayed Al Nahyan, crown prince of Abu Dhabi
- Abdullah bin Zayed Al Nahyan, foreign minister
- Anwar Gargash, diplomatic advisor to Mohammed bin Zayed and former minister of state for foreign affairs
- Nahayan bin Mubarak Al Nahyan, minister of tolerance and coexistence
- Yousef Al Otaiba, minister and ambassador to the United States
- Steven Bondy, chargé d'affaires, U.S. Embassy in the UAE
- Tim Fincher, CEO of the Oasis Hospital (aka Kanad Hospital) in Abu Dhabi
- Ralph Leo, board member of the Oasis Hospital in Abu Dhabi
- Andrew Thompson, priest of St. Andrew's Anglican church in Abu Dhabi
- Jeramie Rinne, former senior pastor of the Evangelical Community Church in Abu Dhabi
- Jim Burgess, senior pastor, Fellowship Dubai evangelical church

UNITED STATES

- Donald J. Trump, forty-fifth president of the United States
- Mike Pence, vice president during the Trump administration
- Mike Pompeo, director of the Central Intelligence Agency and secretary of state during the Trump administration
- Dan Coats, director of national intelligence during the Trump administration
- Jason Greenblatt, former White House special envoy to the Middle East
- General John Abizaid, U.S. Army, retired, and former U.S. ambassador to Saudi Arabia
- Sam Brownback, ambassador for international religious freedom during the Trump administration
- Dan Shapiro, ambassador to Israel during the Obama administration
- Dennis Ross, senior Middle East policy advisor to Presidents Bush, Clinton, and Obama
- David Makovsky, senior advisor to Secretary of State John Kerry

- Porter Goss, former director of the Central Intelligence Agency
- Tom Rose, senior advisor to Vice President Pence
- Sarah Makin, National Security Council
- Kirsten Fontenrose, National Security Council
- K. C. Stevens, National Security Council
- Ludovic Hood, National Security Council
- Hogan Gidley, former deputy White House press secretary
- Lindsey Graham, U.S. senator from South Carolina
- Tom Cotton, U.S. senator from Arkansas
- John Boozman, U.S. senator from Arkansas
- Doug Lamborn, U.S. congressman from Colorado
- Lynn Westmoreland, former U.S. congressman from Georgia
- Jeff Miller, former U.S. congressman from Florida
- Frank Wolf, former U.S. congressman from Virginia
- Jeff Fortenberry, U.S. congressman from Nebraska
- Robert Aderholt, U.S. congressman from Alabama
- Reagan Hedlund, former aide to Mike Pompeo
- Rob Satloff, executive director of the Washington Institute for Near East Policy
- Simon Henderson, Washington Institute for Near East Policy
- Cliff May, founder and president of the Foundation for the Defense of Democracies
- Jonathan Schanzer, senior vice president for research, Foundation for the Defense of Democracies
- Michael Doran, senior fellow at the Hudson Institute
- Arne Christenson, managing director, American Israel Public Affairs Committee

NEAR EAST MEDIA BOARD OF DIRECTORS
- J. Kenneth Blackwell, former U.S. ambassador to the U.N. for human rights and former secretary of state of Ohio
- Michael Little, president of the Christian Broadcasting Network, member of the board of directors of National Religious Broadcasters
- Skip Heitzig, pastor of Calvary Church in Albuquerque

- Joseph Magen, cofounder and chief operating officer of Near East Media, managing editor of All Israel News and All Arab News

ALL ISRAEL NEWS ADVISORY BOARD
- Danny Ayalon, former Israeli ambassador to the United States
- Steve Linde, editor in chief of the Jerusalem Report
- Rivka Kidron, former advisor to Israel's prime minister for diaspora and Christian affairs
- Uri Steinberg, former Israeli tourism commissioner for North America
- Jürgen Bühler, president of the International Christian Embassy Jerusalem
- Mike Huckabee, former governor of Arkansas and presidential candidate
- Anne Graham Lotz, evangelical leader and daughter of Billy Graham
- Jerry Boykin, former commander of Delta Force and former deputy undersecretary of defense for intelligence
- Melody Sucharewicz, former foreign policy advisor to Benny Gantz
- David Shedd, former acting director of the U.S. Defense Intelligence Agency
- Barbara Stevens, former senior officer at the Central Intelligence Agency
- Rick Santorum, former U.S. senator and congressman from Pennsylvania and former member of the Senate Armed Services committee
- Bob Vander Plaats, evangelical leader and president of The Family Leader
- Samuel Rodriguez, president of the National Hispanic Christian Leadership Conference

ALL ARAB NEWS ADVISORY BOARD
- Sheikh Mohammad Al-Issa, secretary-general of the Muslim World League
- Ali Rashid Al Nuaimi, chairman of the Hedayah center, chairman of the defense affairs, interior, and foreign affairs committee of the UAE Federal National Council

- Houda Nonoo, first female Bahraini ambassador to the United States and the first Jewish ambassador from the Arab region
- Khalil Sayegh, Palestinian Christian and advocacy fellow with the Philos Project
- Nadine Maenza, U.S. Commission on International Religious Freedom
- Johnnie Moore, U.S. Commission on International Religious Freedom
- Robert Nicholson, president and executive director of the Philos Project
- A. Larry Ross, media advisor to numerous American evangelical leaders, former spokesman for Billy Graham

I am deeply grateful to the members of each of the six evangelical delegations I led to Arab countries, several of whom have been trusted partners in Near East Media and our two media ventures, All Israel News and All Arab News. Their wise counsel, prayer, and encouragement has been—and continues to be—invaluable.

Scott Miller, my literary agent, has been a trusted friend and professional advisor from the very beginning of my career. I am so thankful for him and his colleagues at Trident Media Group.

The team at Tyndale House Publishers is the best in the business. Thank you to Mark Taylor, Jeff Johnson, Ron Beers, Karen Watson, Jan Stob, Andrea Garcia, Maria Eriksen, the amazing sales force, and all the remarkable professionals who make Tyndale an industry leader. Special thanks to Dave Lindstedt, who edited this book, and Libby Dykstra, who designed the cover. They are consummate professionals and did an amazing job.

To Nancy Pierce and June Meyers—my two heroes—who take care of all my logistical needs, from scheduling and correspondence to flights and finances and so much more. I am so grateful for you both. Your kindness and attention to detail, and to the many curveballs routinely thrown your way (not always by me!), are so impressive. God bless you both.

Thank you so much to Lynn's family and mine for loving us and praying for us and standing with us in countless ways, big and small.

A special shout-out to two of our four sons—Jacob and Jonah—who accompanied me on several of these delegations, took detailed notes, took photos, assisted with logistics, and were a valued source of encouragement and prayer. It was great to work with you both on this project. You both were incredibly helpful. Let's do more together!

Finally, and most importantly, to my amazing wife, Lynn—thank you for being my best friend and greatest ally.

Lynn and I met at Syracuse University in 1986. Began dating in the fall of 1988. Got engaged in the summer of 1989. Married in the summer of 1990, just weeks before Saddam Hussein invaded Kuwait and began transforming the Middle East in ways we hardly could have imagined. What an adventure it has been. I have loved every minute. I'm especially grateful that Lynn was at my side when King Abdullah II invited us to Jordan in the spring of 2006. That trip truly changed the course of our lives. What a joy it was to be there together. I can't wait to see what lies ahead.

About the Author

JOEL C. ROSENBERG is a *New York Times* bestselling author of sixteen novels and five nonfiction books with nearly 5 million copies in print.

Rosenberg's career as a political thriller writer was born out of his film-making studies at Syracuse University, where he graduated with a BFA in film drama in 1989. He also studied for nearly six months at Tel Aviv University during his junior year. Following graduation from Syracuse, he moved to Washington, D.C., where he worked for a range of U.S. and Israeli leaders and nonprofit organizations, serving variously as a policy analyst and communications strategist.

He has been profiled by the *New York Times*, the *Washington Times*, and the *Jerusalem Post* and has appeared on hundreds of radio and TV programs in the U.S., Canada, and around the world. As a sought-after speaker, he has addressed audiences at the White House, the Pentagon, the U.S. Capitol, the Israeli president's residence, the European Union parliament in Brussels, and business and faith conferences in North America and around the world.

The grandson of Orthodox Jews who escaped out of czarist Russia in the early 1900s, Rosenberg comes from a Jewish background on his father's side and a Gentile background on his mother's side.

Rosenberg is the founder and chairman of The Joshua Fund, a non-profit educational and humanitarian relief organization. He is also the founder and editor in chief of All Israel News (allisrael.com) and All Arab News (allarab.news).

He and his wife, Lynn, are dual U.S.-Israeli citizens. They made aliyah in 2014 and live in Jerusalem. They have four sons: Caleb, Jacob, Jonah, and Noah.

For more information, visit joelrosenberg.com and follow Joel on Twitter (@joelcrosenberg) and Facebook (facebook.com/JoelCRosenberg).

Notes

PREFACE

1. "A U.S.-led military coalition invaded the country in 2001 to outset the Taliban regime at the time for sheltering the al-Qaida terrorist network blamed for the terrorist attacks on the United States in September of that year. The war has since reportedly killed more than 150,000 people, including local security forces, civilians, insurgents, and foreign troops." Ayaz Gul, "U.N.: Afghan War Caused 100,000 Civilian Casualties since 2009," Voice of America, December 26, 2019, https://www.voanews.com/south-central-asia/un-afghan-war-caused-100000-civilian-casualties-2009.

2. Estimates vary widely, but one credible estimate puts the number of Iraqi deaths by violence at 240,000 between 2003 and 2011. From 2012 to 2018, the worst years of the Iraqi insurgency, another 82,000 Iraqis were killed. This does not account for the estimated 160,000 Iraqis who may have died from war-related causes, including the lack of food, disease, etc. See Philip Bump, "15 Years after the Iraq War Began, the Death Toll Is Still Murky," *Washington Post*, March 20, 2018, https://www.washingtonpost.com/news/politics/wp/2018/03/20/15-years-after-it-began-the-death-toll-from-the-iraq-war-is-still-murky/. The U.S. Institute of Peace puts the death toll at around 100,000. See Sarhang Hamasaeed and Garrett Nada, "Iraq Timeline: Since the 2003 War," United States Institute of Peace, May 29, 2020, https://www.usip.org/publications/2020/05/iraq-timeline-2003-war. A study cited by the BBC in 2013 estimated total war-related deaths in Iraq at 461,000. See "Iraq Study Estimates War-Related Deaths at 461,000," BBC News, October 16, 2013, https://www.bbc.com/news/world-middle-east-24547256. The cost of the Iraq War is estimated at more than $2 trillion, according to the Costs of War Project through Brown University. See Paulina Cachero, "U.S. Taxpayers Have Reportedly Paid an Average of $8,000 Each and over $2 Trillion Total for the Iraq War Alone," Business Insider, February 6, 2020, https://www.businessinsider.com/us-taxpayers-spent-8000-each-2-trillion-iraq-war-study-2020-2.

3. According to a report published in 2020 by the Syrian Observatory for Human Rights, the group documented 384,660 deaths in Syria from March 15, 2011, to

May 28, 2020. See Syrian Observatory for Human Rights, *2020-2006, 14 Years of Defending Human Rights*, https://www.syriahr.com/en/wp-content/uploads /2020/06/14-y-en.pdf. See also "Syria Death Toll Tops 380,000 in Almost Nine -Year War," Agence France-Presse, April 1, 2020, https://www.france24.com/en /20200104-syria-death-toll-tops-380-000-in-almost-nine-year-war-monitor; Samy Magdy, "Report: Death Toll from Yemen's War Hit 100,000 since 2015," Associated Press, October 31, 2019, https://apnews.com/article /b7f039269a394b7aa2b46430e3d9b6bc.

4. For the number of rockets fired at Israel, see "Weekend of Rockets over Israel," Israel Ministry of Foreign Affairs, May 5, 2019, https://mfa.gov.il/MFA /ForeignPolicy/Terrorism/Pages/Weekend-of-rockets-over-Israel-5-May-2019 .aspx. The accuracy of Palestinian casualty figures is much debated. I used figures from the Israeli human rights group B'Tselem. From 2000 through 2020, the group says 7,480 Palestinians were killed in Gaza by IDF forces and Israeli civilians. See "Fatalities since Operation Cast Lead," B'Tselem, https://www .btselem.org/statistics/fatalities/after-cast-lead/by-date-of-event; "Fatalities during Operation Cast Lead," B'Tselem, https://www.btselem.org/statistics/fatalities /during-cast-lead/by-date-of-event; "Fatalities before Operation 'Cast Lead,'" B'Tselem, https://www.btselem.org/statistics/fatalities/before-cast-lead/by-date -of-event.

5. Bruce Riedel, "The Case of Saudi Arabia's Mohammed bin Nayef," Brookings, February 12, 2021, https://www.brookings.edu/blog/order-from-chaos/2021/02 /12/the-case-of-saudi-arabias-mohammed-bin-nayef/; Jackie Northam, *"Blood and Oil* Traces Mohammed Bin Salman's Rise as a Ruthless Saudi Leader," review of *Blood and Oil* by Bradley Hope and Justin Scheck, NPR, September 1, 2020, https://www.npr.org/2020/09/01/906645954/blood-and-oil-traces-mohammed -bin-salmans-rise-as-a-ruthless-saudi-leader; Donna Abu-Nasr, "Saudi Prince Is 'Toxic,' Graham Says as Pressure Rises on Trump," Bloomberg, October 16, 2018, https://www.bloomberg.com/news/articles/2018-10-16/graham-rips-saudi-crown -prince-as-wrecking-ball-on-world-stage.

6. Bruce Riedel, *Kings and Presidents: Saudi Arabia and the United States since FDR* (Washington, D.C.: Brookings Institution Press, 2017).

7. Ben Hubbard, *MBS: The Rise to Power of Mohammed bin Salman* (New York: Tim Duggan Books, 2020).

8. Bradley Hope and Justin Scheck, *Blood and Oil: Mohammed bin Salman's Ruthless Quest for Global Power* (New York: Hachette, 2020).

9. David D. Kirkpatrick, *Into the Hands of the Soldiers: Freedom and Chaos in Egypt and the Middle East* (New York: Viking, 2018).

CHAPTER 1: WHAT ARE THE MOST SERIOUS THREATS WE FACE TODAY IN THE MIDDLE EAST?

1. "Representative Mike Pompeo on Iran Nuclear Agreement," *Washington Journal*, C-SPAN, July 14, 2015, video, 43:34, https://www.c-span.org/video/?326986-4 /washington-journal-representative-mike-pompeo-r-ks, 00:07–01:16.

2. Tom Cotton and Mike Pompeo, "Release the Secret Iran Deals," editorial, *Wall Street Journal*, August 2, 2015, https://www.wsj.com/articles/release-the-secret -iran-deals-1438551622.

3. At the time, ISIS was sometimes also referred to as ISIL, the Islamic State of Iraq and the Levant. The Levant is an old French term that generally covers the territory we know today as Lebanon, Syria, Iraq, Jordan, the Palestinian Authority, and Israel. Though the terror organization has taken on several forms over the years, it was originally founded as al Qaeda in Iraq (AQI) by Abu Musab al-Zarqawi, a Jordanian-born terrorist, after receiving formal permission and encouragement from Osama bin Laden.

4. David Remnick, "Going the Distance: On and Off the Road with Barack Obama," *The New Yorker*, January 27, 2014, https://www.newyorker.com/magazine/2014/01/27/going-the-distance-david-remnick.

5. Joel C. Rosenberg, "We Are Watching Genocidal Conditions Emerge in Epicenter. U.S. President Orders Airstrikes on ISIS in Iraq [. . .]," blog, August 8, 2014, https://flashtrafficblog.epicentermedia.net/2014/08/08/we-are-watching-genocidal-conditions-emerge-in-epicenter-u-s-president-orders-airstrikes-on-isis-in-iraq-pray-especially-for-iraqi-christians-who-are-being-beheaded-crucified/; Joel C. Rosenberg, "Jihadist Rampage: Hamas Threatens to Relaunch War. ISIS Beheading Children & Christians in Iraq. 170,000 Killed in Syria. [. . .]," blog, August 7, 2014, https://flashtrafficblog.epicentermedia.net/2014/08/07/jihadist-rampage-hamas-threatens-to-relaunch-war-isis-beheading-children-christians-in-iraq-170000-killed-in-syria/.

6. Samuel Smith, "ISIS, Iran Are Agents of 'Apocalyptic Islam' Paving Way for 'Islamic Messiah,' Says NYT Bestselling Author," Christian Post, February 26, 2015, https://www.christianpost.com/news/isis-iran-are-agents-of-apocalyptic-islam-paving-way-for-islamic-messiah-says-nyt-bestselling-author-134746/. See also Joel C. Rosenberg, "The Biggest Threat Now Is Not Radical Islam. It Is 'Apocalyptic Islam.' [. . .]," blog, February 27, 2015, https://flashtrafficblog.epicentermedia.net/2015/02/27/the-biggest-threat-now-is-not-radical-islam-it-is-apocalyptic-islam-let-me-explain-excerpts-from-my-address-to-the-national-religious-broadcasters-convention/; Joel C. Rosenberg, "Fact Sheet: The Islamic State's Apocalyptic Beliefs," September 4, 2015, http://sites.tyndale.com/joelrosenberg/files/2015/09/RESEARCH-ApocalypticBeliefs-ISIS.pdf; Joel C. Rosenberg, "Islamic Extremists Are Trying to Hasten the Coming of the Mahdi," *National Review*, September 11, 2015, https://www.nationalreview.com/2015/09/radical-islam-iran-isis-apocalytpic-messiah-mahdi/; Joel C. Rosenberg, "What Is 'Apocalyptic Islam' and Why Is It So Dangerous? The Research behind My Remarks to the Jerusalem Leaders Summit," blog, November 5, 2015, https://flashtrafficblog.epicentermedia.net/2015/11/05/what-is-apocalyptic-islam-and-why-is-it-so-dangerous-the-research-behind-my-remarks-to-the-jerusalem-leaders-summit/; Joel C. Rosenberg, "Eerie Front-Page NYT Story Examines ISIS Prophecies about an Apocalyptic Showdown in Syrian Town of Dabiq [. . .]," blog, December 8, 2015, https://flashtrafficblog.epicentermedia.net/2015/12/08/front-page-nyt-story-examines-isis-prophecies-about-an-apocalyptic-showdown-in-syrian-town-of-dabiq-story-looks-ripped-from-the-first-hostage-my-forthcoming-novel-about-a-showdown-over-dabiq/; Joel C. Rosenberg, "What the Next U.S. President Will Need to Know about Iran and Islamic State," blog, January 7, 2016, https://flashtrafficblog.epicentermedia.net/2016/01/07/what-the-next-us-president-will-need-to-know-about-iran-and-islamic-state-my-column-in-the-jerusalem-post/; Joel C. Rosenberg, "ISIS Waging

War of Genocide against Christians in the Mideast. New U.N. Report Provides Chilling Details," blog, January 23, 2016, https://flashtrafficblog.epicentermedia .net/2016/01/23/breaking-news-isis-waging-war-of-genocide-against-christians-in -the-mideast-new-un-report-provides-chilling-details/.

7. Expressing the Sense of Congress That the Atrocities Perpetrated by ISIL against Religious and Ethnic Minorities in Iraq and Syria Include War Crimes, Crimes against Humanity, and Genocide, H.Con.Res. 75, 114th Cong. (September 2015), Congress.gov, https://www.congress.gov/bill/114th-congress/house -concurrent-resolution/75/all-info.

8. "Letter to Secretary Kerry—Urge to Include Christians in Designation of ISIS Genocide," Vote Smart, December 8, 2015, https://justfacts.votesmart.org/public -statement/1063268/letter-to-secretary-kerry-urge-to-include-christians-in -designation-of-isis-genocide.

9. Joel C. Rosenberg, "Congress to Obama: Label ISIS Attacks against Christians 'Genocide.' Here's the Latest," blog, March 15, 2016, https://flashtrafficblog .epicentermedia.net/2016/03/15/congress-to-obama-label-isis-attacks-against -christians-genocide-heres-the-latest/.

10. Justin Fishel, "ISIS Has Committed Genocide, Obama Administration Declares," ABC News, March 17, 2016, https://abcnews.go.com /US/secretary-state-john-kerry-declare-isis-committed-genocide /story?id=37713938.

11. Joel C. Rosenberg, "The Obama Administration (Finally) Accuses ISIS of Genocide. Here's the Latest," blog, March 17, 2016, https://flashtrafficblog .epicentermedia.net/2016/03/17/the-obama-administration-finally-accuses-isis-of -genocide-heres-the-latest/.

12. Mike Pompeo, interview by author, September 24, 2020.

13. Zeke Miller, "White House Says bin Laden Son Killed in U.S. Operation," Associated Press, September 14, 2009, https://apnews.com/article /107bb5b28f1c434b91c154e765a80350.

14. "Statement from the President," Archived Trump White House, National Archives and Records Administration, February 6, 2020, https:// trumpwhitehouse.archives.gov/briefings-statements/statement-from-the -president-13/.

15. Andrew Hanna and Garrett Nada, "Jihadism: A Generation after 9/11," Wilson Center, September 10, 2020, https://www.wilsoncenter.org/article/jihadism -generation-after-911.

16. Hanna and Nada, "Jihadism."

17. Matthew Lee and James LaPorta, "U.S., Israel Worked Together to Track and Kill al Qaida No. 2," Associated Press, November 15, 2020, https://apnews.com /article/embassies-israel-iran-dar-es-salaam-tanzania-1df82848c97cb11f0d82f50 055faf7b5.

18. Syrian Observatory for Human Rights, *2020-2006, 14 Years of Defending Human Rights*, https://www.syriahr.com/en/wp-content/uploads/2020/06/14-y-en.pdf.

19. "Secretary Michael R. Pompeo Remarks to Traveling Press," U.S. State Department Archives, September 11, 2020, https://2017-2021.state.gov/secretary-michael -r-pompeo-remarks-to-traveling-press-5//index.html. This marks an improvement from a Defense Intelligence Agency assessment in 2019 that found there were only

three hundred al Qaeda fighters operating in Afghanistan. See *Operation Freedom's Sentinel: Lead Inspector General's Report to the United States Congress* (July 1–September 30, 2019), 19, https://media.defense.gov/2019/Nov/20/2002214020/-1/-1/1/Q4FY2019_LEADIG_OFS_REPORT.PDF.

20. David Shedd, interview by author, November 2, 2020.
21. Bruce Riedel, "Al Qaida Today: 18 Years after 9/11," Brookings Institution, *Order from Chaos* (blog), September 10, 2019, https://www.brookings.edu/blog/order-from-chaos/2019/09/10/al-qaida-today-18-years-after-9-11/.
22. Ben Rhodes, "The 9/11 Era Is Over," *The Atlantic*, April 6, 2020, https://www.theatlantic.com/ideas/archive/2020/04/its-not-september-12-anymore/609502/.
23. Cameron Glenn et al., "Timeline: The Rise, Spread, and Fall of the Islamic State," Wilson Center, October 28, 2019, https://www.wilsoncenter.org/article/timeline-the-rise-spread-and-fall-the-islamic-state.
24. "The United States and Our Global Partners Have Liberated All ISIS-Controlled Territory," Archived Trump White House, National Archives and Records Administration, March 23, 2019, https://trumpwhitehouse.archives.gov/briefings-statements/united-states-global-partners-liberated-isis-controlled-territory/; "U.S. Report: ISIS and al Qaeda Threats in 2019," Wilson Center, June 30, 2020, https://www.wilsoncenter.org/article/us-report-isis-and-al-qaeda-threats-2019; Syrian Observatory for Human Rights, *2020-2006, 14 Years of Defending Human Rights*, https://www.syriahr.com/en/wp-content/uploads/2020/06/14-y-en.pdf.
25. "Remarks by President Trump on the Death of ISIS Leader Abu Bakr al-Baghdadi," Archived Trump White House, National Archives and Records Administration, October 27, 2019, https://trumpwhitehouse.archives.gov/briefings-statements/remarks-president-trump-death-isis-leader-abu-bakr-al-baghdadi/.
26. William McCants, conversations with author. See also William McCants, *The ISIS Apocalypse: The History, Strategy, and Doomsday Vision of the Islamic State* (New York: St. Martin's Press, 2015).
27. David Shedd, interview by author, November 2, 2020.

CHAPTER 2: WHY IS IRAN A THREAT LIKE NO OTHER?

1. Patricia Zengerle and Roberta Rampton, "Congress Invites Netanyahu for Iran Speech, Obama Blindsided," Reuters, January 21, 2015, https://www.reuters.com/article/us-iran-nuclear-israel-congress-idUSKBN0KU1TH20150121. See also Matt Spetalnick and Jeffrey Heller, "Obama Will Not Meet Israel's Netanyahu on U.S. Visit," Reuters, January 22, 2015, https://www.reuters.com/article/us-israel-congress-idUSKBN0KV1UT20150122.
2. Devin Dwyer, "Vice President Biden Won't Attend Bibi Netanyahu Speech to Congress," ABC News, February 6, 2015, https://abcnews.go.com/Politics/vice-president-biden-bails-bibi-netanyahu-speech-congress/story?id=28783882.
3. Joel C. Rosenberg, interview by Glenn Beck, *Glenn Beck*, Fox News Channel, April 14, 2009. A transcript of the interview was posted on Joel C. Rosenberg's blog on April 15, 2009—"Train Wreck Coming in U.S.-Israel Relations over Iran [. . .]," https://flashtrafficblog.epicentermedia.net/2009/04/15/train-wreck-coming-in-us-israel-relations-over-iran-transcript-of-glenn-becks-interview-with-joel/.
4. David E. Sanger, "U.S. May Drop Key Condition for Talks with Iran," *New York*

Times, April 13, 2009, https://www.nytimes.com/2009/04/14/world/middleeast
/14diplo.html.

5. Rosenberg, interview by Glenn Beck, April 14, 2009.

6. For more on this, see Joel C. Rosenberg, *Inside the Revolution: How the Followers of Jihad, Jefferson & Jesus Are Battling to Dominate the Middle East and Transform the World* (Carol Stream, IL: Tyndale, 2009); Joel C. Rosenberg, "Islamic Extremists Are Trying to Hasten the Coming of the Mahdi," *National Review*, September 11, 2015, https://www.nationalreview.com/2015/09/radical-islam-iran-isis-apocalytpic
-messiah-mahdi/; Joel C. Rosenberg, "What the Next U.S. President Will Need to Know about Iran and Islamic State," editorial, *Jerusalem Post*, January 6, 2016, https://www.jpost.com/opinion/what-the-next-us-president-will-need-to-know
-about-iran-and-islamic-state-440672.

7. Rosenberg, interview by Glenn Beck, April 14, 2009.

8. Gil Stern Hoffman, "4% of Israeli Jews: Obama Pro-Israel," *Jerusalem Post*, August 27, 2009, https://www.jpost.com/Israel/4-percent-of-Israeli-Jews-Obama
-pro-Israel. See also Joel C. Rosenberg, "Train Wreck: Netanyahu Heading for U.S. as Israeli Trust in President Obama Plummets," blog, November 3, 2009, https://flashtrafficblog.epicentermedia.net/2009/11/03/train-wreck-netanyahu
-heading-for-u-s-as-israeli-trust-in-the-obama-plummets/.

9. "Transcript of Netanyahu's Speech to Congress," *New York Times*, March 3, 2015, https://www.nytimes.com/2015/03/04/us/politics/transcript-of-netanyahus
-remarks-to-congress.html.

10. Joe Biden, campaign speech, December 3, 2007, Iowa City Public Library.

11. Barack Obama, "Remarks by the President on the Iran Nuclear Deal," Archived Obama White House, National Archives and Records Administration, August 5, 2015, https://obamawhitehouse.archives.gov/the-press-office/2015/08/05/remarks
-president-iran-nuclear-deal.

12. Benjamin Netanyahu, interview by author, January 2007. At the time, Netanyahu was between stints as Israeli prime minister.

CHAPTER 3: THE RISE OF A RUSSIAN-IRANIAN AXIS

1. Some material in this chapter has been drawn from my nonfiction book *Israel at War* (Carol Stream, IL: Tyndale, 2012).

2. Muhammad Sahimi, "Who Murdered Prof. Ali-Mohammadi?" Tehran Bureau, PBS Frontline, January 13, 2010, http://www.pbs.org/wgbh/pages/frontline
/tehranbureau/2010/01/who-murdered-prof-ali-mohammadi.html.

3. Joel C. Rosenberg, "Updated: Covert War Underway in Iran to Sabotage Nuclear Facilities [. . .]," blog, September 29, 2010, http://flashtrafficblog.wordpress.com
/2010/09/29/covert-war-underway-in-iran-to-sabotage-nuclear-facilities-iran
-sentences-blogger-to-19-years-in-prison/.

4. Scott Shane, "Iranian Scientist Gunned Down at Home," *New York Times*, July 24, 2011, https://www.nytimes.com/2011/07/24/world/middleeast/24iran
.html.

5. Julian Borger and Saeed Kamali Dehghan, "Iranian Missile Architect Dies in Blast. But Was Explosion a Mossad Mission?" *The Guardian*, November 14, 2011, http://
www.guardian.co.uk/world/2011/nov/14/iran-missile-death-mossad-mission.

6. Yaakov Katz, "Blast in Iran Struck Uranium Enrichment Facility," *Jerusalem Post*, November 30, 2011, http://www.jpost.com/Defense/Article.aspx?id=247560.

7. "The Wrong Signals to Iran," editorial, *Washington Post*, December 8, 2011, http://www.washingtonpost.com/opinions/the-wrong-signals-to-iran/2011/12/06/gIQAvzNYgO_story.html?hpid=z3.

8. Joel C. Rosenberg, "Covert War Heats Up in Iran and Mideast [. . .]," blog, December 8, 2011, http://flashtrafficblog.wordpress.com/2011/12/08/covert-war-heats-up-in-iran-will-it-be-enough-to-neutralize-nuclear-threat-or-will-israel-launch-preemptive-strikes-in-2012/.

9. Yonah Jeremy Bob, "Yossi Cohen: The Mossad Spy Chief Who Stole Iran's Secret Nuclear Archives," *Jerusalem Post*, September 29, 2019, https://www.jpost.com/israel-news/yossi-cohen-the-mossad-spy-chief-who-stole-irans-secret-nuclear-archives-602811.

10. "PM Netanyahu Presents Conclusive Proof of Iranian Secret Nuclear Weapons Program," Israel Ministry of Foreign Affairs, April 30, 2018, https://mfa.gov.il/MFA/PressRoom/2018/Pages/PM-Netanyahu-presents-conclusive-proof-of-Iranian-secret-nuclear-weapons-program-30-April-2018.aspx. See also David E. Sanger and Ronen Bergman, "How Israel, in Dark of Night, Torched Its Way to Iran's Nuclear Secrets," *New York Times*, July 15, 2018, https://www.nytimes.com/2018/07/15/us/politics/iran-israel-mossad-nuclear.html.

11. David Albright, testimony before the House Subcommittee on National Security, Committee of Oversight and Government Reform, June 6, 2018, https://isis-online.org/uploads/isis-reports/documents/Testimony_albright_june_6%2C_2018.pdf.

12. *What Is New in the Iran Nuclear Archive?* (testimony of David Albright).

13. Michael Crowley, Falih Hassan, and Eric Schmitt, "U.S. Strike in Iraq Kills Qassim Suleimani, Commander of Iranian Forces," *New York Times*, January 2, 2020, https://www.nytimes.com/2020/01/02/world/middleeast/qassem-soleimani-iraq-iran-attack.html.

14. Mark Dubowitz (@mdubowitz), Twitter, January 3, 2020, 1:17 a.m., https://twitter.com/mdubowitz/status/1212996503096221697.

15. Crowley, Hassan, and Schmitt, "U.S. Strike in Iraq Kills Qassim Suleimani."

16. Nabih Bulos and Noga Tarnopolsky, "Gunned-Down Iranian Nuclear Scientist Was an Israeli Target for Years," *Los Angeles Times*, November 27, 2020, https://www.latimes.com/world-nation/story/2020-11-27/iranian-nuclear-scientist-killed-near-tehran-state-media.

17. David E. Sanger and Lara Jakes, "Iran Is Accused of Hiding Suspected Nuclear Activity," *New York Times*, June 19, 2020, https://www.nytimes.com/2020/06/19/us/politics/iran-nuclear-iaea.html.

18. Joel C. Rosenberg, "Iran Is the New Home for al Qaeda Terror Network—Poses 'Grave Threat' to U.S., Israel, Arab Allies—Pompeo Reveals," All Israel News, January 13, 2021, https://www.allisrael.com/iran-is-the-new-home-for-al-qaeda-terror-network-poses-grave-threat-to-us-israel-arab-allies-pompeo-reveals#/.

19. Hans M. Kristensen and Matt Korda, "Status of World Nuclear Forces," Federation of American Scientists, September 2020, https://fas.org/issues/nuclear-weapons/status-world-nuclear-forces/.

20. Kingston Reif, "Russian Strategic Nuclear Forces under New START," Arms Control Association, April 2020, https://www.armscontrol.org/factsheets/Russian-Strategic-Nuclear-Forces-Under-New-START.

21. "Unipolar World Does Not Exist Anymore, Says Putin," TASS Russian news agency, December 19, 2019, https://tass.com/politics/1101097.

22. Aharon Ze'evi-Farkash, interview by author, November 15, 2020.
23. Vladimir Putin with Nataliya Gevorkyan, Natalya Timakova, and Andrei Kolesnikov, *First Person: An Astonishingly Frank Self-Portrait by Russia's President Vladimir Putin*, trans. Catherine A. Fitzpatrick (New York: PublicAffairs, 2000).
24. Putin et al., 139–140.
25. Putin et al., 140.
26. Putin et al., 204.
27. Putin et al., 141, 168.
28. Putin et al., 186.
29. Putin et al., 194.
30. Putin et al., 131.
31. Alexis Mrachek and Shane McCrum, "How Putin Uses Russian Orthodoxy to Grow His Empire," Heritage Foundation, February 22, 2019, https://www.heritage .org/europe/commentary/how-putin-uses-russian-orthodoxy-grow-his-empire.
32. John M. Broder, "Despite a Secret Pact by Gore in '95, Russian Arms Sales to Iran Go On," *New York Times*, October 13, 2000, https://www.nytimes.com/2000/10/13 /world/despite-a-secret-pact-by-gore-in-95-russian-arms-sales-to-iran-go-on.html.
33. Lionel Beehner, "Russia-Iran Arms Trade," Council on Foreign Relations, November 1, 2006, https://www.cfr.org/backgrounder/russia-iran-arms-trade.
34. Anna Borshchevskaya, *Russia in the Middle East: Motives, Consequences, Prospects* (Washington, D.C.: Washington Institute for Near East Policy, February 2016), 24–25. Download pdf of monograph at https://www.washingtoninstitute.org/policy -analysis/russia-middle-east-motives-consequences-prospects.
35. Scott Peterson, "Russian Nuclear Know-How Pours into Iran," *Christian Science Monitor*, June 21, 2002, https://www.csmonitor.com/2002/0621/p01s03-woeu.html.
36. "Russia May Build Eight Nuclear Reactors for Iran," Reuters, May 22, 2014, https://www.reuters.com/article/us-iran-nuclear-russia/russia-may-build-eight -nuclear-reactors-for-iran-idUSBREA4L0KX20140522.
37. "Putin Arrives in Tehran for Summit," Al Jazeera, October 16, 2007, https://www.aljazeera.com/news/2007/10/16/putin-arrives-in-tehran-for-summit.
38. April Brady, "Russia Completes S-300 Delivery to Iran," Arms Control Association, December 2016, https://www.armscontrol.org/act/2016-11/news-briefs/russia -completes-s-300-delivery-iran.
39. Andrew Trotman, "Vladimir Putin Signs $20bn Oil Deal with Iran to Bypass Western Sanctions," *The Telegraph*, August 6, 2014, https://www.telegraph.co.uk /finance/newsbysector/energy/oilandgas/11014604/Vladimir-Putin-signs-historic -20bn-oil-deal-with-Iran-to-bypass-Western-sanctions.html.
40. Paul Sonne, Aresu Eqbali, and Jay Solmon, "Russian President Putin, Iran's Ayatollah Khamenei Meet to Discuss Syria," *Wall Street Journal*, November 23, 2015, https://www.wsj.com/articles/russian-president-putin-irans-supreme -leader-khamenei-meet-over-syria-1448300828.

CHAPTER 4: WHY THE ADDITION OF TURKEY TO THE RUSSIAN-IRANIAN AXIS IS SO DANGEROUS

1. Soner Cagaptay, *The New Sultan: Erdogan and the Crisis of Modern Turkey* (London: I. B. Tauris, 2017), 171–172.

2. "Putin Mends Broken Relations with Turkey's Erdogan," BBC News, August 9, 2016, https://www.bbc.com/news/world-europe-37018562.

3. Joel C. Rosenberg, "Turkey Continues Moving to the Dark Side: Erdogan Cuts Major Military Deal with Russia," blog, July 27, 2017, https://flashtrafficblog .epicentermedia.net/2017/07/27/turkey-continues-moving-to-the-dark-side -erdogan-cuts-major-military-deal-with-russia/.

4. "Ottoman Empire," History.com, last updated February 28, 2020, https://www.history.com/topics/middle-east/ottoman-empire.

5. Cagaptay, *New Sultan*, 7–10. Though I don't agree with all of Cagaptay's conclusions, this book was enormously helpful in understanding Erdoğan's origins, beliefs, and rise to political power. I drew on it heavily for this chapter.

6. Deborah Sontag, "The Erdogan Experiment," *New York Times Magazine*, May 11, 2003, https://www.nytimes.com/2003/05/11/magazine/the-erdogan-experiment .html.

7. Cagaptay, *New Sultan*, 49.

8. Cagaptay, 73.

9. Cagaptay, 75.

10. Sontag, "Erdogan Experiment."

11. Sontag, "Erdogan Experiment."

12. Andrew Purvis, "Turkey's Mystery Man," *Time*, November 18, 2002, 63, https://time.com/vault/issue/2002-11-18/page/65/.

13. Cagaptay, *New Sultan*, 83.

14. See Owen Bowcott, "Islamic Party Wins in Turkey," *The Guardian*, November 7, 2002, https://www.theguardian.com/world/2002/nov/07/turkey.owenbowcott.

15. Soner Cagaptay, "Why Erdogan Wants to Get Along with Trump," Washington Institute for Near East Policy, November 14, 2019, https://www.washingtoninstitute .org/policy-analysis/view/why-erdogan-wants-to-get-along-with-trump.

16. "PM Sharon Meets with Turkish PM Erdogan," Israel Ministry of Foreign Affairs, May 1, 2005, https://mfa.gov.il/mfa/pressroom/2005/pages/pm%20 sharon%20meets%20with%20turkish%20pm%20erdogan%201-may-2005.aspx; Greg Myre, "Turkish Leader Visits Israel, Restoring Friendly Ties," *New York Times*, May 2, 2005, https://www.nytimes.com/2005/05/02/world/middleeast /turkish-leader-visits-israel-restoring-friendly-ties.html.

17. Katrin Bennhold, "Leaders of Turkey and Israel Clash at Davos Panel," *New York Times*, January 29, 2009, https://www.nytimes.com/2009/01/30/world/europe /30clash.html.

18. "Turkish PM Erdogan Slams Shimon Peres for Israeli Killings and Walks off Stage," World Economic Forum, January 29, 2009, video, 3:29, https://www.youtube.com /watch?v=OrbQsHkVQ_4.

19. Kareem Shaheen, "A Year On, Families of 'Martyrs' Who Resisted Turkey Coup Count Cost," *The Guardian*, July 15, 2017, https://www.theguardian.com/world /2017/jul/15/a-year-on-families-of-martyrs-who-resisted-turkey-coup-count-cost.

20. Daniel Moritz-Rabson, "Two Years after Overcoming Attempted Coup, Turkey Plagued by Widespread Arrests and Purges of Civil Servants," *Newsweek*, July 15, 2018, https://www.newsweek.com/arrests-plague-turkey-two-years-after-coup -attempt-1024287.

21. Patrick Kingsley, "Erdogan Claims Vast Powers in Turkey after Narrow Victory in

Referendum," *New York Times*, April 16, 2017, https://www.nytimes.com/2017/04/16/world/europe/turkey-referendum-polls-erdogan.html.

22. Sontag, "Erdogan Experiment."

23. Porter Goss, interview by author, November 11, 2020.

24. Porter Goss, interview by author.

25. "Joel Rosenberg Remarks at 2018 Values Voter Summit," C-SPAN, September 21, 2018, video, 24:54, https://www.c-span.org/video/?c4750649/joel-rosenberg-remarks-2018-values-voter-summit, 23:23-23:35.

CHAPTER 5: I HAD NEVER MET A KING BEFORE

1. "Robert Richer," The Cipher Brief, https://www.thecipherbrief.com/experts/robert-richer.

2. Joel C. Rosenberg, "'The State of the Middle East Is a Catastrophe.' [. . .]," blog, January 12, 2016, https://flashtrafficblog.epicentermedia.net/2016/01/12/the-state-of-the-middle-east-is-a-catastrophe-my-interview-with-cbn-on-the-state-of-the-union-the-presidential-front-runners-the-visit-by-jordans-king-to-washington/; Joel C. Rosenberg, "'Rosenberg Blasts Obama for Snubbing Jordan's King Abdullah,' Reports CBN News," blog, January 12, 2016, https://flashtrafficblog.epicentermedia.net/2016/01/12/rosenberg-blasts-obama-for-snubbing-jordans-king-abdullah/.

3. Mark Thompson, "The Power of Vengeance," *Time*, February 5, 2015, https://time.com/3697760/jordan-isis-revenge/.

4. Khetam Malkawi, "Jordanian Air Force Destroyed '20% of Daesh Capabilities'—Commander," *Jordan Times*, February 8, 2015, http://www.jordantimes.com/news/local/jordanian-air-force-destroyed-20-daesh-capabilities'-commander.

5. See John 1:28.

6. "Letter from HM King Abdullah II," King's Academy, https://www.kingsacademy.edu.jo/about/letter-from-hm-king-abdullah-ii.

CHAPTER 6: WHO IS KING ABDULLAH II?

1. "The Making of Transjordan," History, The Hashemite Kingdom of Jordan, http://www.kinghussein.gov.jo/his_transjordan.html.

2. Pete Moore, "Countries at the Crossroads 2006," Freedom House, European Country of Origin Information Network, July 2006, https://www.ecoi.net/en/document/1258476.html.

3. Gwen Ackerman, "Jordan's King Touches Israelis by Joining Their Mourning," Associated Press, March 16, 1997, https://apnews.com/article/48b26c7e4552c7f935a18a1ec8366885.

4. "98 Press Conference with King Hussein of Jordan and Prime Minister Netanyahu [. . .]," Israel Ministry of Foreign Affairs, March 16, 1997, https://mfa.gov.il/MFA/ForeignPolicy/MFADocuments/Yearbook11/Pages/98%20Press%20Conference%20with%20King%20Hussein%20of%20Jordan%20an.aspx.

5. "98 Press Conference with King Hussein of Jordan and Prime Minister Netanyahu."

6. John F. Burns, "Jordan's King, in Gamble, Lends Hand to the U.S.," *New York Times*, March 9, 2003, https://www.nytimes.com/2003/03/09/world/threats-and-responses-allies-jordan-s-king-in-gamble-lends-hand-to-the-us.html.

7. "The Grand List of Endorsements of the Amman Message and Its Three Points," The Amman Message (website), https://ammanmessage.com/grand-list-of-endorsements-of-the-amman-message-and-its-three-points/.

8. "Introduction to a Common Word between Us and You," A Common Word (website), https://www.acommonword.com/introduction-to-a-common-word-between-us-and-you/.

9. Daniella Diaz, "Obama: Why I Won't Say 'Islamic Terrorism,'" CNN, September 29, 2016, https://edition.cnn.com/2016/09/28/politics/obama-radical-islamic-terrorism-cnn-town-hall/index.html; Jordyn Phelps, "Why President Obama Won't Use the Term 'Radical Islam,'" ABC News, June 13, 2016, https://abcnews.go.com/Politics/president-obama-term-radical-islam/story?id=39815449.

10. King Abdullah II of Jordan, "Jordan's King: Fight on ISIS 'a Third World War,'" interview by Charlie Rose, *CBS This Morning*, CBS News, December 5, 2014, https://www.cbsnews.com/news/jordan-king-abdullah-on-isis-middle-east-conflict/.

11. King Abdullah II of Jordan, interview by Charlie Rose.

12. "Remarks by His Majesty King Abdullah II at the Luncheon after the National Prayer Breakfast," King Abdullah II (website), February 2, 2017, https://kingabdullah.jo/en/speeches/luncheon-after-national-prayer-breakfast.

13. Joel C. Rosenberg, "President Trump Praises Jordan's King Abdullah & Invites Him Back to D.C. for a Summit. [. . .]," blog, February 5, 2017, https://flashtrafficblog.epicentermedia.net/2017/02/05/president-trump-praises-jordans-king-abdullah-invites-him-back-to-d-c-for-a-summit-the-king-delivers-a-powerful-speech-at-the-national-prayer-breakfast-on-opportunity-to-work-together-as-all/.

14. Jeremy M. Sharp, *Jordan: Background and U.S. Relations*, Congressional Research Service, updated June 18, 2020, summary page, https://fas.org/sgp/crs/mideast/RL33546.pdf.

15. Jeremy M. Sharp, *Jordan: Background and U.S. Relations*, Congressional Research Service, April 1, 2013, 17, https://www.refworld.org/pdfid/519cba5b4.pdf.

16. Margaret Talev, "Obama Promises More Aid to Jordan to Cope with Refugees," Bloomberg, February 15, 2014, https://www.bloomberg.com/news/articles/2014-02-15/obama-promises-more-aid-to-jordan-to-cope-with-refugees.

17. Sharp, *Jordan: Background and U.S. Relations*, updated June 18, 2020, 12.

18. "Germany, Jordan Sign Aid Package Worth 462.12 Million Euros," *Jordan Times*, October 23, 2018, http://www.jordantimes.com/news/local/germany-jordan-sign-aid-package-worth-46212-million-euros.

19. "Saudi Transfers Another $334 Million to Jordan in Latest Assistance Package," *The National*, March 4, 2019, https://www.thenationalnews.com/world/mena/saudi-transfers-another-334-million-to-jordan-in-latest-assistance-package-1.832802.

CHAPTER 7: "LET MY PEOPLE COME"

1. Hamza Hendawi, "Kept out of the Obama White House, Egypt's el-Sissi to Test 'Chemistry' with Trump," *Chicago Tribune*, April 2, 2017, https://www.chicagotribune.com/nation-world/ct-egypt-el-sissi-white-house-visit-20170402-story.html.

2. Some elements of this chapter are drawn from a column I wrote on what Egypt was doing right. See Joel C. Rosenberg, "It's Time for Washington to Strengthen Ties with Egypt," editorial, *Jerusalem Post*, March 7, 2017, https://www.jpost.com/opinion/its-time-for-washington-to-strengthen-ties-with-egypt-483412.

3. Hassan al-Banna, quoted in Muslim Brotherhood Terrorist Designation Act of

2014, H.R. 5194, sec. 2, para. 3, 113th Cong., (July 24, 2014), https://www
.govinfo.gov/content/pkg/BILLS-113hr5194ih/html/BILLS-113hr5194ih.htm.

4. Al-Banna, quoted in H.R. 5194, sec. 2, para. 4.

5. Muslim Brotherhood motto, quoted in H.R. 5194, sec. 2, para. 1.

6. H.R. 5194, sec. 2, para. 9.

7. After Tahir, Egyptians Assess Their Government, Their Institutions, and Their Futures (Washington, D.C.: Zogby Research Services, 2013), https://static1 .squarespace.com/static/52750dd3e4b08c252c723404/t/52928b8de4b070ad8ee c181e/1385335693242/Egypt+June+2013+FINAL.pdf.

8. "Egypt Group Claims 22 Million Sign Anti-Morsi Petition," Times of Israel, June 29, 2013, https://www.timesofisrael.com/egypt-group-claims-22-million -sign-anti-morsi-petition/.

9. David D. Kirkpatrick, "Army Ousts Egypt's President; Morsi Is Taken into Military Custody," New York Times, July 3, 2013, https://www.nytimes.com/2013/07/04 /world/middleeast/egypt.html.

10. Kirkpatrick, "Army Ousts Egypt's President."

11. Liam Stack, "Witness Accounts of Sectarian Attacks across Egypt," The Lede (blog), New York Times, August 16, 2013, https://thelede.blogs.nytimes.com/2013 /08/16/witness-accounts-of-sectarian-attacks-across-egypt/.

12. Timothy C. Morgan, "After Military Kills 500 Protesters, Islamists Take Out Anger on Egyptian Christians," Christianity Today, August 15, 2013, https://www .christianitytoday.com/news/2013/july/egypts-pope-praises-recovery-of-stolen -revolution.html.

13. John McManus, "Egypt Crisis: Churches under Attack," BBC News, August 16, 2013, https://www.bbc.com/news/world-middle-east-23727404. See also Martin Chulov, "Egypt's Coptic Christians Report Fresh Attacks on Churches," The Guardian, August 15, 2013, https://www.theguardian.com/world/2013/aug/15 /egypt-coptic-christians-attacks-churches.

14. Barack Obama, "Statement by President Barack Obama on Egypt," Archived Obama White House, National Archives and Records Administration, July 3, 2013, https://obamawhitehouse.archives.gov/the-press-office/2013/07/03 /statement-president-barack-obama-egypt.

15. Mary Beth Sheridan, "U.S. to Expand Relations with Muslim Brotherhood," Washington Post, June 30, 2011, https://www.washingtonpost.com/world/national -security/us-to-expand-relations-with-muslim-brotherhood/2011/06/30/AGVgppsH _story.html.

16. In 1995, the Clinton administration formally declared Hamas, a sister organization of the Muslim Brotherhood, a foreign terrorist organization. In 2001, the Bush administration declared the Kuwaiti branch of the MB a terrorist organization. Since 2001, the U.S. government has put a number of individual members of the Muslim Brotherhood on its list of Specially Designated Global Terrorists. In 2011, then-FBI Director Robert Mueller testified before Congress, "I can say at the outset that elements of the Muslim Brotherhood both here and overseas have supported terrorism." See Muslim Brotherhood Terrorist Designation Act of 2014, H.R. 5194, 113th Cong., (July 24, 2014). The following countries have declared the Muslim Brotherhood a terrorist organization: Egypt, Saudi Arabia, Bahrain, United Arab Emirates, Libya, Russia, Tajikistan, Syria. See "Imams, Politicians,

Professors: Dozens of Muslim Brotherhood Suspects Detained in Tajikistan,"
Radio Free Europe/Radio Liberty, January 9, 2020, https://www.rferl.org/a/dozens
-of-muslim-brotherhood-suspects-detained-in-tajikistan/30368551.html. In 2020,
a Jordanian court banned the Jordanian version of the Muslim Brotherhood from
participating in national elections. See Kamal Taha, "Jordan's Top Court Dissolves
Country's Muslim Brotherhood," Times of Israel, July 16, 2020, https://www
.timesofisrael.com/jordans-top-court-dissolves-countrys-muslim-brotherhood/.

17. "Readout of the President's Call with President-Elect Morsi of Egypt," Archived
Obama White House, National Archives and Records Administration, June 24,
2012, https://obamawhitehouse.archives.gov/the-press-office/2012/06/24/readout
-president-s-call-president-elect-morsi-egypt.

18. "Morsi in 2010: No to Negotiations with the Blood-Sucking, Warmongering
'Descendants of Apes and Pigs'; Calls to Boycott U.S. Products," Middle East
Media Research Institute (MEMRI), March 20, 2010, https://www.memri.org
/tv/morsi-2010-no-negotiations-blood-sucking-warmongering-descendants-apes
-and-pigs-calls-boycott-us.

19. "Morsi in 2010: No to Negotiations."

20. "Morsi in 2010: No to Negotiations."

21. Dashiell Bennett, "Egypt's New President Wants to 'Reconsider' Its Peace Deal
with Israel," The Atlantic, June 25, 2012, https://www.theatlantic.com/international
/archive/2012/06/egypts-new-president-wants-reconsider-its-famous-peace-deal
-israel/326606/.

22. "Mohamed Morsi during Elections Campaign: Jihad Is Our Path, Death for the
Sake of Allah Is Our Most Lofty Aspiration, the Shari'a Is Our Constitution,"
Middle East Media Research Institute (MEMRI), May 13, 2012, https://www
.memri.org/tv/mohamed-morsi-during-elections-campaign-jihad-our-path-death
-sake-allah-our-most-lofty-aspiration.

23. "Mohamed Morsi during Elections Campaign."

24. "Mohamed Morsi during Elections Campaign."

25. "Egypt's Mursi Mulls Cabinet amid Tahrir Sit-In," Daily Star (Lebanon), June 25,
2012, http://www.dailystar.com.lb/News/Middle-East/2012/Jun-25/178060-mursi
-wants-to-expand-ties-with-tehran-to-create-strategic-balance-in-region.ashx.

26. Dudi Cohen, "Morsi Meets Ahmadinejad; Lauds 'Strategic Partnership,'" Ynet
News, August 30, 2012, https://www.ynetnews.com/articles/0,7340,L-4275261
,00.html.

27. "Iran President Ahmadinejad Begins Historic Egypt Visit," BBC News, February 5,
2013, https://www.bbc.com/news/world-middle-east-21336367.

28. Cristiano Lima, "Trump Praises Egypt's al-Sisi: 'He's a Fantastic Guy,'" Politico,
September 22, 2016, https://www.politico.com/story/2016/09/trump-praises
-egypts-al-sisi-hes-a-fantastic-guy-228560.

29. Peter Baker and Declan Walsh, "Trump Shifts Course on Egypt, Praising Its
Authoritarian Leader," New York Times, April 3, 2017, https://www.nytimes.com
/2017/04/03/world/middleeast/-egypt-sisi-trump-white-house.html.

30. Baker and Walsh, "Trump Shifts Course on Egypt."

31. Jacques Neriah, "Egyptian President Sisi Calls for Reform of Islam," Jerusalem
Center for Public Affairs, February 15, 2015, http://jcpa.org/article/sisi-calls
-for-reform-of-islam/.

CHAPTER 8: WHO IS ABDEL FATTAH EL-SISI?
1. The following three sections are adapted from Joel C. Rosenberg, "Meeting Egyptian President Sisi, the Man Who Wants to 'Rebrand' Egypt," editorial, *Jerusalem Post*, April 11, 2017, https://www.jpost.com/opinion/meeting-egyptian -president-sisi-the-man-who-wants-to-rebrand-egypt-486736.
2. "GDP Growth (Annual %)—Egypt, Arab Rep.," GDP data for Egypt, The World Bank, https://data.worldbank.org/indicator/NY.GDP.MKTP.KD.ZG?locations =EG.
3. "Egypt Forecast: Unemployment Rate," International Monetary Fund data published by CEIC, https://www.ceicdata.com/en/indicator/egypt/forecast -unemployment-rate.
4. Amiram Barkat, "OECD Sees Israel's Economy Shrinking 6.2% in 2020," Globes, June 10, 2020, https://en.globes.co.il/en/article-oecd-sees-israels -economy-shrinking-by-62-in-2020-1001331877.
5. *Global Terrorism Index 2019: Measuring the Impact of Terrorism* (Sydney, Australia: Institute for Economics & Peace, November 2019), 13, https://www .visionofhumanity.org/wp-content/uploads/2020/11/GTI-2019-web.pdf.
6. Rosenberg, "Meeting Egyptian President Sisi."
7. See analysis by the Carnegie Endowment for International Peace, "Mohamed Mokhtar Gomaa," September 20, 2013, https://carnegieendowment.org/2013/09/20 /mohamed-mokhtar-gomaa-pub-54933.
8. Mohamed Abdellah, "Egypt Orders Muslim Preachers to Deliver Identical Weekly Sermons," Reuters, July 12, 2016, https://www.reuters.com/article/egypt -islam/egypt-orders-muslim-preachers-to-deliver-identical-weekly-sermons -idINKCN0ZS2FA.
9. "Egypt's Endowments Ministry to Remove 'Extremist Books' from Mosques," Ahram Online, June 22, 2015, http://english.ahram.org.eg/NewsContent/1/64/133418 /Egypt/Politics-/Egypt's-endowments-ministry-to-remove-'extremist-b.aspx.
10. Abdellah, "Egypt Orders Muslim Preachers to Deliver Identical Weekly Sermons."
11. Shawki Allam, *The Ideological Battle: Egypt's Dar al-Iftaa Combats Radicalization* (Egypt: Dar al-Iftaa, n.d.), PDF, https://www.dar-alifta.org/BIMG/The%20 Ideological%20Battle%20(2).pdf.
12. Jehan Sadat, meeting with the author and his first delegation to Egypt, November 1, 2017.
13. Jehan Sadat, *My Hope for Peace* (New York: Free Press, 2009), 16.
14. Sadat, 16.
15. Sadat, 20.

CHAPTER 9: SITTING WITH SISI
1. Some of this chapter is drawn from a column I wrote after we returned home from Cairo. See Joel C. Rosenberg, "Mr. Pence's High-Stakes Trip to Egypt," editorial, *Jerusalem Post*, December 17, 2017, https://www.jpost.com/opinion /mr-pences-high-stakes-trip-to-egypt-518324.
2. "New York Bike Path Truck Rampage: Who Are the Victims?" ABC7 Eyewitness News, November 6, 2017, https://abc7chicago.com/nyc-bike-path-truck-rampage -who-are-the-victims/2589773/.
3. NLT.

CHAPTER 10: THE MEDIA'S WAR AGAINST THE MODERATES

1. Marc Tracy and Lara Jakes, "U.S. Orders Al Jazeera Affiliate to Register as Foreign Agent," *New York Times,* September 15, 2020, https://www.nytimes.com/2020 /09/15/business/media/aj-al-jazeera-fara.html.

2. Khaled Diab, "Egypt's Pharaoh Illusion," Al Jazeera, May 19, 2016, https://www .aljazeera.com/opinions/2016/5/19/egypts-pharaoh-illusion/; Amr Hamzawy, "How Sisi Is Destabilising Egypt," Al Jazeera, April 2, 2017, https://www.aljazeera.com /features/2017/4/2/how-sisi-is-destabilising-egypt; Zena Tahhan, "'Egyptian Society Being Crushed' Five Years after Military Coup," Al Jazeera, July 2, 2018, https://www.aljazeera.com/features/2018/7/2/egyptian-society-being-crushed-five -years-after-military-coup; "Rights Group Says Egypt 'More Dangerous Than Ever' for Critics," Al Jazeera, January 24, 2019, https://www.aljazeera.com/news/2019 /1/24/rights-group-says-egypt-more-dangerous-than-ever-for-critics; Mohamad Elmasry, "Egypt Is a Speeding Train about to Crash," editorial, Al Jazeera, February 28, 2019, https://www.aljazeera.com/opinions/2019/2/28/egypt-is-a -speeding-train-about-to-crash/; "Egypt's el-Sisi Expands Powers, Citing Coronavirus Pandemic," Al Jazeera, May 9, 2020, https://www.aljazeera.com /news/2020/5/9/egypts-el-sisi-expands-powers-citing-coronavirus-pandemic.

3. Merve Şebnem Oruç, "El-Sissi's Pharaoh Complex: How Egypt Ended Up Here," *Daily Sabah,* April 26, 2019, https://www.dailysabah.com/columns/merve-sebnem -oruc/2019/04/26/el-sissis-pharaoh-complex-how-egypt-ended-up-here.

4. Yotam Feldner, "Turkey-Based Muslim Brotherhood TV Channels—an Emerging Hotbed of Extremism, Jihadi Ideology, and Antisemitism," Middle East Media Research Institute (MEMRI), January 8, 2019, https://www.memri.org/reports /turkey-based-muslim-brotherhood-tv-channels-—-emerging-hotbed-extremism -jihadi-ideology-and.

5. Glenn Greenwald, "White House Meeting with Egypt's Tyrant Highlights Key Trump Effect: Unmasking U.S. Policy," The Intercept, April 3, 2017, https://theintercept.com/2017/04/03/white-house-meeting-with-egypts-tyrant -highlights-key-trump-effect-unmasking-u-s-policy/.

6. Jennifer Williams and Zack Beauchamp, "Egypt's President Is a Bloodthirsty Dictator. Trump Thinks He's Done a 'Fantastic Job,'" Vox, April 3, 2017, https://www .vox.com/world/2017/4/3/15160358/trump-egypt-abdel-fattah-el-sisi-white-house.

7. Amira Abo el-Fetouh, "Egypt's Pharaoh Is Trembling," Middle East Monitor, October 1, 2019, https://www.middleeastmonitor.com/20191001-egypts-pharaoh -is-trembling/.

8. Michelle Boorstein, "President Trump's Evangelical Advisers Meet with Egyptian Leader Sissi in Cairo," *Washington Post,* November 3, 2017, https://www .washingtonpost.com/news/acts-of-faith/wp/2017/11/03/president-trumps -evangelical-advisors-meet-with-egyptian-leader-al-sissi-in-cairo/; Sarah Jones, "Why Is Trump Sending Michele Bachmann to Meet Egypt's Abdel Fattah al -Sisi?" *New Republic,* November 3, 2017, https://newrepublic.com/article/145649 /trump-sending-michele-bachmann-meet-egypts-abdel-fattah-al-sisi.

9. Samuel Smith, "Egypt's President Sisi Meets with U.S. Evangelical Leaders for First Time in Cairo," Christian Post, November 2, 2017, https://www.christianpost .com/news/egypts-president-sisi-meets-us-evangelical-leaders-cairo.html.

10. Chris Mitchell, "Egyptian President Meeting with U.S. Evangelicals 'Prophetic'

and 'Historic,'" CBN News, November 3, 2017, https://www1.cbn.com/cbnnews
/israel/2017/november/egyptian-president-meeting-with-us-evangelicals-prophetic
-and-historic.

11. Mitchell, "Egyptian President Meeting with U.S. Evangelicals."

12. Mohamed Abdelaziz and David Pollock, "Half of Egyptians Value U.S. Ties, but
Few Want Normalization with Israel," Fikra Forum, Washington Institute for
Near East Policy, January 15, 2021, https://www.washingtoninstitute.org/policy
-analysis/half-egyptians-value-us-ties-few-want-normalization-israel.

13. David Pollock, "In Egypt, One-Third Still Like the Muslim Brotherhood; Half
Call U.S. Ties 'Important,'" Fikra Forum, Washington Institute for Near East
Policy, December 10, 2018, https://www.washingtoninstitute.org/fikraforum/view
/in-egypt-one-third-still-like-the-muslim-brotherhood-half-call-u.s.-ties-im.

14. Mark E. Neely Jr., "The Lincoln Administration and Arbitrary Arrests: A
Reconsideration," *Journal of the Abraham Lincoln Association* 5, no. 1 (1983): 6–24,
https://quod.lib.umich.edu/j/jala/2629860.0005.103/--lincoln-administration
-and-arbitrary-arrests?rgn=main;view=fulltext. Neely writes that Lincoln "did
not apologize" for "arbitrary arrests in the North during the Civil War," and even
went so far as to write in a letter dated June 12, 1863, "The time [is] not unlikely
to come when I shall be blamed for having made too few arrests rather than too
many." Neely writes: "He [Lincoln] argued that the Confederate States, when
they seceded, had been counting on being able to keep 'on foot amongst us a most
efficient corps of spies, informers, suppliers, and aiders and abettors of their cause'
under 'cover of "Liberty of speech," "Liberty of the press," and "*Habeas corpus*."'"

15. "Egypt's President Sisi Pardons Over 330 Mostly Youth Prisoners," Reuters,
May 16, 2018, https://www.reuters.com/article/us-egypt-rights/egypts-president
-sisi-pardons-over-330-mostly-youth-prisoners-idUSKCN1IH1LD; "Egyptian
President El-Sisi Pardons 712 Prisoners," *Arab News*, June 6, 2018, https://www
.arabnews.com/node/1317011/middle-east; "Egypt's President Sisi Pardons 560
Prisoners," Reuters, May 17, 2019, https://www.reuters.com/article/us-egypt
-politics/egypts-president-sisi-pardons-560-prisoners-idUSKCN1SN20L; "Egypt
Releases 4,011 Inmates for Sinai Liberation Day," *Egypt Independent*, April 25,
2020, https://egyptindependent.com/egypt-releases-4011-inmates-for-sinai
-liberation-day/; "Presidential Pardon for 3,157 Prisoners," *Egypt Today*, May 23,
2020, https://www.egypttoday.com/Article/1/87992/Presidential-pardon-for-3157
-prisoners.

CHAPTER 11: CROSSING THE JORDAN

1. *Hearing on Global Health Programs, before the State, Foreign Operations Subcommittee*, 114th Cong. (May 6, 2015) (testimony of Dr. Rick Warren, pastor),
https://www.appropriations.senate.gov/imo/media/doc/hearings/050615%20
Dr.%20Warren%20Testimony%20-%20SFOPS.pdf.

2. See, for example, Leviticus 19:18; Matthew 22:37-39; Mark 12:31; Luke 10:27.

3. See Romans 10.

4. "King Receives Delegation of U.S. Evangelical Leaders," King Abdullah II
(website), November 7, 2017, https://kingabdullah.jo/en/news/king-receives
-delegation-us-evangelical-leaders.

5. "Delegation of American Evangelicals Travels to Jordan to Thank King Abdullah II

for Advancing Peace, Caring for Refugees, Fighting Radicalism & Protecting Christians," A. Larry Ross Communications, November 8, 2017, https://alarryross .com/joel-c-rosenberg-news/2018/11/27/delegation-of-american-evangelicals-travels -to-jordan-to-thank-king-abdullah-ii-for-advancing-peace-caring-for-refugees-fighting -radicalism-amp-protecting-christians.

6. "Delegation of American Evangelicals Travels to Jordan."
7. "Delegation of American Evangelicals Travels to Jordan."
8. *Public Opinion Survey: Residents of Jordan, June 20–29, 2018* (Washington, D.C.: International Republican Institute, 2018), https://www.iri.org/sites/default /files/2018.11.6_jordan_poll_presentation.pdf.
9. "Unemployment Continues to Rise in 2019, Hitting 19%," *Jordan Times*, June 4, 2019, http://www.jordantimes.com/news/local/unemployment-continues-rise -2019-hitting-19.
10. "Jordan Unemployment Rate Reaches 'Historic High'—JEF [Jordan Economic Forum]," *Jordan Times*, September 16, 2020, https://www.jordantimes.com/news /local/jordan-unemployment-rate-reaches-historic-high'-—jef.
11. *Public Opinion Survey: Residents of Jordan, November 14–22, 2019* (Washington, D.C.: International Republican Institute, 2019), https://www.iri.org/sites/default /files/jordan_scrubbed_slides_3.27.20_1.pdf.
12. "New Poll: Jordanians Remain Frustrated with the Economy and Government," International Republican Institute, March 31, 2020, https://www.iri.org/resource /new-poll-jordanians-remain-frustrated-economy-and-government.
13. *Public Opinion Survey: Residents of Jordan, November 14–22, 2019.*
14. *Public Opinion Survey: Residents of Jordan, November 14–22, 2019.*
15. David Pollock, "Jordan's Public Internally Focused, but Shares U.S. View on Iran and Regional Peace," Fikra Forum, Washington Institute for Near East Policy, February 26, 2019, https://www.washingtoninstitute.org/fikraforum/view/jordans -public-internally-focused-but-shares-u.s.-view-on-iran-and-regional.
16. Pollock, "Jordan's Public Internally Focused."
17. Pollock, "Jordan's Public Internally Focused."
18. Pollock, "Jordan's Public Internally Focused."
19. David Pollock and Catherine Cleveland, "Comparing Arab Polls on Trump, U.S. Policy, Israel, Iran, and More," Fikra Forum, Washington Institute for Near East Policy, May 9, 2019, https://www.washingtoninstitute.org/fikraforum/view/comparing -arab-polls-on-trump-u.s.-policy-israel-iran-and-more.
20. Richard Barrett, *Beyond the Caliphate: Foreign Fighters and the Threat of Returnees* (The Soufan Center and The Global Strategy Network: October 2017), 12, http:// thesoufancenter.org/wp-content/uploads/2017/11/Beyond-the-Caliphate-Foreign -Fighters-and-the-Threat-of-Returnees-TSC-Report-October-2017-v3.pdf. David Schenker, director of the Beth and David Geduld Program on Arab Politics at the Washington Institute, put the number at approximately 2,500 in his assessment titled "The Growing Islamic State Threat in Jordan," Washington Institute for Near East Policy, January 10, 2017, https://www.washingtoninstitute.org/policy-analysis /view/the-growing-islamic-state-threat-in-jordan.
21. Pollock, "Jordan's Public Internally Focused."
22. Maayan Groisman, "Jordanian Parliament Speaker: We Oppose the Peace Treaty with Israel," *Jerusalem Post*, May 15, 2016, https://www.jpost.com/arab-israeli

-conflict/jordanian-parliament-speaker-we-oppose-the-peace-treaty-with-israel-454002.

23. Smadar Perry, "Jordan's MPs Oppose Appointing New Envoy to Israel," Ynet News, August 24, 2018, https://www.ynetnews.com/articles/0,7340,L-5334440,00.html.

24. Daniel Siryoti, "Report: Jordanian MPs Demand Review of Peace Treaty with Israel," Jewish News Syndicate, October 24, 2018, https://www.jns.org/report-jordanian-mps-demand-review-of-peace-treaty-%E2%80%8Ewith-israel-%E2%80%8E/.

25. Mohammad Ghazal, "Jordan Terminates Baqoura, Ghumar Annexes in Peace Treaty with Israel," *Jordan Times*, October 22, 2018, https://www.jordantimes.com/news/local/jordan-terminates-baqoura-ghumar-annexes-peace-treaty-israel.

26. "Jordan—Lower House Rejects Gas Deal with Israel, Calls for Terminate It," Jordan News Agency, March 27, 2019, https://menafn.com/1098306384/Jordan-Lower-house-rejects-Gas-Deal-with-Israel-calls-for-terminate-it.

27. David Pollock, "Two-Thirds in Jordan Fear U.S.-Israeli Plans, but Domestic Issues Rank First," Fikra Forum, Washington Institute for Near East Policy, July 1, 2020, https://www.washingtoninstitute.org/fikraforum/view/Jordan-Public-Opinion-Middle-East-USA-Israel-Annexation; Pollock, "Jordan's Public Internally Focused."

CHAPTER 12: "I AM READY TO MAKE PEACE"

1. "Sheikh Khalifa Stable after Recovering from Stroke," *The National*, January 25, 2014, https://www.thenationalnews.com/uae/sheikh-khalifa-stable-after-recovering-from-stroke-1.686381.

2. Matthew Amlôt, "Here Are the Top 10 Sovereign Wealth Funds in the Arab World," Al Arabiya, August 29, 2019, https://english.alarabiya.net/en/business/economy/2019/08/28/Here-are-the-top-10-sovereign-wealth-funds-in-the-Arab-world.

3. Mansour al-Nogaidan, "The Rise of the UAE and the Meaning of MbZ," Fikra Forum, Washington Institute for Near East Policy, September 15, 2020, https://www.washingtoninstitute.org/fikraforum/view/rise-the-uae-meaning-mbz.

4. "UAE Economy 36 Times Bigger since 1971 Union," *Gulf News*, December 2, 2001, https://gulfnews.com/uae/uae-economy-36-times-bigger-since-1971-union-1.431538.

5. "Mohamed bin Zayed Receives U.S. Evangelical Christian Delegation," Emirates News Agency, October 29, 2018, http://wam.ae/en/details/1395302716899.

CHAPTER 13: WHO IS MOHAMMED BIN ZAYED?

1. Daniel Sanderson, "Christian Evangelicals Describe UAE as a 'Fantastic Friend' to the West," *The National*, October 30, 2018, https://www.thenational.ae/uae/government/christian-evangelicals-describe-uae-as-a-fantastic-friend-to-the-west-1.786096.

2. Yousef Al Otaiba, interview by author, July 30, 2020.

3. Andrea Koppel and Elise Labott, "UAE Cuts Ties with Taliban," CNN.com, September 22, 2001, http://edition.cnn.com/2001/WORLD/asiapcf/central/09/22/ret.afghan.taliban/index.html; Jack Moore, "NATO Officially Initiates UAE into Afghan Mission," *The National*, July 12, 2018, https://www.thenationalnews.com/world/europe/nato-officially-initiates-uae-into-afghan-mission-1.749833.

4. "List of Groups Designated Terrorist Organisations by the UAE," *The National*, November 16, 2014, https://www.thenationalnews.com/uae/government/list-of -groups-designated-terrorist-organisations-by-the-uae-1.270037.

5. Anwar Gargash, interview by author, December 8, 2020.

6. Chris Mitchell, "Freedom Is Unfolding in This Arab Country: U.S. Evangelicals Find UAE 'Treasure of Moderation,'" CBN News, October 31, 2018, https:// www1.cbn.com/cbnnews/world/2018/october/freedom-is-unfolding-in-this-arab -country-us-evangelicals-find-uae-treasure-of-moderation.

7. Mitchell, "Freedom Is Unfolding."

8. Mitchell, "Freedom Is Unfolding."

9. Mitchell, "Freedom Is Unfolding."

10. Mitchell, "Freedom Is Unfolding."

11. Joel C. Rosenberg, "In the UAE's Year of Tolerance, Please Come to Jerusalem," editorial, *Jerusalem Post*, February 6, 2019, https://www.jpost.com/opinion/in-the -uaes-year-of-tolerance-please-come-to-jerusalem-579904.

CHAPTER 14: THE ROAD TO RIYADH

1. "Jews Barred in Saudi Tourist Drive," BBC News, February 27, 2004, http:// news.bbc.co.uk/2/hi/middle_east/3493448.stm.

2. Jim Collins, "First Who, Then What," excerpts from *Good to Great* (New York: HarperBusiness, 2001), Jim Collins (website), https://www.jimcollins.com/concepts /first-who-then-what.html.

3. Bruce Riedel, *The Prince of Counterterrorism*, Brookings Essay (Washington, D.C.: Brookings, September 29, 2015), e-book, http://csweb.brookings.edu/content /research/essays/2015/the-prince-of-counterterrorism.html.

4. Rahima Nasa, "Timeline: The Rise of Saudi Arabia's Prince Mohammed bin Salman," PBS Frontline, October 1, 2019, https://www.pbs.org/wgbh/frontline /article/timeline-the-rise-of-saudi-arabias-prince-mohammed-bin-salman/.

5. Ben Hubbard, "Saudi King Rewrites Succession, Replacing Heir with Son, 31," *New York Times*, June 21, 2017, https://www.nytimes.com/2017/06/21/world /middleeast/saudi-arabia-crown-prince-mohammed-bin-salman.html; "The New, Young Crown Prince Reshaping Saudi Arabia," Reuters, June 21, 2017, https:// www.reuters.com/article/us-saudi-succession-mohammedbinsalman/the-new -young-crown-prince-reshaping-saudi-arabia-idUSKBN19C1RV.

6. Joel C. Rosenberg, "Rosenberg: Trump Goal Is to Build Israel, Sunni Alliance against Iran," interview by Gary Lane, *Global Lane*, CBN News, April 11, 2017, https://www1.cbn.com/globallane/archive/2017/04/11/rosenberg-trump-goal-is-to -build-israel-sunni-alliance-against-iran; Joel C. Rosenberg, "President Arrives in Saudi Arabia to Meet with Arab & Muslim Leaders. [. . .]," blog, May 21, 2017, https://flashtrafficblog.wordpress.com/2017/05/21/president-arrives-in-saudi -arabia-to-meet-with-arab-muslim-leaders-heres-the-latest-including-his-itinerary/.

7. Rosenberg, interview by Gary Lane, April 11, 2017.

8. Rosenberg, interview by Gary Lane.

9. Joel C. Rosenberg, "Confirmed: President Will Visit Israel, Saudi Arabia & the Vatican This Month. [. . .]," blog, May 5, 2017, https://flashtrafficblog .epicentermedia.net/2017/05/05/confirmed-president-will-visit-israel-saudi -arabia-the-vatican-this-month-trip-designed-to-reach-out-to-jews-muslims -christians-strengthen-u-s-alliances-advance-peace/.

10. Carol E. Lee and Margherita Stancati, "Donald Trump, Saudi Arabia Sign Agreements in Move to Counterbalance Iran," *Wall Street Journal*, May 20, 2017, https://www.wsj.com/articles/president-donald-trump-arrives-in-saudi-arabia-as-overseas-trip-starts-1495263979; Ian Black, "Obama's Chilly Reception in Saudi Arabia Hints at Mutual Distrust," *The Guardian*, April 20, 2016, https://www.theguardian.com/world/2016/apr/20/barack-obama-saudi-arabia-visit-king-salman-relationship.

11. Donald Trump, "President Trump's Speech to the Arab Islamic American Summit," Archived Trump White House, National Archives and Records Administration, May 21, 2017, https://trumpwhitehouse.archives.gov/briefings-statements/president-trumps-speech-arab-islamic-american-summit/. Words in all caps in the original.

12. Trump, "President Trump's Speech to the Arab Islamic American Summit."

13. Trump, "President Trump's Speech to the Arab Islamic American Summit."

14. Anwar Gargash (@AnwarGargash), Twitter, May 21, 2017, 10:08 a.m., https://twitter.com/AnwarGargash/status/866309612336709634.

15. Noor Zahid, "Many Muslims Hopeful, Some Wary after Trump's Saudi Speech," Voice of America (VOA), May 21, 2017, https://www.voanews.com/middle-east/many-muslims-hopeful-some-wary-after-trumps-saudi-speech.

16. Zahid, "Many Muslims Hopeful."

17. Joel C. Rosenberg, "Mohammed bin Salman Is 33—Here Are 21 Impressive Reforms Already Underway," editorial, Fox News, August 31, 2018, https://www.foxnews.com/opinion/joel-c-rosenberg-mohammed-bin-salman-is-33-here-are-21-impressive-reforms-already-underway.

18. Martin Chulov, "I Will Return Saudi Arabia to Moderate Islam, Says Crown Prince," *The Guardian*, October 24, 2017, https://www.theguardian.com/world/2017/oct/24/i-will-return-saudi-arabia-moderate-islam-crown-prince.

19. CNN Wire, "If You're Surprised by Saudi Arabia's Fight with Canada, You Haven't Been Paying Attention," WTHI-TV10, August 9, 2018, https://www.wthitv.com/content/national/490370171.html.

20. Jeffrey Goldberg, "Saudi Crown Prince: Iran's Supreme Leader 'Makes Hitler Look Good,'" *The Atlantic*, April 2, 2018, https://www.theatlantic.com/international/archive/2018/04/mohammed-bin-salman-iran-israel/557036/.

21. Embassy of the Kingdom of Saudi Arabia, "His Royal Highness the Crown Prince Meets with Religious Leaders in the United States," press release, March 30, 2018, https://www.saudiembassy.net/news/his-royal-highness-crown-prince-meets-religious-leaders-united-states.

22. Goldberg, "Saudi Crown Prince."

CHAPTER 15: AN INVITATION TO THE FORBIDDEN KINGDOM

1. Joel C. Rosenberg, "After Weeks of Wild Rumors and Salacious Allegations, Here's What We Actually Now Know about the Death of Jamal Khashoggi—and What We Don't," blog, October 21, 2018, https://flashtrafficblog.wordpress.com/2018/10/21/after-weeks-of-wild-rumors-and-salacious-allegations-heres-what-we-actually-now-know-about-the-death-of-jamal-khashoggi-and-what-we-dont/.

2. David Ignatius, "Jamal Khashoggi's Long Road to the Doors of the Saudi Consulate," editorial, *Washington Post*, October 12, 2018, https://www.washingtonpost.com/opinions/global-opinions/jamal-khashoggis-long-road-to-the-doors-of-the-saudi

-consulate/2018/10/12/b461d6f4-ce1a-11e8-920f-dd52e1ae4570_story.html?utm
_term=.1fce97bc2fe3.

3. Margherita Stancati and Nancy A. Youssef, "Missing Journalist Was an Insider
Willing to Cross Saudi Red Lines," *Wall Street Journal*, October 12, 2018, https://
www.wsj.com/articles/missing-journalist-was-an-insider-willing-to-cross-saudi-red
-lines-1539376391; Ben Hubbard and David D. Kirkpatrick, "For Khashoggi,
a Tangled Mix of Royal Service and Islamist Sympathies," *New York Times*,
October 14, 2018, https://www.nytimes.com/2018/10/14/world/middleeast/jamal
-khashoggi-saudi-arabia.html; Guy Taylor, "Perceived Threat: Long, Tangled History
Put Khashoggi in Crosshairs," *Washington Times*, October 17, 2018, https://www
.washingtontimes.com/news/2018/oct/17/jamal-khashoggi-killing-sparked-muslim
-brotherhood/; Melanie Phillips, "The Story behind the Story of Jamal Khashoggi,"
MelaniePhillips.com, October 19, 2018, https://www.melaniephillips.com/story
-behind-story-jamal-khashoggi/; Yigal Carmon, "Does the *Washington Post* Have a
Blind Spot for the Muslim Brotherhood?" Middle East Media Research Institute
(MEMRI), November 13, 2018, https://www.memri.org/reports/does-washington
-post-have-blind-spot-muslim-brotherhood; David Reaboi, "Khashoggi: Qatari Asset
in Life; Qatari Asset in Death," Security Studies Group (SSG), December 23,
2018, https://securitystudies.org/jamal-khashoggi-and-qatar-in-the-echo-chamber/;
"Khashoggi Columns Shaped by Qatar Foundation Director, Reports *Washington
Post*," *Gulf News*, December 23, 2018, https://gulfnews.com/world/gulf/saudi
/khashoggi-columns-shaped-by-qatar-foundation-director-reports-washington-post
-1.61092405; Jim Hanson, "Bombshell: New Info Says Khashoggi Was a Foreign
Influence Agent," The Federalist, December 27, 2018, https://thefederalist.com
/2018/12/27/bombshell-khashoggi-foreign-governments-influence-agent/; Seth J.
Frantzman, "The Anti-Semitic Tweets of Murdered Saudi Writer Jamal Khashoggi,"
Middle East Forum, April 19, 2019, https://www.meforum.org/58237/antisemitic
-tweets-jamal-khashoggi.

4. Ben Hubbard and David D. Kirkpatrick, "For Khashoggi, a Tangled Mix of Royal
Service and Islamist Sympathies," *New York Times*, October 14, 2018, https://www
.nytimes.com/2018/10/14/world/middleeast/jamal-khashoggi-saudi-arabia.html.

5. Jamal Khashoggi, "The U.S. Is Wrong about the Muslim Brotherhood—and
the Arab World Is Suffering for It," editorial, *Washington Post*, August 28, 2018,
https://www.washingtonpost.com/news/global-opinions/wp/2018/08/28/the-u-s-is
-wrong-about-the-muslim-brotherhood-and-the-arab-world-is-suffering-for-it/.

6. Souad Mekhennet and Greg Miller, "Jamal Khashoggi's Final Months as an Exile
in the Long Shadow of Saudi Arabia," *Washington Post*, December 22, 2018,
https://www.washingtonpost.com/world/national-security/jamal-khashoggis-final
-months-an-exile-in-the-long-shadow-of-saudi-arabia/2018/12/21/d6fc68c2
-0476-11e9-b6a9-0aa5c2fcc9e4_story.html.

7. Joel C. Rosenberg, "After Weeks of Wild Rumors and Salacious Allegations."

CHAPTER 16: MEETING MBS

1. "Saudi Royal Air Defense Forces Intercept a Ballistic Missile Launched by
Yemen's Houthi Militia toward Jazan," *Arab News* (Pakistan), September 16,
2018, https://www.arabnews.pk/node/1373051/saudi-arabia.

2. Alan Rappeport, "Saudi Crown Prince Calls Khashoggi's Death 'Heinous,'" *New*

York Times, October 24, 2018, https://www.nytimes.com/2018/10/24/world/middleeast/saudi-khashoggi-crown-prince.html.

CHAPTER 17: READING MBS
1. Matthew 19:19; 22:39; Mark 12:31.
2. "Evangelical Delegation Meets with His Royal Highness Mohammed Bin Salman, Crown Prince of the Kingdom of Saudi Arabia," A. Larry Ross Communications, November 1, 2018, https://alarryross.com/joel-c-rosenberg-news/2018/11/1/evangelical-delegation-meets-with-his-royal-highness-mohammed-bin-salman-crown-prince-of-the-kingdom-of-saudi-arabia.
3. "Saudi Arabia Hosts Rare Visit of U.S. Evangelical Christian Figures," Reuters, November 1, 2018, https://www.reuters.com/article/us-saudi-christians/saudi-arabia-hosts-rare-visit-of-u-s-evangelical-christian-figures-idUSKCN1N6675.
4. Michelle Boorstein, "Trump's Evangelical Advisers Meet with Saudi Crown Prince and Discuss Jamal Khashoggi's Murder, 'Human Rights,' Spokesman Says," *Washington Post*, November 2, 2018, https://www.washingtonpost.com/religion/2018/11/01/it-is-our-desire-lift-up-name-jesus-trumps-evangelical-advisers-meet-with-saudi-crown-prince-mohammed-bin-salman/.
5. Sigal Samuel, "Trump's Evangelical Advisers Hear from the Saudi Crown Prince on Khashoggi," *The Atlantic*, November 9, 2018, https://www.theatlantic.com/international/archive/2018/11/saudi-khashoggi-evangelicals/575509/.
6. Samuel, "Trump's Evangelical Advisers Hear from the Saudi Crown Prince."
7. Samuel, "Trump's Evangelical Advisers Hear from the Saudi Crown Prince."
8. Chris Mitchell, "Exclusive Video: Christian Leaders Meet with Saudi Crown Prince in Historic Step," CBN News, November 3, 2018, https://www1.cbn.com/cbnnews/world/2018/november/exclusive-video-christian-leaders-meet-with-saudi-crown-prince-in-historic-step.
9. Dan Falvey, "Saudi Arabia MURDER: Crown Prince Bursts into FURIOUS RANT after Khashoggi Death," *Express*, November 9, 2018, https://www.express.co.uk/news/world/1042956/saudi-arabia-murder-mohammed-bin-salman-anger-jamal-khashoggi. Words in all caps in the original.
10. Falvey, "Saudi Arabia MURDER."
11. Travis Gettys, "Michele Bachmann and Other End-Times Evangelicals Turn Up in Saudi Arabia," Salon, November 2, 2018, https://www.salon.com/2018/11/02/michele-bachmann-and-other-end-times-evangelicals-turn-up-in-saudi-arabia_partner/.
12. Jerome Socolovsky, "Evangelicals Seek Détente with Mideast Muslim Leaders as Critics Doubt Motives," *Morning Edition*, NPR, January 2, 2019, https://www.npr.org/2019/01/02/681200155/evangelicals-seek-detente-with-mideast-muslim-leaders-as-critics-doubt-motives.
13. "Netanyahu Asks U.S. to Continue Support for MBS," *Kayhan International*, November 2, 2018, http://kayhan.ir/en/news/59216/netanyahu-asks-us-to-continue-support-for-mbs.

CHAPTER 18: LUNCH AT THE WHITE HOUSE
1. Barak Ravid, "White House Working to Reassure Evangelicals on Middle East Peace Plan," Axios, March 9, 2019, https://www.axios.com/trump-kushner-middle-east-peace-plan-evangelicals-5337c4f7-0f91-489c-baad-7799f63baed7.html.
2. This section is adapted from Joel C. Rosenberg, "Will Trump's Middle East

Peace Plan Really Be 'Dead on Arrival'?—Opinion," editorial, *Jerusalem Post*, March 11, 2019, https://www.jpost.com/opinion/will-trumps-middle-east-peace -plan-really-be-dead-on-arrival-opinion-583054.

CHAPTER 19: 9/11 IN SAUDI ARABIA
1. Isaiah 43:18-19, NIV.
2. "Raif Badawi," United States Commission on International Religious Freedom, https://www.uscirf.gov/religious-prisoners-conscience/current-rpocs/raif-badawi.
3. Hebrews 13:3, NIV.
4. 1 Kings 10:6-9, NIV.
5. See Daniel 2:21; Esther 4:14.

CHAPTER 20: SITTING WITH SHEIKH MOHAMMAD AL-ISSA
1. Sheikh Mohammad Al-Issa, "One of the World's Most Influential Muslim Leaders Tells All Arab News How the 9/11 Attacks Gave Him a Life Mission [. . .]," interview by Joel C. Rosenberg, part 1, All Arab News, September 1, 2020, https://allarab .news/one-of-the-worlds-most-influential-muslim-leaders-tells-all-arab-news-how-the -9-11-attacks-gave-him-a-life-mission-to-combat-violent-extremists-build-bridges -with-jews-and-christians-and-pro/; Sheikh Mohammad Al-Issa, "Leading Saudi Sheikh Tells All Arab News Why He Led First-Ever Muslim Delegation to Auschwitz, [. . .]," interview by Joel C. Rosenberg, part 2, All Arab News, November 24, 2020, https://allarab.news/leading-saudi-sheikh-tells-all-arab-news-why-he-led -first-ever-muslim-delegation-to-auschwitz-and-why-saudis-crown-prince-welcomed -first-ever-group-of-evangelical-christians-to-the-palace/.
2. Norah O'Donnell, "Mohammad bin Salman Denies Ordering Khashoggi Murder, but Says He Takes Responsibility for It," *60 Minutes*, CBS News, September 29, 2019, https://www.cbsnews.com/news/mohammad-bin-salman-denies-ordering -khashoggi-murder-but-says-he-takes-responsibility-for-it-60-minutes-2019-09-29/.
3. Nic Robertson and Eliza Mackintosh, "Khashoggi's Children Could Get as Much as $70 Million in Compensation for His Killing," CNN, April 2, 2019, https:// www.cnn.com/2019/04/02/middleeast/jamal-khashoggi-children-intl.
4. Greg Miller, "Khashoggi Children Have Received Houses in Saudi Arabia and Monthly Payments as Compensation for Killing of Father," *Washington Post*, April 1, 2019, https://www.washingtonpost.com/world/national-security /khashoggi-children-have-received-houses-in-saudi-arabia-and-monthly-payments -as-compensation-for-killing-of-father/2019/04/01/c279ca3e-5485-11e9-8ef3 -fbd41a2ce4d5_story.html.
5. Tim Lister, "Saudi Death Sentence Wipes MBS's Fingerprints in Khashoggi Killing," CNN, December 23, 2019, https://www.cnn.com/2019/12/23/middleeast /saudi-khashoggi-verdict-analysis-intl/index.html.
6. Marwa Rashad and Raya Jalabi, "Saudi Arabia Jails Eight over Khashoggi Murder, Fiancée Decries Trial," Reuters, September 15, 2020, https://www.reuters.com /article/saudi-khashoggi-int/saudi-arabia-jails-eight-over-khashoggi-murder -fiancee-decries-trial-idUSKBN25Y1YH.
7. "Jamal Khashoggi Murder: Saudi Court Commutes Death Sentences," BBC News, September 7, 2020, https://www.bbc.com/news/world-europe-54061597.
8. Warren P. Strobel, "CIA Intercepts Underpin Assessment Saudi Crown Prince

Targeted Khashoggi," *Wall Street Journal*, December 1, 2018, https://www.wsj.com
/articles/cia-intercepts-underpin-assessment-saudi-crown-prince-targeted
-khashoggi-1543640460.

9. Strobel, "CIA Intercepts Underpin Assessment."

10. Strobel, "CIA Intercepts Underpin Assessment."

11. *Annex to the Report of the Special Rapporteur on Extrajudicial, Summary or Arbitrary Executions: Investigation into the Unlawful Death of Mr. Jamal Khashoggi*, report to the Human Rights Council, 41st session, A/HRC/41/CRP.1 (June 19, 2019), 53; Agnes Callamard, "Khashoggi Killing: UN Human Rights Expert Says Saudi Arabia Is Responsible for 'Premeditated Execution,'" Office of the High Commissioner Human Rights (OHCHR), June 19, 2019. See press release and link to the full report at https://www.ohchr.org/EN/NewsEvents/Pages/DisplayNews.aspx?NewsID =24713.

12. *Annex to the Report of the Special Rapporteur*, 50.

13. *Assessing the Saudi Government's Role in the Killing of Jamal Khashoggi*, Office of the Director of National Intelligence, February 11, 2021 (released on February 25, 2021), https://www.dni.gov/files/ODNI/documents/assessments /Assessment-Saudi-Gov-Role-in-JK-Death-20210226v2.pdf.

14. *Assessing the Saudi Government's Role in the Killing of Jamal Khashoggi.*

15. *Assessing the Saudi Government's Role in the Killing of Jamal Khashoggi*, italics added.

16. An unofficial English translation of the Charter of Makkah can be viewed at the Embassy of the Kingdom of Saudi Arabia website, https://www.saudiembassy.net /statements/charter-makkah.

17. Charter of Makkah, unofficial English translation.

18. Tariq Al-Thaqafi, "Prominent Muslim Figures: Religious, Cultural Diversity Does Not Justify 'Conflict,'" *Arab News*, May 30, 2019, https://www.arabnews.com/node /1503946/saudi-arabia.

19. "Progress under Vision 2030," fact sheet, Saudi Embassy, Washington, D.C., November 2019; "Human Rights Reforms in Saudi Arabia," fact sheet, Saudi Embassy, Washington, D.C., May 2020; "Recent Human Rights Reforms in the Kingdom of Saudi Arabia," Saudi Embassy, Washington, D.C., 2020. See "Saudi Arabia's Reforms and Programs to Empower Women," Embassy of the Kingdom of Saudi Arabia, August 2019, https://www.saudiembassy.net/sites/default/files /Factsheet%20on%20Progress%20for%20Women%20in%20Saudi%20Arabia.pdf.

20. "Progress under Vision 2030," "Human Rights Reforms in Saudi Arabia," and "Recent Human Rights Reforms in the Kingdom of Saudi Arabia."

21. U.S. Embassy, Saudi Arabia, *2020 Investment Climate Statements: Saudi Arabia*, U.S. Department of State, https://www.state.gov/reports/2020-investment-climate -statements/saudi-arabia/.

22. "Saudi Arabia Releases 250 Immigration Offenders amid Coronavirus Outbreak: Statement," Reuters, March 26, 2020, https://www.reuters.com/article/us-health -coronavirus-saudi-prisoners/saudi-arabia-releases-250-immigration-offenders-amid -coronavirus-outbreak-statement-idUSKBN21D1J9.

23. Sarah Dadouch, "Saudi Arabia Has Been Scrubbing Its Textbooks of Anti-Semitic and Misogynistic Passages," *Washington Post*, January 30, 2021, https://www .washingtonpost.com/world/middle_east/saudi-arabia-textbooks-education -curriculum/2021/01/30/28ebe632-5a54-11eb-a849-6f9423a75ffd_story.html.

24. Dadouch, "Saudi Arabia Has Been Scrubbing Its Textbooks."

25. Ghaida Ghantous, "With Eye on U.S. Ties, Saudi Arabia Leads Pack on Gulf Détente," Reuters, January 6, 2021, https://www.reuters.com/article/gulf-qatar -int-idUSKBN29B2FM.

26. Isabel Debre, "Prominent Saudi Women's Rights Activist Released from Prison," Associated Press, February 10, 2021, https://apnews.com/article/loujain-al-Hathloul -released-prison-8732416346416c4e05707cfdd813eacd; Joel C. Rosenberg, "Saudi Government Releases 3 Political Prisoners, Including a Women's Rights Activist, Drawing Praise from President Biden," All Arab News, February 11, 2021, https:// allarab.news/saudi-government-releases-3-political-prisoners-including-a-womens -rights-activist-drawing-praise-from-president-biden/.

CHAPTER 21: THE ABRAHAM ACCORDS

1. Joel C. Rosenberg, "Israel-UAE Peace Deal May Cripple Iran's Influence over Region," interview by Shannon Bream, *Fox News at Night*, Fox News Channel, August 14, 2020, video, 6:00, https://video.foxnews.com/v/6181021512001#sp =show-clips, 2:14-3:40.

2. Joel C. Rosenberg, "Who Will Be Next to Make Peace with Israel?" All Israel News, September 2, 2020, https://www.allisrael.com/who-will-be-next-to-make -peace-with-israel.

3. Salman bin Hamad al-Khalifa, "The Arab Peace Initiative for Israel and the Palestinians," editorial, *Washington Post*, July 16, 2009, https://www.washingtonpost .com/wp-dyn/content/article/2009/07/16/AR2009071602737.html.

4. Donald Trump, "Remarks by President Trump, Prime Minister Netanyahu, Minister bin Zayed, and Minister Al Zayani at the Abraham Accords Signing Ceremony," Archived Trump White House, National Archives and Records Administration, September 15, 2020, https://trumpwhitehouse.archives.gov /briefings-statements/remarks-president-trump-prime-minister-netanyahu -minister-bin-zayed-minister-al-zayani-abraham-accords-signing-ceremony/.

5. Benjamin Netanyahu, "Remarks by President Trump, Prime Minister Netanyahu, Minister bin Zayed, and Minister Al Zayani at the Abraham Accords Signing Ceremony."

6. Abdullah bin Zayed, "Remarks by President Trump, Prime Minister Netanyahu, Minister bin Zayed, and Minister Al Zayani at the Abraham Accords Signing Ceremony."

7. Abdullatif Al Zayani, "Remarks by President Trump, Prime Minister Netanyahu, Minister bin Zayed, and Minister Al Zayani at the Abraham Accords Signing Ceremony."

8. William Daroff, interview by author, September 15, 2020.

9. John Hagee, interview by author, September 15, 2020.

10. Mike Pence, interview by author, David Brody, and Erick Stakelbeck, September 15, 2020.

11. Mike Pence, interview by author, David Brody, and Erick Stakelbeck.

12. Joel C. Rosenberg, interview by Shannon Bream, *Fox News at Night*, Fox News Channel, September 15, 2020, Internet Archive, video clips starting at 8:04 p.m., https://archive.org/details/FOXNEWSW_20200916_030000_Fox_News _at_Night_With_Shannon_Bream/.

CHAPTER 22: NOBEL PRIZE OR NO BIG DEAL?

1. John Kerry, *13th Annual Saban Forum: Challenge for the Trump Administration in the Middle East, a Conversation with U.S. Secretary of State John Kerry* (U.S. Department of State: Washington, D.C., December 4, 2016), 6, 8, https://www.brookings.edu/wp-content/uploads/2016/12/cmep_20161204_kerry_transcript.pdf.

2. Zachary Crockett, "Donald Trump Is the Only U.S. President Ever with No Political or Military Experience," Vox, January 23, 2017, https://www.vox.com/policy-and-politics/2016/11/11/13587532/donald-trump-no-experience.

3. Ali Khamenei (@khamenei_ir), Twitter, February 5, 2020, 4:29 a.m., https://twitter.com/khamenei_ir/status/1225003515858374657; 4:18 a.m., https://twitter.com/khamenei_ir/status/1225000782900146176; 5:03 a.m., https://twitter.com/khamenei_ir/status/1222475353156964353?lang=en.

4. "Trump's Middle East Plan: Starting Point or Dead End?" *New York Times*, editorial, January 30, 2020, https://www.nytimes.com/2020/01/30/opinion/peace-plan-trump.html.

5. Paul Waldman, "The Trump Administration's New Mideast 'Peace' Plan Is Absurd," *Washington Post*, editorial, January 28, 2020, https://www.washingtonpost.com/opinions/2020/01/28/trump-administrations-new-mideast-peace-plan-is-absurd/.

6. "Sanders Statement on Trump's Middle East Plan," press release, Bernie Sanders U.S. Senator for Vermont (website), January 28, 2020, https://www.sanders.senate.gov/press-releases/sanders-statement-on-trumps-middle-east-plan/.

7. Aaron David Miller, "I'm a Veteran Middle East Peace Negotiator. Trump's Plan Is the Most Dangerous I've Ever Seen," editorial, Jewish Telegraphic Agency, February 27, 2020, https://www.jta.org/2020/02/27/opinion/im-a-veteran-middle-east-peace-negotiator-trumps-plan-is-the-most-dangerous-ive-ever-seen.

8. Joe Biden (@JoeBiden), Twitter, January 28, 2020, 4:58 p.m., https://twitter.com/joebiden/status/1222323147418017794?lang=en.

9. Ron Kampeas, "At White House, U.S. Jews Offer Little Resistance to Obama Policy on Settlements," *Jewish Journal*, July 14, 2009, https://jewishjournal.com/news/united-states/71341/.

10. Tom Cherones, director, "The Opposite," *Seinfeld*, season 5, episode 21, NBC, aired May 19, 1994.

11. Mike Pence, interview by author, David Brody, and Erick Stakelbeck, September 15, 2020.

12. Mike Pompeo, interview by author, September 24, 2020.

13. Jason Greenblatt, interview by author, February 3, 2021.

14. Thomas L. Friedman, "The Love Triangle That Spawned Trump's Mideast Peace Deal," editorial, *New York Times*, September 15, 2020, https://www.nytimes.com/2020/09/15/opinion/trump-israel-bahrain-uae.html.

15. "9/16/20: Press Secretary Kayleigh McEnany Holds a Press Briefing," Trump White House Archived, September 16, 2020, video, 24:38, https://www.youtube.com/watch?v=WlRmWLkJFPk, 23:50–24:38.

16. Ezzedine C. Fishere, "Opinion: The UAE-Bahrain-Israel Accords Are a Big Step—in the Wrong Direction," editorial, *Washington Post*, September 21, 2020, https://www.washingtonpost.com/opinions/2020/09/21/uae-bahrain-israel-accords-are-big-step-wrong-direction/.

17. Meghan McCain, conversation with Whoopi Goldberg on *The View*, season 24, episode 7, ABC, aired September 16, 2020. See also "Mainstream Media Asks Zero Questions about Abraham Accords at Press Briefing," All Israel News, September 17, 2020, https://www.allisrael.com/media-bias-alert-not-one-question -by-the-mainstream-media-about-the-abraham-accords-to-the-whitehouse-press -secretary/.

18. "Iran Responds to Bahrain and UAE Normalization with Israel: Israel's Destruction Is Near, the Gulf State Regimes Are in Danger," Middle East Media Research Institute (MEMRI), November 2, 2020, https://www.memri.org/reports/iran -responds-bahrain-and-uae-normalization-israel-israels-destruction-near-gulf-state.

19. "Iran Responds to Bahrain and UAE Normalization with Israel."

20. Qais Abu Samra, "Palestine Hails Erdogan's Speech to U.N.," Anadolu Agency, September 23, 2020, https://www.aa.com.tr/en/middle-east/palestine-hails -erdogan-s-speech-to-un/1983143; Daren Butler and Tuvan Gumrukcu, "Turkey May Suspend Ties with UAE over Israel Deal, Erdogan Says," Reuters, August 14, 2020, https://www.reuters.com/article/us-israel-emirates-turkey/turkey-may -suspend-ties-with-uae-over-israel-deal-erdogan-says-idUSKCN25A0ON.

21. Butler and Gumrukcu, "Turkey May Suspend Ties with UAE."

22. Joshua Shuman, "Turkish-Israel Trade on the Rise as Diplomatic Relations Hit Bottom," *Jerusalem Post*, October 16, 2020, https://www.jpost.com/middle-east /turkish-israel-trade-on-the-rise-as-diplomatic-relations-hit-bottom-645852.

23. Stephen Farrell, "Israel Hails UAE Deal but Palestinians—and Settlers— Dismayed," Reuters, August 13, 2020, https://www.reuters.com/article/uk-israel -emirates-trump-reactions-idINKCN2592RE.

24. Marwan Bishara, "The UAE Makes Peace with Israel's War on the Palestinians," editorial, Al Jazeera, August 14, 2020, https://www.aljazeera.com/opinions/2020 /8/14/the-uae-makes-peace-with-israels-war-on-the-palestinians.

25. Marwan Bishara, "Trump's 'Peace Plan': The Farce, the Fraud and the Fury," editorial, Al Jazeera, January 29, 2020, https://www.aljazeera.com/opinions /2020/1/29/trumps-peace-plan-the-farce-the-fraud-and-the-fury.

26. Joel C. Rosenberg, "Sudan Is About to Normalize Relations with Israel, Well- Placed Israeli Source Tells All Arab News," All Arab News, October 22, 2020, https://allarab.news/sudan-is-about-to-normalize-relations-with-israel-well-placed -israeli-source-tells-all-arab-news/.

27. Joel C. Rosenberg, "White House Confirms Sudan Will Join Abraham Accords and Make Peace with Israel—3rd Arab-Israeli Normalization Deal since August," All Arab News, October 23, 2020, https://allarab.news/white-house-confirms -sudan-will-make-peace-with-israel/.

28. All Israel News, "Israel-Morocco Agreement Report," Facebook, December 10, 2020, https://www.facebook.com/watch/?v=880523566027872; Nicole Jansezian, "Morocco to Declare Peace with Israel: Fourth Arab-Israeli Peace Deal in Four Months," All Israel News, December 10, 2020, https://www.allisrael.com /trump-announces-morocco-to-declare-peace-with-israel.

29. See, for example, Joel C. Rosenberg, "Israel's Momentous Decision: The Settlements or the Saudis?" editorial, *Jerusalem Post*, June 2, 2020, https://www .jpost.com/opinion/israels-momentous-decision-the-settlements-or-the-saudis -629969; Joel C. Rosenberg, "Will American Evangelicals Support Immediate

Annexation?" editorial, *Jerusalem Post*, June 14, 2020, https://www.jpost.com /opinion/will-american-evangelicals-support-immediate-annexation-631362.

30. Rosenberg, "Will American Evangelicals Support Immediate Annexation?"

31. Anwar Gargash, interview by author, December 8, 2020.

32. Daniel Estrin, "As Thousands of Israeli Tourists Visit Dubai, a Small Jewish Community Gets a Boost," NPR, December 29, 2020, https://www.npr.org/2020 /12/29/950818576/as-thousands-of-israeli-tourists-visit-dubai-a-small-jewish -community-gets-a-boo.

33. Abdullah bin Rashid Al Khalifa, interview by author, September 29, 2020.

34. Khalid bin Ahmed Al Khalifa, interview by author, December 15, 2020.

35. Joel C. Rosenberg, "All Israel News Confirms: Netanyahu, Mossad Chief Made Secret Trip to Meet with Saudi Crown Prince, U.S. Officials," All Israel News, November 23, 2020, https://www.allisrael.com/all-israel-news-confirms-netanyahu -mossad-chief-made-secret-trip-to-meet-with-saudi-crown-prince-us-officials.

36. Joel C. Rosenberg, "Groundbreaking New Poll Finds Nearly 8-in-10 Americans Want Saudi Arabia to Be the Next Country to Make Peace with Israel," All Arab News, November 13, 2020, https://allarab.news/new-poll-finds-nearly-8-in-10 -americans-want-saudi-arabia-to-be-the-next-country-to-make-peace-with-israel/.

CHAPTER 23: WHAT IS THE FUTURE OF FAITH IN THE MIDDLE EAST?

1. International Religious Freedom Act of 1998, H.R. 2431, 105th Cong. (1998), https://www.congress.gov/bill/105th-congress/house-bill/2431/text.

2. "2019 Ministerial to Advance Religious Freedom," U.S. Department of State, July 16–18, 2019, https://2017-2021.state.gov/2019-ministerial-to-advance -religious-freedom//index.html.

3. See adaptation of my address at Joel C. Rosenberg, "What Is the State of Religious Freedom in Israel & the Arab World? Here's What the Media Is Not Telling You. [. . .]," blog, July 18, 2019, https://flashtrafficblog.epicentermedia .net/2019/07/18/what-is-the-state-of-religious-freedom-in-israel-the-arab-world -heres-what-the-media-is-not-telling-you-my-keynote-address-to-the-state -departments-conference-on-religious-freedom/.

4. Joel C. Rosenberg, "Game-Changing Moment: Egyptian President Sisi Makes History Building Largest Church in the Mideast [. . .]," blog, January 7, 2019, https://flashtrafficblog.wordpress.com/2019/1/07/game-changing-moment-egyptian -president-sisi-makes-history-building-largest-church-in-the-mideast-our-evangelical -delegation-was-honored-to-be-here-for-the-opening-a-few-thoughts/.

5. Chris Mitchell, "Egypt's El Sisi Builds Middle East's Largest Church, a 'Game Changer' in the Region," CBN News, January 7, 2019, https://www1.cbn.com /cbnnews/israel/2019/january/egypts-el-sisi-builds-middle-easts-largest-church-a -game-changer-in-the-region.

6. Mitchell, "Egypt's El Sisi Builds Middle East's Largest Church."

7. "Full Text: Mike Pompeo's Cairo Speech on Mideast Policy and Obama," Haaretz, January 10, 2019, https://www.haaretz.com/us-news/full-text-secretary-of-state -pompeo-s-speech-at-the-american-university-in-cairo-1.6829117.

8. Emily Jones and Chris Mitchell, "Exclusive: Pompeo Vows U.S. to Stand with Persecuted Believers: 'Christians Central to Middle East,'" CBN News, January 10, 2019, https://www1.cbn.com/cbnnews/israel/2019/january/greatest-threat-of-all-in -the-middle-east-pompeo-pinpoints-top-foe-calms-fears-among-us-allies.

CHAPTER 24: WHAT IS THE FUTURE ROLE OF EVANGELICAL CHRISTIANITY IN THE MIDDLE EAST?

1. "Pastor Andrew Brunson," U.S. Commission on International Religious Freedom, https://www.uscirf.gov/religious-prisoners-conscience/released-rpocs/pastor-andrew-brunson.

2. W.J. Hennigan, "Why Trump Imposed Sanctions on a Key NATO Ally," *Time*, August 1, 2018, https://time.com/5355883/donald-trump-turkey-sanctions-andrew-brunson/.

3. Jacob Pramuk, "Why Trump Is Attacking Turkey with Sanctions and Tariffs," CNBC, August 10, 2018, https://www.cnbc.com/2018/08/10/why-trump-is-attacking-turkey-with-sanctions-and-tariffs.html.

4. Laura Pitel, "Erdogan Says Detained U.S. Pastor Has 'Dark' Ties to Terrorism," *Financial Times*, October 1, 2018, https://www.ft.com/content/51f74fde-c592-11e8-8670-c5353379f7c2.

5. Andrew Brunson, interview by author, November 9, 2020.

6. Andrew Brunson, interview by author.

7. Andrew Brunson, interview by author.

8. Andrew Brunson, interview by author.

9. "What Is an Evangelical?" National Association of Evangelicals (NAE), https://www.nae.net/what-is-an-evangelical/.

10. "What Is an Evangelical?"

11. NIV.

12. Mark Hitchcock, *The End: A Complete Overview of Bible Prophecy and the End of Days* (Carol Stream, IL: Tyndale, 2012), 4.

13. Hitchcock, 4–5.

14. See Matthew 24:10-12; 2 Timothy 3:1-5.

15. See Matthew 24:14; Romans 11:26; Revelation 7:9-10.

16. Jayson Casper, "The Top 50 Countries Where It's Hardest to Be a Christian (2020)," *Christianity Today*, January 15, 2020, https://www.christianitytoday.com/news/2020/january/top-christian-persecution-open-doors-2020-world-watch-list.html. Casper is citing data from the World Watch List, published by Open Doors USA.

17. "Ambassador Samuel Brownback Remarks at the 2019 IDC Solidarity Dinner," September 10, 2019, In Defense of Christians, Washington, D.C., video, 13:35, May 15, 2020, https://www.youtube.com/watch?v=eylOig6HOuo.

18. Joel C. Rosenberg, *Epicenter: Why the Current Rumblings in the Middle East Will Change Your Future* (Carol Stream, IL: Tyndale, 2006). See also J. Dwight Pentecost, *Things to Come: A Study in Biblical Eschatology* (Grand Rapids, MI: Zondervan, 1958); Tim LaHaye, *The Coming Peace in the Middle East* (Grand Rapids, MI: Zondervan, 1984); John F. Walvoord, *Every Prophecy of the Bible: Clear Explanations for Uncertain Times* (Colorado Springs: David C Cook, 2011); Walter C. Kaiser Jr., *Preaching and Teaching the Last Things: Old Testament Eschatology for the Life of the Church* (Grand Rapids, MI: Baker Academic, 2011); and Mark Hitchcock, *The End: A Complete Overview of Bible Prophecy and the End of Days* (Carol Stream, IL: Tyndale, 2012).

19. See *Jewish Encyclopedia Online*, s.v. "Gog and Magog," by Emil G. Hirsch and Mary W. Montgomery, https://www.jewishencyclopedia.com/articles/6735-gog-and-magog; Naftali Silberberg, "The Battle of Gog and Magog," Chabad.org,

https://www.chabad.org/library/article_cdo/aid/1108919/jewish/Gog-and-Magog
.htm; "Speech of Rabbi Yisrael Meir Yad Vashem Chairman of the Council,
Holocaust Survivor at the Memorial Service on the Occasion of the 70th
Anniversary of Kristallnacht," World Holocaust Forum Foundation, November 9,
2008, https://worldholocaustforum.org/press/speeches/speech-of-rabbi-yisrael
-meir-yad-vashem-chairman-of-the-council-holocaust-survivor-at-the-memorial
-service-on-the-occasion-of-the-70-anniversary-of-kristallnacht/; Gil Ronen,
"Rabbis: Clash Signals Gog, Magog," Arutz Sheva (Israel National News),
June 3, 2010, https://www.israelnationalnews.com/News/News.aspx/137869.
20. *Encyclopedia Britannica Online*, s.v. "Yājāj and Mājāj," last updated October
29, 2015, https://www.britannica.com/topic/Yajuj-and-Majuj. See also Maulana
Muhammad Ali, *The Antichrist and Gog and Magog* (Columbus: Ahmadiyya
Anjuman Isha'at Islam, 1992), https://www.aaiil.org/text/books/mali/gog
/antichristgogmagog.pdf; David Cook, *Contemporary Muslim Apocalyptic
Literature* (New York: Syracuse University Press, 2005); Jean-Pierre Filiu,
Apocalypse in Islam (Berkeley: University of California Press, 2011).
21. See Matthew 5:43-48; 22:39; Mark 12:31; Luke 6:27-36; 10:25-37.
22. NIV.
23. NIV.
24. Luke 4:18-19.
25. Ephesians 3:20, NIV.

CHAPTER 25: WHAT IS THE FUTURE OF SECURITY AND PROSPERITY IN THE MIDDLE EAST?

1. Spencer Bokat-Lindell, "Are Biden and Sanders Too Old to Be President?" editorial,
New York Times, September 19, 2019, https://www.nytimes.com/2019/09/19
/opinion/president-age-limit-biden.html.
2. Jack Shafer, "Is Joe Biden Too Old?" *Politico*, August 2, 2019, https://www
.politico.com/magazine/story/2019/08/02/joe-biden-age-media-227499.
3. Shafer, "Is Joe Biden Too Old?"
4. Joel C. Rosenberg, "Kamala Harris, Biden's VP Pick, Is Actually More Moderate
on Israel Than Many Democrats," All Israel News, October 7, 2020, https://
www.allisrael.com/kamala-harris-bidens-vp-pick-is-actually-more-moderate-on
-israel-than-many-democrats.
5. Tovah Lazaroff, "Biden, Netanyahu Will Be Frenemies from the Start on
Settlements," *Jerusalem Post*, November 10, 2020, https://www.jpost.com/israel
-news/politics-and-diplomacy/biden-netanyahu-will-be-frenemies-from-the-start
-on-settlements-648655.
6. Lazaroff, "Biden, Netanyahu Will Be Frenemies from the Start on Settlements."
7. Ashley Killough, "Joe Biden: Bibi and I Are 'Still Buddies,'" CNN, November 10,
2014, https://www.cnn.com/2014/11/10/politics/biden-netanyahu/index.html.
8. Jeremy M. Sharp, *Israel's Iron Dome Anti-Rocket System: U.S. Assistance
and Coproduction*, Congressional Research Service, September 30, 2014,
EveryCRSReport.com, https://www.everycrsreport.com/reports/IN10158.html. See
also Yonah Jeremy Bob, "Getting the U.S. to Fund Iron Dome against All Odds,"
Jerusalem Post, October 24, 2017, https://www.jpost.com/israel-news/senior-defense
-official-tells-jpost-how-he-convinced-white-house-to-fund-iron-dome-508254.
9. Jennifer Epstein, "Biden Says He Wouldn't Move U.S. Embassy from Jerusalem,"

Bloomberg, April 29, 2020, https://www.bloomberg.com/news/articles/2020-04
-29/biden-says-he-wouldn-t-move-u-s-embassy-from-jerusalem.

10. "Statement by Joe Biden on the Agreements between Israel, the UAE, and Bahrain,"
Biden-Harris (website), September 15, 2020, https://joebiden.com/2020/09/15
/statement-by-joe-biden-on-the-agreements-between-israel-the-uae-and-bahrain/.

11. "Joe Biden: Former Vice President of the United States," editorial, *New York Times*,
January 17, 2020, https://www.nytimes.com/interactive/2020/01/17/opinion/joe
-biden-nytimes-interview.html.

12. "Joe Biden: Former Vice President of the United States."

13. Evan Osnos, "The Biden Agenda," *The New Yorker*, July 20, 2014, https://www
.newyorker.com/magazine/2014/07/28/biden-agenda.

14. Joseph R. Biden Jr., *A Vision for the Future of the Transatlantic Partnership*,
transcript of address to the Chatham House (London: Chatham House, Royal
Institute of International Affairs, October 10, 2018), 3, https://chathamhouse
.soutron.net/Portal/DownloadImageFile.ashx?objectId=1733.

15. Robert M. Gates, *Duty: Memoirs of a Secretary at War* (New York: Alfred A.
Knopf, 2014), 288.

16. Salvador Rizzo, "Joe Biden's Claim That He Got '150,000 Combat Troops out of
Iraq,'" *Washington Post*, July 22, 2019, https://www.washingtonpost.com/politics
/2019/07/22/joe-bidens-claim-that-he-got-combat-troops-out-iraq/.

17. Leon Panetta with Jim Newton, *Worthy Fights: A Memoir of Leadership in War
and Peace* (New York: Penguin, 2014), 392.

18. Glenn Kessler, "Biden's Claim That He Didn't Tell Obama Not to Launch bin Laden
Raid," *Washington Post*, January 8, 2020, https://www.washingtonpost.com/politics
/2020/01/08/bidens-claim-that-he-didnt-tell-obama-not-launch-bin-laden-raid/.

19. Tom Cohen, "Obama Calls for Israel's Return to Pre-1967 Borders," CNN,
May 20, 2011, https://edition.cnn.com/2011/POLITICS/05/19/obama.israel
.palestinians/.

20. See responses by the Democratic candidates to questions on Israel at "Israel,"
New York Times, February 6, 2020, https://www.nytimes.com/interactive/2020
/us/politics/2020-democrats-israel-foreign-policy.html.

21. Suzanne Maloney, *Major Beneficiaries of the Iran Deal: The IRGC and Hezbollah*,
testimony before the U.S. House Committee on Foreign Affairs Subcommittee
on the Middle East and North Africa, 114th Cong., published by the Brookings
Institution, September 17, 2015, https://www.brookings.edu/testimonies/major
-beneficiaries-of-the-iran-deal-the-irgc-and-hezbollah/.

22. See responses by the Democratic candidates to questions on Iran at "Iran," *New
York Times*, February 6, 2020, https://www.nytimes.com/interactive/2020/us/politics
/2020-democrats-iran-foreign-policy.html.

23. Judah Ari Gross, "Gantz Appears to Rebuke IDF Chief over Public Criticism of
U.S., Threat to Iran," Times of Israel, January 27, 2021, https://www
.timesofisrael.com/gantz-appears-to-rebuke-idf-chief-over-public-criticism
-of-us-threat-to-iran/.

24. Benny Gantz, interview by author, February 5, 2021.

25. Judah Ari Gross, "Gantz: Israel Will Take Military Action against Nuclear Iran If
Needed," Times of Israel, February 1, 2021, https://www.timesofisrael.com
/gantz-israel-will-take-military-action-against-nuclear-iran-if-needed/.

26. Gross, "Gantz: Israel Will Take Military Action against Nuclear Iran If Needed."

368 || ENEMIES AND ALLIES

27. Lara Jakes and Eric Schmitt, "Biden Reverses Trump Terrorist Designation for Houthis in Yemen," *New York Times*, February 5, 2021, https://www.nytimes.com/2021/02/05/us/politics/biden-houthi-yemen-terrorist-designation.html.

28. Ellen Knickmeyer, "Biden Ending U.S. Support for Saudi-Led Offensive in Yemen," Associated Press, February 4, 2021, https://apnews.com/article/biden-end-support-saudi-offenseive-yemen-b68f58493dbfc530b9fcfdb80a13098f.

29. Ismaeel Naar, "Saudi Arabia Has Intercepted 526 Drones, 346 Ballistic Missiles So Far," Al Arabiya, February 28, 2021, https://english.alarabiya.net/News/gulf/2021/02/28/Saudi-Arabia-has-intercepted-526-drones-346-ballistic-missiles-so-far-Spokesperson#.

30. Miriam Berger, "FAQ: What Biden Did—and Didn't Do—After U.S. Report on Khashoggi's Killing by Saudi Agents," *Washington Post*, February 27, 2021, https://www.washingtonpost.com/world/2021/02/27/faq-what-biden-did-didnt-do-after-us-report-khashoggis-killing-by-saudi-agents/.

31. Robin Wright, "The Sweeping Impact of a Broken Biden Campaign Promise," *The New Yorker*, March 1, 2021, https://www.newyorker.com/news/our-columnists/biden-betrayed-his-promise-to-defend-human-rights-and-jamal-khashoggi.

32. Fred Ryan, "Opinion: Say It Ain't So, Joe," editorial, *Washington Post*, March 1, 2021, https://www.washingtonpost.com/opinions/2021/03/01/fred-ryan-biden-promises-jamal-khashoggi/.

33. Raf Sanchez, "Biden Looks to Recalibrate Relationship with Saudi Arabia and Crown Prince Mohammed bin Salman," NBC News, February 20, 2021, https://www.nbcnews.com/news/world/biden-looks-recalibrate-relationship-saudi-arabia-crown-prince-mohammed-bin-n1258354.

34. John Hudson and Karen DeYoung, "Inside the Biden Team's Deliberations over Punishing the Saudi Crown Prince," *Washington Post*, March 1, 2021, https://www.washingtonpost.com/national-security/khashoggi-killing-intelligence-report-mbs-saudi-arabia/2021/03/01/5bdebe68-7ae1-11eb-b0fc-83144c02d676_story.html.

35. Joel C. Rosenberg, "Are U.S.-Saudi Ties Heading for a Train Wreck? Biden to Make Major Announcement Monday, After Releasing Report Accusing MBS of Ordering Khashoggi Murder," All Arab News, February 28, 2021, https://allarab.news/are-us-saudi-ties-heading-for-a-train-wreck-biden-to-make-major-announcement-monday-after-releasing-report-accusing-mbs-of-ordering-khashoggi-murder/.

36. Kelsey Warner, "Israel's OurCrowd and UAE's Al Naboodah Create $100 Million Fund for Gulf Tech Investors," *The National*, October 6, 2020, https://www.thenationalnews.com/business/technology/israel-s-ourcrowd-and-uae-s-al-naboodah-create-100m-fund-for-gulf-tech-investors-1.1089017.

37. Jason Greenblatt, interview by author, February 3, 2021.

38. NASDAQ Stock Screener, https://www.nasdaq.com/market-activity/stocks/screener.

39. NIV.

CHAPTER 26: WHAT IS THE FUTURE OF PEACE IN THE MIDDLE EAST?

1. Michael Hirsh, "Clinton to Arafat: It's All Your Fault," *Newsweek*, June 26, 2001, https://www.newsweek.com/clinton-arafat-its-all-your-fault-153779. See also David Shyovitz, "2000 Camp David Summit: Background & Overview," Jewish Virtual Library, https://www.jewishvirtuallibrary.org/background-and-overview-of-2000-camp-david-summit.

2. David Shyovitz, "2000 Camp David Summit: Background & Overview."

3. Bill Clinton, *My Life* (New York: Alfred A. Knopf, 2004), 944–945.

4. Tamara Zieve, "This Week in History: The Arab League's Three No's," *Jerusalem Post*, August 26, 2012, https://www.jpost.com/features/in-thespotlight/this-week -in-history-the-arab-leagues-three-nos.

5. "Arab Peace Initiative," S. Daniel Abraham Center for Middle East Peace, https://centerpeace.org/explore/arab-peace-initiative/.

6. "Arab Peace Initiative."

7. "Full transcript: Prince Bandar bin Sultan's Interview on Israel-Palestine Conflict," Al Arabiya, October 5, 2020, https://english.alarabiya.net/features/2020/10/05/Full -transcript-Part-one-of-Prince-Bandar-bin-Sultan-s-interview-with-Al-Arabiya.

8. Ghaith Al-Omari, "Israel-UAE Deal Achieves a Middle East Rarity: It's Win-Win-Win, Palestinians Included," "Think," NBC News, August 13, 2020, https:// www.nbcnews.com/think/opinion/israel-uae-deal-achieves-middle-east-rarity-it-s -win-ncna1236694.

9. "Ghaith Al-Omari on the Palestinian Negotiation, with Joel C. Rosenberg," All Arab News, September 14, 2020, video, 20:54, 1:43–3:20, https://www.youtube .com/watch?v=Im_SuuFb0xU.

10. "Ghaith Al-Omari on the Palestinian Negotiation," 6:05–6:41.

11. David Horovitz, "Abbas Couldn't Make Peace with the Jews; He Believes His Own Lies about Us," Times of Israel, January 16, 2018, https://www.timesofisrael .com/abbas-couldnt-make-peace-with-the-jews-he-believes-his-own-lies-about-us/.

12. "Ghaith Al-Omari on the Palestinian Negotiation," 5:40–5:49.

13. "Ghaith Al-Omari on the Palestinian Negotiation," 9:23–10:29.

14. "Ghaith Al-Omari on the Palestinian Negotiation," 13:50–14:02.

15. "Ghaith Al-Omari on the Palestinian Negotiation," 16:43–17:49.

16. Israeli President Reuven Rivlin, interview by author, November 26, 2020.

17. "Rivlin Condemns 'Terrible Crime' of Kfar Kassem Massacre," Times of Israel, October 26, 2014, https://www.timesofisrael.com/rivlin-to-address-ceremony -marking-kfar-kassem-massacre/.

18. 1 Chronicles 12:32, NIV.

Sign up for Joel's *What's the Story* e-newsletter to receive exclusive insights from a bestselling thriller writer.

Visit **JOELROSENBERG.COM** to sign up for the monthly newsletter.

CP1456